LIFE STRESS

VOLUME III
OF A COMPANION
TO THE LIFE SCIENCES

PROFESSOR HANS SELYE   (Photo by Laszlo)

LIFE STRESS

VOLUME III
OF A COMPANION
TO THE LIFE SCIENCES

Edited By

STACEY B. DAY, M.D., PH.D., D.SC.

Clinical Professor of Medicine, Department of Medicine,
Division of Behavioral Medicine, New York Medical College,
Valhalla, New York; President, International Foundation
for Biosocial Development and Human Health, New York;
Retired Professor of Biology, Sloan Kettering Division, Cornell University
Medical College, New York and lately Member and Head,
Biosciences Communications and Medical Education,
Sloan Kettering Institute for Cancer Research, New York.

VNR VAN NOSTRAND REINHOLD COMPANY
NEW YORK   CINCINNATI   TORONTO   LONDON   MELBOURNE

Manufactured in the United States of America

Published by Van Nostrand Reinhold Company Inc.
135 West 50th Street, New York, N.Y. 10020

Van Nostrand Reinhold Limited
1410 Birchmount Road
Scarborough, Ontario M1P,2E7, Canada

Van Nostrand Reinhold Australia Pty. Ltd.
17 Queen Street
Mitcham, Victoria 3132, Australia

Van Nostrand Reinhold Company Limited
Molly Millars Lane
Wokingham, Berkshire, England

15 14 13 12 11 10 9 8 7 6 5 4 3 2 1

Library of Congress Cataloging in Publication Data
Main entry under title:

A companion to the life sciences.

Includes index.
  1. Life sciences. I. Day, Stacey B.
[DNLM: 1. Biology. 2. Science. 3. Behavioral
sciences. 4. Medicine. QH307.2 C737]
QH307.2.C65   574   78-8300
ISBN 0-442-22010-3 (v.1)
ISBN 0-442-25163-7 (v.2) Integrated Medicine
ISBN 0-442-26294-9 (v.3) Life Stress

This book is dedicated to

PROFESSOR HANS SELYE

whose entire life work has been to account,
to simplify, and to teach the evolution
and management of stress.

INTRODUCTION

STACEY B. DAY, M.D., PH.D., D.SC.
Clinical Professor of Medicine
Division of Behavioral Medicine
Department of Medicine
New York Medical College
Valhalla, New York

Stress and life? The growing inability of health services generally, throughout the world, to deliver better health for more money or to appreciably cure chronic disease, regardless of increasingly sophisticated and expensive technological price tags, continues to point up problems of human happiness and equitable quality of life, in a world of nonpareils and often arbitrary standards. Economists have argued that medical professions "operate a cartel or play on human anxieties," thus driving up costs. An alternative view, while certainly not eliminating economic viewpoints, could arguably advance the thesis that neither the public nor physicians have responsibly appreciated the changing concepts of health that rigid traditionalism, under the thrust of contemporary machine society and the Age of Information, has shown itself to be quite incapable of managing. The notion of life stress, set forth in the papers in this small volume, focuses on the perspective of health and the human being in terms of health communications and biopsychosocial limits.

The two previous volumes of the *Companion to the Life Sciences* set the pattern of interdisciplinary integration of information based on educational concepts of polypolarity, analysis, and synthesis of information content, developed over a 12-year period in an effort to utilize wisely the exponential flood of so-called research knowledge that has almost drowned the academic professions. During these years, our efforts have been to integrate the morphologic and dynamic matrix of the life sciences into the natural holism and cultural concepts which not only recognize the human personality as an experiential force, but acknowledge him both through his physiological being and through his self-image: man and anti-man, the whole being less a summation of fragments than a vision of a human being in general harmony with the universality of nature.

In effect the living organism is an integrated hierarchical system, unified, regulated, and controlled, ideally in harmony with both an internal and an external environment.

In any system, matter and energy are an integral part of both the system itself and its environment. The living self is an open system—as I discussed in my view of death as failure to direct energy flow and an expression of disorganization at the molecular level (Day, 1970, 1975)—the input and output of which are continually cycling. This system receives energy from the environment, uses it, and transforms it as needed.

The implicit birth of these concepts can certainly be found as early as 55 B.C., in the writings of T. Lucretius Carus (*De Rerum Naturae*), and later as a most brilliant introduction to the molecular era, by Erwin Schrödinger, in his unsurpassed intellectual primer for all molecular science, *What Is Life?* (1944).

On reflection, we understand that environment is both internal and external to man, and since man is a living system, intake and output of matter and energy, feedback, steady states, sine curve rhythms in repair and in regeneration, and adaptation not only follow the physical laws of the universe (after Schrodinger and Lucretius), but in the spiritual sense also relate to the selective psychophysiological control which each individual may exert in a dynamic interchange of matter and energy that forms and patterns each unique holistic environment. This integrated whole, this whole person, can be described within a personal biologos—in the sense that as a living being the person is part of the bios; as an intellectual being the person is constituted of the logos. All life—individual, cultural, and social—through its interrelationships and range of human functions, both physiological and intellectual, we believe, involves the biologos. A simple extension of this view is that there can be no evolution based solely on the bios. In the case of the human animal, bios and logos are one, and evolution, no matter on what grounds (intermarriage, migration, selection for the common gene pool), must be understood to include the sociological process content, the logos, the intellectual potential, no less than the hierarchical realities of the living cell understood in the bios.

Augmentation of concepts of systems theory include, notably, the basic contributions of Ludwig von Bertanlaffy, modified and advanced in recent years by contemporary thinkers, including James Grier Miller under the influence of Whitehead of Harvard University. Reference to Miller's work provides an updated description of the living organism as an integrated hierarchy of molecules, cells, organs, and organ systems, which not unwisely predicts that man, like all other life forms, is subject to the universal laws of nature.

In our own thinking, it has long been unacceptable, even foolish, to fragment or dismember the biologos or human whole, including the patient in critical illness, in an effort to heal a crisis, no matter what it may be. It is our view, indeed, that such an approach may actually provoke deterioration rather than refortification. The human person is more than a marching band of disarticulated limbs, hands, legs, feet, thighs, head, eyes, nose, ears, and organs—a biologic cacophony of severed parts rendering man no longer man but a comprehension of disunited anatomicities of a once associated whole. This whole exists, in fact, because of the unlimited interrelationships which give both morphologic and psychospiritual form to the hierarchy of molecules and molecular compounds that represent, in symbol, man the human being.

Man is not structure and function alone. In a simplistic way, the person represents an external physical information world dissolved in a unique spiritual and existential personal world. That is our view.

Over the last two decades, with colleagues, we have sought to understand how this system is best organized. Systems theory (matter-energy concepts) teaches that organization as such can only arise from information. Information comprises the total content of the biosphere. The processing of information is termed communication. For the self *to be,* a person must have access to information, which in good health or in sickness may traffic via interactive processes recognizable within health communications—between the person and his society (family, class, group, etc.), culture (agrarian, urban, technologic, etc.), and environment or biosphere.

These forces for human health and quality of life are reinforced by cultural/sociological aspects imprinted in the biologos. The social foundation of health we view as biopsychosocial in nature. While there are, at this time, variable views of a precise definition of biopsychosocial health, we believe that all must recognize that true health is created within a framework of cultural diversity and intercultural communications. All concepts are integrated within an umbrella of *biosocial development* that, simply put, presents health as a synthesis between health communications and biopsychosocial limits.

Man is a cultural animal. He may become sick in body, psyche, or both. Disease, including stress aberrations, may effect any or all of these configurations. The life force merges into the dynamics of all components. Where the interface is made manifest, the dynamics define the nature of human action or human behavior.

From this point, in our view (Day and Lolas, 1981), concepts of biopsychosocial health imply comprehension of problems translating biologic or life rules, principally between analyses (scientific factorial approaches) and syntheses (practical modes of action).

Quite evidently, the life force, influenced by stress in the terms discussed in the following papers, is best considered from the prospect of the biologos, and emerging ideas are best evaluated within the concepts set forth here.

In an evolutionary sense, the breadth of all associations rendered here incorporates the interrelationship of both psychic and physical events within man, including his mysticism, religion, culture, and symbolism, as well as the biologic potential of his genes. It is our view that evolutionary concepts based on biologic principles alone provide insufficient understanding of the normal context of human life. It is our tenet, based on 12 years of thought, that a connecting acausal principle, such as the principle of *synchronicity* elaborated by Jung, observed in our teaching, will serve to elucidate a more meaningful view of man. The concept of *synchronicity* indicates a *meaningful coincidence of two or more events,* in which something other than the probability of chance alone is involved. This must be so for evolution where biopsychosocial dynamics and psychophysiological forces, hand in hand with traditional Darwinian perspectives, together contribute to survival of the total gene pool. In effect, the human individual is, and can only be, a product of both sides of the coin, so to say. The human animal is explicable through a working harmony of both biologic *and* cultural/social dynamics. In this view, selection for species survival is and can only be a synthesis derived from the common gene pool, modified and selected for survival through and by the cultural and social dynamics within the group or society under review. Within these givens, stress may interface at any point within the dimensions of space and time, in a multiplicity of forms, to add its impact, good or bad, to the evolutionary momentum.

References

Day, S. B. Death: Failure to direct energy flow and an expression of disorganization at the molecular level. In *Molecular Pathology* (R. A. Good, S. B. Day, and J. J. Yunis, (eds.), ch. 31. Springfield: Charles C. Thomas, 1975.

Day, S. B. and Lolas, F. Biopsychosocial health (editorial). *Foundation One* (The International Foundation For Biosocial Development and Human Health) 3(1) 1–2 1980.

Day, Stacey B., Yunis, E. J., and Dubey, D. P.; An Overview of Stress and the Immune System. In *Social Pediatrics,* Edited by Robert J. Schlegel. Foundation Monograph No. 2., International Foundation for Biosocial Development And Human Health, New York, 1981.

Day, Stacey B.: Stress And Cancer. Presented at the Third International Symposium on the Management of Stress, The Hans Selye Foundation, Tokyo, 1981.

Dorsey, J. M.: The Psychic Nature of Physiology. Center For Health Education, Detroit, Michigan, 1977.

Jung, C. G. *Synchronizität als ein Prinzip akausaler Zussamenhänge.* Zurich: Studien aus dem C. G. Jung-Institut 1V, 1952.

Lucretius, Titus Carus. *De Rerum Naturae* ca. 55 B.C.

Miller, J. G. *Living Systems.* New York: McGraw-Hill, 1978.

Rybak, B.: Paris 1979. Originated word *Biologos,* used by John M. Dorsey and many other workers over long years as *BIOS* and *LOGOS.* (Personal correspondence). Although Rybak claims to have "invented" the word, he has not demonstrated philosophical usage and comprehension of the *biologos* as did Professor John Dorsey, of Wayne State University, in his psychophysiological writings over many years since 1964.

Schrödinger, E. *What Is Life?* (The Physical Aspect of the Living Cell), 1st ed. U.K. Cambridge University Press, 1944.

Contents

III LIFE STRESS AND THE PERSON (HUMANISM)

IV LIFE STRESS, THE CHILD, THE WOMAN,
AND THE FAMILY

LIFE STRESS

VOLUME III
OF A COMPANION
TO THE LIFE SCIENCES

I
BASIC SCIENCE

Stress: Eustress, Distress, and Human Perspectives

Hans Selye, M.D., Ph.D., D.Sc., C.C.
International Institute of Stress
Montreal, Canada

It was exactly four decades ago that we performed those first primitive experiments which led to the publication of a "Letter to the Editor" of *Nature* entitled "A Syndrome Produced by Diverse Nocuous Agents." Since that time we at the International Institute of Stress have been able to collect more than 200,000 publications in our Library and Documentation Center which deal with various aspects of what is now known as the stress concept, not only in virtually all fields of medicine, pathology,biochemistry, and medical jurisprudence, but also in the behavioral sciences and philosophy.

A panoramic overview of the subject, provided by the reexamination of all aspects of stress research, was necessary for the presentation of this chapter in Professor Day's *Life Stress* text. The compilation of this survey, also made it possible at this time to crystallize the main points of the concept.

Experiments on various species of experimental animals showed, in 1936, that the organism responds in a stereotyped manner to such diverse factors as infections, intoxications, trauma, nervous strain, heat, cold, muscular fatigue, and x-irradiation. The specific actions of all these agents are quite different. Their only common feature is that they place the body in a state of stress. Hence, we concluded that the stereotyped response—which is superimposed upon all specific effects—represents a reaction to stress as such. *Stress, then, is the nonspecific response of the body to any demand.*

But what is nonspecific stress? The term had long been used in physics to denote the results of the interaction between a force and the resistance opposed to it. For instance, pressure and tension cause stress in inanimate matter. We thought that the above-mentioned nonspecific response represents the biologic equivalent of such physical stress. The term has now been quite generally accepted in this sense not only in English, but—since

3

attempts to translate "stress" led to much confusion—also in most other languages. We regard as specific actions those which can be elicited by only one or a few agents (e.g., the effect of thyrotrophic hormone on the thyroid). Conversely, nonspecific actions are those which can be elicited by many agents (e.g., shock, loss of body weight, inflammation, tissue necrosis). Stress is the sum of the nonspecific biologic phenomena (including damage and defense), and consequently, a stressor agent is by definition nonspecific since it produces stress.

The Concept of the General Adaptation Syndrome

The most outstanding manifestations of this stress response were: adrenocortical enlargement with histologic signs of hyperactivity, thymicolymphatic involution with certain concomitant changes in the blood count (eosinopenia, lymphopenia, polynucleosis), and gastrointestinal ulcers, often accompanied by other manifestations of damage or shock.

We were struck by the fact that, while during this reaction all the organs of the body show involutional or degenerative changes, the adrenal cortex actually seems to flourish on stress. We suspected this adrenal response of playing a useful part in a nonspecific adaptive reaction, which we visualized as a "call to arms" of the body's defense forces and, therefore, designated the *alarm reaction.*

However, it soon became apparent that this alarm reaction was not the entire response. Upon continued exposure to a stressor capable of eliciting the initial reaction, a *stage of adaptation* or resistance ensued. In other words, no organism can be maintained continuously in a state of alarm. If the stressor is so severe that continued exposure becomes incompatible with life, the animal dies within a few hours or days. If it does survive, the initial response is necessarily followed by a *stage of resistance* during which the symptoms subside (Fig. 1).

The manifestations of this second phase are quite different from and, in many instances the exact opposite of, those which characterize the alarm reaction.

Curiously, after still more exposure to the noxious agent, the acquired adaptation is lost again. The animal enters into a third phase, the *stage of exhaustion,* which inexorably follows as long as the stressor is severe enough and applied for a sufficient length of time.

The GAS, then, is made up of three stages:

1. *Alarm Reaction.* This occurs upon sudden exposure to diverse stimuli to which the organism is not adapted. This reaction has two phases:

    a. *Shock phase,* the intitial and immediate reaction to the noxious agent. Various signs of injury such as tachycardia, loss of muscle tone, and decreased temperature and blood pressure are typical symptoms. Here, too, the characteristic triad first appears.

    b. *Countershock phase,* a rebound reaction marked by the mobilization of defensive phase, during which the adrenal cortex is enlarged and secretion of corticoid hormones is increased. (Most of the acute stress diseases correspond to these two phases of the alarm reaction.)

2. *Stage of Resistance.* This is characterized by full adaptation to the stressor and by the improvement or disappearance of symptoms. There is, however, a concurrent decrease in resistance to most other stimuli.

3. *Stage of Exhaustion.* Since adaptability is finite, exhaustion inexorably follows if the stressor is sufficiently severe and prolonged. Symptoms reappear, and if stress continues unabated, death ensues.

With this formulation, the vague outlines of primitive man's intuitive perception of stress were brought into sharper focus and translated into precise scientific terms that could be appraised by the intellect and tested by reason.

Adapation Energy

Because of its great practical importance, it should be pointed out that the triphasic nature of the GAS gave us the first indication that the body's adaptability, or adaptation energy, is finite since, under constant stress, exhaustion eventually ensues. We still do not know precisely what is lost, except that it is not merely caloric energy, since food intake is normal during the stage of resistance.

Our reserves of adaptation might be compared to an inherited fortune from which we can make withdrawals but to which there is no evidence that we can make additional deposits.

After exhaustion from excessively stressful activity, sleep and rest can restore resistance and adaptability almost to previous levels, but the emphasis here is on the word *almost.* Just as any machine eventually wears out even if it has enough fuel, so does the human body sooner or later become the victim of constant wear and tear.

The stages of the GAS are analogous to the three stages of a man's life: childhood (with its characteristic low resistance and excessive responses to any kind of stimulation), adulthood (during which adaptation to most commonly encountered agents has occurred and resistance is increased),

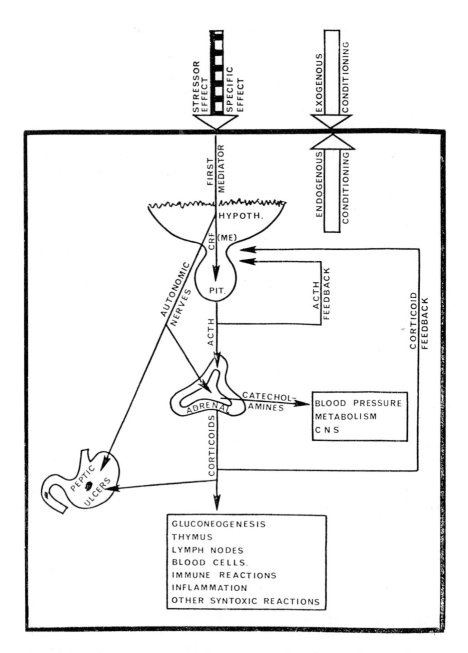

FIG. 1. *Principal pathways mediating the response to a stressor agent and the conditioning factors which modify its effect.* As soon as any agent acts upon the body (thick outer frame of the diagram), the resulting effect will depend upon three factors (broad vertical arrows pointing to the upper horizontal border of the frame). All agents possess both nonspecific stressor

and senility (characterized by irreversible loss of adaptability and eventual exhaustion ending with death).

Every biological activity causes wear and tear, and leaves some irreversible "chemical scars" which accumulate to constitute the signs of aging. Thus, adaptability should be used wisely and sparingly, rather than being recklessly squandered by "burning the candle at both ends."

Mechanisms of Stress

Discoveries since 1936 have linked nonspecific stress with numerous biochemical and structural changes of previously unknown origin. There has also been considerable progress in analyzing the mediation of stress reactions by hormones. However, the carriers of the alarm signals which first relay the call for adaptation have yet to be identified. Perhaps they are metabolic by-products released during activity or damage, or perhaps what is involved is the lack of some vital substance consumed whenever any demand is made upon an organ. Since the only two coordinating systems which connect all parts of the body with one another are the nervous and the vascular systems, we can assume that the alarm signals use one or both of these pathways. Yet, while nervous stimulation may cause a general stress response, deafferented rats still show the classic syndrome when exposed to demands; thus, the nervous system cannot be the only route. It is probable that often, if not always, the signals travel in the blood.

The facts which led us to postulate the existence of the alarm signals would be in agreement with the view that the various cells send out different messengers. In that case, the messages must somehow be tallied by the organs of adaptation.

Whatever the nature of the *first mediator*, however, its existence is assured by its effects, which have been observed and even measured. The discharge of hormones, the involution of the lymphatic organs, the enlargement of the adrenals, the feeling of fatigue, and many other signs of stress, can all be produced by injury or activity in any part of the body.

---

effects (solid part of arrow) and specific properties (interrupted part of arrow). The latter are variable and characteristic of each individual agent; they are not discussed here, other than to state that they are inseparably attached to the stressor effect and invariably modify it. The other two heavy vertical arrows pointing toward the upper border of the frame, represent exogenous and endogenous conditioning factors which largely determine the reactivity of the body. It is clear that since all stressors have some specific effects, they cannot elicit exactly the same response in all organs. Furthermore, even the same agent will act differently in different individuals, depending upon the internal and external conditioning factors which determine their reactivity. (Reprinted by courtesy of Butterworths, Reading, Mass., from H. Selye, *Stress in Health and Disease, 1976)*

Through the first mediator, the agent or situation disruptive of homeostasis eventually excites the hypothalamus, a complex bundle of nerve cells and fibers that acts as a bridge between the brain and the endocrine system. The resulting nervous signals reach certain neuroendocrine cells in the median eminence (ME) of the hypothalamus, where they are transformed into CRF (corticotrophic hormone releasing factor), a chemical messenger which has not yet been isolated in pure form but is probably a polypeptide. In this way a message is relayed to the pituitary, causing a discharge into the general circulation of ACTH (adrenocorticotrophic hormone).

ACTH, reaching the adrenal cortex, triggers the secretion of corticoids, mainly glucocorticoids such as cortisol or corticosterone. Through gluconeogenesis these compounds supply a readily available source of energy for the adaptive reactions necessary to meet the demands made by the agent. The corticoids also facilitate various other enzyme responses, and suppress immune reactions and inflammation, thereby helping the body to coexist with potential pathogens.

Usually secreted in lesser amounts are the pro-inflammatory corticoids, which stimulate the proliferative ability and reactivity of the connective tissue, enhancing the "inflammatory potential." Thus, they help to build a strong barricade of connective tissue through which the body is protected against further invasion. Because of their prominent effect upon salt and water metabolism, these hormones have also been referred to as mineralocorticoids (e.g., desoxycorticosterone, aldosterone). The somatotrophic hormone (STH) or growth hormone of the pituitary likewise stimulates defense reactions.

This chain of events is cybernetically controlled by several feedback mechanisms. For instance, if there is a surplus of ACTH, a short-loop feedback returns some of it to the hypothalamus-pituitary axis and this shuts off further ACTH production. In addition, through a long-loop feedback, a high blood level of corticoids similarly inhibits too much ACTH secretion.

Simultaneously with all these processes, another important pathway is utilized to mediate the stress response. Hormones such as catecholamines are liberated to activate mechanisms of general usefulness for adaptation. Adrenaline in particular is secreted, to make energy available, to accelerate the pulse rate, to elevate the blood pressure and the rate of blood circulation in the muscles, and to stimulate the central nervous system (CNS). The blood coagulation mechanism is also enhanced by adrenaline, as a protection against excessive bleeding if injuries are sustained in the encounter with the state of affairs eliciting stress.

Countless other hormonal and chemical changes during stress check and balance the body's functioning and stability, constituting a virtual arsenal of weapons by which the organism defends itself. The facts known today may lead us to believe that the anterior pituitary and the adrenal cortex play the cardinal roles in stress, but this is probably due to the syndrome's having been studied primarily by endocrinologists. Also, the techniques required to investigate the role of the nervous system are much more complex. It is considerably easier, for example, to remove an endocrine gland and substitute for its hormones by injecting extracts, than it is to destroy minute nervous centers selectively and then restore their function to determine the role they may play.

Adaptability Is Probably the Most Distinctive Characteristic of Life

In maintaining the independence and individuality of natural units, none of the great forces of inanimate matter is as successful as the alertness and adaptability to change which we designate as life, the loss of which is death. Indeed, there is probably a certain parallelism between the degree of aliveness and the extent of adaptability in every animal, in every man.

Many maladies are due not to any particular pathogen but to a faulty adaptive response by the body to the stress induced by the pathogen. Such maladaptations are brought about by derangements in hormonal secretion, and we have called the resulting ailments "diseases of adaptation." Included in this category are insomnia, indigestion, high blood pressure, gastric and duodenal ulcers, and certain allergies, as well as cardiovascular and kidney diseases. Ideally, adaptation consists of a balanced blend of submission and defense. Some ailments are due to an excess of defensive, others to an overabundance of submissive, bodily reactions.

Within the body there are two types of chemical messengers: the so-called messengers of peace, or syntoxic stimuli, which tell the tissues not to fight, and the messengers of war, or catatoxic agents, which signal the body to attack or to defend itself. Unfortunately, an agent may sometimes elicit a response from the wrong messenger. If, for example, we inject a drop of an irritant into the hind paw of a rat, the whole leg will become inflamed. Inflammation is a defense reaction, and if the irritant is potentially harmful, it is a good reaction, for it delimits the injured area. This would be beneficial, for instance, if we injected leprosy bacillus or tuberculosis bacillus. However, if a harmless irritant was applied, such as a drop of dilute formalin solution, it would become innoxious immediately upon contact with living tissues. It might kill a few adjacent cells which the rat would not even notice, but the actual disease would be a result of the rat's reaction. People who suffer from hay fever give evidence of this. Although there is nothing inherently dangerous in pollen, if one is allergic to it, it will provoke inflammation, sneezing, etc.; in other words, a faulty adaptive reaction ensues.

The indirect production of disease by inappropriate or excessive adaptive reactions can be further illustrated by an example drawn from daily life. If we meet a loudly insulting, but obviously harmless drunk, nothing will happen if we take a syntoxic attitude and go past and ignore him. However, if we respond catatoxically—by fighting, or only by preparing to fight—the outcome may be tragic. We will discharge adrenaline-type hormones that increase blood pressure and pulse rate, while our whole nervous system becomes alarmed and tense. If this happens to a coronary candidate, he may end up with a fatal heart attack or brain hemorrhage. In that case, death will have been caused by a biologically suicidal choice of the wrong reaction. The proper response to a stressor always depends on the particular circumstances involved.

A New Code of Behavior

Fundamentally, it is our ability to cope with the demands made by the events in our lives, not the quality or intensity of the events, that counts. What matters is not so much the things that happen to us, but the way we take them—whether they are primarily desired or undesired conditions. That is why I recommend that in everyday normal life, you should judge how you are taking the stress of your life at any particular moment; if there are too many signs of distress in your feelings and behavior, here are a few thoughts that could be useful in dealing with the stresses of daily life:

- Admit that there is no such thing as perfection; be satisfied to strive for improvement, but do not always feel you must "prove" yourself to be worthwhile.
- Whatever your goals, consider first whether they are really worth fighting for; do not waste your efforts on unrealizable goals.
- Do try to keep your mind on the pleasant aspects of life; we all have much to be thankful for and hopeful about.
- Nothing paralyzes a person's efficiency more than frustration; nothing helps it more than success. Even after the greatest of defeats, the depressing thought of being a failure is best combated by taking stock of your past achievements which no one can deny you. Such conscious

stocktaking is most effective in reestablishing the self-confidence necessary for future success.

• When faced with a task which is painful yet indispensable, don't procrastinate; get right to it and get it done, instead of prolonging the stress by agonizing delays.

Some of the unfortunate results of the distress encountered in daily life can be treated with standard medicines; others cannot. To counteract the effects of mental distress, people try out various techniques which claim to eradicate the ill effects or at least help us to cope with them. This is why so many people turn to psychotherapy, medication techniques, tranquilizers—the number of anti-stress medications and psychological techniques grows every day. When nothing seems to work, some find an outlet for their energy only in violence, drugs, or alcohol, thus creating still another problem for themselves and for society.

To my mind, the root of the problem lies in the lack of a proper code of motivation that gives our lives purpose.

I, therefore, started analyzing the thing in an honest, objective way, and I realized that the values by which we were brought up as children, the absolute faithfulness and belief in a certain divinity, in a certain political leader, have just lost their impact. Even money, which was considered the dirtiest aim to make in your life, has lost its value to a large extent. It is always losing its value.

So, what is a permanent value, and what can be offered instead? And I thought that there are certain laws which everyone can accept. For example, the laws of Nature. You see, we are all part of Nature, products of Nature, and we cannot deny Nature. If a glass is filled with water, and at sea level I bring it up to 100°C, it will boil. It always did, and it always will, irrespective of what infallible leader you believe in.

The laws—values—of Nature seem to be absolute, unlike some other social values. What about values based on natural law? What might those be? Might a code of ethics based not on traditions of our society, inspiration, or blind faith in the infallibility of a particular prophet, religious leader, or political doctrine, but on the scientifically verifiable laws that govern the body's reactions in maintaining homeostasis and living in satisfying equilibrium with its surroundings be more enduring? I thought that could be a solution, so I started collecting examples, and I collected more and more of them. I thought that you could work it out by analogy. In my book *Stress without Distress*,[1] which was my first attempt to show this, and in my autobiography *The Stress of My Life*,[2] I attempted to show in more detail how we can adjust our personal reactions to enjoy fully the eustress of success and accomplishment without suffering the distress commonly generated by frustrating friction and purposeless aggressive behavior against our surroundings.

It is a biologic law that man—like the lower animals—must fight and work for some goal that he considers worthwhile. We must use our innate capacities to enjoy the eustress of fulfillment. Only through effort, often aggressive egoistic effort, can we maintain our fitness and assure our homeostatic equilibrium with the surrounding society and the inanimate world. To achieve this state, our activities must earn lasting results; the fruits of work must be cumulative and must provide a capital gain to meet future needs. To succeed, we have to accept the scientifically established fact that man has an inescapable natural urge to work egoistically for things that can be stored to strengthen his homeostasis in the unpredictable situations with which life may confront him. These are not instincts we should combat or be ashamed of. We can do nothing about having been built to work, and it is primarily for our own good. Organs that are not used (muscles, bones, even the brain) undergo inactivity atrophy, and every living being looks out first of all for itself. There is no example in Nature of a creature guided exclusively by altruism and the desire to protect others. In fact, a code of universal altruism would be highly immoral, since it would expect others to look out for us more than for themselves.

How, then, can we develop a code of ethics that accepts egoism and works to hoard personal capital as morally correct? I shall summarize my main conclusions in the form of three basic guidelines:

1. *Find your own natural predilections and stress level.* People differ with regard to the amount and kind of work they consider worth doing to meet the exigencies of daily life and to assure their future security and happiness. In this respect, all of us are influenced by hereditary predispositions and the expectations of our society. Only through planned self-analysis can we establish what we really want; too many people suffer all their lives because they are too conservative to risk a radical change and break with traditions.

2. *Altruistic egoism.* The selfish hoarding of the goodwill, respect, esteem, support, and love of our neighbor is the most efficient way to give vent to our pent-up energy and create enjoyable, beautiful, or useful things.

3. *Earn thy neighbor's love.* This motto, unlike "love thy neighbor as thyself," is compatible with man's biological structure, and although it is based on altruistic egoism, it could hardly be attacked as unethical. Who would blame him who wants to assure his own homeostasis and happiness

by accumulating the treasure of other people's benevolence toward him? Yet this makes him virtually unassailable, for nobody wants to attack and destroy one upon whom he depends.

Application of this code would maximize the adaptability which is our most precious resource in dealing with the stress of life.

References

1. Selye, H. *Stress without Distress*. Philadelphia-New York: Lippincott, 1974.
2. Selye, H. *The Stress of My Life: A Scientist's Memoirs*. New York: Van Nostrand Reinhold, 1979.

Stress as a Factor in Human Evolution

Peter N.O. Mbaeyi, Ph.D.

Universitat Tuebingen
Federal Republic of Germany

Director
International Foundation for Biosocial Development and Human Health
New York, New York

This contribution aspires to a simple objective—the prescription of a precise conceptual framework for the investigation of the stress phenomenology in human life and evolution. This aim will be pursued from the viewpoint of analytic neurosciences (quantitative analysis of neural phenomena). In seeking to achieve this, something contrary to widely and commonly held views and attitudes, the neccessary and appropriate setting, must first be created (by way of analogies with some other appropriate phenomena). This paper will be devoted entirely to this process of constructing analogies.

Stress is used in an everyday colloquial way to circumscribe a multitude of (neurologically determined) behaviors—irrateness, hectic behavior, restlessness, nervousness—and to account for a number of events—overwork, exhaustion, disordered actions, etc. As a result of this, stress has acquired a negative image, forcing its positive aspects into the background.

This positive side is given by the fact that a certain measure of stress is significant, in fact necessary, for growth and development understood in the broad sense of adaptation—the ability to adjust to and accommodate changing conditions and environment, in short to evolve. For example, stress is in many cases essential for promoting learning; here, stress will appear in the form of acceptable motivations and incentives. The converse of this holds in some cases, namely, that the removal of stress may hinder learning. Therefore, the circumstantial connotations which colloquial language associates with stress are merely circumscriptions of symptoms relating only to one extreme aspect of stress.

An analysis of stress as a phenomenology must be made with precision in such a way that the circumstantial descriptions emerge as part of the general characterizations. Henri Poincaré, in one of his celebrated treatises (of general character) *Science and Methods,* observed that science grows largely through the careful distillation and formulation of analogies. This advice will be followed and practiced here.

In conjunction with the related concept of strain, stress is a terminology and concept which occurs in one area of the classical natural sciences, namely continuum mechanics (mechanics of continua). The following examples of simple objects define what is classically understood as a continuum: a thin rod, a membrane or plate, a beam. When these are subjected to some external force, such forces are measured and given as force per unit length, force per unit area, or force per unit volume and are called *strain.* These force applications lead to deformations of these bodies; such deformations are measured and given as *stress.* Consequently, there exist some relationships between strain and stress.

However, stress is not only dependent on strain but also on the elastic character of the continua; this describes the rate at which a continuum gives way (i.e., produces stress) to the applied strain. With this aid, it is possible to learn the limit point at which a particular strain produces so much stress that the entire original composition of the continua is completely altered. Thus, the *elasticity* of a continuum is the measure of its adaptiveness (indicated by regulated stresses) to the strain imposed on it by external factors. By careful trimming and training of the stress, strain, and elastic characteristics, it is well known that continua with various properties can be produced; this is the principle of what may be termed metallurgical "alchemy"—the fabrication of materials with different properties for different purposes.

From the foregoing discussion, it is clear that a material that is required to withstand high strain must have low stress properties (i.e., show little or no deformation by being highly resistant to external forces). On the other hand, a material required for detection of the smallest external force changes must have high stress properties (i.e., exhibit large deformations by having low resistance to external forces). It is therefore clear that a body with high stress properties will, under great strain, break faster than one with low stress characteristics. Two examples will illustrate this point:

1. Let increasing temperature (heat) be the external force generated; since metal structures are affected by heat treatment, metals with particularly low stress properties toward heat treatment (temperature rises and drops) are the only ones useful for the construction of combustion chambers (e.g., car engines).
2. The detection of detonations is based on monitoring the pressure waves which these generate in air, water, or the earth's crust. For spots far away from the detonation point or for weak detonations, highly sensitive materials, i.e., materials with high stress properties, are needed for the construction of detection equipment.

Other finer aspects of these stress, strain, and elastic properties will be encountered below in conjunction with developing neural analogues of the pattern of application of external forces on a continuum.

QUESTION: Is the excursion into the rudimentary framework of continuum mechanics useful and relevant to understanding the stress phenomenology of human life and evolution on the basis of neural phenomena?

ANSWER: Yes. Under the following conditions:

1. View the stress phenomenology of human life from the point of view of neural behaviors, where neural behaviors are taken to correspond to the behavorial states of a realistic neural network, representing and reproducing the (entire) natural linkages in a nervous system.
2. Construct, through careful building of analogies, neural network equivalents of the functional roles of strain, stress, and elastic characteristics of continua.

Under these premises, the stress phenomenology of human life and evolution can then be defined as functions of the neural network equivalents of strain and elastic properties.

The way toward achieving this will now be delineated, together with an exposition of the open questions. Before doing this, an advance remark will be made: very often in colloquial phraseology, a person showing symptoms of the circumstantial description called stress would often also be said to be under (great) strain. So that intuitively, the association of these dual concepts—strain and stress—is imbedded in the imagination about stress phenomenology in human life and is implicitly present when people talk of stress. Similarly, it is often said that someone who breaks under a stress situation is less resistant or adaptive to strain; here again, there is the implicit measure of how adaptive i.e., elastically accommodating, we are to strains generated by everyday life. Consequently, the transpositions that will be made precise here are not totally foreign to the intuitive feelings about stress phenomenology.

Some human behaviors are governed by synchronizations of the neuromuscular networks. Therefore, we will first dispose of the muscular system: when the muscular network is subjected to strains beyond its capability, muscular rupture occurs in the same way that a continuum breaks or its matter flows when it is subjected to strains beyond those admissible for the retention of its elastic limits. Thus, the behavior of the muscular network does not differentiate itself very much from that of the elements of classical continuum mechanics.

Therefore, our attention will now be turned to the neural networks whose components are simply the neurons (comparable to active transmitter cables), the synaptic modulators, etc. Henceforth, all references to neural networks should be taken to imply this type of network.

STRAIN CONCEPT IN NEURAL BEHAVIORS

From now on, we will be concerned with the neural networks, dealing purely with the transmission, processing, and accumulation (i.e., storage) of information. This network is assumed to consist of a finite number of subunits with specific functions within the whole network. Furthermore, behaviors in these neural networks are assumed to occur when these are subjected to external forces, called *excitations* (it should be noted, however, that neural behaviors do not only emerge as a result of external forces, since self-excitation of neural networks is also admissible under certain conditions).

DEFINITION 1: The *strain* on a neural network is the *density of excitations* per distinct subunit (of the neural network) per unit time.

DEFINITION 2: The density of excitation in a subunit is measured by the number of potential (i.e., latent) and active neural waves contained in that subunit.

Definition 2 above is intended to incorporate the effects of chemical information coding in neural nets.

In everyday language, this may be formulated as follows: With what frequencies (i.e., regularities ≡ intervals of time) and intensities do excitations arrive at various neural subunits?

In order to illustrate the conceptual sense of the above definitions, we will return to the example given by classical continuum mechanics. The strain applied to a continuum need not necessarily be a one time act or simply a continuous act. A third possibility is often employed as follows: the strain is a sequence of varying or constant external forces, applied with certain frequencies (i.e., at certain time intervals), so that for any given time span taken as a measure, the average strain, for example, measures the density of strain applied within the time span. This procedure is used very often in the heat and pressure treatment of materials in the fabrication of metals with different properties. Within this context, the conceptual framework is fairly simple: by subjecting a continuum to waves of certain strains, it is expected that a material can be so conditioned that it acquires certain exploitable properties—certain elastic and stress reaction capabilities to externally applied strains.

STRESS CONCEPT IN NEURAL BEHAVIORS

Returning to neural phenomena, we find that Definitions 1 and 2 define the excitability of a neural network in a way that embodies analogues of the preceding paragraph. We are, therefore, now in a position to introduce stress and elastic (accommodation) concepts for neural networks.

DEFINITION 3: A neural network is in a behavioral undifferentiated state if all its subunits are uniquely synchronized.

Assume that a neural network is prescribable by a system of autonomous differential equations with $(N + 1)$ components corresponding to its N (finite) subunits, while the extra dimension represents the network taken as a whole. Then,

DEFINITION 4: The N subunits of a neural network are uniquely synchronized if the system of autonomous differential equations describing the neural network does not admit a canonical decomposition.

An autonomous system of differential equations is said to be canonically decomposed, if there exists a so-called linear transformation such that it can be transformed into a set of decoupled equations. The canonical decomposition may be whole [i.e., cover all (N + 1) components] or partial (i.e., cover only some but not all sets of subunits). On this basis, we now have:

DEFINITION 5: The *stress* on a neural network is given by the *extent of the canonical decomposition* of the system of autonomous differential equations prescribing its state at any given time.

On the basis of this, stress will be classified into three basic types—positive, negative, and neutral stress.

DEFINITION 6: The stress on a neural network will be called a *positive stress,* if the function which measures the output of the network (taken as whole) grows (i.e., increases) continuously with time under continuous or intermittent applications of strain (according to Definition 1).

DEFINITION 7: The stress on a neural network is *negative stress,* if the function which measures the output of the network (taken as whole) decreases continuously with time under continuous or intermittent applications of strain.

DEFINITION 8: The stress on a neural network is a *neutral stress* if the function which measures the output of the network (taken as a whole) remains continuously constant with time under the application of strain.

A discussion of the implications of the above definitions will follow after the introduction of the third factor needed for the limitations with basic characteristic elements of continuum mechanics.

ACCOMMODATION OR ELASTICITY IN NEURAL BEHAVIORS

The specification of this entity will complete the analogies needed for understanding stress phenomenology in human life.

ASSUMPTION 9: The *strain density* on a neural subunit is *controlled* by a set of *neural time scales,* which control the *activation and deactivation (i.e., refraction)* of the *chemical dynamics* of a neural unit containing biochemical elements.

ASSUMPTION 10: The intervals of the neural time scales of neural phenomena are not fixed constants; they admit fluctuations, i.e., movements above and below certain "average" values.

An immediate consequence of Assumption 10 is: neural time scales are defined by what are called half-open intervals.

Assumptions 9 and 10 lead to the following conclusion: neural networks can be conditioned using varying strain densities arising from the variability of the neural time scales.

DEFINITION 11: A neural network will be said to have the *property of accommodation* or *to be elastic,* if the *neural time scales* associated with it are *defined by half-open intervals.*

For a discussions of time in terms of neural phenomena, we refer to the following: Haefner,[1] Hallen,[2] Hufschmidt,[3] Magun,[4] Schaltenbrand,[9,10] and Strauss;[11] for the analytical precision of these time problems, we refer to Mbaeyi.[5,6]

The next step is to put this in obvious linkage with stress phenomenology. In a nutshell, this is given by varying the neural time scales differently for all the subunits, a process that leads eventually to the achievement of Definition 5. The frequencies of these variations will inevitably produce variability of stress; i.e., for a given time interval, stress will vary by having differing sets of subunits which satisfy Definition 5. In other words, the partial canonical decomposition of neural networks will fluctuate with time. It is the rate of this fluctuation that gives stress phenomenology its negative connotation in colloquial language and understanding. These fluctuations, depending on their frequencies, may produce any situations defined by Definitions 6 through 8; the negative connotations are particularly associated with Definition 7.

THE OPEN QUESTIONS

It is not possible to expand this discussion on stress phenomena without becoming technical (analytically or otherwise). For example, it is necessary to introduce queuing and scheduling problems in order to expand on the role of variable neural time scales as pacers of accommodation (elasticity) in neural behaviors. Attention will therefore be focused on pointing out some of the open questions. The requirements prescribed by Assumptions 9 and 10 are analytically settled.[6,7] Apart from these, the open questions embrace particularly the construction of analytical frameworks which satisfy the requirements specified in Definitions 1 through 5; in addition to this, there is the need to specify and make precise the types of queuing and scheduling problems which are most suited to analytical specifications of neural behaviors. All of these are very largely dependent on the careful construction of neural networks that are realistic reproductions of the nervous system—the dendrites, the peripheral nerves, the spinal cord, etc.—both as individual systems and as integral parts of an organic entity.

ACKNOWLEDGMENT. I wish to thank my friend, Professor Stacey B. Day, President and Executive Director of the International Foundation for Biosocial Development and Human Health, for the invitation to contribute to this volume on stress appearing under the auspices of the foundation.

References

1. Haefner, H. Zeitlichkeit und physikalische Zeit. In *Zeit in Nervenaertzlicher Sicht* (G. Schaltenbrand, ed.), pp. 11–14. Stuttgart: Ferdinand Enke Verlag, 1963.
2. Hallen, O. Ueber Stoerungen des Zeiterlebens in epileptischen Aura. In *Zeit in Nervenaetzlicher Sicht* (G. Schaltenbrand, ed.), pp. 104–111. Stuttgart: Ferdinand Enke Verlag, 1963.
3. Hufschmidt, H. J. Die Zeitfaktor in der physiologischen und pathologischen Willkuermotorik. In *Zeit in Nervenaertzlicher Sicht* (G. Schaltenbrand, ed.), pp. 123–125. Stuttgart: Ferdinand Enke Verlag, 1963.
4. Magun, R. Die Zeitmessung in der Neurologie. In *Zeit in Nervenaertzlicher Sicht* (G. Schaltenbrand, ed.), pp. 111–123. Stuttgart: Ferdinand Enke Verlag, 1963.
5. Mbaeyi, P.N.O. Information capacity of neural network I—the single neuron. To appear *Proc. 5th European Congress on Cybernetics and Systems Research, Vienna* (April 1980).
6. Mbaeyi, P.N.O. Information capacity of neural network II—the one dimensional network. To appear *Proc. Intern. Symp. on Math. Methods in Biology and Medicine, University Salerno, Salerno, Italy* (April 1980).
7. Mbaeyi, P.N.O. Information capacity of neural networks III—the two and three dimensional networks (in preparation; to appear autumn/winter 1981).
8. Poincare, H. *Science and Methods.* Dover Publications.
9. Schaltenbrand, G. (ed.). *Zeit in Nervenaertzlicher Sicht.* Stuttgart: Ferdinand Enke Verlag, 1963.
10. Schaltenbrand, G. Die Krisis des Zeitbegriffs. In *Zeit in Nervenaertzlicher Sicht* (G. Schaltenbrand, ed.), pp. 1–11. Stuttgart: Ferdinand Enke Verlag, 1963.
11. Strauss, E. Ueber die Stoerungen des Zeitlebens be Seelischen Erkr Erkrankungen. In *Zeit in Nervenaertzlicher Sicht* (G. Schaltenbrand, ed.), pp. 14–15. Stuttgart: Ferdinand Enke Verlag, 1963.

The Brain and Stress

Henry Tamar, Ph.D.
Indiana State University
Terre Haute, Indiana

STRESS-ASSOCIATED FOCI AND PATHWAYS

The routes which transmit stress-engendered nerve impulse discharges through the brain can be said to eventually converge on the hypothalamus. This is the outlet by which the brain can call forth the autonomic nervous system and hormonal aspects of the nonspecific stress reaction. The stress-related roles of brain structures are covered below.

Association Cortex

This is the part of the cerebral cortex devoted to the higher mental faculties—reasoning, judgment, memory, etc. The prefrontal areas of the association cortex can directly transmit impulses to the hypothalamus, or can send nerve activity to it indirectly by way of the thalamus. There seem to also be efferent connections to the limbic system. Thus, higher mental activity can lead to the nonspecific stress reaction.

Sensory Cortex

The sensory cortex apparently conveys nerve impulses to the association cortex by poorly known fiber connections. It possibly also transmits impulses directly to the hypothalamus. The afferent and efferent connections with the thalamus at least mainly serve sensory functions.

Limbic System

The limbic system (here excluding the thalamus and hypothalamus) is important in the development of a large variety of homeostatic responses. It is so involved in the control of numerous autonomic and endocrine effects that it is known as the "visceral brain." The limbic system is the primary seat of strong emotions, and affects drinking and eating. It plays a role in

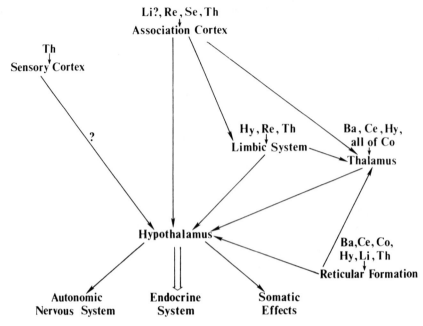

FIG. 1. Scheme of many important nerve connections between brain centers concerned with stress. The further actions of the hypothalamus in mediating stress responses are also included. Abbreviations: Ba, basal ganglia; Ce, cerebellum; Co, cortex; Hy, hypothalamus; Li, limbic system; Re, reticular formation; Se, sensory cortex, Th, thalamus.

high-level integration of visceral with olfactory and somatic inputs, and probably contributes to arousal.

The chief efferent outflows run to the hypothalamus (amygdalar-hypothalamic tracts, etc.). There are afferent and efferent connections with the thalamus, and major connections of these types with the reticular formation. an apparent direct afferent inflow from the cortex's frontal lobe is weak.

Thalamus

This structure, consisting of numerous nuclei, gives rise to the nonspecific system of thalamocortical pathways, regarded as a projection from the ascending reticular activating system. The nonspecific system may determine the cortex's level of excitability and control the intensity of the input to the cortex. Several thalamic nuclei apparently contribute to the control of visceral efferent, endocrine, and emotional behavior mechanisms. These nuclei receive, from the hypothalamus, the mamillothalamic tract which has a role in autonomic control and apparently also in homeostatic cycles. The habenular nucleus, by efferent pathways to lower centers such as the reticular formation, exerts an influence on autonomic centers controlling digestive secretion and motility. Removal of the habenular nuclei in animals affects endocrine and temperature regulation, and metabolism. The posterior nuclear complex may have a significant role in central pain mechanisms. The thalamus is a center for integration, especially of visceral, olfactory, and somatic inputs. More complex and varied patterns of information result and are widely distributed.

The thalamus has afferent and efferent connections with the cerebral cortex, limbic system, hypothalamus, basal ganglia, and reticular formation, and receives tracts from the cerebellum.

Reticular Formation

This long column in the central brain stem is probably involved in controlling numerous autonomic functions and the endocrine hypothalamic-pituitary mechanisms. It contains the cardiomotor, vasopressor, vasodepressor, and possibly gastrointestinal "centers," and the inspiratory and expiratory neurons. It participates in the development of emotions and in body temperature regulation. The reticular formation's ascending activating system connects to the nonspecific thalamocortical system and is the main origin of arousal.

The reticular formation receives afferent fibers from the cerebral cortex, cerebellum, limbic system, basal ganglia, thalamus, and hypothalamus. Collateral branches from the afferent systems and the spinoreticular pathways pass to it. In turn, it has direct or indirect efferent connections with the named systems and areas. There are efferent outflows to brain stem and spinal cord autonomic centers.

Hypothalamus

The hypothalamus, which is composed of numerous nuclei, is significant in the operation of almost all body systems. Most of its many functions are important in homeostasis and in the responses to stress. It is an outstanding integration center, integrating activity from many parts of the nervous system as well as nerve discharges from external and internal sources. Thus it integrates the processes necessary for energy balance. It further integrates efferent activities of the autonomic nervous, endocrine, and somatic nervous systems. The hypothalamus is a relay station that influences nervous system function in all directions, and it in turn is directly or indirectly affected by virtually all portions of the brain. The key actions exerted by the hypothalamus on the endocrine system via the pituitary gland will be covered in the next section.

The hypothalamus has a central role in mediating both the autonomic nervous system and the endocrine system phases of the nonspecific stress response. The autonomic (sympathetic) phase appears first and may initiate the only general response (the "fight or flight" reaction discussed in the following chapter) if the stressor is not too strong or lasting. Otherwise, the endocrine phase (see the next section) will follow.

In animals, ablation of the brain above the hypothalamus does not prevent the autonomic nervous system from functioning in a relatively normal fashion. However, higher brain centers provide better autonomic control and greater effectiveness of autonomic responses by acting on, or in conjunction with, the hypothalamus. Stressor action can call forth changes in the limbic system, etc., which precede or are concomitant with effects on the hypothalamus, and which are then transmitted to it.

The hypothalamus is the chief center for temperature regulation. Ablation of the brain areas superior to it in mammals causes minor impairment of temperature control but does not terminate the homeothermic condition. Impulse activity from temperature receptors in the body surface, viscera, spinal cord, and medulla oblongata is channeled to the hypothalamus, which possesses thermal sensors itself. The hypothalamic receptors are dominant.

The hypothalamus is also important in thirst perception, drinking, and the control of water loss, the last primarily through the kidneys. Direct stimulation of hypothalamic regions, raised tissue fluid osmotic pressure, and high temperatures stimulate drinking. If the body must conserve water, cells of the supraoptic hypothalamic nuclei produce antidiuretic hormone which acts in the kidneys. Water retention by the kidneys is also part of the general stress syndrome.

Renin and angiotensin act not only on the hypothalamus but also on the limbic system to elicit signs of thirst, and the control of water intake is now believed to involve the mesencephalon, limbic system, and cerebral cortex as well.

The hypothalamus is also significant in the control of body weight. It has hunger and satiety centers which interact, and may have glucose receptor or akin receptor cells. Hypoglycemia is an effective and typical stressor.

However, the limbic system and other brain structures may instead primarily control food intake.

It is certain that the hypothalamus takes part in emotional reactions. It contributes to the exhibition of rage, defensive behavior (fear and such), pleasure, etc. The hypothalamus seems to integrate emotional responses. However, the reticular formation may contribute significantly to anger and fear, the limbic system gives rise to pleasant sensations, and the limbic system may greatly add to the autonomic phase of the nonspecific stress response, as well as to the somatic reactions, produced by emotions. The limbic system may also be integrative in this regard.

Somatic responses as well are partially regulated by the hypothalamus. It helps to integrate reflex activities and gives rise to directional movements. In its presence, body movements remain fundamentally effective and coordinated, and such movements can be part of the response to stressors.

Besides many afferent connections from the limbic system, thalamus, and reticular formation, the hypothalamus also receives afferent ascending somatosensory, visceral, and gustatory tracts as well as olfactory pathways. Direct afferent pathways from the cerebral cortex and from the cerebellum have not been as firmly established. Efferent routes radiate from the hypothalamus to the limbic system, thalamus, reticular formation, primary somatomotor cortex (MSI), lower motor and autonomic centers, and the posterior lobe of the pituitary gland. There is a vascular link with the anterior pituitary.

The Hypothalamic-Pituitary System

All of the functions of the pituitary gland, which lies directly beneath the hypothalamus, are controlled by the latter.

The antidiuretic hormone (ADH) and oxytocin are produced in different neurosecretory neurons of the hypothalamus and pass down the axons of these neurons, through the pituitary stalk, into the posterior (neural) lobe of the pituitary gland. Here the hormones are stored in the axon terminals, to be released into the circulation when nerve impulses are conducted through the neurosecretory neurons. Both excitatory and inhibitory humoral and neural influences determine the level of impulse activity in the neurons which make ADH and, thus, the rate of release of this substance. The impulse discharges acting on the ADH-producing neurons can originate in the hypothalamus or in other nervous system structures. Such stressors as thirst, exercise, hemorrhage, and emotions increase ADH secretion.

The release of larger amounts of glucocorticoids is the chief factor leading to the second, endocrine system phase of the nonspecific stress response (the alarm reaction). The mechanisms responsible for the increased secretion of these hormones are of a different nature from those enhancing the amount of circulating ADH.

Stressors act directly on the hypothalamus and/or lead to increased nerve activity in other portions of the brain. In any case, the elicited neural activity appears to eventually stimulate neuroendocrine cells whose axons terminate in the ventral hypothalamus, especially the median eminence (the last forms the lower surface of the pituitary stalk where this stalk joins the main hypothalamus). Many neuroendocrine cells react by secreting the corticotrophic hormone releasing factor (CRF) from their axon endings. This releasing factor enters a surrounding capillary bed and is then carried in the blood through hypothalamic-hypophyseal portal vessels into another capillary bed in the anterior lobe of the pituitary gland. Now CRF stimulates anterior lobe cells to release adrenocorticotrophic hormone (ACTH) into the circulation. The ACTH is brought to the adrenal cortex and stimulates it to release corticoids, especially the glucocorticoids.

Among the many other releasing factors made in the hypothalamus is thyrotrophic hormone releasing factor (TRF). This substance is believed to function in a manner parallel to CRF in causing thyroid stimulating hormone (TSH) to be liberated from the anterior lobe. Although TRF production is stimulated by a number of stress conditions, cold is a specific agent for its formation and secretion.

The pineal gland is presently considered to function, through its peptides, in controlling the secretion of hormone releasing factors in the hypothalamus. At the same time it appears to be under the control of the hypothalamus (the source of pineal circadian rhythms) and other brain structures by way of sympathetic nerve fibers. It could thus be seen as a neurochemical transducer.

BRAIN PEPTIDE TRANSMITTERS

The chemical transmitters which convey nerve impulses across synaptic clefts in the brain are thought to include peptides, and many more peptides are likely to be suspected as such mediators in the future. These neuropeptides are especially interesting because stress-related functions, such as transmission of pain, have been attributed to many of them.

Not all the neuropeptides can be expected to act as transmitters in a normal sense—some may turn out merely to modulate impulse transmission by affecting membrane ion channel properties, the quantity of a neurotransmitter released, etc.

Many peptides function as both brain transmitters and as hormones elsewhere, making the differentiation of these two classes of substances indistinct. Thus substance P, modified cholecystokinin, neurotensin, enkephalins, etc., act in the brain and also as hormones or transmitters in the digestive system. Adrenocorticotrophic hormone, antidiuretic hormone, oxytocin, and thyrotrophic hormone releasing factor, all covered earlier, are included among the neuropeptides.

Neuropeptides are unlike other transmitter-type substances in that they apparently trigger complex response entities. For example, ADH greatly improves memory in animals, while injecting the neuropeptides angiotensin II and luteinizing hormone releasing factor into the brains of animals, respectively, arouses strong thirst and female reproductive behavior.

Substance P is commonly found in brain areas that contain much serotonin (5-HT), a monoamine neurotransmitter, and both are important in pain perception. Substance P is concentrated in the mesencephalon's substantia nigra, in pathways in the limbic system (emotional behavior), and in the axon terminations of first-order pain fibers. It is released from the last to excite dorsal spinal cord neurons that are particularly reactive to pain-eliciting input. Substance P has also been implicated in tooth pain and in the vasodilation surrounding injured regions.

Two differently localized brain peptides called enkephalins (in one, the last of five amino acids is methionine; in the other, leucine) bind strongly to opiate receptors and thus show morphine-like activity. Similar peptides obtained from the pituitary gland have been named endorphins. Beta-endorphin, present at near 10% of the enkephalin concentration in specific brain neuron systems (excepting enkephalin neurons), is even more potent than the enkephalins. All these substances seem to naturally inhibit pain reception by binding to the opiate receptors. Acupuncture, subjecting the brain to low-frequency electric current, and hypnosis may all mitigate chronic pain by causing the release of enkephalins and endorphins in the brain and spinal cord.

Enkephalin localized in spinal cord interneurons appears to modulate the substance P–requiring transmission of pain discharges from first-order pain fibers by interacting with opiate receptors on the fibers' terminations (morphine and other opiates are effective here too). This inhibits the release of substance P. The presence of enkephalin fibers and opiate receptors in the emotion-controlling limbic system could explain why opiate drugs bring about euphoric states.

The opiate-like peptides variously change the excitability of different CNS neurons. Injected beta-endorphin produces a marked and lasting catatonic state. Beta-endorphin also greatly stimulates ADH secretion, probably by acting in the hypothalamus.

Neurotensin has powerful analgesic action that is not related to that of opiates. Neurotensin is found in highest amounts in the hypothalamus and the basal ganglia.

BRAIN RECEPTORS

In this section, after a brief overview, opiate receptors will serve as an illustrative example.

Neural transmitters, in order to have an effect, must react with receptor molecules on postsynaptic neural cell membranes. Each receptor molecule, presumably of protein, is specifically structured for interaction with a particular transmitter. Neurons producing a specific transmitter are differentially distributed in the brain, and the neurons possessing receptors with which this transmitter can interact are localized accordingly, so that a transmitter stored in axon terminations is near receptors suitable for it. Commonly a transmitter can interact with several differently—but properly—structured receptors, and each such receptor subtype may have a characteristic distribution.

There appear to be several different opiate receptors. Thus it is postulated that the benzomorphan drugs act at kappa receptors and morphine at mu receptors, and that hallucinogenic opiates affect sigma receptors. An additional, delta receptor selectively binds the leu- over the met-form of the peptide transmitter enkephalin, while met-enkephalin more often interacts with the mu receptor.

The mu receptors are concentrated in brain regions receiving sensory input (cerebral cortex layer 4, some sensory nuclei of the thalamus). These receptors may be particularly concerned with pain perception and perhaps specifically with opiate analgesia.

Parts of the limbic system, which regulates emotions, contain especially many delta receptors.

Opiate receptors in general are concentrated in the parts of the spinal cord and brain contributing to the perception or integration of pain and emotions. Less localized, dull, chronic pain is transmitted to the cerebral cortex by the paleospinothalamic pathway, which extends through the spinal cord, reticular formation, hypothalamus, central thalamus, and limbic system. This pathway is rich in opiate receptors, and therefore chronic pain is successfully relieved with opiate analgesics such as morphine. However, the pathway for localized, momentary pain lacks concentrations of opiate receptors.

References

1. Brooks, C. M. and Koizumi, K. The hypothalamus and control of integrative processes. In *Medical Physiology* (V. B. Mountcastle, (ed.),14th ed., vol. 1, pp 923–947. St. Louis: C. V. Mosby, 1980.
2. Iversen, L. L. The chemistry of the brain. *Sci. Amer.* 24: 134–149 (1979).
3. Snyder, S. H. Brain peptides as neurotransmitters. *Science* 209: 976–983 (1980).
4. Snyder, S. H. and Goodman, R. R. Multiple neurotransmitter receptors. *J. Neurochem.* 35: 5–15 (1980).

The Autonomic Nervous System

Henry Tamar, Ph.D.
Indiana State University
Terre Haute, Indiana

GENERAL DESCRIPTION

Definition

The human nervous system can be divided according to function into two major portions, the somatic nervous system and the autonomic nervous system.

The somatic nervous system innervates the voluntary muscles and thus is the part of the nervous system through which we carry out the activities we can (consciously) control. The somatic nervous system includes most elements of the brain and the cranial nerves connected to it, the spinal cord, and the spinal nerves.

The autonomic nervous system, instead, consists of nerve cells which are devoted to regulating the activity of a series of organs that are not normally under conscious control. These automatically functioning organs contain one or more of three tissues: smooth or involuntary muscle, cardiac muscle, and glandular epithelium.

General Composition and Function

The autonomic nervous system *sensu stricto* includes primarily motor (efferent) neurons—nerve cells which carry nerve impulses (action potentials) originating in the brain stem or spinal cord toward the automatically active organs. However, the autonomic system, like the somatic system, acts on the basis of reflex arcs, and therefore sensory neurons (visceral afferents) play a key role in its activity. Yet these sensory neurons cannot be included in the autonomic system because such a sensory neuron can be part of both an autonomic and a somatic nervous system reflex arc.

In the autonomic nervous system we find both nerve ganglia (masses of neuron cell bodies) and nerves (which may consist of hundreds of thousands of nerve axons). The neurons themselves are almost entirely either preganglionic (and therefore transmit impulses from the brain stem or spinal cord to synapses with neurons in autonomic ganglia) or postganglionic (and thus carry nerve messages from autonomic ganglia to effector organs). There is integrative activity, some involving interneurons, in autonomic ganglia.

The autonomic nervous system is made up of two divisions, the sympathetic system and the parasympathetic system. The sympathetic system or thoracolumbar outflow originates from the thoracic and three or four upper lumbar segments of the spinal cord, while the parasympathetic or craniosacral outflow arises from cranial nerve nuclei in the brain stem and from the second, third, and fourth sacral segments of the spinal cord. Most automatic organs are innervated by both the sympathetic and parasympathetic systems, and these two systems usually affect organ function in opposing ways (the principle of autonomic antagonism). At the same time, however, generally one of the systems exerts a dominant influence on an organ.

Since the autonomic nervous system plays a vital role in maintaining homeostasis, many autonomic neurons exhibit constant (tonic) impulse activity; the dually innervated organs receive continuous streams of both sympathetic and parasympathetic nerve impulses. Evidence for interaction between sympathetic and parasympathetic terminations in dually innervated organs has been reported.

Chemical Transmitters

In the autonomic nervous system only sympathetic postganglionic neurons, and not even all of these, release noradrenaline (norepinephrine) from their axon terminals. Noradrenaline, on crossing the subsequent neuroeffector junctions, combines with two types of receptors, the alpha and beta receptors, in the effector cell membranes.

Some sympathetic postganglionic neurons, those having neuroeffector junctions with sweat glands, in the external genitalia or with smooth muscle cells in skeletal muscle blood vessels, instead release acetylcholine from their axon terminals. The parasympathetic postganglionic neurons, and all sympathetic and parasympathetic preganglionic neurons, also release acetylcholine.

Acetylcholine combines with at least nicotinic and muscarinic receptors in post-gap cell membranes. Autonomic postganglionic neurons possess nicotinic receptors, so named because nicotine also interacts with them. Curare blocks nicotinic receptors. Effector cell membranes stimulated by autonomic cholinergic postganglionic neurons have muscarinic receptors, which are also stimulated by muscarine and are blocked by atropine.

It is now believed that ATP is the chemical transmitter released by a special group of distal autonomic neurons that inhibit digestive smooth muscle, and a number of other substances are suspected to be autonomic transmitters. There also appear to be additional membrane receptor types.

RELATIONS WITH THE SOMATIC NERVOUS SYSTEM

The term autonomic nervous system is really a misnomer. Although the autonomic system acts to influence automatic organs, it is actually integrated with somatic nervous system centers in the brain stem and spinal cord. These centers themselves are only the lowest level of a hierarchy of the somatic nervous system's so-called autonomic centers.

The highest level of somatic system autonomic centers lies in the cerebral cortex. Impulses from cortical autonomic centers descend to trigger or inhibit activity in limbic (rhinencephalic) autonomic centers, and these in turn transmit nerve messages to autonomic centers in the hypothalamus. These send impulses to lowest-level autonomic centers—the parasympathetic centers of the brain stem or sacral spinal cord and/or to the sympathetic centers of the thoracolumbar spinal cord. These lowest-level autonomic centers then act on the autonomic nervous system proper, stimulating or inhibiting parasympathetic or sympathetic activity (and thus indirectly automatic organs).

By means of the close relationship between the somatic nervous system and the autonomic nervous system described above, conscious mental states readily affect the activities of automatic (visceral) organs. In the last 20 years it has further been shown that humans, by use of biofeedback equipment, can learn to make specific desired responses with automatic organs.

Recent thought tends to emphasize a general body role for the autonomic system (Fig. 3). It is considered to act in parallel with the somatic system. Also, the somatic autonomic control centers are no longer seen as separately devoted to the autonomic system.

SYMPATHETIC SYSTEM

Structure

The sympathetic division is larger than the parasympathetic division of the autonomic nervous system and has a considerably greater distribution.

One chain of sympathetic ganglia lies on each side of the anterior surface of the vertebral column, extending from the level of the second neck vertebra to the coccyx. Each chain typically has 3 cervical ganglia, 11 thoracic ganglia, 4 lumbar ganglia, and 4 sacral ganglia, or a total of 22 ganglia. All these ganglia are connected to each other, as well as to the spinal cord, by short nerve tracts.

There are also a number of collateral (subsidiary) sympathetic ganglia, which with little exception are situated closer to the vertebral column than to the effector organs to which they send nerve fibers. Among these are the two celiac ganglia, which form much of the celiac or solar plexus, are sizable and flat, and lie on each side of the celiac artery immediately beneath the diaphragm. Another collateral ganglion is the small superior mesenteric ganglion, near the start of the superior mesenteric artery. The small inferior mesenteric ganglion, near the start of the inferior mesenteric artery, is not usually present as a single entity in man.

The chains of sympathetic ganglia give off the splanchnic nerves, which connect them with collateral ganglia. Three splanchnic nerves (the greater, lesser, and lowest) leave the thoracic part of each chain, and four the lumbar portion. The thoracic splanchnic nerve–collateral ganglia routes are the chief avenues by which sympathetic impulses reach abdominal automatic organs. However, the splanchnic nerves also contain sensory, afferent fibers.

The cell bodies of the sympathetic preganglionic neurons lie in the lateral columns (horns) of the butterfly-shaped central gray matter of the spinal cord's thoracic and first two or three lumbar segments. The myelinated axons of these neurons leave the spinal cord in the anterior roots of the 14 corresponding spinal nerves on each side. They continue through the spinal nerve trunks (and the beginning of the spinal nerves' anterior rami), but then leave the spinal nerves by way of short branches known as *white rami communicantes*. True white rami are only associated with the mentioned 14 spinal nerves on each side, or only with the sympathetic outflow. The white rami carry the sympathetic preganglionic axons to the sympathetic ganglion chains.

When a preganglionic fiber enters a sympathetic chain, it may synapse with sympathetic postganglionic neurons in a ganglion at its level, may continue in the chain and end in either a higher or a lower ganglion, or may eventually pass out of the chain in a splanchnic nerve to synapse with postganglionic neurons in a collateral ganglion (Fig. 1).

The cell bodies of sympathetic postganglionic neurons are located in the ganglia of the sympathetic chains or in collateral ganglia and give rise to usually thin, unmyelinated axons, the postganglionic fibers. Some axons from sympathetic chain ganglia travel toward automatic effector organs in spinal nerves, while the other axons course through autonomic nerves (some of both groups after first ascending or descending in the sympathetic chain).

The sympathetic chain–spinal nerve routes involve a *gray ramus communicans* which enters the spinal nerve immediately proximal to the white ramus (there are some mixed rami). The postganglionic fibers pass through

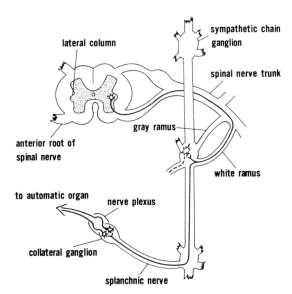

FIG. 1. Diagrammatic representation of a route of sympathetic nerve impulses from the spinal cord to an automatic effector organ by way of postganglionic neurons in a collateral ganglion.

the anterior and posterior rami of the spinal nerve and its branches, and
serve a zone of blood vessels, arrector hair muscles, sweat glands, etc.

The postganglionic axons which follow an autonomic nerve route diffuse
through complex plexuses before reaching effector organs. Some of these
plexuses surround the corresponding collateral ganglia. There are celiac
ganglia or superior mesenteric ganglion–celiac plexus–abdominal viscera,
inferior mesenteric ganglion-hypogastric plexus-abdominal or pelvic
viscera, cervical ganglion (in the sympathetic chain)–cardiac plexus–heart,
etc., autonomic nerve routes. There appears to be important neuronal interaction in enteric plexuses.

Postganglionic sympathetic axons innervate the smooth muscle of a
variety of blood vessels and hollow internal organs, and also terminate in a
number of glands.

Exceptionally, the sympathetic innervation of the adrenal medullae consists of preganglionic fibers which travel without interruption from the
lateral columns of the spinal cord to specialized medulla cells of nervous
origin that produce adrenaline and noradrenaline.

Function

The sympathetic system greatly increases its activity in response to emergency or stress conditions. This role in stress is so clear-cut that the
physiologist Walter B. Cannon described the general body response to an
upsurge in sympathetic activity as the "fight or flight" reaction. The group

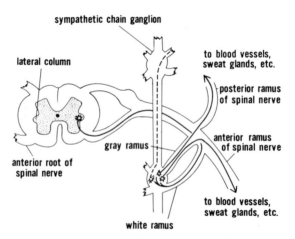

FIG. 2. Diagrammatic representation of two routes of sympathetic nerve impulses from the
spinal cord to automatic effector organs via, respectively, the anterior ramus and the posterior
ramus of a spinal nerve. An additional spinal nerve route is indicated by a dashed line.

of body changes included in this reaction sets the stage for high levels of energy release and physical exertion by the organism. The sympathetic system is mobilized to call forth the "fight or flight" reaction by direct physical factors such as extreme temperatures and lack of water, or by emotional states, and its resultant activity is normally generalized to a series of automatic organs.

The responses of automatic organs to an increased level of arriving sympathetic impulses are often best understood in terms of the "fight or flight" concept. Thus the dilation of skeletal (voluntary) muscle blood vessels initiated by heightened sympathetic activity increases the blood flow to these muscles and provides the extra oxygen and glucose required for greater muscular exertion. The faster and stronger heartbeat produced (by action on the s.a. node, the a.v. node, and the cardiac muscle) enhances the circulation and serves the same purposes. Dilation of the coronary vessels to increase the coronary circulation seems to accompany the stimulation of the heart. Constriction of most blood vessels, such as those of the skin, cerebrum, and abdominal viscera, raises the blood pressure and facilitates circulation to the musculature. It also makes more red cells available to the musculature. Vasoconstriction further is a response to cold. The increase in liver glycogenolysis makes more blood glucose available, as does the often concomitant inhibition of pancreatic insulin secretion, and muscle glycogenolysis rises as well. The slight dilation of the bronchi enhances respiratory exchange and allows the blood to pick up extra oxygen. Both the basal metabolic rate and mental activity are increased. Greater secretion by the sweat glands can prevent overheating. Also, the meridional muscle fibers of the iris of the eye are stimulated, resulting in dilation of the pupil, which should lead to momentarily greater visual acuity.

Further, the sympathetic system, by stimulation of the hairs' arrector pili (smooth) muscles, can cause erection of the hair of the skin, and this can be mechanically protective in animals or can reduce their heat loss at low temperatures.

All of the above effects are strengthened and maintained by the sympathetic action on the adrenal medulla, which is to stimulate significant secretion of adrenaline and noradrenaline (the output of adrenaline averages four times that of noradrenaline, but proportions vary). Even a special adrenergic sweating and a predominant dilation of the skeletal muscle blood vessels are called forth. The adrenal medullae's noradrenaline has essentially the same effects as that released from sympathetic postganglionic axon terminations, but it acts ten times longer since it remains in the circulation for some time. Adrenaline stimulates body metabolism and the heart to a greater extent than noradrenaline, but causes much less constriction of skeletal muscle blood vessels than the latter.

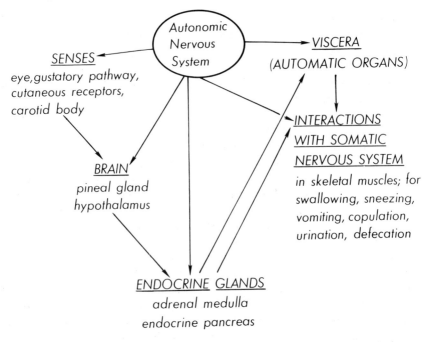

FIG. 3. Generalized scheme of the effects of the autonomic nervous system on the body as a whole. Some autonomic system targets are listed in lower-case letters.

At the same time, the sympathetic system inhibits momentarily nonessential vegetative functions. The activity of the smooth muscle of the digestive tract and of the urinary bladder is reduced preventing, respectively, peristaltic movements and bladder contraction. However, the sphincters of the digestive and urinary systems are stimulated to constrict. The gall bladder is relaxed. Further, the salivary and gastric glands are often affected, especially by vasoconstriction of their blood vessels.

In the male, sympathetic impulses also initiate emission of spermatozoa during the sexual act.

PARASYMPATHETIC SYSTEM

Structure

The myelinated axons of the parasympathetic outflow are found in two widely separated locations. The axons of the preganglionic neurons whose cell bodies lie in the brain stem's cranial nerve nuclei pass peripherally in the III, VII, IX, and X cranial nerves. Those arising from cell bodies in the lateral columns (horns) of the gray matter of the second to fourth sacral segments of the spinal cord pass through the anterior rami of the second, third, and fourth sacral spinal nerves in the lower back. They then extend through visceral branches of these spinal nerves, branches known as the pelvic splanchnic nerves.

The sacral part of the parasympathetic system serves organs in the lower abdomen, including the descending colon, rectum, and urinary bladder, and also the genitalia. The parasympathetic fibers supplying organs superior to the transverse colon (in the head, neck, thorax, and abdomen) instead belong to the cranial portion of the system.

Parasympathetic preganglionic axons are long. Most run to the short dendrites and the cell bodies of postganglionic neurons which lie in peripheral ganglia located relatively close to the served automatic organs. Others contact postganglionic neurons whose cell bodies are somewhat scattered in the walls of the automatic effector organs themselves. Since the preganglionic neurons terminate and synapse only close to or in the affected organs, each just contacts postganglionic neurons influencing one organ. This contributes to the generally localized nature of parasympathetic effects.

Unlike the preganglionic neurons, parasympathetic postganglionic neurons usually possess short, unmyelinated axons.

Function

As would be deduced from the principle of autonomic antagonism, the parasympathetic system generally acts to oppose the sympathetic system's mobilization of the body. The parasympathetic system calls forth conservation of body energy and stimulates visceral functions of less immediate significance. In the absence of abnormal stimuli, it is the principal regulator of numerous automatic organs such as the heart, the parts of the digestive tract, and the pancreas. These organs ordinarily are subject to more parasympathetic than sympathetic activity.

The parasympathetic system reduces the heart's rate and strength of contraction. It may also initiate constriction of coronary vessels, although innervation of the last has not been fully demonstrated. Blood vessels in the cerebrum and in some abdominal viscera may be dilated, but there is no parasympathetic innervation of the blood vessels (1) of skeletal muscles or (2) of the skin in general. The bronchi are slightly constricted. Peristalsis and glandular secretion (including of saliva) in the digestive tract are stimulated, and the digestive system sphincters are inhibited and thus caused to open. Pancreatic juice and insulin secretion are increased. Secretion by the tear glands and nasal glands, contraction of the urinary bladder, and turgidity of erectile tissues (by arterial dilation and venous constriction) are stimulated. The urinary sphincters are inhibited and thus allowed to relax. Also, the pupil of the eye is constricted, and the ciliary muscle contracts and thus accommodates the lens for near vision. There is no parasympathetic innervation of the liver, adrenal medulla, sweat glands, or the hairs' arrector pili muscles.

Surprisingly, emotional stress can often lead to greater stomach activity, while long-continued stress may bring about excess stomach acidity and eventually peptic ulcer. Both phenomena appear to result from a stress-induced increase in parasympathetic impulses to the stomach.

Reference

Brooks, C. McC., Koizumi, K., and Sato, A. (eds.). *Integrative Functions of the Autonomic Nervous System*. Tokyo: University of Tokyo Press, and Elsevier/North-Holland Biomedical Press, 1979.

Stress and Animal Models of Disease

Malcolm P. Rogers, M.D.
Associate in Medicine (Psychiatry) Division of Psychiatry
Department of Medicine, Brigham and Women's Hospital
Boston, Massachusetts

Assistant Professor of Psychiatry
Harvard Medical School
Boston, Massachusetts

Introduction

In recent years, evidence has accumulated that the brain and emotional states can modify the functioning of the immune system.[1] Direct brain stimulation, conditioning, hypnosis, neurotransmitter stimulation of lymphocytes, and the impact of stress on immune responses have all provided support for this hypothesis. The latter has included both human and animal studies. Emotional changes, such as grief and anxiety, may affect immune responses directly or indirectly by altering sleep, diet, and perhaps other behaviors. This chapter will focus on several animal experiments which have shown definite but, in many cases, complex effects of stress on susceptibility to diseases that are closely linked with failures in immune regulation.

The Concept of Stress

The term *stress* is widely used but unfortunately with variable meanings. Some have used it to mean a noxious and threatening stimulus; others, such as Selye, have used it to mean the response of the organism to such a stimulus, either physiologically, psychologically, or both. For the purpose of this chapter, and in general, we would define stress in terms of the stimulus rather than the response (which, as others have suggested, might best be called strain). Clearly, in human beings, the degree to which a particular event is stressful will depend on its meaning for a particular individual. For experimental animals we have no direct way of knowing the animal's inner experience except through behavioral and physiological measures, such as defecation and neuroendocrine changes.

Infection

Experimental stress in rodents, typically created either by physical restraint or by avoidance conditioning using electrical shocks, has been associated with increased susceptibility to numerous viral illnesses, including herpes simplex, poliomyelitis virus, Coxsackie B virus, and polyoma virus. Other stressful manipulations, such as exposure to high-intensity sound, overcrowding, or a predator, have also increased susceptibility to certain infections. In the latter study,[2] Hamilton showed that exposure to a predator (cat) increased dramatically the rate of reinfection of mice with tapeworm, and was also correlated with adrenal hypertrophy and splenic atrophy, including an atrophy of splenic germinal centers containing high concentrations of lymphocytes.

To add to the complexity, however, it has also been observed in at least two studies that stress may have a protective effect against infection. Thus, the exact nature of the stress and the timing of its application in relation to the biology of the host and the microorganism are all important factors in determining the effect which stress will have on susceptibility to infection.

Cancer

The incidence and rate of growth of experimental animal tumors have been altered by stress. A strain of mice carrying the Bittner oncogenic virus usually develops mammary tumors within 8 to 18 months after birth. Riley demonstrated that the usual stressful housing of laboratory mice was associated with a 92% incidence of tumors, whereas only 7% developed tumors in a special nonstressful environment.[3] Elevated cortisol levels and involution of the thymus gland were also found in the stressed animals, and were hypothesized to have mediated the stress-induced effects on tumor development. One theory of immune surveillance holds that cancerous cells occurring in the body are recognized and destroyed by cells of the immune system, in particular the Natural Killer cells (NK). This study suggests that stress may impair this surveillance function.

Another study, by Ader and Friedman, showed that stimulation by handling during the first three weeks of life shortens the survival time of mice after transplantation of lymphoid leukemia. Recently Plaut and his associates demonstrated that anticipation of a noxious stimulus (shock preceded by a warning signal) could increase the resistance to spontaneously occurring leukemia in AKR mice. Thus, as with infectious disease models, different stresses in animal tumor systems can either protect against or accelerate tumor growth.

Arthritis

Physicians have commented that emotions occasionally appear to influence diseases with autoimmune manifestations, such as rheumatoid arthritis.

In one animal model for rheumatoid arthritis, adjuvant-induced arthritis in rats, Amkraut and his colleagues have reported that group housing stress significantly increases the intensity of this disease in male rats. They also showed that group housing stress accelerates the time of maximal disease and the rate of recovery.

Recently, an experimental model of autoimmune arthritis has been described in rats or certain strains of mice. In rats, intradermal injection of native heterologous or homologous type II collagen, prepared from cartilage, can initiate a chronic polyarthritis 11 to 21 days later.[4] The arthritis can be passively transferred by spleen and lymph node cells sensitized to type II collagen, which indicates that immunologic hypersensitivity to this protein induces the disease. A proliferative synovitis is found in this model which histologically resembles that observed in rheumatoid arthritis. Humoral and cellular immunologic responses to collagen are present in collagen-induced arthritis and rheumatoid arthritis. These shared features suggest that this may be an appropriate animal model for human arthritis. Approximately 40% of collagen-injected outbred Wistar rats develop arthritis.

We have investigated the susceptibility of this model to experimentally induced psychological stress. The primary stress modality that we chose was exposure to a predator, since rats appear to possess an innate fear of cats. This is evidenced by a freezing response to the sight or smell of a cat. We also chose what appeared to be a symbolic stress, rather than a physically noxious one.

The following experiment was performed twice: 60 female outbred Wistar rats were placed in groups of five in plastic cages. On day 0, we immunized the rats with type II collagen, emulsified in incomplete Freund's adjuvant. Care was taken to immunize all rats in a similar manner.

Our stress protocol involved dividing the rats into three equal groups. Beginning three days prior to immunization, the 20 rats in Group A were exposed to a cat for a 10-minute period four times a day. Exposure to the cat involved the following procedure. The four cages housing the 20 Group A rats were transported by cart to the exposure room. A cat was brought into the room and put in a large metal cage, into which was placed a smaller cage containing the Group A rats. After 10 minutes, the rats were returned to their housing cages.

The 20 rats in Group B served as a control for any effects attributable to handling and transporting the Group A rats. The experimental stresses were stopped on day 10, just prior to the usual time for the onset of arthritis. Except for bedding changes and immunization, the 20 rats in Group C were left undisturbed during this period.

Beginning on day 11 and continuing until day 28 when the study was terminated, each rat was examined daily for the development of arthritis. The severity of arthritis was rated by an evaluator blinded to the protocol and by caliper measurements of the ankles. On day 21, blood was collected by distal tail amputation for serum antibodies to type II collagen. On day 28, intradermal delayed-type hypersensitivity reactions to collagen were quantitifed using a radiometric ear assay.

Similar results were obtained in the two separate experiments, so the data were combined and are shown in Table 1. In contrast to the 40% incidence of arthritis in the undisturbed Group C, only one rat in the cat-exposed Group A developed arthritis. The incidence of arthritis was also significantly decreased in the transported and handled Group B. Histologic evidence of synovitis was found in each rat with the clinical diagnosis of arthritis and, additionally, in only one rat clinically adjudged to be nonarthritic.

Stress dissociated the development of immunologic sensitivity to collagen from the occurrence of arthritis. As has been found in previous studies, greater humoral and cellular repsonses to collagen correlated with the oc-

TABLE 1. Effects of Various Stresses on Collagen-induced Arthritis.

Group	Stress	Number of Arthritic/Nonarthritic Rats	P Value*
A	Cat Exposure	1/39 (3%)	0.001
B	Transportation, handling	4/39 (10%)	
C	Undisturbed	16/40 (40%)	

* Degree of significance compared to the incidence of arthritis in Group C.

curence of arthritis in Group C. In contrast, the nonarthritic rats in the two stressed groups frequently exhibited high antibody titers and delayed hypersensitivity to collagen.

This study[5] demonstrates that psychological stress, produced either by exposure to a predator or by transportation and handling, can profoundly suppress the clinical and histologic manifestations of arthritis in this model. The mechanisms by which stress abrogates the development of synovitis—but not immunologic sensitivity to collagen—remain to be defined. An elevation in glucocorticoids resulting from stress may have been an important mediator, and perhaps catecholamine increases as well. However, we have recently found that stress produced by auditory stimulation (an automobile siren) can exacerbate the clinical features of collagen-induced arthritis.[6] A hypothesis involving glucocorticoids or other possible mediators must reconcile the paradoxical effect of different stress modalities on collagen-induced arthritis.

Summary

The dichotomous responses to different stresses in this model of autoimmune arthritis are similar to those described above in infectious disease and cancer models, and reiterate the complexity of stress effects on animal models of disease, especially those involving the immune system. However, the central importance of the studies described above lies in their demonstration of the capacity of mind-body interactions to alter in a fundamental way immunologically mediated biological disease processes.

References

1. Rogers, M. P., Dubey, D., and Reich, P. The influence of the psyche and the brain on immunity and disease susceptibility: a critical review. *Psychosom. Med.* **41**:147–164 (1979).
2. Hamilton, D.R. Immunosuppressive effects of predator induced stress in mice with acquired immunity to *Hymenolepis nana*. *J. Psychosom. Res.* **18**:143–150 (1974).

3. Riley, V. Mouse mammary tumors: alteration of incidence as apparent function of stress. *Science* **189**:465–467 (1975).
4. Trentham, D. E., Townes, A. S., and Kang, A. H. Autoimmunity to type II collagen: an experimental model of arthritis. *J. Exp. Med.* **146**:857–868 (1977).
5. Rogers, M. P., Trentham, D. E., McCune, W. J. et al. Effect of psychological stress on induction of arthritis in rats. *Arthritis Rheum.* **23**: 1337–42 (1980).
6. Rogers, M. P., Trentham, D. E., Dynesius, R. A., et al. Exacerbation of type II collagen-induced arthritis by auditory stress (abstract). *Clin. Res.* **28**:508 (1980).

Stress-induced Deficits in Animal Behavior

Barbara A. Regan, M.A.
Central Nervous System Disease Therapy Section
Lederle Laboratories
Pearl River, New York

During the past two decades, many studies have been undertaken in an attempt to correlate psychological and/or physiological variables and behavior. The rationale for these investigations is twofold: first, to gain insight into the normal behavior of an organism and, second, to attempt to explain behavior disorders in terms of aberrant processes within the central nervous system. This has led to a growing belief that deficits in laboratory animals ensuing from exposure to stress may be analogous to clinical depression in man. The stressors used in this area of research include confinement of infrahuman primates, inescapable electric shock in dogs and rats, and forced swimming in rodents; the behavioral variables measured relate to motor activity and avoidance responding.

Harlow and his co-workers have shown that early separation of monkeys from their mothers or peers can result in prolonged abnormal behaviors reminiscent of behavior observed in human depression, particularly anaclitic depression.[1,2] Consequently, they suggest that this may be an animal model of depression. This aberrant behavior, characterized by decrements in motor activity and social interactions, can also be induced in monkeys by confinement in a vertical chamber.[3]

In early studies by Seligman and his co-workers at the University of Pennsylvania, dogs were exposed to inescapable (noxious) electric shocks.

In subsequent testing, these dogs failed to learn escape and avoidance responding in a conventional shuttlebox situation, whereas animals not previously exposed to shock readily acquired this behavior. Further studies showed that dogs receiving the same amount of shock, which they were able to avoid or escape, did not show these behavioral decrements.[4,5] This indicates that it was the inescapability of the shock, rather than the shock per se, that was an important contingency in the induction of these deficits. This phenomenon disappeared within 48 hours after exposure to the stressor, and dogs initially tested 72 hours after inescapable shock did not show these deficits. A similar profile of behavioral responding deficits, a concomitant decrease in locomotor activity, and a parallel time course of decay were observed in rats following inescapable electric shock. Agents that are effective in the treatment of human clinical depression also prevent these stress-induced deficits in laboratory animals. Seligman has theorized that these decrements in behavior are produced because the animals learn that their behavior is not instrumental in the termination of the shock. He has termed this aberrant behavior *learned helplessness* and suggests that it may be analogous to clinical depression, which is characterized by feelings of "helplessness and hopelessness" because the patient feels he has no control over his environment.

In more recent studies, forced swimming in mice and rats has been used as a stressor, and resultant deficits in motor activity and avoidance responding have been observed. One of the most salient effects observed is that this stress-induced immobility is prevented by the prior administration of clinically effective antidepressive agents or treatments.[6] However, Weiss and his co-workers have performed a number of experiments utilizing either inescapable shock or cold swimming as stressors to further characterize the nature of these ensuing deficits. The results of these experiments show that the failure to escape and/or avoid electroshock is directly related to the degree of motor activity required by the operant task.[7] In a conventional shuttlebox paradigm, the effects of inescapable stress are robust on subsequent avoidance behavior. In contrast, in a test which required minimal skeletal muscle activity to terminate the shock (i.e., the "nosing" response, whereby the rat simply has to poke its nose through a hole a short distance in front of its head), animals preexposed to cold swimming showed no deficits. Repeated exposure to the stressor attenuated the deficits observed, rather than reinforcing them (contrary to what the learned helplessness theory would predict). Similar behavioral deficits can also be induced by the administration of tetrabenazine, a pharmacological agent that depletes norepinephrine. Also, animals can be protected from these decrements in behavior following inescapable stress by the prior administration of clinically effective antidepressant agents (either a monoamine oxidase inhibitor or a tricyclic norepinephrine uptake inhibitor).

Neurochemical assays were also conducted in an attempt to correlate the deficits in behavior with specific neurotransmitters in the central nervous system.[8] The results of these studies indicate that deficits in motor activity and avoidance learning are associated with decreased levels of brain norepinephrine, but not of dopamine; furthermore, this effect may be due to enhanced uptake of norepinephrine. Repeated exposure to the stressor attenuates this decrease, and the time course of decay of this effect parallels the time course of decay of the behavioral deficits observed after inescapable stress. This indicates that these behavioral deficits may be mediated by a functional decrease in brain norepinephrine activity.

The integration of these behavioral, biochemical, and pharmacological data with those from the previously described studies of Seligman has led Weiss to formulate the *motor activation deficit* hypothesis as an alternative to the learned helplessness theory. In brief, this hypothesis states that deficits in escape and avoidance responding observed after inescapable stress are due to the inability of the subject to initiate the necessary amount of motor activity to learn and perform the task.

This hypothesis does not preclude the possibility that learning may have an effect in stress-induced deficits, nor does it eliminate the possibility that neurotransmitters other than norepinephrine are involved in the mediation of these behaviors. However, it appears that the induction of the deficits described in this paper may be due at least in part to a decrease in norepinephrine function in the central nervous system.

References

1. Alexander, B. K. and Harlow, H. F. Social behavior of juvenile rhesus monkeys subjected to different rearing conditions during the first six months of life. *Zool. Jb. Physiol. Bd.* **71**: 489-508.
2. Harlow, H. and Suomi, S. Production of depressive behavior in young monkeys. *Journal of Childhood Autism and Schizoprhenia* **1**: 246-255 (1971).
3. Suomi, S. and Harlow, H. Depressive behavior in young monkeys subjected to vertical confinement. *J. Comp. Physiol. Psych.* **180** (1): 11-18 (1972).
4. Overmeier, J. and Seligman, M. Effects of inescapable shock upon subsequent escape and avoidance responding. *J. Comp. Physiol. Psych.* **63**: 28-33 (1967).
5. Seligman, M., Maier, S., and Solomon, R. Unpredictable and uncontrollable aversive events. In *Aversive Conditioning and Learning* (F. R. Brush, ed.) pp. 347-400. New York: Academic Press, 1971.
6. Porsolt, R., Anton, G., Blavet, N., and Jalfre, M. Behavioral despair in rats: a new model sensitive to antidepressant treatments. *Europ. J. Pharmacol.* **47**: 379-391 (1978).

7. Weiss, J., Bailey, W., Porhorecky, L., Korzeniowski, D., and Grillione, G. Stress-induced depression of motor activity correlates with regional changes in brain norepinephrine but not in dopamine. *Neurochem. Res.* **5** (1): 9-22 (1980).
8. Weiss, M., Glazer, H., and Pohorecky, L. Coping behavior and neurochemical changes: an alternative explanation for the original "learned helplessness" experiments. In *Animal Models in Human Psychobiology* (G. Serban and A. Kling, eds.), pp. 141-173. New York: Plenum Press, 1976.

Stress and Anxiolytics in Animal Experiments

Ivana P. Day, Ph.D.
Central Nervous System Disease Therapy Section
Medical Research Division of American Cyanamid Co.
Pearl River, New York

This paper explores a possible role for anxiolytic drugs in the treatment of stress as evidenced by experimental work in laboratory animals. In the physiological and neuropharmacological sense, stress and anxiety are not to be considered synonymous phenomena. A clear concept of the differences between these paradigms becomes of increasing importance, particularly in view of the proliferation of arbitrary classifications such as appear in the *Index Medicus,* where under the headings "Stress," "Psychological Stress," and "Emotional Stress," the distinctions to be drawn between stress and anxiety are far from clear. Day[1] has pointed out that the human handling of anxiety and stress is likely to vary with the intellectual and educational endowment of the individual. Anxiety can be viewed through a series of vectors that qualify "a specific conscious inner attitude." These include:

1. A physically and mentally painful awareness of being powerless to resolve a crisis at hand
2. The psychophysiological impending premonition of what the organism recognizes as danger
3. The neurophysiological and psychophysiological exhaustion or stages of demand associated with crises as in emergency reactions faced by the body

4. Excess preoccupation with introspective solution of "reality" problems; self-created irresoluble doubt

Anxiety may exist by itself, it may accompany depression or psychosis, or it may be a secondary factor in concomitant organic illness. Anxiety requires medication when it interferes with moderately optimal functioning in everyday life.

Stress is a nonspecific response of the body to any demand made upon it. Life crises and problems of living cause stress, which in turn produces the alarm reaction and the General Adaptation Syndrome.[2] The founder of stress theory, H. Selye, says: "Stress is not nervous tension or emotional arousal, it is not something to be avoided. Complete freedom from stress is death."

Anxiolytics

According to a definition of the World Health Organization, anxiolytics are substances which reduce pathological anxiety, tension, and agitation without therapeutic effect on cognitive or perceptual processes. A few examples of typical chemical structures of anxiolytic drugs are presented in Fig. 1.

Mephenesin was the first drug with recognized antianxiety properties. It was described in 1946 as "a substance causing in animals tranquilization, muscle relaxation and sleep like condition from which the animals could be roused."[3] A short duration of action was a disadvantage. Numerous chemical modifications and intensive pharmacological research ultimately resulted in the synthesis of meprobamate which was introduced clinically in 1955. Chlordiazepoxide, synthesized by Sternbach et al.,[4] was introduced as a new anxiolytic in 1960. A number of analogues followed, six of which are currently available in the US (chlorazepate, chlordiazepoxide, diazepam, lorazepam, oxazepam, and prazepam). The name benzodiazepines has become synonymous with the term anxiolytics. At the present time, benzodiazepines are the most widely used drugs ever. The consumption of these drugs has reached dimensions unique in the history of drug therapy. The effort undertaken to understand how anxiolytics produce their characteristic effect has resulted in an enormous volume of scientific literature.

Anxiolytics form a distinct class of compounds with a characteristic profile of action in laboratory animals.[5,6] They are all anticonvulsants, muscle relaxants, and sedatives. They inhibit aggressive behavior, increase food intake, and disinhibit suppressed behavior. They are relatively safe, with a

1. Propanediol Carbamates
    Mephenesin

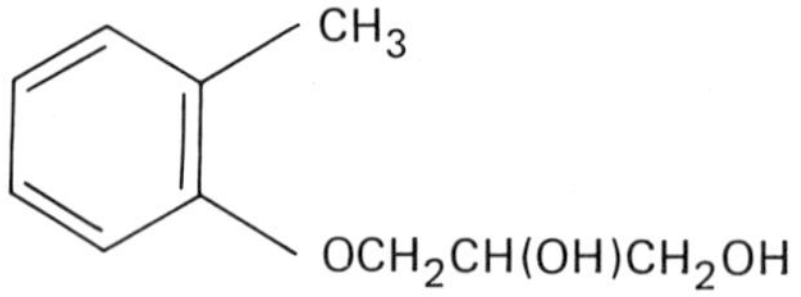

CH$_3$

OCH$_2$CH(OH)CH$_2$OH

Meprobamate

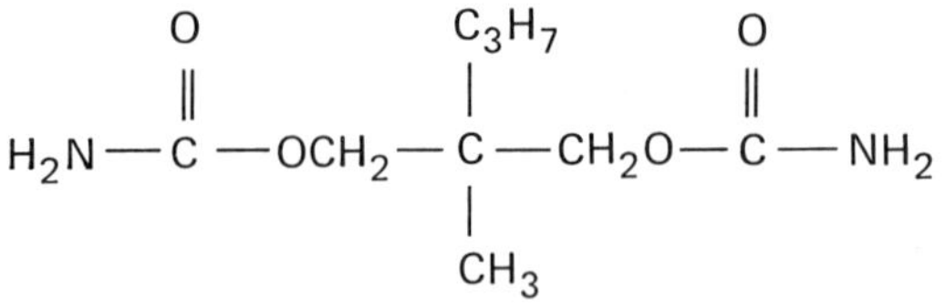

2. Benzodiazepines
    Chlordiazepoxide

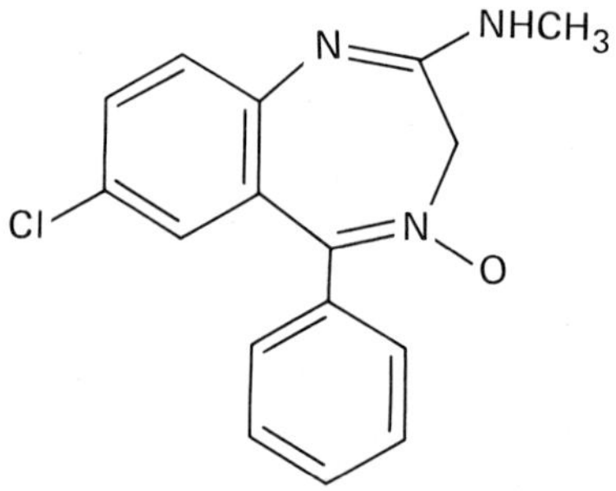

Diazepam

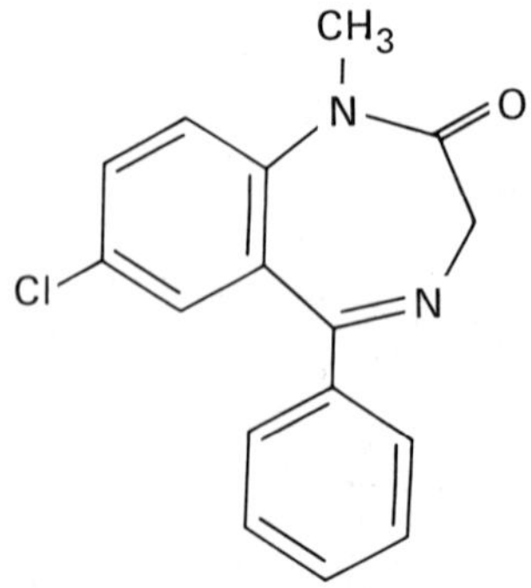

FIG. 1. Chemical structures of anxiolytics.

high therapeutic index. In comparison with phenobarbital which also possesses anxiolytic properties, benzodiazepines exhibit a clear separation between therapeutic doses and doses causing sleep (hypnotic doses). Benzodiazepines have no effect on endogenous levels of biogenic amines in the brain, but they decrease the turnover rates of norepinephrine (NE), dopamine, serotonin, and histamine. They inhibit cyclic-3'5'-adenosine monophosphate phosphodiesterase and increase the activity of gamma-aminobutyric acid (GABA). Interactions with the GABA system may explain the muscle relaxant and anticonvulsant properties of benzodiazepines but not necessarily their anxiolytic properties. Recent reports [7,8] of specific binding sites in the brain for 3H-diazepam suggest the existence of a neurohumoral system controlling states of anxiety analogous to the opiate-like endogenous peptides. The endogenous ligand for benzodiazepine receptors in the brain is yet to be discovered. This area of research can bring an understanding of the mechanisms and systems involved in anxiety.

Benzodiazepines prevent or ameliorate biochemical changes induced by stress.[9] They inhibit the increase of plasma corticosteroids which occurs in situations involving uncertainty and unpredictability. The stress-activated increase of NE turnover is prevented by chlordiazepoxide or diazepam, as is the increase of plasma free fatty acids, glucose, and lactate. The high incidence of gastric erosions and the increased gastric secretion of hydrochloric acid caused by noxious optic and acoustic stimuli in rats are reduced by pretreatment with diazepam.

Stress-induced changes in animal behavior are frequently studied in psychopharmacological laboratories and are believed to be experimental models of depression.[10,11] Behavioral deficits caused in rats by inescapable stress (e.g., forced swimming) are prevented by antidepressants but not by anxiolytics.[12] An apparent difference exists between stress in which the animal has at least partial control over the situation and stress which is inescapable and induces helplessness and hopelessness.

Disinhibitory action, typical of anxiolytics, occurs when any kind of behavior is suppressed by variable factors. The most common suppressing factor used in the laboratory is electrical shock presented together with a reward (food or water) to food- or water-deprived animals.[13] The situation is stresssful to the animal, but at the same time such animals have a choice—to take punishment together with a reward, or to stay hungry or thirsty. Control animals always prefer the second choice and take only few shocks. Animals pretreated with anxiolytics are willing to take punishment with their food or with water. Under these conditions, diazepam significantly increases the behavioral response (measured by the number of shocks taken) and decreases the level of plasma corticosterone elevated by the conflict situation.[14] In case of inescapable electrical shock, anxiolytics have no effect; the animals do not try to escape from hopeless situations and their behavior is not dissimilar to that of untreated controls. The original question was: Is there experimental evidence of the usefulness of anxiolytics in stress? A conclusion follows: anxiolytics, mainly benzodiazepines, inhibit the biochemical response of organisms to stress. However, the behavioral studies are not conclusive. Benzodiazepines disinhibit behavior suppressed by stress induced in conflict situations, but they have no effect on behavior resulting from inescapable stress.

References

1. Day, S. B. Death not the mysterium tremendum. In *Cancer, Stress and Death* (J. Taché, H. Selye, and S.B. Day, eds.), p. 213. Plenum Medical Book Company, 1979. New York, NY.
2. Selye, H. *The Stress of Life.* New York: McGraw-Hill, 1956.
3. Berger, F. M. and Bradley, W. The pharmacological properties of alpha:beta dihydroxy-gamma-(2-methylphenoxy)-propane (myanesin). *Brit. J. Pharmacol.* 1: 265-272 (1946).
4. Sternbach, L.H., Randall, L.O., Gustafson, S.R. 1-4-Benzodiazepines (chlordiazepoxide and related compounds). In *Psychopharmacological Agents* (M. Gordon, ed.), Vol. I, pp. 175-281. New York: Academic Press, 1974.
5. Anxiolytics. *Industrial Pharmacology* (S. Fielding and H.Lal. eds.). New York: Futura Publishing Company, 1979.
6. Schallek, W., Horst, W. D., and Schlosser, W. Mechanisms of action of benzodiazepines. *Adv. Pharmacol. Chemother.* 16: 45-87 (1979).
7. Squires, R. and Braestrup C., Benzodiazepine receptors in rat brain. *Nature* 266: 732-734 (1977).
8. Lippa, A. S., Klepner, C. A., Yunger, L., Sano, M. C. Smith, W. V., and Beer, B. Relationship between benzodiazepine receptor and experimental anxiety in rats. *Pharmacol. Biochem. Behav.* 9: 853-856 (1978).
9. Greenblatt, D. J. and Shader, R. I. *Benzodiazepines in Clinical Practice.* New York: Raven Press, 1974.
10. Regan, B. A., Stress-induced deficits in animal behavior. This volume, p. 43.
11. Everitt, B. J. and Keverne, E. B. Models of depression based on behavioral observations of experimental animals. In *Psychopharmacology of Affective Disorders* (E.S. Paykel and A. Coppen, eds.) pp. 41-59. London: Oxford University Press, 1979.
12. Porsolt, R. D., Anton, G., Blavet, N., and Jalfre, M. Behavioral despair in rat: a new model sensitive to antidepressant treatments. *Eur. J. Pharmacol.* 47: 379-391 (1978).
13. Vogel, J. R., Beer, B., and Clody, D. E. A simple and reliable conflict procedure for testing anti-anxiety agents. *Psychopharmacologia* 21: 1-7 (1971).
14. Lippa, A. S., Greenblatt, E. N., and Pelham, R. The use of animal models for delineating the mechanisms of action of anxiolytic agents. In *Animal Models in Psychiatry and Neurology.* (Hanin and Usdin, eds.), pp. 279-292. New York: Pergamon Press, 1979.

Benzodiazepines: Mechanism of Action and Appropriate Use

Nelson Hendler, M.D., M.S.
Assistant Professor of Psychiatry
Psychiatric Consultant, Pain Treatment Center
Johns Hopkins Hospital
Baltimore, Maryland

Clinical Director
Mensana Clinic
Stevenson, Maryland

Why does man need a tranquilizer? Basically, we are functioning with a Stone Age physiology in a Space Age society. Evolution has prepared our body for flight or fight. In response to tension, anxiety, danger, or fear, cavemen would either attack the object of their fear or run away from it. Unfortunately, this is not particularly acceptable or functional in our society; we can't punch our adversary in the face or physically run away from confrontations when they occur. Evolution has not caught up with our current needs for a less excitable physiology. Consequently, anxiety and tensions build up within our body on a purely hormonal basis, based on accumulations of epinephrine, norepinephrine, and a variety of other agents from the adrenal glands and the pituitary. Therefore, modern man has a strong need to calm this fear and anxiety, which has been evident throughout history.

HISTORY

The first reported use of a drug in this capacity was alcohol. Certainly, there are many biblical indications that tension was soothed by either playing a lyre or having drinks of wine. The use of *Rauwolfia* alkaloids, the serpent plant of India, was reported in ancient Hindu Ayurvedic writings. It was this snakeroot, chewed by the fakirs and medicine men of India, that later gave rise to the medical use of reserpine, one of the earliest tranquilizers. Tobacco has long been reported a useful tranquilizer and, in fact, has been called "sotweed" because of the heady stupor that it produced. Marijuana has been used by modern man and even by animals, and the literature is full of references to "locoweed" or to smoking hemp. Certainly the opium den of the Chinese is well known. However, it wasn't until 1864, when Adloph von Bayer discovered the chemical formula of barbiturates, with their subsequent clinical application in 1902, that man was first really able to use mind-altering drugs on a widespread basis. Barbiturates, which consist of Seconal, Amytal, phenobarbital, Nembutal, Tuinal, and other drugs of that class, were the first widely prescribed tranquilizers in modern medicine. Unfortunately, there was a very small therapeutic margin, so the difference between the therapeutic and lethal dosages was only five- to tenfold. As a result of this, many accidental and purposeful suicides occurred with the use of this medication, and this was especially true when it was combined with alcohol. In 1954, meprobamate was discovered. It has been been marketed as Miltown or Equanil, and has proved somewhat less lethal with less of an addictive potential than the barbiturates. The next major breakthroughs occured in 1960 with the introduction of Librium, in 1964 with the introduction of Valium, and in 1970 with the introduction of Dalmane. These drugs and others like them (see Table 1) constitute a class of drugs called benzodiazepines.

This class of drugs has a very safe and wide margin between the therapeutic and the lethal doses. Also, these drugs are particularly effective in reducing anxiety and tension. These two factors have led to their widespread use and acceptance by the medical community. Physicians were finally given an effective drug that was also safe. However, it was easy to abuse and overutilize these drugs: patients began to demand them, while at the same time physicians found how convenient they were for solving many complaints.

CURRENT USE OF BENZODIAZEPINES

A variety of sources have quoted the ubiquity of benzodiazepines in the American market. Tallman et al. reported in 1977 that 54 million prescrip-

TABLE 1. Benzodiazepines.

Generic Name	Brand Name of Drug or Combination Preparations Containing the Drug
Diazepam	Valium
Chloridazepoxide	Librium, Librax, Limbitrol, Libritabs, Menrium
Oxazepam	Serax
Prazepam	Centrax, Verstan
Lorazepam	Ativan
Chlorazepate	Azene, Tranxene
Flurazepam	Dalmane

tions were written for diazepam and 13 million for chlordiazoxide.[13] Flurazepam, specially marketed in North America as a hypnotic, accounted for 53% of all hypnotic prescriptions written, which translated into 13.6 million prescriptions. The retail cost of these drugs was approximately 240 million dollars according to a recent *Newsweek* article. Another article indicates that 97% of all general physicians in the United States prescribed benzodiazepines.[4] In fact, Louis Lasagna cites the *National Drug and Therapeutic Index* in a June 1977 article in the *American Journal of Psychiatry.*[7] He indicates that from 1974 to 1975, general practitioners wrote 15.5 million prescriptions for oral benzodiazepines, or approximately 36% of all benzodiazepine prescriptions. The next group of physicians to utilize benzodiazepines were internists, who prescribed 22% of all the benzodiazepines in that year. Psychiatrists prescribed only 15% of the benzodiazepines, while surgeons prescribed approximately 10%, as did osteopaths and OB-gyn physicians combined. Therefore, a full 85% of all benzodiazepine prescriptions are written by nonpsychiatrists.[7] These figures do not take into account injectable benzodiazepines given as preoperative sedation or prior to a variety of diagnostic procedures, including mylogram, I.V.P., cystoscopic exam, proctoscopic evaluation, etc. However, even more distressing were recent studies which cited the lack of knowledge of the mechanism of action of psychotropic drugs by the people who use them, other than psychiatrists. In fact, the lay public has gotten into the act, and very often tranquilizers are freely exchanged amongst friends the way one might try a new brand of Scotch. No doubt we all recall the scene from a recent movie when the friend of an anxious character asks a group of people who has a Valium and 20 bottles appear from the gathered crowd. Lasagna's article further defines the reasons for which physicians prescribe benzodiazepines. Most disappointingly, psychiatrists *inappropriately* prescribed benzodiazepines for anxiety associated with depression (the rationale for this is not clear). However, the next most frequent reason was the treatment of anxiety alone. The general practitioners, osteopaths, and internists felt that 25 to 33% of their patients had anxiety, but they also prescribed benzodiazepines to an equal number of patients (25 to 33%) for circulatory disorders, digestive disorders, tension headaches, or pain in the chest or back. Surgeons prescribed benzodiazepines for disc problems and "sprains and strains," while OB-gyn doctors used it for genitourinary disorders. The major effect sought by all *specialists* was tranquilization (45 to 67%, depending on the specialty). The next most sought after effect was sleep induction (8 to 29%, varying with specialty), while the only significant difference existed between medical specialists and surgeons when prescribing the drug for muscle relaxation (1 to 8% for the medical group vs 30% for surgeons). Neurologists used benzodiazepines for muscle relaxation 22% of the time. Women get benzodiazepines twice as frequently as men, and the 40 to 59 year age group receives 40% of the prescriptions.[7] This is not surprising since many of the intended uses were for circulatory disorders such as hypertension, postmyocardial infarction, post-operative, and angina patients. Since benzodiazepines are so widely used, it is incumbent upon a psychiatrist to be totally familiar with the mechanism of action of these drugs so he can assist his medical colleagues in selecting the appropriate drug for the appropriate indication. This brings us to the topic of drug metabolism.

PHARMACOKINETICS

The two leaders in the field of benzodiazepine pharmacokinetics research, Richard Shader and David Greenblatt, have elucidated the major clinical features of within-class differences of benzodiazepines that are based on studies dealing with absorption, routes of administration, metabolism, and active metabolites. In two articles, Shader's group studied the effect of routes of administration on bioavailability and blood levels of both chlordiazepoxide and diazepam, and found that two models exist for the rate of decay (or disappearance from the plasma) of chlordiazepoxide.[3,9] The first group of subjects had a biexponential decay, which assumes that the drug is distributed into two separate compartments of the human body, or the so-called *two compartments open pharmacokinetic model.* This may be conceptualized as drug distribution involving (1) absorption across the gut, and then distribution into (2) the bloodstream and, (3) perhaps the fat of the body; each compartment, blood or fat, then gives up the chlordiazepoxide at a different rate, thereby producing a two-compartment decay curve or biexponential. This is typically found with anesthetic agents or sulfur containing (fast-acting) barbiturates. However, chlordiazepoxide also exhibits a triexponential (three-compartment) decay in other subjects, which may involve the exchangeable portion of the bone.[3] This has clinical significance, since a simple 50 mg I.V. injection of chlordiazepoxide (slowly over one hour) has an elimination half-life of 13 hours in a biexponential decay, but half-lives of 18 to 20 hours are recorded in the triexponential group. This says that two pharmacologically distinct groups of people exist, one of whom has a rapid (13 hours) metabolism of chlordiazepoxide and in whom the drug completely disappears in 48 hours. The other group takes longer to degrade chlordiazepoxide, and the drug has an 18- to 20-hour half-life, with clinically significant levels being found at even 72 hours, which was the extent of time for sampling.[3] Thus we can see that at least two distinct groups of patients exist with different metabolisms of chlordizepoxide.

More interestingly, it seems that the normal rules of pharmacokinetics are violated when one considers the routes of administration of diazepam and chlordiazepoxide. For most drugs, inhalation is usually as fast as interarterial administration, followed normally by I.V., then I.M., subcutaneous, oral, and rectal routes. The two drugs frequently used for preoperative medication, alcohol withdrawal, and acute anxiety episodes seem to be better absorbed *orally* than when given I.M. In fact, oral doses of both drugs seem to be more rapidly absorbed and have a higher serum level (two times high plasma level initially), rising to nearly 3.5 to 4 times the I.M. dose over ½ to 2 hours. In fact, blood levels for the I.M. dose do not approximate the oral dose until about 15 hours after administration. After oral administration of diazepam and chlordiazepoxide their absorbsion in the gastrointestinal tract is nearly complete, but the I.M. route results in only partial and unpredictable absorption. The use of I.M. diazepam and chlordiazepoxide bears reexamination, especially when they are used in repeated injection at high doses. Shader and Greenblatt are especially concerned when these drugs are injected every 3 to 6 hours for the treatment of alcohol withdrawal.[9] The cumulative effect of multiple doses that are slowly absorbed could lead to excessive sedation of a delayed onset, a situation not infrequently encountered by clinicians treating delirium tremens. The unknown cause of the excessive sedation (due to benzodiazepines or a natural sign of delirium tremens) may lead a clinician to mistakenly oversedate an already excessively medicated patient.

Other factors influence blood levels of benzodiazepines. Patients who are taking antacids, at clinically effective levels, alter the pH of their gastric contents. As the acidity is neutralized, and the pH rises from 3.0 to 7.0, the rate of hydrolysis of chlorazepate changes from 48.8 *seconds* to 9.0 *hours.*[9] The reduced hydrolysis prevents the formation of the active metabolite desmethyldiazepam (also the active metabolite of diazepam). The clinical significance of this finding is evident—anxious persons with peptic ulcer disease take concomitant doses of antacid or anticholinergic drugs which could reduce the absorption or hydrolysis of benzodiazepines, thereby reducing their blood levels and effectiveness.

Once the benzodiazepines are in the system, 98% of the drug is metabolized, and Kornetsky reports only 2% is excreted unchanged by the gut and kidneys.[5] The major site of biotransformation of benzodiazepines is the liver. This occurs after the initial hydrolysis of most benzodiazepines by an acidic stomach. Kyriakopoulos reports that approximately 60% of an oral does of lorazepam is conjugated to the glucuronide in the liver and eliminated from the urine in 24 hours; 75% of the dose was collected in the urine at the end of 120 hours.[6] Fecal elimination was negligible. The unconjugated drug is eliminated through urinary excretion, with a half-life of 12 to 18 hours. Significantly, it is reasonable to assume that a patient receiving no more than 8 mg of lorazepam a day would not be expected to accumulate lorazepam or its glucuronide, based on pharmacokinetic studies by Kyriakopoulos.[6] In contrast, chronic administration of chlordiazepoxide at the dosage of 50 mg/day over a 15-day period gave different results. The unconjugated levels of chlordiazepoxide diminished over a 15-day period, starting at 0.55 μg/cc and *falling* to 0.18 μg/cc, or nearly a 66% *reduction* of the free drug in the plasma. However, the two active metabolities, desmethylchlordiazepoxide and demoxepam slowly began to rise in the plasma, nearly doubling their initial blood level after 15 days. The half-life for unaltered chlordiazepoxide was 9 hours, and all detectable levels were eliminated by 36 hours. However, the half-life of desmethylchlordiazepoxide was approximately 38 hours, not 9, and it was detectable in the urine for as long as 84 hours (3½ days) after the last oral dose. Even more distressing were the findings regarding demoxepam; after stopping the drug, the blood level *rose* from the steady-state level of approximately 0.52 μg/cc, and continued to *rise* to a peak of 0.82 μg/cc 48 hours after discontinuing the drug. Thereafter, a decay occurred in which the steady-state level was reached at 60 hours, and only after 108 hours (4½ days) from the time of stopping the drug was the quantity of the active metabolite *one-half* the steady-state level; i.e., the active metabolite of demoxepam has a half-life of 108 hours or 4½ days![3] This finding by Greenblatt and Shader suggests two critical concepts. The first is simple—that the accumulation of chlordiazepoxide, its active metabolites, *or both* during chronic therapy is a potentially important clinical problem. Therefore, a patient may unwittingly be accumulating a larger dose of drug than was anticipated because of these cumulative effects. Finally, when withdrawing a patient from a drug, the physician must be aware of the potential appearance of side effects, 3 to 7 days after discontinuance, due to the active metabolites; all drugs in the benzodiazepine catagory should be tapered over 1 to 1½ weeks. The second concept imparted by Greenblatt and Shader's work may be inferred from the fact that the blood levels of chlordiazepoxide *went down* by nearly two-thirds of the original level after 5 days.[3] This suggests a concept of enzyme induction described by Ebert and Shader.[8] Many drugs induce their own destruction by exciting drug-metabolizing enzymes in the liver microsomes. The psychotropic drugs which do this are numerous—several barbiturates, glutethimide, meprobamate, haloperidol, chlorpromazine, and chlordiazepoxide.[8] This microsomal enzyme induction is a well-know phenomenon, and over 200 drugs have been reported to produce this effect. This reaction can create many clinical complications due to drug interaction, but this will be discussed later. For the moment, let us only consider the fact that enzyme induction in the liver, a phenomenon called *tachyphylaxis* by pharmacologists, begins to *lower* the serum level of a drug when a standard dose is given chronically, i.e., over more than 10 to 15 days. This may mean that a benzodiazepine might begin to lose its effectiveness over time, a phenomenon called for *tolerance*. However, it seems that only the benzodiazepines which are hydroxylated and demethylated by the liver are subject to trachyphylaxis and subsequent tolerance.[8] These are diazepam, proazepam, chlordiazepoxide, and flurazepam, the last of which takes 7 days before the major active metabolite reaches steady-state levels in the serum and has a half-life of 47 to 100 hours (2 to 4 days). Restated for emphasis, diazepam, chlordiazepoxide, and flurazepam are metabolized by the liver and, in the process, create enzyme induction that results in lower plasma levels of these drugs when given chronically (10 to 15 days or more). Also, the major metabolites of these drugs may last as long as 2 to 4 days, or more, and still exert a clinicial effect. As Shader and Greenblatt point out, this contrasts with oxazepam and lorazepam which *are not* hydroxylated or demethylated by the liver.[9] This difference has clinical significance, since one must be more concerned that there will be reduced degradation of diazepam, chlordiazepoxide, and flurazepam in persons with liver disease, older persons, and alcoholic patients who have already overtaxed their liver microsomal system. Therefore, dosages of the three drugs previously mentioned must be concomitantly reduced in elderly or alcoholic patients. Clinical studies confirm this statement, with significantly higher plasma levels of diazepam being found in elderly or alcoholic patients than in healthy controls.[9] This is not true of oxazepam. Finally, the different metabolic routes may explain why the glucuronide metabolite of lorazepam reaches a higher plasma concentration than lorazepam itself, but follows the same decay curve with only a slightly larger half-life than the original drug (i.e., a half-life of 12 hours for free lorazepam and 17 hours for the glucuronide metabolite).[6] This is in contradistinction to chlordiazepoxide which has a free drug half-life of 9 hours, while the demethylated metabolites have half-lives of up to 108 hours.[3] Clearly then, there are two distinct groups of benzodiazepines. The first group contains those that are not hydroylated and demethylated by the liver, do not accumulate in the body, and do not require dosage adjustment for elderly or liver-damaged patients. These drugs are lorazepam and oxazepam. A second group of drugs exist that do get hydroxylated and demethylated by the liver, accumulate in the system, induce tachyphylaxis and tolerance, and require lower doses in elderly and liver-damaged patients. These drugs are diazepam, chlordiazepoxide, flurazepam, and proazepam. Other significant differences exist between these groups in terms of the need for more frequent administration and the occurrence of fewer drug interactions in the former group, while only a once daily administration may be needed, but with a greater possiblity of drug interaction, in the second group (see Table 2).

Now that we know a little of the pharmacokinetics of benzodiazepines, we should pay strict attention to their *mechanism of action.* In order to appreciate how benzodiazepines work, we need to review briefly the location of various neurosynaptic transmitters in the central nervous system (CNS), and examine how benzodiazepines affect each one of these transmitters. From this information, we can deduce several behavioral effects as well as side effects.

Benzodiazepines have an effect on gamma-aminobutyric acid (GABA), indoleamines (serotonin), catecholamines such as norepinephrine and dopamine, and an unrelated drug glycine.[11] Approximately 25 to 40% of all synapses in the central nervous system use GABA as a transmitter. GABA is the major inhibitory transmitter in the central nervous system since, in most areas of the cortex, GABA-containing nerve terminals synapic on cell bodies whose membrane potential is hyperpolarized by

TABLE 2 Benzodiazepine Metabolism.

A) Drugs that are hydroxylated and demethylated in the liver, accumulate in the body, and should be reduced in elderly or hepatically impaired patients:

Generic Name	Half–Life	Metabolite(s) Half–Life
Diazepam	20–50 hr	
Chlordiazepoxide	9–30 hr	38–108 hr
Flurazepam	47–100 hr	
Prazepam	63 hr	
Clorazepate	30–60 hr	

B) Drugs that are not degraded by liver enzymes, that have a short half-life, do not accumulate in the body, and do not require dosage adjustment in elderly or liver-damaged patients:

Generic Name	Half–Life	Metabolite(s) Half–Life
Lorazepam	12 hr	17 hr
Oxazepam	5–12 hr	

GABA release. This postsynaptic inhibition is found in the cortex and is enhanced by benzodiazepines. However, at certain spinal cord and brain stem or reticular activating system (RAS) synapses, GABA promotes presynaptic inhibition. GABA neurons synapse on primary sensory afferent fibers and partially depolarize the presynaptic nerve terminals.[1] This results in a reduced release of neurosynaptic transmitter from these nerve endings; thus, less of an effect is seen. GABA activity is enhance by benzodiazepines and, therefore, reduces synaptic transmission of brain stem neurons, specifically those that release serotonin and norepinephrine, which are synaptic transmitters found in high concentration in the RAS and brain stem. This action can reduce the amount of sensory input, and according to Snyder and his co-workers, barbiturates, benzodiazepines, and other sedatives are equally effective in producing GABA-mediated presynaptic inhibition of the release of RAS biogenic amine transmitters, i.e. norepinephrine and serotonin.[11] Therefore, one may infer that *enhancing* GABA-induced synaptic inhibition by *either* benzodiazepines or barbiturates will produce *sedation* and *anticonvulsant* effects. This mechanism also establishes the rationale for cross tolerance between benzodiazepines and barbiturates. However, benzodiazepines seem to have a specific effect on glycine, which is an inhibitory neurosynaptic transmitter in the brain stem and spinal cord. Benzodiazepines seem to postsynaptically bind to the glycine receptor and function as a partial agonist, i.e., mimic the action of glycine, thereby producing *muscle relaxation*. Similiar effects in the limbic system and brain stem could account for its *antianxiety action*. In summary, GABA activity enhancement is a feature shared by both benzodiazepines and barbiturates, and produces sedation and anticonvulsant activity. However, the glycine-mimetic effect of benzodiazepines seems to be specific and may account for the muscle relaxing and antianxiety activity. Moreover, there are other consequences of GABA excitation and glycine enhancement. Snyder et al.[11] and Stein et al.[12] emphasize that both norepinephrine and serotonin cells receive GABA and glycine mediation. The net effect of benzodiazepines on these neurosynaptic transmitters is to reduce the release of serotonin presynaptically and to reduce serotonin turnover. This reduced turnover has also been reported by Robert C. Smith at the University of Chicago, for both norepinephrine and dopamine, and is more evident in stressed subjects.[10] In a preliminary study, Smith and his co-workers found elevated MHPG in the urine of patients receiving diazepam. Since MHPG is indicative of the amount of CNS degradation of norepinephrine, one may infer that there was a reduction in CNS levels of norepinephrine due to increased degradation. The clinical significance of this finding becomes apparent if one examines the role of biogenic amines in the CNS. Only 2% of the neurosynaptic transmitters in the CNS are biogenic amines, i. e., either an indoleamine like serotonin, or a catecholamine such as norepinephrine and dopamine. However, 90% of these biogenic amine neurosynaptic transmitters are found in the hypothalamus, median forebrain, bundle, paraventricular area of the hypothalamus, and the reticular activating system of the brain stem. These are parts of the archeo-cortex (old brain) which comprises the limbic system. This concept is critical, since these areas are intimately associated with emotion, sleep and wakefulness, sex, eating, drinking, aggressive behavior, etc. Since benzodiazepines excite GABA production, they inhibit the presynaptic release of serotonin and, to a variable degree, norepinephrine. Stage 3 and 4 sleep needs serotonin to be effected, and REM sleep requires both Ach (acetylcholine) and norepinephrine which has been reported by Sitaram, working with Wyatt's group,[16] and by others.[15] Therefore, the use of benzodiazepines to induce sleep has no pharmacological rationale. In fact, most of the benzodiazepines seem to inhibit REM sleep and stage 3/4 sleep, just as phenobarbital does. The only exception to this seems to be flurazepam which only inhibits stage 3/4 sleep. Nonetheless, when one considers the number of available medications that augment both REM and stage 3/4 sleep, such as the sedative trycyclic antidepressants like doxepin and amitriptyline, one wonders why benzodiazepines should ever be rationally considered as a sleeping aid (see Table 3).

One cannot conclude a discussion of benzodiazepines without making

TABLE 3. Hypnotic Drugs or Those that Exert Hypnotic Effects. *†

	Effect on Serotonin	Effect on Rem Sleep ‡	Effect on Stage 3/4 (Slow Wave) Sleep§
L-Tryptophan	+ + +	+ + +	+ + +
Doxepin	+ + + +	+	+ + +
Amitriptyline	+ + + +	+	+ + +
Imipramine	+ + +	+ +	+ +
Phenobarbital	− −	− − −	−
Flurazepam	− −	0	− − −
Diazepam	− − −	− −	− −
Chlorpromazine	0	+ + +	0
Desipramine	0	+ + +	0

* From Chapter 14, "The Psychopharmacology of Chronic Pain," in *The Diagnosis and Non-surgical Management of Chronic Pain* by Nelson Hendler, M.D., Raven Press, New York, 1981.

† + = augmentation; − = inhibition.

‡ REM sleep needs ACTH and norepinephrine.

§ 5-HT needed to get slow wave (stage 3/4) sleep.

mention of the recently discovered benzodiazepine receptor site in the CNS. Tallman, Paul, Skolnick, and Gallager have written a very fine review article on this topic.[13] In 1977, Braestrip, Albrechtsen, and Squires, as well as Mahler and Okade, reported specific benzodiazepine receptors in the CNS. The receptors were located throughout the cortex, as are GABA receptors, and are found in high density in the cerebellum. Interestingly, receptor sites for benzodiazepines have also been found in the kidney, liver, and lung of animals, but significantly , the pharmacologic specificty of these sites is different from the CNS. Also, there is little correlation between the affinity of the peripheral binding sities and the clinical or behavioral effects of benzodiazepines. One final concept can be derived from the idea of a benzodiazepine receptor. There is suggestive evidence that, in a fashion analogous to the enkephalins and β endorphins, there seem to be endogenous substances that can specifically bind to the benzodiazepine receptor site, and the purines and nicotinamide have been implicated.

After reviewing the mechanism of benzodiazepine action, a review of benzodiazepine side effects is in order. First and foremost are the cross tolerance and additive effects that occur if two benzodiazepines are coadministered. While this may seem improbable, it is not uncommon to see a patient on diazepam (or Valium) for anxiety and also Librax (for irritable bowel syndrome). Additionally, one occasionally encounters patients who are prescribed benzodiazepines during the day and flurazepam, or Dalmane, at night. Since really all the benzodiazepines are degraded by demethylation by the same liver enzymes, with the exception of lorazepam and oxazepam, it stands to reason that one benzodiazepine will reduce the degradation of another by overloading the enzyme system. Even with tachyphylaxis, this overload seems to have clinical significance. Additionally, the combination of benzodiazepines with a tricyclic antidepressant may create additive effects on hypotension and sedation. Pharmacologically, it seems antithetical to give a benzodiazepine that reduces norepinephrine and serotonin turnover, with a trycyclic designed to augment the action of these two biogenic amines. Additionally, this combination of diazepam and amitriptyline has been reported to cause a toxic psychosis.[2] Benzodiazepines, given in combination with phenytoin, increase on a mutual basis the degradation of each drug.[2] However, at a recent meeting of the American Neurological Association in Boston (1980), several authors indicated that there was no indication for the adjunctive effect of benzodiazepines in the treatment of epilepsy.

Another serious reaction, of importance to psychiatrists, is the prolongation of neuromuscular blockade caused by diazepam, which interacts with gallamine and succinyl-choline.[2] If a patient is to receive ECT, diazepam should be discontinued at least one week prior to treatment, or protracted recovery from anesthesia could result. In operations, preoperative medication with diazepam or a history of oral administration prior to a surgical procedure in which succinylcholine is used could also create problems in the recovery room. Finally, the coadministration of chlordiazepoxide with disulfiram results in reduced degradation of chlordiazepoxide, resulting in stuporous states at times indistinguishable from delirium tremens; this in turn, can lead to the inappropriate increase of benzodiazepines, when in effect the problem is toxic benzodiazepine levels.[9] Other, more subtle changes can be attributed to benzodiazepines. Hendler and his co-workers at Johns Hopkins Hospital found that there was a significant degree of correlation among patients between a great deal of diffuse (15 to 25 cps) beta activity on EEG, compatible with a sedative effect due to benzodiazepines, and impaired performance on tests of intellectual functioning such as the WAIS, Bender Gestalt, and the Memory Quotient test.[4] In fact, of the thirteen patients who were taking therapeutic does of benzodiazepines for one month or more, 70% had indications of cognitive impairment, while only 35% of a group of 13 patients taking only narcotics had the same degree of impairment. Other side effects have been reported for benzodiazepines and are well described in Shader and DiMasio's book *Psychotropic Drug Side Effects*.[8] In children, approximately 10% developed paradoxical rages, while approximately 5% developed depression when treated with chlordiazepoxide. In adults, both diazepam and chlordiazepoxide have been reported to produce rage, hostility, aggression, and even murder and suicide. Unfortunately, no quantification has been placed on this reaction, other than terms like *many, frequent, not uncommon,* etc. Depression in adults has been reported, with the onset occurring with as litle as 2 mg. of diazepam after only one dose, or be due to a slow insidious process. Pharmacologically, this may be explained by the reduced biogenic amine turnover created by GABA excitation, and one should always suspect diazepam as a causative agent if a patient reports feeling depressed. Typically this occurs in cardiac patients receiving both diazepam and propranolol (Inderal), both of which can inhibit biogenic amine activity. For the same reason, withdrawal of benzodiazepines can create a sleeplessness for up to two weeks after discontinuing the drug; the active metabolites of the longer half-life benzodiazepines continue to exert activity on GABA inhibition of biogenic amines even after the drug is discontinued. This mechanism may be due to enzyme inhibition, and during the recovery phase, there may still be reduced serotonin and norepinephrine. Since the pharmacological mechanisms of sleep involve serontonin accumulation in the dorsal median rephe nuclei of the RAS of the brain stem, any continued serotonin blockage can produce sleeplessness.[15] While the active forms of benzodiazepines are in the system, they drug the patient to sleep, like phenobarbital with which they may cross-tolerate. When discontinued, rebound REM sleep and sleeplessness are frequent side effects. Finally, tremors, seizures, and hallucinations have been reported. Galactorrhea and amenorrhea have also been reported secondary to benzodiazepines, but their incidence is rare.

How should benzodiazepines be used? A recent FDA recommendation limits the consecutive prescription of benzodiazepines to four months. In fact, clinical usefulness is not evident beyond *two* months. Benzodiazepines should not be used to aid sleep, nor should they be used in the treatment of depression. The use of benzodiazepines as a muscle relaxant in chronic pain patients seems to aggravate the perception of pain, and their use in phobic anxiety has been supplanted by tricylics and MAO inhibitors. The appropriate uses are best divided into hyperacute, acute, and subacute. For hyperacute, medical emergencies, I.V. diazepam for status epilepticus or tetanus is safe and effective in dosages between 5 and 10 mg. However, there have been reported incidences of respiratory arrest in status epilepticus with dosages as low as 2 mg I.V. As an acute medication for preoperative sedation or prior to procedures, diazepam is safe and effective if given orally or intravenously. Unfortunately the I.M. rate of absorption is less reliable. For acute anxiety attacks, a dose of 2 to 5 mg I.V. is useful, and dosages between 10 and 20 μg I.V. have been used in psychiatry for narcosynthesis. Alcohol withdrawal, impeding or acute delirium tremens, and hallucinosis respond well to 2 mg to 10 mg I.V. diazepam. For withdrawal from alcohol, either diazepam or chlordiazepoxide is useful, at 5 to 19 mg each 4 to 6 hours maintenance dosages. Anxiety states are well managed by any benzodiazepine, but care must be taken to limit the treatment to one to four months. Sprains and strains repond well to diazepam, but some orthopedic surgeons suggest treating these with codeine and allow the spasm to remain as protective splinting. Finally, stiff-man syndrome responds well to diazepam at dosages between 10 and 40 mg each, although baclofen may replace the benzodiazepines.

In summary, there are many potentially appropriate uses for benzodiazepines, but care and judgement must be exercised in their prescription. They do not replace psychotherapy in the treatment of anxiety, and they should not be used for sleep and depression. Their use should be limited to a course of treatment no longer than three to four months. Used properly and wisely, they are a safe and effective clinical tool for all physicians, and a great advance over previous forms of antianxiety therapy.[14]

References

1. Bloom, F. E., Neural mechanisms of benzodiazepine actions. *American Journal of Psychiatry* **134**(6): 669–672 (1977).
2. Gaultieri, C. T., and Powell, S. F. Psychoactive drug interactions. *Journal of Clinical Psychiatry,* **39**(9): 62/720–729/71 (1978).
3. Greenblatt, D. J., Shader, R. I., and Koch-Weser, J. Clinical pharmacokinetics of chloridazepoxide. In *Pharmacokinetics of Psychoactive Drugs: Blood Levels and Clinical Response,* (L. A. Gottschalk and S. Merlis, eds.), Ch. 8. New York: Spectrum Publications, 1976.
4. Hendler, N., Cimini, C., Ma, T., and Long, D. A comparison of cognitive impairment due to benzodiazepines and to narcotics. *American Journal of Psychiatry,* **137**(7): 828–830 (1980).
5. Kornetsky, C. *Pharmacology: Drugs Affecting Behavior,* New York: John Wiley and Sons, 1976.
6. Kyriakopoulos, A. A. Bioavailability of Lorazepam in Humans. In *Pharmacokinetics of Psychoactive Drugs: Blood Levels and Clinical Response,* L. A. Gottschalk, and S. Merlis, eds.) Ch. 5. New York: Spectrum Publications, 1976.
7. Lasagna, L. The role benzodiazepines in nonpsychiatric medical practice. *American Journal of Psychiatry* **134**(6): 656–658 (1977).
8. Ebert, M. and Shader, R. Hepatic effects. In *Psychotropic Drug Side Effects: Clinical and Theoretical Perspectives* (R. Shader and A. DiMascio, eds.), Ch. 19. Baltimore: Williams & Wilkins, 1970.
9. Shader, R. I. and Greenblatt, D. J. Clinical implications of benzodiazepine pharmacokinetics. *American Journal of Psychiatry* **134**(6): 652–656 (1977).
10. Smith, R. C., Dekirzenjian, H., Davis, J., Casper, R., Fosenfield, L., and Tsai, C. Blood level, mood, and MHPG responses to diazepam in man. In *Pharmacokinetics of Psychoactive Drugs: Blood Levels and Clinical Response* (L. A. Gottschalk and S. Merlis, eds.), Ch. 9. New York: Spectrum Publications, 1976.
11. Snyder, S. H., Enna, S. J., and Young, A. B. Brain mechanisms associated with therapeutic actions of benzodiazepines: focus on neurotransmitters. *American Journal of Psychiatry* **134**(6): 662–665 (1977).
12. Stein, L., Belluzzi, J. D., and Wise, C. D. Benzodiazepines: behavioral and neurochemical mechanisms. *American Journal of Psychiatry* **134**(6): pp. 665–669 (1977).
13. Tallman, J. F., Paul, S. M., Skolnick, P., and Gallager, D. W. Receptors for the age of anxiety: pharmacology of the benzodiazepines. *Science* **207**: 274–281 (January 18, 1980).
14. Uhlenhuth, E. H. Evaluation of antianxiety agents in humans: experimental paradigms. *American Journal of Psychiatry* **134**(6): 659–662 (1977).
15. Williams, R. L. and Karacan, I. (eds.). *Pharmacology of Sleep.* New York: John Wiley and Sons, 1976.
16. Sitaram, N., Wyatt, R. Jed., Dawson, S., and Gillim, J. C. REM sleep induced by physostigmine infused during sleep. *Science* **191**: 1281–1283 (March 26, 1976).

Stress and Disease: An Immunologic* Perspective

Devendra P. Dubey, Ph.D.
Don Staunton, Ph.D.
Edmond J. Yunis, M.D., Ph.D.

Sidney Farber Cancer Institute
Harvard Medical School
Boston, Massachusetts

The importance of psychosocial and physical stress in the etiology of a variety of illnesses including cancer, allergy, arthritis, and infectious diseases, has been emphasized in the past two decades. Serious effort to understand the contribution of stress (a noxious and threatening stimulus) to the development of these diseases, in terms of different physiologic components such as neuroendocrine and immune systems, has just begun.[1] In higher organisms, the nervous, endocrine, and immune systems are examples of complex regulatory networks that coordinate and integrate body function. Each contains a self-regulatory system and an integrative regulatory or interface system. Physical and psychological trauma affects the neuroendocrine network profoundly, while in turn, the neuroendocrine system moderates the immune function and thus modifies, increasing [2] or decreasing,[3] the susceptibility to infection and the risk factor for neoplastic disease. On the other hand, antigenic stimulation may be followed by alternations in hormone levels and/or nerve firing.[2] Taken together, the evidence supports a bidirectional regulation between immune and neuroendocrine systems.

It is clear that the immune response is precisely regulated by multiple positive and negative feedback loops, involving various cell interactions and soluble mediators. A network theory has been developed by Jerne and modified by others.[4] Basically, an environmental antigen can activate specific antigen reactive T or B cells that preexist in the organism. These cells, possessing receptor molecules for the antigen (idiotypes), are activated to undergo clonal expansion. Interacting T cells must also recognize

*This work has been supported by grants from the National Institute of Health, NCI CA 27063, 19589, CA 06516.

self major histocompatibility (MHC) antigens in order to react with the antigen. The expanded population, which may exhibit a suppressor or helper function, activates a second population possessing receptors for the idiotype of the first (anti-idiotype). These T or B cells may abrogate the activities of the first set and, in turn, stimulate proliferation of a third clone possessing anti-anti-idiotypes, and so on.

This complex network depends on the thymus for development and maintenance. Removal or malfunctioning of the thymus, as in advanced age or stress, may lead to an apparent increase or decrease in the reponse to antigenic challenge. The consequences may be the development of autoimmunity or increased vulnerability to attacks by viruses, bacteria, neoplastic diseases, etc. Recent evidence also implicates immunological factors controlled by the major histocompatibility gene complex in a variety of diseases such as arthritis, diabetes mellitus, demyelinating diseases of the central nervous system, malignancies, and infections.

Evidence presented below, of the tight integration of the immune and neuroendocrine system, may be found in ontogeny, in the correlation between altered states within each normally operating system, and in pathology.[2,10]

There exists near parallel development of the immune and endocrine systems. In various mammals, the state of maturity of one system at birth is mirrored by the other.

In the germ-free animal, lymphoid tissue mass and immunoglobulin levels are decreased. These animals are also reported to exhibit thyroid, adrenal, and testicular insufficiency. Neonatally thymectomized or congenitally athymic mice kept in a germ-free environment display a T-cell deficiency, hypothyroidism, alteration of gonadal normal levels, a delayed puberty in females, and other endocrine disturbances.[2] In the congenitally hypopituitary Snell (dw) dwarf mice, an immunodeficiency develops which may be corrected by treatment with growth hormone.[10]

In the hyperthyroid patient, one may observe elevated serum immunoglobulin, lymphoid hyperplasia, strong allergic reactions, and increased risk of malignant lymphoma, whereas thymectomized animals show a generalized immunodepression. Adrenalectomy in animals allows for an overproliferation of lymphatic tissues, including the thymus. Various experiments in neonatal and adult animals support a lifelong requirement for thyroxine and corticosteroids for maintenance of the immune system. At least one of the sex hormones (progesterone) has been shown to possess an immunopotentiating effect.[10]

Animals injected with antigens such as SRBC or trinitrophenylhemocyanin exhibit an elevated serum corticosterone level (two- to threefold) and, in some cases, a decreased serum thyroxine level concomitant with antibody production. Also concomitant with peak antibody production and endocrine fluctuation is a threefold increase in the firing rate of neurons in the ventromedial nuclei of the hypothalamus. Lesions in the posterior ventral hypothalamus of rabbits completely suppressed the production of antibodies allowing longer retention of antigen in the blood. Destruction of other parts of the immune system had no effect on the immune response.[5]

The concentration of neurotransmitters, norepinephrine, and biogenic amines in the hypothalamus is particularly high. Stein et al.[5] have shown that lesions in the hypothalamus modify immune responsivity via neural and hormonal pathways. There also exists evidence of increased brain norepinephrine turnover in experimental stress,[6] as well as in man during high stress situations.[7]

Adrenocorticotropic hormone (ACTH), growth hormone, prolactin, thyroid stimulating hormone and other thyroid hormones, and gonadotropins all demonstrate altered levels in response to stress.

The effect of stress on antibody production has been studied by a number of investigators. When stressed animals were immunized with bacterial flagellin, the antibody production was observed to be significantly reduced.[7] Also, when animals were subjected to severe sound stress, the response of lymphocytes to PHA in vitro, was significantly decreased, suggesting an effect of stress on T cells. These and similar experiments using animals demonstrate a depressed response by B as well as T cells in humoral and cellular immunity following stressful life experiences. The exact mechanisms by which stress alters immune status, and may act as an immunosuppressant in some conditions and an immunopotentiating factor in other conditions, is unknown, although some general models have been proposed.

Acetylcholine, β-adrenergic catecholamines, prostaglandins, insulin, histamine, and glucocorticoid hormones all seem to have specific receptor sites on lymphocytes through which they may regulate immune activity. [1,6] Recently, evidence for opiate receptors for morphine and met-enkephalin on T lymphocytes has been presented.[11] Circulating endogenous opiates have been shown to regulate cell-mediated immune function. All these receptors exert their influence through an intracellular cAMP and cGMP.

CONCLUSION

An understanding of the phenomena of disease requires a multidisciplinary approach. A disturbed network of immune-neuroendocrine interactions resulting from stress may have pervasive effects on the body that leads to the waning of physiologic controls. Chronological age-related changes in physiology are reflected in thymic involution, loss of immune capacity, and increased susceptibility to viral and bacterial infections. Viral infection of lymphoid cells may in itself produce alterations in the functional capacity of regulator cells, which may further lead to immunodeficiency and autoimmune diseases, cancer, and many other diseases associated with aging. Be it man or mouse, the speed with which a particular organism traverses his life trajectory depends partly on genetic inheritance and partly on environmental factors, i.e., psychosocial factors. Psychosocial trauma may affect longevity through disturbed neuroendocrine and immune functions. However, the ability to adjust to changes is partly determined by genetics. Association of the major histocompatibility complex with diseases exhibiting altered immunoregulation has been observed. Further investigation is needed to answer the question of how much control this gene complex actually does exert on the response or absence of response to environmental load. It would be of great interest, for instance, to investigate the changes of immune parameters following stress in individuals of different HLA phenotypes.

References

1. Rogers, M.P., Dubey, D., and Reich, P. The influence of the psyche and the brain on immunity and disease susceptibility: a critical review. *Psychomatic Medicine* **41**: 147-164 (1979).
2. Besedovsky, H. and Sorkin, E., Network of immune-neuroendocrine interactions. *Clin. Exp. Immunol.* **27**: 1-12 (1977).
3. Rogers, M.P. Stress and animal models of disease. This volume, p. 38.
4. Golub, E.S. Idiotypes and the network hypothesis. *Cell* **22**: 641-642 (1980).
5. Stein, M. et al. Influence of brain and behavior on the immune system. *Science* **191**: 435-440 (1976).
6. Smookler, H. et al. *Int. J. Neuropharmacol.* **8**: 33 (1969).
7. Rubin, R. et al. *Psychosom. Med.* **32**: 589 (1970).
8. Schlessinger, J. et al. Insulin and antibodies against insulin cap on the membrane of cultured human lymphocytes. *Nature* **286**: 729-731 (1980).
9. Solomon, G.F. *Int. Arch. Allergy* **35**: 97 (1969).
10. Makinodan, T. and Yunis, E.J. *Comprehensive Immunology: Immunology of Aging*, vol. 1, pp. 73-85. New York, N.Y. 1976.
11. Wybran, J. et al. *J. Immunol.* **123**: 1068-1070 (1979).

II
STRESS AND LIFE EVENT TERRITORIES

Bases and Methodology Problems of Life Event Research

H. Hönmann, M.D.
H. Schepank, M.D.
Psychosomatic Clinic (Head: H. Schepank)
Zentralinstitut für Seelische Gesundheit
Mannheim, Federal Republic of Germany

FUNDAMENTAL HYPOTHESES OF LIFE EVENT RESEARCH

Considered from the historical point of view, life event research dates back to the Swiss-American psychiatrist Adolf Mayer who, about 1900, in his "psychobiologic psychiatry" regarded social, psychic, and somatic factors as equal causes for the rise of psychiatric diseases. In the past 15 years the development of life event research has continued primarily in the Anglo-American region. According to its actual concept of methods, the life event theory can in part be attributed to Brown and coauthors [1] and to Rahe and Holmes. [2]

Based on the hypothesis of a negative influence on health as a result of the onset of increased stress, instruments were developed which survey the stress impact on a person caused either by a single considerable stress situation or by general daily stress, i.e., the total stress impact resulting from general daily events or changes of life situation.

It has been suggested that with a certain temporary accumulation (the more quantitative aspect) or intensity of the stress impact (the more qualitative aspect), an individual adaptation to the change caused by life events is no longer possible and the probability of the onset of psychic and physical diseases will increase. [3-5]

Also the psychoanalytical conception of illness contains hypotheses of modern life event research. Here we have in mind, for example, the importance which life events of early childhood can have on the further course of life, or the severity of traumatization by acute life events which can be explained by the existence of previous individually specific life events. In this context we should mention the concept of the trigger-situation of Schultz-Hencke, which starts with a certain life event specificity after a certain previous experience of life events, or the hypothesis of a certain determination for psychic disorders by infant life events. In general, psychoanalysis, however, lays more stress on the long-term effect of imporant life events.

Today, life event investigation inquires about the extent of the injurious habit of life events from a quantitative point of view. Its basic hypothesis is that the outbreak of an illness is directly preceded by an exceptional stress impact caused by life events. Neglecting combinations of events and the temporal succession of these events, the intensity of the global stress so caused is examined. As life events, comparatively ordinary changes in life are measured relative to the expected horizon of events of the person investigated. Some studies exclusively investigate the results that certain events can have on the health of a person, e.g., death of one's partner, problems of migration, unemployment, catastrophes, etc. It is not the social situation, but its change as psychosocial reason for an illness, that is relevant in this research.

Life events may produce stress:

1. if the events are threatening (which means they cannot be controlled, foreseen, or mastered by activities, but force a person to interrupt his everyday routine;
2. if the general psychophysical condition is impaired;
3. if the social context does not offer help.

The stress of a person suffers from a life event may be measured within the limits of a stress impact which gives information about the stress situation of a person caused by the life event. It may be suggested that chronic and acute strains accumulate. From experience, a person having to cope with constant stress impact shows more acute stress symptoms, too. Besides answering the question of which specific life events, by means of which specific mechanisms and under which specific circumstances, lead to which diseases, there is the question of the relative risk: e.g., judging the extent of the effect of true part life events on the onset of the psychiatric disorders.

The following hypotheses are possible:

1. Life events are necessary and sufficient to produce an illness.
2. Life events are necessary, but not sufficient to produce an illness.
3. Life events are not necessary, but are sufficient to produce an illness;

instead of life events, however, a different factor (e.g., other causes
of diseases) can produce an illness.
4. Mere life events are neither necessary nor sufficient to produce an illness. Connected with certain factors of context and individual production of symptoms, life events will have a particular pathogenic effect.

Probably many life events in one respect have no noxious consequences on
health. It also seems that psychic and probably psychosomatic disorders
may occur without life events having preceded them. Presumably, mere life
events are neither a necessary nor a sufficient cause of psychic and
psychosomatic disorders and only show their pathogenic effect in connection with other factors.

The following intervening variables come into consideration first of all:

1. Individual variables (coping mechanisms, actual attitudes and personality patterns, physiological dispositions etc.)
2. Context variables (demographic variables, sociocultural and sociopsychological factors, vulnerability factors)

Life event research investigates the events of a defined period of
time—an independent variable—relative to their comparatively direct consequences—a dependent variable.

All life event inventories presently applied may be attributed to the additive model laid down for example by Rahe and Holmes, or the threshold
model established by Brown.

THE MEASURING STANDARD OF DIFFERENT
LIFE EVENT INSTRUMENTS

The measuring of the stress impact caused by a single life event is possible
on different levels of differentiation.[3] We must make a fundamental
distinction between:

1. the measuring of stress impact based on expert rating, and
2. the measuring of stress impact in the course of self-rating of the subject.

In the following, the life events "birth of a child" and "death of a child"
will be used as an example.

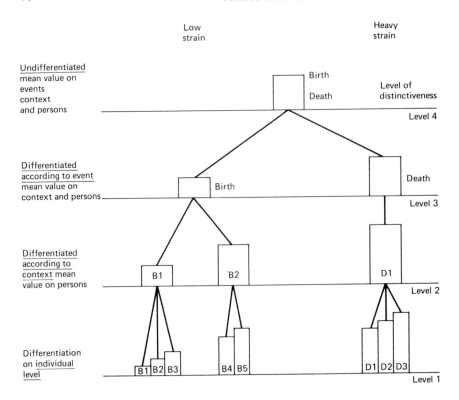

FIG. 1. Events on various levels of differentiation. The height of the column corresponds to the intensity of the experienced stress impact (in imitation of Katschnig, 1980).[3]

First Level

Different mothers will subjectively feel relieved or impaired by the birth or death of their children to different extents; a differentiation on subject level seems possible. The standard of this level of differentiation as expert rating, according to our opinion, is actually not achieved sufficiently by any instrument. The self-rating method used by Siegrist[4] at least comes close to this differentiation level.

The methodological problems of direct and indirect contamination, and the questions of reliability and validity which are obvious in this procedure, actually, however, are unresolved. The stress impact here results not only from the social context but also from individual experiences gained during life, from disposable strategies of mastering life, and from individual patterns of experience and attitude. The measuring is based on the hypothesis that a person is able and willing to indicate the results of experienced stress impact in a retrospective way.

Second Level

In comparable social situations, with a comparable notice of events and event frequency, considering the individual context for the typical woman or typical mother, we assume a typical stress impact. The stress impact values for "birth of a child" or "death of a child" here refer to a group of persons with the same social context. The quantitative dimension may be regarded as a mean value based on persons with the same context. The life event schedule of Brown is a typical instrument of this differentiation level.

Third Level

Independent from the context, a constant stressing dimension is attributed to a special life event. This results from the mean value of the stress impact which a life event receives in a standard random sample. Here the point is the mean value of the total stress impact dimension for typical persons (not typical women or mothers) in different contexts (not a determined context). Differentiation is executed on event level. The measuring number represents a mean value of context and persons. The life event "death of a child" is considered as constant stress impact and gets a certain stress impact value. The same is true for the stress impact value which is presumed for the life event "birth of a child." There are numerous such instruments which were preceded by calibration studies, e.g., by Dohrenwend and coauthors, Paykel and coauthors, and Tennant and Andrews.

Fourth Level

All kinds of life events are regarded here as equal stress factors. The number of life events is simply additive. "Birth of a child" is equal to "death of a child." There is no differentiation of life events. The measuring number represents a mean value of event, context, and persons.

METHODOLOGICAL PROBLEMS IN THE COURSE OF LIFE EVENT RESEARCH

The Problem of Direct Contamination

Independent and dependent variables influence each other by the measuring procedure itself. The stress impact caused by a life event is retrospectively interpreted by the knowledge of a later illness or recovery; we assume causal relations when a statistical association is really existent.

Indirect Contamination

It is conceivable that a pronounced obsessive brooding not only leads to illness but also to an increased tendency to report life events. Personality factors can thus influence both the answering of the life event inventory and the illness itself, which produces the problem of a pseudocorrelation.

Problem of Rare Events

Furthermore, we refer to the statistical analysis of the data which represents an additional general problem of evaluation in the course of life event research.

The usual univariate and multivariate procedures are based on the assumption of relatively frequent events. As to content, however, life events are principally rare events, and frequently it is the nonoccurrence of a life event which counts here. Furthermore, within the limits of the addition model, a number of particular problems of evaluation arise.

The Zero Error

In general, according to the life event concept, the number of zero codings in the life event inventories is large since, as is well known, only really rare events are to be surveyed. In case, however, zero codings are included in the stress impact qualities, large numerical correlations may have its cause in the respective nonoccurrence of a life event. In comparing groups relative to the same variables, differences in the stress impact strength are also determined by the number of events which have occurred. The larger the number of nonoccurring events, the smaller the mean values will necessarily be, as far as the stress impact strength is concerned.

In order to eliminate this zero error, only events which have really occurred can be considered when calculating the strength of stress impact caused by life events.

The Number Error

If one takes into account only those events which have really happened, a number error becomes the consequences. Differences between subjects or between groups depend on the number of events which have occurred. A possible correction would be the equation of one stressing event; this, on the other hand, would lead to a leveling of life events which, of course, stress different people in different ways.

The Combination Error

As a further methodological problem we must mention the combination error. The number of stressing events may be the same; their combination, however, different. In this case, differences in the total stress impact are based on different combinations of life events, for instance. While leveling in one stressing event will correct the number error in a certain way, the compensation of the combination error will be realized by forming pairs, a fact which, as experience shows, is exceptional.

RELIABILITY AND VALIDITY OF THE LIFE EVENT INVENTORIES

The reliability of a life event instrument for test and retest purposes should be proved not only on the group level, but also on the individual level. In any case, it would be desirable to check the reliability on the level of each item, and not simply relative to the general stress impact value.

As far as the validity of the life event inventories is concerned, there are scarcely any results at hand. It is necessary to investigate:

1. the real onset of a life event;
2. the objective stress impact caused by a life event at the time of its onset and the extraction of distortion effects which resulted from the consequences of the life event later on (this problem is the same in the self-rating scales as in the expert ratings, if the expert knows the life story of a subject);
3. the question of acceleration of illness or real cause of an illness, based on the onset of one or a group of life events.

With regard to the number of actually existing life event inventories, the question arises as to what extent the results of different life event studies can be compared with each other. Katschnig contributed an interesting abstract to this question.[3] On 42 patients who had attempted suicide, a cross-evaluation of the Schedule of Recent Experience (Holmes and Rahe, 1977) and the Life Event Schedule (Brown, 1968) was performed. The results were as follows: in both measuring instruments, the groups of investigated subjects show an increase of general stress impact caused by life events before the suicide attempt. For the increase of the stress impact score of the total population investigated, however, different persons are responsible in each case, i.e., the methods score different phenomena.

References

1. Dohrenwend, B. S. and Dohrenwend, B. P. (eds.). *Stressful Life Events: Their Nature and Effects.* New York: John Wiley, 1974.
2. Gunderson, E. K. E. and Rahe, R. H. (eds.). *Life Stress and Illness.* Springfield: Thomas, 1974.
3. Katschnig, K. (ed.). *Sozialer Streß und psychische Erkrankung.* München-Wien-Baltimore: Urban und Schwarzenberg, 1980.
4. Siegrist, J., Dittmann, K., Rittner, K., and Weber, J. *Lebensverändernde Ereignisse, Psychosoziale Dispositionen u. Herzinfarkt.* Marburg: University Press, 1979.
5. Joraschky, P. and Köhle, K. Maladaption und Krankheitsmanifestation. In *Lehrbuch der psychosomatischen Medizin* (Th. v. Uexküll, ed.). München-Wien-Baltimore: Urban und Schwarzenberg, 1979.

Behavior, Cognition, Emotion: A Note on the Psychosomatic Approach

Fernando Lolas, M.D.
Psychophysiology Unit
Faculty of Medicine
University of Chile at Santiago North
Santiago, Chile

The gaps in factual knowledge related to psychosomatic conditions are usually filled by theories which try to interconnect phenomena observed at different levels. The literature is filled with studies on personality structure, specific conflicts, ecological conditions, constitution, stressful stimuli, and endless lists of metapsychological constructs. The associations between these features and physiological derangement are usually of the interpretative type. Their predictive power is scarce. Ad hoc hypotheses have to be developed for discrepant cases. What is more important, however, is that most of the theories beg the question of *how* inner experience, "psychic" phenomena, and cultural influence are transformed into bodily pathology. The mechanisms which would make "the mysterious leap from the mind into the body" possible have not received, so it seems, due attention.

The main point to be made here is that the ways in which the question is usually put are caught in the traditional practical dualism of most psychosomatic approaches. When associated with a definite theoretical orientation, usually dependent upon selective and extensive training, this can lead to one-sided perspectives and ill-directed interdisciplinary approaches. The latter—when unsuccessful—end up in the meaningless juxtaposition of data.

We wish to return to a very simple formulation of the problem at hand. For us, the psychosomatic approach is characterized by an attitude which considers physical disease in the light of the *behavior* of the person.[9] We purposely employ the word person, indicating a system (that is, a cohesive arrangement of elements which preserves self-identity) which represents the highest level of organismic organization and the lowest level of the social hierarchy. From a very general point of view, behavior is any change of an entity with respect to its environment.[8] This classical definition might be usefully applied here, with the reservation that environment—a coextensive system, developed vis-a-vis an organism—need not be conceived solely as composed of objects and forces, but as a true, significant *situation*.[11] In point of fact, the distinction between concrete, abstract, and conceptual systems should be examined more carefully before proceeding to an orderly inquiry, but for the present purpose if would suffice to state that the system "person" may be profitably studied as a concrete one, concrete meaning the "real substance or thing as opposed to abstracted quality."[7] The sum total of organism-environment *transactions* (in Dewey's and Bentley's sense [3]) is behavior.

The term behavior may not be the most fortunate one, for it is laden with much ideological connotation. Suffice it to say that at the level of generality implied here, it resembles the concept of system performance proposed by others,[12] and its usefulness should prove itself by providing a meeting ground for different disciplines and unifying descriptive frameworks. Moreover, if metaphysical behaviorism is distinguished from methodological behaviorism, misunderstandings could be, to some extent, avoided. By behavior we mean to imply *all* transactions performed by the system under consideration as a whole. Living systems theory has incorporated the notion that organisms are essentially information processing systems striving for homeostasis. If this is accepted, all behavior is concerned in one way or another with preserving homeostasis. In simplified terms, this may occur by means of internal (under the skin) processes or through environment-oriented processes. The first constitute *covert behavior;* the second, *overt behavior.*

This categorization of behavior runs the risk of appearing too abstract and devoid of any practical implication. We wish to add that the basis for it does not rest solely upon the visibility of the behavior in question. It has also to do with the much more complicated issue of its meaning for an external observer. The position of the observer is clinically relevant insofar as aside from the system "person," the systems "group" and the system "two persons" lie at the core of psychosomatic theorization. At these two levels, behavior can have meaning for an external observer. This means that he can, consciously or unconsciously, process signals and signs, make use of symbolic devices, and put to work the behavior observed in terms of his own experience and previous history. Meaning is thus a shorthand expression for potential operation. In this sense, then, overt behavior is behavior with immediate meaning-valence.

The distinction proposed does not do justice to the complexities involved in the study of overt behavior.[6] The point to be emphasized, however, is that within the descriptive framework employed here, there is no need to assume a causal hierarchy between covert behavior and overt behavior. Both are, so to speak, at the same level and are simply complementary aspects of the total behavior. One of the main hindrances to effective experimentation in psychosomatic research has been either the notion that overt behavior is caused by invisible agencies (such as instincts, emotions, and so forth) or the assumption that covert and overt domains must be isomorphic (thus leading to endless "games in correlations"). Covert refers here to those behaviors which cannot be directly observed in the group or in the dyadic situation, or which have to be inferred from manifest behavior. At this point, we do not wish to differentiate further between "intervening variables" or "mediating mechanisms."

In preserving homeostasis and self-identity, living systems engage in matter-energy and information transactions. Stress, emotion, and activation are among the many different, though related, terms that describe states of disequilibrium. It is noteworthy that the main failure of energetic and economic theories of affect (related to the heat engine analogy or to the hydraulic model) lies precisely in the chain of events that would convert energy into affect. Affects and emotion are viewed as discharge phenomena, essentially discontinuous, having a causative role in behavior.[5] Another weakness of these theories is the cleavage they take for granted between affect and cognition. Psychoanalysts and behavioral scientists have recognized the problems for empirical research which derive from such positions.[5,10] They have come to the conclusion that there are affective components to every mental event, that affect is thus a quality of all experience, that clinical experience does not support a discharge view of psychic energy, and that behavior is not better predicted or explained by hypostatizing forces or ad hoc instincts. When these views are linked to the notion that the system "person" (like any living system) is essentially an information processor, then it would appear that there is no need to draw distinctions between affect and cognition, except as some form of taxonomy of behavioral events. Affect has been conceived as a stage in the processing of information or some quality derived from information-processing activities. This does not rule out the possibility that certain inputs may be associated more often with feeling states or subjective experience, or that built-in or acquired characteristics of the system may enhance the epiphenomenal affective consequences of a given set of cognitive processes. On the contrary, since all aspects of behavior are complementary, one should expect that a better definition and delineation of states could only be achieved by taking into consideration the past history of both the organism and the environment. Feeling states would not be an automatic outcome of any input but the result of active organizing processes derived from a confrontation between present demands and stored cognitive strategies designed to meet them (programs) that could be reflected, albeit differently, in psychological or physiological operations. It is probably necessary to postulate a comparator mechanism or an appraisal device to accomplish this. Some authors have proposed that precisely what we call *emotions* in our everyday language are means (socially established) for problem solving or rules for the organization of cognitive processes.[1] Insofar as we are here considering as cognitive process the reception, transmission, and processing of information, emotional meaning is the result of a program for guiding and organizing overt behavior.

If the foregoing discussion is brought to bear on the problem of *how* the so-called psychosomatic patients express themselves, it would probably take us too far to try to reinterpret the wealth of clinical descriptions. We have been repeatedly confronted with a dimension of analysis stressing the apparent lack of verbal mediation of affect experience in some individuals (alexithymia, pensée operatoire).[2] The question of whether this feature is causally related to somatic disease has not been answered yet, and for the present purpose is immaterial. We are much too dependent on the notion that affect precedes expression, and so the controversy goes on about whether these persons do not experience affect at all or are unable to convert it into words. From a research perspective, it might be worthwhile to explore the hypothesis that emotional words are in themselves organizing and controlling devices for emotion, and that in these individuals the primary deficit is a cognitive one. There are by now resourceful experimental designs which make use of the principles outlined above. To formulate and test hypotheses will depend upon abandoning or reformulating the framework of reference in which most of these descriptions have been made and upon developing research strategies that are able to accommodate different observational techniques. To the extent that overt and covert behavior are complementary aspects, there should be no difficulty in tackling the problem of mediating pathogenetic mechanisms from a more neutral standpoint. The development of an effective behavioral medicine is critically dependent on this unifying neutrality.

Acknowledgment. This manuscript was prepared under support of the Humboldt Foundation, Federal Republic of Germany.

References

1. Averill, J. R. Emotion and anxiety: sociocultural, biological, and psychological determinants. In *Emotions and Anxiety* (M. Zuckerman and C. D. Spielberger, eds.). New York: Wiley, 1976.
2. Bräutigam, W. and von Rad, M. *Toward a Theory of Psychosomatic Disorders*. Basel: Karger, 1977.
3. Dewey, J. and Bentley, A. F. *Knowing and the Known*. Boston: Beacon Press, 1949.
4. Engel, G. L. The clinical application of the biopsychosocial model. *Amer. J. Psychiat.* **137**: 535-544 (1980).
5. Krystal, H. Aspects of affect theory. *Bull. Menn. Clin.* **41**: 1-26 (1977).
6. Lolas, F. and Ferner, H. Zum Begriff des impliziten Verhaltens. *Z. kli. Psychol. Psychother.* **26**: 223-233 (1978).
7. Miller, J. G. *Living Systems*. New York: McGraw-Hill, 1978.
8. Rosenblueth, A., Wiener, N., and Bigelow, J. Behavior, purpose and teleology. *Phil. Sci.* **10**: 18-24 (1943).
9. Ruesch, J. *Semiotic Approaches to Human Relations*. The Hague: Mouton, 1972.
10. Sandler, J. The role of affects in psychoanalytic theory. In *Physiology, Emotion and Psychosomatic Illness,* Ciba Foundation Symposium. Amsterdam: Elsevier-Excerpta, 1972.
11. Üexküll, Th. v. *Lehrbuch der psychosomatischen Medizin*. München-Wien: Urban und Schwarzenberg, 1979.
12. Warren, C. E., Allen, M., and Haefner, J. W. Conceptual frameworks and the philosophical foundations of general living systems theory. *Behav. Sci.* **24**: 296-310 (1979).

Activation, Emotion, Stress: The Need for a Unified Approach *

Fernando Lolas, M.D.

Universitat Heidelberg
Federal Republic of Germany

Although *stress* has become some sort of key word for professionals and layment alike, it is a poorly defined phenomenon. Positively considered, it has created an interest in areas of research which can only be approached in an interdisciplinary fashion. On the negative side, its very broadness has been partly responsible for many terminological confusions and much criticism.

It has been proposed to define stress as an alteration of psychological homeostasis. This definition is adopted in order to circumvent the difficulties associated with a purely physiological one. Such difficulties make it unrealistic to support unspecificity on the response side as a definitory characteristic, and since any stimulus provokes homeostatic changes, the ad hoc differentiation between eustress and distress had to be advanced. Some authors, in view of the confusion, have even proposed to abandon the term at all or to use it to designate a problem area. Although psychological stress and social stress constituted important expansions of the original concepts, for they represented the fusion of the old psychiatric with the physiological tradition, most of the criticisms voiced against the stress concept can be traced back to the point in time when these expansions took place.

The emphasis on the psychological aspect of homeostasis and the resulting redefinition of stress phenomena have uncovered striking similarities between stress research and traditional problem areas in psychophysiology, such as activation and emotion. As a matter of fact, the very notion of psychological homeostasis refers to the maintenance of the normal mood state of an individual at rest; emotions are then viewed as alterations from this state. It should be pointed out that homeostatic concepts have been repeatedly employed in stress theories (as, for example, by Cofer and Appley, and Lazarus) although no adequate description of the

*This manuscript was prepared while the author's research was supported by the Alexander von Humboldt Foundation, Federal Republic of Germany.

basic equilibrium is provided. Despite the fact that stress, in common parlance, has come to be viewed as a relatively unspecific, intense, and unpleasant emotional activation, it has been this notion of homeostasis which basically has led to the distinction between eustress and distress (that is, reactions of the living organism to *all* stimuli which tend to disturb the dynamic homeostasis of psychological, biochemical, and physiological processes). It should be added at this point that researchers have often directed their attention to different types of experimental situations, which may not necessarily involve the same mechanisms, such as acute stress, chronic stress, and chronic intermittent stress.

Arousal and Activation

The wealth of theoretical elaborations on arousal and activation shows the convergence of different research traditions. One of these derived from the work of Cannon on the generalized response of the sympathetic nervous system to threatening stimuli, which was related to an arousal model combining the notions of threatening stimuli, autonomic arousal, and the activation of adaptive overt behavior. Another tradition may be viewed in the notions of generalized drive from Hullian learning theory and central motive state from Morgan. It had in common with the first tradition the assumption that a nonspecific component associated with drive energized behavior, incorporating this hypothesis into a formal theory of behavior, and suggesting in addition that arousal was associated with appetitively, as well as aversively, based drives. The third tradition may be linked to neurophysiological work on the reticular activating system, which seemed to offer an anatomical substrate for nonspecific arousal as indicated by electroencephalographic activation (Hebb, Lindsley, etc.).

Although many other research viewpoints have contributed to the development of arousal theory, effort has been directed toward assimilating them into a single model in which the reticular activating system has been assumed to serve as a generalized arousal mechanism, responding to sensory inputs of all kinds, energizing behavior, and producing both EEG and sympathetic nervous system activation. Classical activation theory thus viewed the organism as a functional unit, implying intraindividual constancy or stable relationships between autonomic, central nervous system, and behavioral indicators. A second major assumption related the general notion of activation to behavioral performance in a descriptive way, such as the well-known Yerkes-Dodson inverted U relationship between them.

It is meanwhile an established experimental fact that autonomic, electrocortical, and behavioral indicators can show dissociations depending upon situation and idiosyncratic response tendencies. This could, however, be valid only for phasic reaction patterns, whereas the general theory of activation concentrated on tonic central processes. It should be useful to distinguish between activation as a variable and its empirical indicators. In this regard, activation could be viewed as a background phenomenon not necessarily linked linearly with any of its quantifiable peripheral manifestations, but more or less a state of potential energy mobilization. The low intercorrelations between indicators could then be explained by different time courses in the activation of subsystems (which could be out of phase at any given point in time), by regulatory antagonistic regulation between subsystems, or by peculiar adaptive demands interacting with stored (constitutional and dispositional) action programs. Whether the different subsystems act in parallel or are interactive is still an open experimental question. It should be noted, nevertheless, that some evidence seems to point toward the complementarity of the different subsystems, so that the notion that some definable state might be delimited on the basis of activation pattern is still a tenable one.

The above-mentioned criticism led to reformulations of the classical problems, which in the main have relied upon defining more than one activating system. Whereas in some early work no distinction was made between arousal and activation, this distinction has been used by many theorists. In Eysenck's personality theory, for instance, the formal distinction between activation and arousal is made. The first could be traced back to the activity of portions of the limbic system and underlies the dimension "neuroticism" or stress vulnerability, while the second would be mediated by the ascending reticular system and would be related to the extraversion dimension. Similar statements and experimental support have been provided by others. If the construct attention is viewed as selective activation (related to cue properties and informational aspects of behavior), several models designed to account for it can also be cited. In many of them, two or more systems are assumed in order to account for experimental findings. Pribram and McGuinness refer to arousal as tonic responses to environmental input, to activation as phasic preparedness to response, and to effort as a coordinating process. This position exemplifies a major direction in current theorization. As Fahrenberg points out, two- or multiple-component systems can be useful only insofar as the components are seen as partially independent, otherwise are they simply "metaphors." It should also be added that any model must provide working hypotheses on how the component subsystems interact or influence each other. This applies particularly to inhibition effects and—to cite only an example—behavioral inhibition systems (such as the one in Gray's model).

Emotion and Stress

The foregoing presentation is relevant insofar as many of the empirical relationships studied within the framework of activation theory could also hold true for stress research, if this can be conceived of as an independent research area at all. The literature on emotion is also plagued with terminological difficulties, for here subjective states (feelings) have played a prominent role and should be taken into account. Emotion theories have oscillated between the emphasis on *peripheral* as opposed to *central* mechanisms and between psychologically minded as opposed to physiologically minded interpretations. The most widely discussed theory at present is intermediate between reductionistic approaches (all emotions being only stages in the activation continuum) and psychological-interpretative ones. Such cognitive emotion theory (for instance, Arnold's, with its emphasis on felt action tendency) closely resembles the cognitive stress theories (such as those emphasizing appraisal and coping), so that a formal distinction between the two fields is sometimes difficult to draw. Some theoreticians insist upon prior experience, fantasies, and intentions, while others stress situational cognitions (e.g., Schachter and Singer). A certain degree of proximity seems to exist between cognitive emotion theories and unidimensional activation theories, especially if they insist upon a dimensional approach. Categorial approaches—which try to develop a taxonomy of differentiable emotional patterns—are closer to selective or fractionated response systems.

Both in stress as well as in emotion research, the role of cognitive mechanisms has been emphasized. In many formulations the nature and mode of operation of these mechanisms are left unexplained (black box approach). From a psychophysiological perspective, they can be viewed as patterns of operations within the central nervous system associated with the reception, transmission, and processing of information. One recently proposed theory of emotional imagery (Lang's) conceives of the image in the brain as a conceptual network controlling specific somatovisceral patterns and constituting a prototype for overt behavioral expression. It has become a widely held view that the stressful character of any given situation does not depend on the stimulus alone but on organismic factors related to cognitive organization, such as anticipation of threat, object loss, appraisal, and coping. However different the frameworks of reference for these conceptions may be—they may accord more or less importance to developmental factors, for example—the general point is that the stimulus object is not exclusively the primary initiator of the response program (be it called stress, strain, or emotion). Upon receiving a stimulus, in Lang's words, "what is constructed . . . is not an internal stimulus . . . what the subject does is to generate a conceptual structure which contains stimulus and response information, both embedded in a more or less elaborate semantic network." One of the implications of this view is that emotional behavior may begin at any point in the conceptual network, in what we could call a nonlinear stimulus-response relationship.

Dimensions of Behavior

It seems that the concepts outlined above could be treated within a single framework. The differences reside more in emphasis and vocabulary than in basic principles. Whether the entire field should be termed "stress research," "activation research," or "emotion research" is a matter of individual preference.

What we are dealing with is, essentially, adaptive behavior. Adaptive behavior is a feature present in all living systems. Sometimes, partial aspects of behavior are emphasized at the expense of others. Words are coined which open new avenues of inquiry, refer in a shorthand way to complex phenomena, and bring these phenomena to public attention. Emphasis on partial aspects is responsible for the fact that we have many theories about behavior but no science of behavior. An epistemological imperative for developing useful research strategies is to strive for unifying principles.

In reviewing the literature, it appears that the basic dimensionality of behavior has been treated under one or more of the following headings: intensity, direction, valence, and selectivity (specificity).

It seems that the first of these dimensions—*intensity*—has received special attention in physiological studies. It refers to those energizing aspects that account for differences in activity and reactivity between organisms or in an organism at different times. Parameters for intensity are more or less easily derived from physiological processes.

Direction refers to steering mechanisms and processes, which account for some of the most general teleonomic aspects of adaptive behavior. Whether an animal goes to sleep or searches for food surely depends not only upon the internal state of activation but also upon external clues which become relevant in terms of stored information and action programs. The directedness of behavior received attention in studies dealing with cognitive aspects.

Valence refers to the experiential character of any given behavioral transaction. Although classical introspectionist psychology based its research program on this aspect of behavior, interest in "mentalistic" constructs (such as pleasure or fear) faded away from some extended period of time. Insofar as the valence aspect of behavior is a demonstrable fact, it should be approached with the same tools—in the sense of conceptual operations—as the other aspects and integrated with them.

Selectivity—or, better, *specificity*—refers to patterning. It introduces the notion that specific stimuli, specific organism, and specific situation might interact in complex forms to give rise to any given behavioral performance. Whether or not this notion permits a taxonomy of the behavioral domain that fits the exigencies of an idiographic (individualizing) approach (as is needed in clinical medicine) is again a problem in experimentation. Another experimental question is whether a demonstrated specificity at the physiological level correlates with valence aspects of the total behavior exhibited by an organism.

Concluding Remarks

Experimental studies can be classified according to the emphasis they place upon one or the other of these four dimensions. It should be kept in mind that only rarely do behavioral studies take all four into consideration. Most often, they concentrate on one of them, neglecting the others. If these results are then extrapolated and given predictive character, misunderstandings arise. It is perhaps not too farfetched to state that this has happened not infrequently in the areas of stress and emotion research. The added problem of the use of idiosyncratic jargon to refer to the same phenomena obscures still more the basic commonalities, shared assumptions, and overall goals. To learn how organisms interact with their environments in an adaptive way, and how the processes involved are affected by their previous history, changes in the surroundings, and situational determinants, is certainly the goal of a unified perspective, still in need of unifying principles.

References

1. Burchfield, S. R. The stress response: a new perspective. *Psychosomatic Medicine* **41**: 661-672 (1979).
2. Fahrenberg, J. Psychophysiologie. In *Psychiatrie der Gegenwart*. K. P. Kisker, J. E. Meyer, C. Müller and E. Strömgren (eds.), 2nd ed., vol I/1. Berlin-Heidelberg: Springer, 1979.
3. Lang, P. J. A bio-informational theory of emotional imagery. *Psychophysiology* **16**: 495-512 (1979).
4. Levi, L. (ed.). *Emotions: their Parameters and Measurement*. New York: Raven Press, 1975.
5. Selye, H. *Stress in Health and Disease*. London: Butterworth, 1976.

Basic Concepts in Psychophysiological Personality Research*

Fernando Lolas, M.D.
Universitat Heidelberg
Federal Republic of Germany

There are two major ways of approaching the problem of individual differences in behavior. One of them stresses the roles a personality plays within a group, focusing upon interpersonal transactions. The other emphasizes the fact that personality can be viewed as an individually developed somatopsychological pattern of structural-functional characteristics.

Although there is no basic antagonism between these two approaches, considerable disagreement may arise if the framework of reference is not appropriately stated. Under similar terms, reference may be made to altogether different processes.

When we refer to psychophysiological personality research, we mean to imply a way of describing and analyzing behavior which takes into account both its covert and overt aspects, and aims to develop a conceptual system of abstracted relationships and interactions among long-term subject variables. The term *behavior* designates any transaction performed by a living system. Covert behavior is equated—for the purposes of simplicity—with concrete or abstracted physiological processes.

The point of departure for any theory of personality is the recognition of individual behavioral differences. Idiographic approaches would try to emphasize the individualizing, idiosyncratic properties of behavior. Nomothetic approaches would search for commonalities. There exists the possiblity of adopting a *typological* or a *dimensional* framework. The first consists in defining mutually exclusive, more or less rigid categories to which individual subjects can be ascribed. The second deals with quantitative continua along which any individual subject may be positioned. Although psychophysiological research can proceed on both a typological and a dimensional basis, the second permits a more differentiated description involving quatitative assessment and leads to a better integration between data of different kinds.

*This manuscript was prepared while the author's work was supported by the Alexander von Humboldt Foundation, Federal Republic of Germany

The latter is an important point, since in any theory of personality the notion of *trait* has to be elaborated. Traits are enduring, long-term behavioral characteristics exhibited by a subject, albeit differently, in diverse situations. On the other hand, trait also refers to relationships of similarity indentifiable in different behavioral performances. Observe that the second connotation refers to the establishment of regularities or isomorphisms across observational levels (e.g., language, manifest behavior, imagery). This pervasiveness of traits may not—theoretically at least—be uniform for all of them, so that some can be evinced more readily with one observational technique than with others. In this sense, one of the major problems in psychophysiological personality research is the specification of trait systems that can incorporate both physiological and other types of descriptors. Depending upon the researcher's habit of thought, the circumstance may arise that some personality theories are simply not amenable to certain types of experimental or descriptive approaches. On such occasions, a reformulation of the basic tenets might be necessary.

Differential psychophysiology (that is, the psychophysiology of individual differences) should be qualified in a further direction. Since not all differences that can be observed can be attributed to traits, the problem of separating them from short-term, context-dependent changes in *state* may be considerable. The state-trait dichotomy (in some respects similar to the structure-process one) would be too lengthy a topic to deal with here. Suffice it to say that it is not only a problem in the temporal dimension (that is, traits are not simply more enduring and states more short-lived); it is also a problem in defining levels and techniques of observation (that is, a conceptual as well as an empirical one). Since changes of state can sometimes be evinced at one observational level and not at another (due, for instance, to the appropriateness of the assessment instrument, "time-resolution" of the observation technique, or real dissociations such as those occurring between physiological and psychological phenomena), it is perhaps advisable to keep in mind tht personality therories are conceptual systems and traits are abstractions. The latter implies that their presence may also be inferred from temporal or spatial patterning across obervational domains or by intensity characteristics of changes in state.

From the standpoint of physiological methodology, a further distinction may be established. Some researchers have directed their attention to the effector organ functioning, that is to say, striated and smooth muscle contraction, heart rate, autonomic responses, and the like. This approach extends behavioral analysis to somatic functions explored at the periphery. We may call it *behavioral psychophysiology* or *peripheral psychophysiol-*

ogy, where it should be noted that behavior here connotes observable events. Other workers have studied the central nervous system mechanisms which may account for mediating processes or intervening variables between inputs and outputs. There exists the hope that complex psychological constructs might be reformulated in terms of cerebral physiology. Central nervous system indicators related to information processing or to encoding mechanisms can then be explored and the data so obtained linked with other types of information, such as that derived from psychometric assessment. If we agree that cognition involves all the processes associated with reception, storage, and retrieval of information, then such an approach could be termed *cognitive psychophysiology* or, more neutrally, *central psychophysiology.* In both approaches, the basic endeavor consists of expanding the descriptive data base on which to anchor theorization and empirical work on individual differences. We have already alluded to the possibility of defining traits from *both* a physiological and, say, a psychometric standpoint, framing both sources of data within a single point of departure. Most frequently, however, the psychometric definition of traits precedes physiological research, so that a correlative approach ensues. Researchers may try to validate a certain paper-and-pencil trait by means of physiological measurements or to demonstrate its predictive validity. Again, not all theories of personality developed so far can easily be investigated from the physiological standpoint without losing their meaningfulness. This is due to the fact that some theories have developed with a predominant sociopsychological orientation and cannot easily incorporate the intraindividual source of information.

In terms of the research output generated, Eysenck's theory of personality has been one the most popular. Eysenck's theory is a dimensional theory making explicit reference to physiological correlates, although its most important descriptive concepts are said to be valid for both laboratory conditions and social interaction. The major dimensions, introversion-extra-version and neuroticism-stability (or emotionality vs nonemotionality), have emerged from the most diverse types of studies of both adults and children, and could be compared with similar factorially derived dimensions described by others (e.g., Cattell's exvia-invia and anxiety). *E* (extraversion-introversion) and *N* (neuroticism) could be traced back to the operation of at least two distinct activation mechanisms, one related to the reticular formation (arousal) and the other to portions of the limbic system (activation). These systems are postulated to be independent for most of the time, except on occasions when strong emotions are produced in the individual; such strong emotions produce strong arousal in the cortex, either directly or through the reticular formation, so that a com-

bination of strong emotion–low arousal is impossible, although the combination high arousal–little emotion is possible. Several other writers have
elaborated on two (or perhaps more) distinct systems or dimensions in
order to account for individual behavioral variance. Not all of them
elaborate on the important problem of the interaction between arousal and
emotion. This point deserves emphasis, for although Eysenck's E and N
dimensions are orthogonal factors, mathematically independent as has
been repeatedly shown, the indicators provided by central nervous system
functioning usually show various degrees of interaction between the
physiological systems assumed to be related to the overt manifestations of
personality traits. Eysenck himself has observed that a direct measurement
of the assumed nervous system correlates to the personality dimensions is a
doubtful, if not an erroneous, objective, since much work has been done at
the physiological level which throws doubt on any simplistic or schematic
view of nervous system operations. What is important, however, is that
when people labeled "high neuroticism subjects" are stimulated, they will
show a different pattern of somatic reactivity. Although the same holds
true for the extraversion demension, some contradictory findings have been
reported, and criticism against the unidimensionality of this construct has
been voiced. Eysenck's theory, by incorporating features of Pavlov, Hull,
and Jung, made at the beginning an original description in terms of a single
dimension of excitation-inhibition, weak excitation meaning strong inhibition. This view is at variance with other currents of thought (also derived
from Pavlov's work) which maintain that excitation and inhibition are processes in the central nervous system that can vary independently in
strength. This is a highly appealing conceptual framework, provided that
empirical referents for the two processes can be reliably established. Gray's
model has been presented as a heuristically useful theory for developing experimental research strategies.

   No justice can be done to the wealth of empirical studies in this area.
Personality factors probably need to be conceived of as largely innate
determinants of resting level of arousal, which interact with stimulus-
produced arousal in complex forms. It is perhaps useful to draw the
distinction between *arousal*, as tonic level, and *arousability,* that is, the
degree to which the individual can be aroused by stimulation. The level he
attains might be different from his prevailing state at a particular time,
which may not reflect his maximum potential (in terms of reactivity). This
is again important insofar as the tasks employed in some experimental settings may vary greatly in complexity, indexed either in terms of previously
established habits or in terms of interference factors. All this, in turn,
should lead to the proposition that intrasubject measures of momentary

state of arousal (particularly under conditions of demand) may or may not be correlated with psychometric personality features. A further interacting factor could be the temporal rhythm of arousal, which may be different for different subjects and which may interact with task and other factors. It should also be observed that the degree of equilibrium or homeostasis at which the organism operates in maintaining the relationships between two (or more) arousal systems may have important methodological implications.

If we examine succinctly what the aims of psychophysiological personality research are, it appears that the first of them should be the definition of appropriate dimensional frameworks which take into consideration all possible sources of individual behavioral diversity. This should allow a reliable classification of subjects on the basis of measurable properties. In turn, such classification should yield testable predictions concerning behavior or prognosis regarding the effects of certain behavioral manipulations. This is also a task related to the need for appropriate categorization of normal and abnormal ways of interacting with the environment and their possible modification.

Because of the multiplicity of interacting variables, many of which are difficult to measure, prediction can only proceed on the basis of conscious choice of experimental settings and careful extrapolation of data. Not all theories of personality (personality being left here undefined) can be approached from a psychophysiological point of view unless they are reformulated. Despite all its weaknesses, we have selected Eysenck's theory as an example to illustrate some points because it explicitly incorporates the physiological dimension as one of its empirical referents. Although this happened at the beginning mostly in analogical terms, this theory offers the advantage of its simplicity and of its modifiability on the basis of experimental data. It is thus designed to guide research into fruitful channels and not to establish once and for all eternal truths.

We have not attempted here a summary which could by no means do justice to the rich and diversified literature in this field. Our main point is the notion of individual differences in behavior, which may be approached by taking into consideration intrasubject (physiological) processes. We have distinguished different forms of approaching this problem and referred briefly to the state-trait dichotomy. Peripheral and central psychophysiology have been distinguished from the methodological point of view. Different interacting variables in the experimental validation of conceptual personality frameworks have been mentioned, and the example of Eysenck's dimensions has been used to illustrate the main issues involved. The main conclusion to be derived from this exposition is that a sophisticated body of knowledge, empirically grounded, has tackled the issue of individual differences and that personality factors (psychophysiologically conceived) are to be taken into account in any experimental work and not relegated to the status of error term. Trivial as this statement might appear, a brief look at the psychopharmacological, physiological, and medical literature demonstrates that they are not taken into account in a considerable proportion of cases. Perhaps a further background conviction should be mentioned. There is great need for more detailed and long-ranging theoretical conceptions in psychophysiology in general, and in the area of individual differences in particular. This is not to be misconstrued as a plea to abandon detailed and specific experimental inquiry. Data collection, however, unless informed by hypotheses can have only a very limited value. The many different theoretical frameworks provide disparing and antagonical views and irreconcilable jargons. Along with further experimentation, attention must be devoted to the ways in which differing views can be meaningfully integrated and general hypotheses formulated.

References

1. Callaway, E. Brain electrical potentials and individual psychological differences. New York: Grune and Stratton, 1975.
2. Cattell, R. B. and Dreger, R. M. (eds.). *Handbook of Modern personality Theory.* Washington: Halsted Press, 1977.
3. Eysenck, H. J. (ed.). *Handbook of Abnormal Psychology,* 2nd ed. London: Pitman Medical, 1973.
4. Fowles, D. C. The three arousal model: implications of Gray's two-factor learning theory for heart rate, electrodermal activity, and psychopathy. *Psychophysiology* 17: 87–104 (1980).
5. Lolas, F. and de Andraca, I. Neuroticism, extraversion, and slow brain potentials. *Neuropsychobiology* 3 :12–22 (1977).

The Experiential Approach: The Core of Monistic Health

Yujiro Ikemi, M.D., Ph.D.
Professor Emeritus, Kyushu University Faculty of Medicine
Director, Kitakyushu City Kokura Hospital
Kyushu, Japan

Akira Ikemi, M.A.
Clinical Psychologist
Kita-Kyushu City Kokura Hospital
Kyushu, Japan

INTRODUCTION

The development of modern psychosomatic medicine signifies, for one, the attempt to restore a human quality to the study of the body and diseases. In part, it attempts to overcome the dualism set forth by Descartes and to replace it with the unity of human existence. In this sense, psychosomatic medicine represents a "re-search" for the *whole person* out of the fragments of mind and body, out of the ideas of the mind over body or body over mind. The core of the monistic view is unfragmented human existence.

Human existence has been fragmented by the style of thought which Descartes led. Following this line of thought, medicine has conceived of human existence by its fragmentation into body and mind. With this dualistic view, the body has been conceptualized as a mechanical object which exists independently of consciousness, and as such it was studied by its reduction to the most elementary components. Though this reductionism and compartmentalization have led to great progress in the medical sciences, there reached a point in this line of research where it became evident that the body was not an isolated mechanism but part of a greater whole—of the whole living person, of the environment, and of nature itself. Modern medicine has recognized the primordial interrelatedness of the world through the body.

Psychosomatic medicine, as its name implies, has had a tendency to reduce this primordial interrelatedness into compartments—*psyche* and *soma*—and to apply two conceptual systems, two approaches, two languages systems to the study of diseases. In this regard, unless the two approaches of psyche and soma are well integrated, dualism is created rather than being overcome. Furthermore, in recent years, psychosomatic medicine has advocated a "biopsychosocial" approach which may help to cover the wide range of interrelatedness evident in the body and diseases, but may also proceed to further confuse and fragment the unity of human bodily existence into different sets of concepts, approaches, and technical languages. Psychosomatic medicine now seeks a way of integrating different concepts and methods into its theory, research, and practice.

Meanwhile, for the psychosomatic practitioner, it is clear that his endeavor addresses human *existence*. The different concepts and methods of psychosomatic medicine are used in some way to address existence, the living reality of the patient. Existence, as we shall describe later, is not itself a concept, but a preconceptual whole from which concepts emerge. The core of the monistic psychosomatic approach aims at a direct experiential awareness of this preconceptual whole.

A person is not a biopsychosocial unit, but his existence is a *whole* that exists before these conceptual differentiations. Concepts and methods are neither valid nor invalid to begin with, but they become so in the process of existential explication (Gendlin, 1965). In other words, a certain technique may "fit" or "make sense" to a particular patient but may not to another patient with a similar symptom. This does not mean that the technique itself was valid or not valid but that in the first case it *became* valid in the process of the patient's explication of his existence while it did not in the latter. Human existence is not a passive object to be worked on by the practitioner, but it actively creates concepts and tries to understand itself. The different concepts and methods in psychosomatic medicine become *real* to the patient only when they experientially resonate with the patient's own existence. The integration of different concepts in psychosomatic medicine may occcur on the grounds of this real experience of the patient, on the grounds of his existence. The heart of the psychosomatic approach aims directly at existence. Only when the patient has become aware of his own existence is authentic self-control possible.

The oriental way of life has given birth to a variety of exercises whose aim was to directly experience an existential awareness of life. Philosophy and the arts did not remain a scholastic endeavor but developed into ways of direct experiencing.

Zen, Yoga, tea ceremony, martial arts, etc., are valued as a *way* to that experience. Psychosomatic medicine has now come to a point of searching for a way to awaken existential awareness; in this paper, we shall state more precisely how this is so. At first, we shall attempt to grasp more clearly what we mean by existence.

EXISTENCE

By existence, we do not mean a particular theoretical concept. Rather, we mean the concrete living of reality, lived through *experiencing*. In this discussion on existence, we follow the lead of the American psychologist, Eugene Gendlin (1979).

(1) Existence is lived through experiencing. One's existence here and now is his experiencing here and now. (Of course, here and now implies a past facility and a future possibility.) Existence is found in here-and-now experiencing. (2) Experiencing is *bodily felt*. My experiencing here and now, my reading this paper, may be experienced as a sense of something like excitement in my body. Implicit in this slice of experiencing is the past effort that culminates in this work and the future possibilities that unfold with this work. All this (and more) is experienced bodily as a sense of something (like excitement). (3) Experiencing is *preconceptual*. From it arises concepts, but concepts cannot capture all of experiencing. A person's experiencing is not ready-made into categories, into a biopsychosocial unit, for example. Rather, the explication of his experiencing can be studied biologically, psychologically, and sociologically, but his experiencing itself is none of these conceptual frameworks. From this, it can be said that experiencing is internally differentiable; that is, it can be explicated and differentiated into concepts. (4) Experiencing is a process. We do not speak here of "an experience of . . . ." Experiencing is not isolated in time. An experience of anxiety, for example, points to a process where something isn't fine and something like this, which is not yet clear, should be done. Once that something is done, anxiety will *shift*. Experiencing is not static, it joins a flow, a process. (5) In experiencing there is an implicit authenticity. In the above example of anxiety, we mentioned that experiencing points toward that something which is not clear now but should be done. This "what should be done" is an authentic possibility that is implicit in experiencing. (6) Experiencing is *of something*. Experiencing, although it is internally felt, is not a purely subjectivist phenomenon. Experiencing is of something in the world (intentionality). Hence, the world and human existence cannot be severed insofar as experiencing points to the world.

The notion of existence elaborated by Gendlin brings us close to the oriental notion of existence as experiencing, as a process, and as a bodily felt reality in the world. It is, however, evident that many psychosomatic patients have not been awakened to this level of experiencing. A case in point is alexithymia, a condition observed in psychosomatic disorders in which patients have difficulty articulating feelings or sensing them bodily. Further, there are patients who appear to be bound to a certain conceptualization of themselves and of the world, and thereby lose a sense of process, fluidity, and authenticity in their lives. Moreover, there are patients who distrust their experiencing process and tend to intellectualize rather than feel their problems deep inside. Hence, it is proper to speak of raising the patient's level of experiencing as an aim of psychosomatic therapy. Once the patient is able to experience at a high level, he is able to explore and conceptualize the nature of his problem, which facilitates understanding and self-control.

HIGHER LEVELS OF EXPERIENCING

Higher Levels of Experiencing and Psychotherapy

Klein et al. (1969) have devised an Experiencing Scale based on levels of experiencing conceptualized from psychotherapy recordings.

At low levels of experiencing, psychotherapy clients talk only of external events in a detached manner, while at higher levels, clients describe freely and frequently in a propositional manner, their personal experiences. Briefly, Klein's stages are shown in Fig. 1. Note that in Stage 1, the client is impersonal and detached from the problem. In Stages 2 through 4, the client is attached and involved in the experiencing described. Yet at higher levels, once again, the client is able to feel the problem, yet be detached enough to be exploratory or hypothetical about it. This is the experience which is frequently described as "full," "calm detachment," or an "observing self."

Further studies with the Experiencing Scale indicate that in most cases of successful psychotherapy of any style, clients speak with a high level of experiencing (Stage 4 and above), while at low levels of experiencing, psychotherapy often fails (Gendlin et al.,) This study indicates that the success or failure of psychotherapy is related to the client's level of experiencing and not merely to the therapist's qualities or to the style of therapy. It showed, furthermore, that psychotherapy does not, by itself, raise the level of experiencing. A high level of experiencing is a key to successful psychotherapy. How can the level of experiencing be raised?

Higher Levels of Experiencing and Altered States of Consciousness

Gendlin has devised a specific technique called "focusing" to raise the client's level of experiencing. Without elaborating about focusing, it should

Stages	Content	Manner
1	External events; refusal to participate	Impersonal, detached
2	External events; intellectual self-description	Interested, personal, self-participation
3	Personal reactions to external events; limited self-descriptions; behavioral description of feelings	Reactive, emotionally involved
4	Description of feelings and personal experiences	Self-descriptive, associative
5	Problems or propositions about feelings and personal experiences	Exploratory, elaborative, hypothetical
6	Synthesis of readily accessible feelings and experiences to resolve personally significant issues	Feelings vividly expressed, integrative, conclusive or affirmative
7	Full, easy presentation of experiencing all elements confidently	Expansive, illuminating, confident, buoyant

FIG. 1 (Klien et al., 1969)

be said that it is not the only way to raise the level of experiencing. Other techniques such as those of meditation (e.g., Zen) also aim at raising the level of experiencing so that one can become aware of what one is feeling, thinking, sensing, etc. (mindfulness). This experience of being in a clear "space" and at the same time "watching" feelings and thoughts is essential to both meditation and focusing, and facilitates psychotherapy. This high level of experiencing, which may be conceptualized as an "altered state of consciousness," serves as a groundwork for successful psychotherapy.

In the altered state of consciousness, it has been reported that psychologically there is a maximal level of attention (Chauchard, 1979). Attention is maximal in this state since there is an optimal balance of attention and inhibition. Too much attention implies a lack of attention, while too little attention cannot obviously effect attention. In an EEG study of Zen monks (Hirai, 1978), the monks in meditation were repeatedly presented with a sound stimuli. The EEG patterns of those who experienced themselves as being in an optimal meditation situation manifested slow alpha waves that moved into beta waves only at the time that the stimuli were presented. Beta waves rapidly returned to alpha waves each time the stimuli were withdrawn. Those who were too relaxed in meditation did not attend to the stimuli (did not show beta waves), while those who were too tense attended to each stimulus with prolonged beta waves that did not return easily to an alpha state. After a number of stimuli presentations, these subjects got habituated to the stimuli and did not return to the alpha state. It is clear then, that in the optimal Zen meditation, the Zen monk is able to fully attend to each stimulus while being in a relaxed condition.

These altered states of consciousness are effected by bodily exercises, posture, and breathing in particular. Oriental culture has been fertile with the development of many bodily exercises to arrive at this state of consciousness.

The altered states of consciousness not only serve as groundwork for successful psychotherapy but also have positive and de-stressing effects on the whole organism. Gelhorn and Kiely (1972) reviewed the works of Hess and others to show the mutual interplay of the ergotropic and trophotropic systems. Body-oriented approaches (somatopsychic) apparently alter proprioceptive afferent discharge to the reticulohypothalamic activating system through relaxation of the muscular system, and control of breathing in particular, inducing an optimal state of hypothalamic (ergo-tropic-trophotropic) balance.

In such a state of balance, hypothalamic-cortical discharges are diminished, resulting in lowered cortical excitation and dominance of the trophotropic system. Gelhorn has referred to this as "a state of emptiness of consciousness without loss of consciousness" (Gelhorn and Kiely, 1972). The emptiness of consciousness is the psychological concomitant of the shift to the trophotropic side. To maintain this state requires conscious effort, which may be reflected in a mild stimulation of the ergotropic system. He has noted that in none of the techniques of autogenic training, progressive relaxation, and systematic desensitization has there been reported such a remarkable subcortical-cortical patterning change of electrical activity as there has been in the case of Zen meditation and Yoga exercises. The altered state of consciousness induced by such methods activates the natural pro-homeostatic, de-stressing, and self-regulating functions and is itself therapeutic to many psychosomatic disorders. From this point of view, these self-activated altered states of consciousness may not be *altered* states of consciousness, but in fact the *natural* state of consciousness.

An Integrated Approach to Psychosomatic Therapy

It has already been mentioned that a high level of experiencing is essential to successful psychotherapy. A high level of experiencing, in turn, is

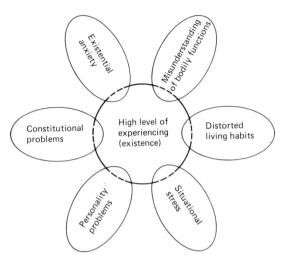

FIG. 2.

facilitated by techniques of bodily exercises and certain meditation techniques which are, in themselves, therapeutic to many cases of psychosomatic disorders.

Hence, successful psychological or psychosomatic approaches require their foundation a body-oriented or somatopsychic approach to raise the level of experiencing. Once a high level of experiencing is reached in the somatopsychic approach, the psychosomatic approach may help to clarify, conceptualize, and articulate the experiencing process. Thus the psychosomatic approach and the somatopsychic approach serve as complements to each other. Together, the two approaches facilitate holistic understanding, grounded in bodily felt experiencing.

It is at a high level of experiencing that the psychosomatic patient can come to understand the dynamics of his illness in a full way. Usually, the patient, with the help of the therapist, arrives at one of the following conceptualizations of his illness experience (see Figs. 2 and 3): (1) misunderstanding of bodily functions, (2) situational stress, (3) distorted living habits, (4) personality problems, (5) constitutional problems, (6) existential anxiety.

Once the patient is able to understand his problems fully, the psychosomatic practitioner can facilitate therapy by administering the most effective approach to the particular patient's problem. Here again, the psychosomatic approach and the somatopsychic approach can be used concomitantly, so that therapeutic work can be done in a physiologically optimal state of consciousness and brain functioning.

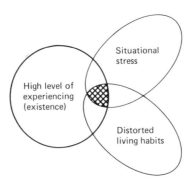

FIG. 3. A particular patient's explication of his experiencing may show, for example, that both situational stress and distorted living habits operate in his illness.

TOWARD PSYCHOSOMATIC HEALTH

Our approach to psychosomatic therapy aims at raising the patient's level of experiencing which facilitates physiological homeostasis as well as existential awareness. This approach promotes health and self-actualization, rather than being only a specific "cure" for a specific condition. Our approach promotes the realization of human potentials inherent in experiencing, rather than mechanically readjusting the person to "normality." The approach rejoins the patient with the process of life's unfolding fluidity. In this manner, psychosomatic medicine may be conceptualized as a *way* to healthy living.

SUMMARY

Despite the abundance and frequent confusion of different concepts and approaches in psychosomatic medicine, our psychosomatic approach addresses the patient's lived reality, his concrete existence. Existence is lived through experiencing. Hence, our psychosomatic approach attempts to raise the level of experiencing through various somatopsychic approaches which in turn facilitate psychosomatic approaches. Once a high level of experiencing is achieved, the patient can understand holistically the nature of the most effective techniques of therapy. We recommend that such techniques should consist selectively (not eclectically) of both psychosomatic and somatopsychic approaches. Finally, such an integration therapy program aims not only at restoring health but points out a way to holistic health.

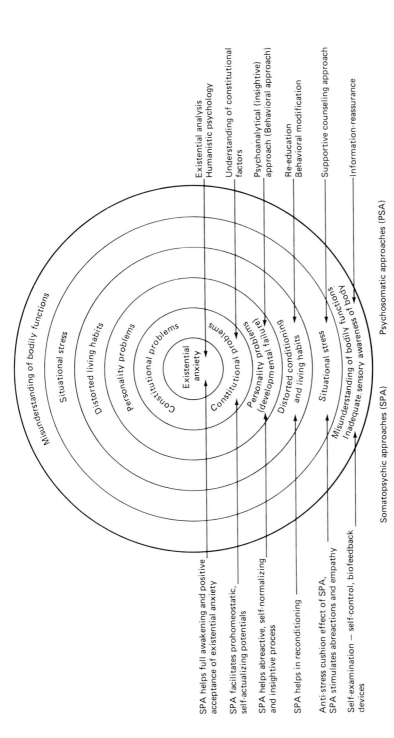

FIG. 4. Therapeutic approaches according to the level of the psychological problem (anxiety, frustration, etc.). To be read from outside to inside of circle (Ikemi and Ishikawa, 1975).

Existential analysis
Humanistic psychology

Understanding of constitutional factors

Psychoanalytical (insightive) approach (Behavioral approach)

Re-education
Behavioral modification

Supportive counseling approach

Information-reassurance

Misunderstanding of bodily functions
Situational stress
Distorted living habits
Personality problems
Constitutional problems
Existential anxiety
Constitutional problems
Personality problems (developmental failure)
Distorted conditioning and living habits
Situational stress
Misunderstanding of bodily functions
Inadequate, sensory awareness of body

Somatopsychic approaches (SPA)

Psychosomatic approaches (PSA)

Whenever necessary, psychopharmaceuticals can also be used to help control different levels of anxiety.

SPA helps full awakening and positive acceptance of existential anxiety

SPA facilitates prohomeostatic, self-actualizing potentials

SPA helps abreactive, self-normalizing and insightive process

SPA helps in reconditioning

Anti-stress cushion effect of SPA, SPA stimulates abreactions and empathy

Self-examination — self-control, biofeedback devices

103

References

Gendlin, E. T. Existential explication and truth. *Journal of Existentialism* 6 (22) (winter 1965/ 6).

Gendlin E. T. Experiential psychotherapy. In *Current Psychotherapies* (R. Corsini, ed.). Ithaca: F. E. Peacock, 1979.

Gendlin, E. T., Beebe, J., Cassens, J., Löien, M., and Oberlander, M. Focusing ability in psychotherapy, personality, and creativity. In *Research in Psychotherapy,* J. M. Shlien, (ed.), vol. 2. Washington: American Psychological Association.

Ikemi, Y. and Ishikawa, H. Integration of occidental and oriental psychosomatic treatments. *Psychother. Psychosom.* 31: 324-333 (1979).

Klein, M. H., Mathieu, D. L., Gendlin, E. T., and Kiesler, D. J. *The Experiencing Scale: A Research and Training Manual.* Wisconsin Psychiatric Institute, 1969.

How to Be Happy in Spite Of Life's Vicissitudes

Frank M. Berger, M.D.

Professor of Psychiatry
Department of Psychiatry and Behavioral Sciences
University of Louisville School of Medicine
Louisville, Kentucky

The view that stress and unpleasant emotional experiences may cause physical disease is now widely accepted in spite of the fact that most of the available evidence supporting it is either indirect or conjectural. The confusion and lack of progress existing in this field may be primarily due to our neglect in defining our terms rigorously (what do we mean by words such as *stress*?), our inability to measure objectively the presence and intensity of emotions, and our lack of understanding of the conditions that are required to make emotions trigger the appearance of organic disease. The following is an attempt to clarify and to sum up our knowledge in this field as I see it.

Emotions are the feelings we experience when we are moved or stirred up. Emotions, whether pleasant or unpleasant, cause certain physical responses in the body which in a medical or scientific context are referred to as stress. In everyday English, the word *stress* is used to describe an emotional state in which a person is subjected to mental tension and strain. In a scientific context, the word *stress* does not pertain to emotional states, but is used to describe the bodily responses to stimuli that alter the existing equilibrium (Selye, 1956). Stress is induced by stressors, which are any stringent demands that impinge on the organism. These stress-producing stimuli may be pleasurable, (e.g., music, sex, smoking, or accepting honors) or unpleasant (e.g., excessive noise, marital discord, death of a loved one, or disease). Stress is the stereotyped nonspecific bodily response to these stimuli. It is the same whether induced by pleasant or unpleasant emotions, life crises, or mental or organic disease.

The Measurement of Stress and Emotion

Stress-inducing stimuli will cause release of adrenocorticotropic hormone, norepinephrine, epinephrine, endorphins, and other as yet unidentified substances which in turn will bring about a number of readily measurable physiological responses, such as an increase of blood pressure and heart rate, changes in the coagulability of blood, dilation of the bronchioles, a rise in the level of free fatty acids in the blood, and many others. It is possible to evaluate the presence and extent of stress objectively by measuring the blood levels of substances released in response to stress-inducing stimuli, such as norepinephrine, epinephrine, and cortisol, or by evaluating the physiological responses induced by the release of these neurotransmitters and hormones.

Emotions manifest themselves not only by subjective feelings, but also by a variety of bodily manifestations which are similar to the physiological responses observed in persons under stress. These symptoms are not characteristic of any specific emotion and may accompany pleasant or unpleasant emotional states. We may weep with joy or sorrow, or may feel faint from pleasure or fear. It appears that all intense emotions will act as stressors and cause stress. The psychological and physiological changes that accompany emotional states are merely manifestations of stress. The evaluation of these changes does not capture the essential element of emotional states, which cannot be fully understood until experienced. The physical and psychological changes which are observed during the emotional states may be just epiphenomena that usually accompany, but are not the primary or critical, events in the brain that make us experience the emotion. At present we do not know what these essential events are because we do not have any understanding of the physical basis of emotions. We do not know what happens in the brain when we experience an emotion.

Pharmacologic Manipulations

One way of showing that the experiencing of an emotion is a different and separate event from the somatic and psychological changes that accompany it is the administration of beta-adrenoreceptor-blocking drugs, such as propranolol, to patients suffering from pathologic neurotic anxiety. These drugs, usually referred to as beta-blockers, relieve most of the somatic symptoms present in these patients without affecting the feeling of anxiety itself (Kielholz, 1977).

The beta-blockers can also protect the heart and blood vessels from the deleterious effects of catecholamines, and in this manner counteract in predisposed individuals some of the harmful effects of stress. They antagonize the stress-induced sympathetic stimulation of the heart that may lead to an increase of blood pressure, which constitutes a risk factor for patients with coronary disease.

There are drugs that are able to relieve inappropriate and maladaptive emotions, such as those experienced by patients suffering from anxiety states or endogenous depression. Antianxiety drugs, such as meprobamate or diazepam, relieve the pathologic anxiety characteristic of the psychoneurotic state and, at the same time, eliminate the somatic manifestations of anxiety in these patients. These drugs, however, are ineffective in relieving other kinds of anxiety, such as that present in schizophrenia or other organic mental disorders, or apprehension due to organic diseases. They also do not affect the normal fear responses (Berger, 1980). Antidepressants will relieve the symptoms of endogenous depression, but will be of little or no value in situational depression.

Emotions occuring in healthy people, as a rule, cannot be affected by drugs without seriously altering the state of awareness. There are no pills that will counteract anger or hate, just as there are no pills that can make us love or worship. The feeling of contentment induced by alcohol or certain other drugs is the result of an abnormal state of consciousness in which unpleasant and painful memories can be disregarded.

Under certain circumstances, it is possible to induce emotions by the administration of drugs. Thus administration of epinephrine can produce anxiety. However, the epinephrine-induced emotions differ from naturally occurring anxiety in a subtle way, in having an "as if" quality. Similarly, fear induced by mescaline differs from fear induced by real danger in that it is accompanied by a feeling of unreality, just as the sense of well-being experienced as a result of achieving a desired goal differs from the state of euphoria attained by digesting of alcohol or opium.

Psychosomatic Diseases

Psychosomatic medicine relates to the study and treatment of disorders in which emotions and stress play a prominent part and in which they exert an important effect on the functions of the body. Among the conditions included in this group of disorders are hypertension, peptic ulcer, asthma, rheumatoid arthritis, ulcerative colitis, migraine, and various dermatoses. There is no complete proof that psychic factors are the cause of any of these disease entities. It has, however, been well substantiated that psychogenic factors can aggravate or ameliorate psychosomatic diseases to a greater extent than is the case with other diseases.

In psychosomatic diseases, emotions or stress can function as a trigger to aggravate the condition and bring about an acute attack. Bronchial asthma is a case in point. An attack of asthma is produced by a release of mediators from the sensitized cells. Such a release can be triggered not only by exposure to the specific allergen, but also by exposure to irritant gases, by infections, or by excitement. Bronchoconstriction can be brought about by any of these events, but it does not necessarily and invariably occur in the presence of these factors. Why this should be so we do not know, but we suspect that the emotional equilibrium of the subject greatly affects the occurrence or nonoccurrence of the bronchospasm. Similarly, acute attacks of migraine, ulcerative colitis, lower-back pain, as well as attacks of pain and stiffness in rheumatoid arthritis, appear to be influenced by the emotional state of the patient.

Stress by itself, in the absence of strong emotional feedback, does not cause any symptom or disease. The presence of strong and sustained unpleasant emotions will cause stress, and the combined presence of these two factors appears to make people more susceptible to any and all diseases and less able to handle life crises in an appropriate way. Conversely, pleasant emotions such as caring, love, or joy—whether given or received—make us less susceptible to all kinds of diseases and increase our ability to deal with the vicissitudes of life. These conclusions appear to be borne out by the study of death rates in the United States according to marital status. In almost every case, widowed, divorced, and single people have significantly higher death rates than married people. This appears to be true in a variety of unrelated conditions, such as coronary heart disease, stroke, cancer, rheumatic fever, pneumonia, suicides, and accidents. It is possible that the higher mortality rate of people living alone is caused by the loneliness of their existence (Lynch, 1979).

Relief of Distress

Stress is the natural and appropriate adaptive response to change. It is unavoidable and need not lead to distress unless it is sustained beyond endurance by inappropriate emotional responses. As we have to live with stress, we should learn how to handle the emotional states that may make it damaging. Although we all are, by and large, exposed to similar external events, some of us get much more distressed than others. Thus it cannot be just the nature of the events that make us unhappy and sick, but our perception of them. Our perception of events and the distress they cause will, in turn, depend on our educational background, our temperament, our beliefs and prejudices, and our genetic background. While we can do nothing about the automatic, stereotyped stress responses, it is within our power to alter our emotional responses, and this is the aim of the various psychotherapeutic techniques that have become so popular during the recent past. Among these are the cognitive, existential, gestalt, rogerian, directive and nondirective, transactional, and many other forms of psychotherapy, as well as various biofeedback and relaxation techniques. It appears that all these forms of treatment are about equally effective in enabling people to handle more adequately the problems of daily living without undue distress. The results obtained appear to depend more on the personality of the therapist and his ability to establish a good relationship with the patient than on the treatment used. Often no therapist is needed; a spouse or trusted friend who is always available can help to overcome most emotional turmoils.

Most of our distress is due to three factors succinctly summarized by Ellis (1972): misperception of reality, unrealistic expectations of ourselves and the world, and unrealistic demands. We misperceive and distort reality by seeing what we would like to see or what we fear instead of what is there. We get disturbed if our expectations are not fulfilled and our demands not met. The impact of these bad mental habits can be lessened by recognizing them and by realizing that it is not stress that makes us sick and unhappy, but our inappropriate and maladaptive emotional responses. Many disturbing emotions can be controlled by putting them in the proper perspective. One way of doing this is to use one's reason. "Human bondage consists in the impotence of man to govern or restrain the affects . . . for a man who is under their control is not his own master. A free man is one who lives according to the dictates of reason alone" (Spinoza, 1670). To do this is not easy, but Spinoza's dictum will help us to avoid irrationality, which has been defined as any thought, emotion, or behavior that significantly interferes with our survival and happiness. Why not try to be happy?

References

Berger, F. M. Effect of antianxiety drugs on fear and stress. *Behavioral Sciences* 25: 315 (1980).

Ellis, A. *Humanistic Psychotherapy: The Rational-emotive Approach.* New York: Julian Books and McGraw-Hill Paperbacks, 1973.

Kielholz P. (ed.). *Beta-blockers and the Central Nervous System.* Berne: Hans Huber Publishers, 1977.

Lynch, J. J. *The Broken Heart, the Medical Consequences of Loneliness.* New York: Basic Books, 1979.

Selye, H. *The Stress of Life.* New York: McGraw-Hill, 1956.

Recent Life Events and Illness Onset*

John Petrich, M.D.
Clinical Associate Professor

Cheryl A. Hart, B.S.
Research Assistant

Thomas H. Holmes, M.D.
Professor
Department of Psychiatry and Behavioral Sciences
University of Washington School of Medicine
Seattle, Washington

Introduction

Traditionally, psychiatrists have looked to life experience for understanding patients' symptoms. This report summarizes a body of research which evolved from the systematic methods of Thomas H. Holmes and his co-workers and focuses upon the relation between life events and illness susceptibility. Illness is defined broadly to include disorders of behavior, thought, and feelings, as well as other medical and surgical diseases.

Methods

Beginning in 1949 in Holmes' laboratory, the Meyerian life chart [1] was used to record the psychologic, sociologic, and medical histories of over 5000 patients. These records provided the basis for a selection of 43 life

* This research was supported in part by the O'Donnell Psychiatry Research Fund.

events which clustered prior to illness onset in patients with tuberculosis, hernia, cardiovascular and skin disease, and pregnancy. [2,3] The single theme common to all the events was that each represented a change in the ongoing life pattern of the patient. Using a method from sensory psychology,[4] Holmes and Rahe [5] quantified the magnitude of change and readjustment associated with each of the 43 events in the Social Readjustment Rating Scale (SRRS; see Table 1).

The Schedule of Recent Experience (SRE) is a questionnaire which elicits data about the frequency of occurrence of the 42 life events from the SRRS (excluding Christmas). Frequency data from the SRE are used to calculate the life change score in Life Change Units (LCU) according to the formula:

$$LCU = \Sigma(\text{item frequency} \times \text{scale value})$$

LCU scores are usually calculated for each of any number of one-year periods.

Epidemiologic Studies of Health Change and Health Care Seeking Behavior

In a pilot application of the SRE, Rahe [6] compared health changes to life changes reported by 88 resident physicians. Each subject was asked to complete the SRE for each of ten preceding years. The LCU score was then calculated for each year. A health history was also obtained. Of the 96 reported health changes, including allergic, infectious, psychosomatic, and

TABLE 1. The Social Readjustment Rating Scale.*

Life Event	Mean Value
1. Death of spouse	100
2. Divorce	73
3. Marital separation from mate	65
4. Detention in jail or other institution	63
5. Death of a close family member	63
6. Major personal injury or illness	53
7. Marriage	50
8. Being fired at work	47
9. Marital reconciliation with mate	45
10. Retirement from work	45
11. Major change in the health or behavior of a family member	44
12. Pregnancy	40
13. Sexual difficulties	39
14. Gaining a new family member (e.g., through birth, adoption, oldster moving in, etc.)	39

(continued)

TABLE 1. (Continued)

Life Event	Mean Value
15. Major business readjustment (e.g., merger, reorganization, bankruptcy, etc.)	39
16. Major change in financial state (e.g., a lot worse off or a lot better off than usual)	38
17. Death of a close friend	37
18. Changing to a different line of work	36
19. Major change in the number of arguments with spouse (e.g., either a lot more or a lot less than usual regarding child rearing, personal habits, etc.)	35
20. Taking on a mortgage greater than $10,000 (e.g., purchasing a home, business, etc.)	31
21. Foreclosure on a mortgage or loan	30
22. Major change in responsibilities at work (e.g., promotion, demotion, lateral transfer)	29
23. Son or daughter leaving home (e.g., marriage, attending college, etc.)	29
24. In-law troubles	29
25. Outstanding personal achievement	28
26. Wife beginning or ceasing work outside the home	26
27. Beginning or ceasing formal schooling	26
28. Major change in living conditions (e.g., building a new home, remodeling, deterioration of home or neighborhood)	25
29. Revision of personal habits (dress, manmers, associations, etc.)	24
30. Troubles with the boss	23
31. Major change in working hours or conditions	20
32. Change in residence	20
33. Changing to a new school	20
34. Major change in usual type and/or amount of recreation	19
35. Major change in church activities (e.g., a lot more or a lot less than usual)	19
36. Major change in social activities (e.g., clubs, dancing, movies, visiting, etc.)	18
37. Taking on a mortgage or loan less than $10,000 (e.g., purchasing a car, TV, freezer, etc.)	17
38. Major change in sleeping habits (a lot more or a lot less sleep, or change in part of day when asleep)	16
39. Major change in number of family get-togethers (e.g., a lot more or a lot less than usual)	15
40. Major change in eating habits (a lot more or a lot less food intake, or very different meal hours or surroundings)	15
41. Vacation	13
42. Christmas	12
43. Minor violations of the law (e.g., traffic tickets, jaywalking, distrubing the peace, etc.)	11

* Holmes and Rahe,[5] complete wording of Table 3, p. 216.

musculoskeletal disorders, 93% occurred within two years of a life change score of 150 LCU or more.

Further analysis of the data showed a direct relation between the magnitude of life change and the chance for health change. Of the individuals reporting less than 200 LCU in a year, 37% reported health changes the following year; scores from 200 to 299 LCU in a year were associated with a 51% chance for health change the subsequent year. Seventy-nine percent of subjects reported health changes secondary to a yearly score over 300 LCU.

In a prospective continuation of this study, 84 of the residents gave information about the state of their health during an eight-month follow-up period.[6] The LCU score from the preceding year was used to study risk for health change during the study interval. At the end of the follow-up, 49% of the highest risk group (over 300 LCU), 25% of the medium risk group (150 to 299 LCU), and 9% of the low risk group (less than 150 LCU) reported illness during the study period.

Episodes of minor illness, health care seeking behavior, and life change were the foci of a series of prospective studies of Navy personnel, both in the United States and in Norway.[7] The SRE was administered to over 4000 enlisted men prior to naval cruises and summed for six-month intervals for the preceding three years. The younger, predominantly single men experienced more life changes overall than the older, married, senior enlisted men. Those enlisted men with a peak in life change in the six months preceding the cruise demonstrated increased frequency of visits to the ship physician for predominantly minor illness.

Life change was, however, only one of many factors associated with visits to sick call on naval cruises. Factors such as the men's location on the ship (engine room or deck) and the overall difficulty rating of the cruise were important in determining the probability of health care seeking.

Casey et al.[8] examined sick-call visiting behavior in relation to life change among men at army boot camp. Initial visits could not be predicted from the life change score at the onset of training. Subsequent visits and referrals for further care, however, were twice as likely for men whose first visit occurred in a setting of high life change. These data suggest that health care seeking, per se, is distinct from symptom onset and is not necessarily associated with the same predictor variables.

Hart, Masuda, and Holmes[9] analyzed utilization data from a health maintenance organization as a function of life change, type of care, payment plan, and gender of the patients. Utilization was found to be most strongly related to LCU scores six months prior. Significant correlations (0.20 to 0.30) were found between the six-month LCU score and help seeking for people with both prepaid and federally subsidized fee programs. This relation held for patients visiting both the general medical and the mental health service.

Among patients on a fee-for-service payment schedule, a positive relationship between medical service utilization and life change was obtained. There was, however, no correlation between life change and utilization of the mental health service. The net zero correlation resulted from differences in the behavior of males and females in this sample. Females on a fee-for-service payment schedule showed a positive correlation between life change and utilization, whereas males showed a negative correlation.

Accidental Injury

The role of psychosocial factors in athletic injuries was examined by Bramwell et al.[10] In a prospective study of 79 varsity college football players, the results from the Athletic Schedule of Recent Experience (ASRE) and the season injury record were compared. The risk for injury (three or more missed practices, or one or more missed games because of a specific injury) was proportional to the accumulated life change. The injured group included 26 players with a mean life change score of 632 per year, while the noninjured group included 46 men with a mean life change score of 494. This difference is significant at $p = 0.05$.

In a study of 37 hospitalized fracture patients, Tollefson[11] demonstrated moderate to major life crises in 30 of the patients during the year prior to fracture injury. Other workers have since confirmed this direct association between life change and accidental burn injury.[12]

The relation between life change and traffic accidents has also been examined. Selzer and Vinokur[13] compared the driving records and SRE scores of 532 alcoholic and nonalcoholic drivers. A significant relationship between the accumulation of life changes and traffic accidents was demonstrated for the alcoholic group.

A prospective study relating accident frequency in children with life change and personality variables confirmed that life change scores did correlate directly with accident frequency while personality variables did not.[12]

Cardiovascular Disease

It has been estimated that 12% of the time lost by the working population is attributable to cardiovascular disease and its sequelae. Today, after several decades of intensive research, the best combinations of standard risk factors fail to predict satisfactorily populations at risk for these diseases. Fresh efforts are increasingly directed to the psychological, social, and behavioral conditions associated with risk for clinical disease.

From a list of 67 persons who experienced sudden cardiac death in Stockholm, Rahe and Lind [15] were able to interview 39 next of kin who reported to the decedents to have experienced three times the magnitude of life change in the last six months of life as compared to earlier periods. Theorell and Rahe [16] studied a cross section of patients with coronary disease and found that surviving patients maintained steady levels of life change whereas those dying of coronary disease showed peaks of life change 7 to 12 months before death, with a decrease to average levels over the last 6 months before death.

A study of 54 survivors of myocardial infarction [17] showed a crescendo of life change in the six months before the infarction, but only for the patients with no previous history of heart disease. Those with prior heart disease had generally higher life change scores at all previous periods covered in the interview assessment.

A comparable project [18] conducted among 279 survivors of myocardial infarction in Helsinki showed a rising rate of life change for the six months immediately before infarction. Dividing the patients into those with and without other serious illness before the index infarction revealed nearly twice as much life change in the previously ill group as in the previously well group in earlier six-month periods. Increases in life change for the last six months characterized both groups with coronary disease. The same study showed that obtaining data about patients from their spouses generated similar average life change scores as asking the patients themselves.

Lundberg et al., [19] using a matched control group in their retrospective study of life changes and myocardial infarction, found no statistically significant differences between patients with infarction and the control group when total life change units were calculated. They found, however, that when each person assigned weights reflecting his or her own perception of the impact of each event, the patients with infarction generated significantly higher mean values than controls. It can be hypothesized either that more distressing life events were more likely to precede myocardial infarction or that the crisis of a coronary disease episode sensitized patients to attach more importance to earlier life events than persons without a recent life-threatening illness.

In a prospective study of life change and cardiovascular disease in over 6000 Swedish construction workers, 41 to 61 years of age, Theorell, Lind, and Floderus [20] found no association between elevated life change scores and the incidence of acute myocardial infarction over the next 12 to 15 months. Elevated scores, however, did predict development of neuroses and several chronic diseases.

Since 1970, studies from many research centers have supported earlier reports that higher risk of coronary disease is present in persons manifesting a "coronary-prone" behavior pattern, Type A. This style of behavior is characterized by some or all of the following: intense striving for achievement, easily provoked impatience, time urgency, abruptness in gestures and speech, overcommitment to vocation or profession, and excesses of drive and hostility.

In the aforementioned study of Swedish workers,[20] patients with myocardial infarction reported more hostility when slowed by others, but showed no differences on expressed need to rush against time deadlines. Behavioral style and attitudes were measured in this study by means of a ten-question, paper-and-pencil test. From these and other psychosocial and demographic variables, only two were associated with risk of myocardial infarction: hostility when held in queues and recent increased responsibility at work.

In summary, ongoing research suggests an interaction between recent life experience and behavioral style in the genesis of cardiovascular disease. In patients whose attitude features marked striving and time urgency, a crescendo of life change, especially in the area of work and career responsibilities, is associated with increased risk for clinical disease onset.

Depression

Paykel et al.[21] have studied the relationship between life events and depressive disease. Attempting to isolate life changes independent of the symptoms of depression and focusing closely on clinical interview data, they derived a listing of events which cluster prior to the onset of depression. A preliminary study of the six-month interval prior to illness onset showed that depressives report three times the numbr of life events as a group of matched controls. Increased total event frequency was reflected uniformly in most individual events. For eight events, differences between depressives and general population controls reached statistical significance. These events were increased arguments with spouse, marital separation, changing or starting a new type of work, death of an immediate family member, serious illness of family member, departure of family member from home, serious personal illness, and substantial change in work conditions.

Depressives reported significantly more events which could be identified as "undesirable," wheras there was no difference between depressives and normals in the reported number of "desirable" events.

Another dimension of life experience could be defined as the loss or gain of people in the social field. Exits, or events involving clear departures, were reported more frequently by depressives than controls. Entrances, or introductions of new persons to the social field, were equally frequent in both groups. Exits from the social field correspond to the familiar psychiatric concept of loss, which has been particularly linked with depression.

The data of Paykel et al.[21] suggest that special kinds of life events precede episodes of depression. Increasing magnitude of life change alone does not fully describe this cluster. Recent work in scaling perceptions of life events shows that almost all the exit events were scaled high and all the entrances were scaled low, when subjects were asked to rate the degree to which each event was "upsetting" on a 0 to 20, equal interval scale.[22] Thus, both the loss and the magnitude of impact are dimensions of the life experience prior to clinically manifest depression.

Since the original studies, Paykel and his co-workers [23] have extended their work to include suicide. People who attempt suicide tend to be a special group, younger than most depressives, with a background of disturbed social relations and personality disorders. In a study of 53 patients, aged 18 to 65 years, life event information was obtained by interview within one week following a suicide attempt. The time period under consideration in this study was the six months prior to the attempt. For a control, patients were matched for age, sex, marital status, social class, and race with two other groups: depressives from the earlier study and a general population sample.

In the preceding six-month study period, suicide attempters reported four times the number of life events as did the general population sample (3.3 vs 0.8 event) and 50% more than the depressives. Suicide attempters, however, reported more entrances than did depressives, but the same number of exits. Instead of the specific relationship to exits found for depression, entrances were just as strongly associated with attempted suicide. On the desirable-undesirable dichotomy, attempters reported an excess of the undesirable events. The pattern for suicide attempters was an exaggeration of that found earlier for depressives, although the attempters did report more desirable events than depressives.

Each of the six months in the study interval was also examined for trends in the mean number of life events. For the general population sample, events were spread evenly over the entire period. For depressives, while there was a mild peaking the month before onset, the excess of events reported was spread over the entire six-month interval. The suicide attempters showed a marked peak only the month preceding the attempt, and a detailed analysis showed this peaking to be particularly marked in the week immediately prior to the attempt.

The data suggest, then, that the temporal pattern of life events surrounding suicide is different from that prior to the onset of depression. The link between life changes and attempted suicide is much more immediate than is that for depression in general.

Seriousness of Illness

Data obtained during the course of investigations in the laboratory of T. H. Holmes and his co-workers [2,3] suggest a direct relation between the severity of illness and the magnitude of life change experienced during the year prior to symptom onset. Since there was no statisfactory or quantitative measure of the relative severity of different diseases, Wyler, Masuda, and Holmes [24] constructed a list of illnesses commonly seen in the doctor's office.

The list of 125 illnesses was then rated by physicians and laymen in a test similar to that employed in the development of the SRRS. Peptic ulcer was arbitrarily assigned a value of 500, and raters were asked to give number estimates for the relative ''seriousness'' of each remaining disease. Physicians and laymen agreed strongly about the rank ordering of these illnesses, and subsequent comparisons with the ranking of Spanish and Irish laymen [25,26] suggested that there is a broad cross-cultural consensus about the relative severity of different diseases.

Using the Seriousness of Illness Rating Scale, Wyler, Masuda, and Homes [27] assigned appropriate values to 42 diseases experienced by 232 hospitalized patients. These values were compared with the life change magnitude that occurred in the two-year period preceding onset of disease. The correlation between life change and disease severity was highly significant for chronic diseases ($r_s = 0.648$).

These data suggest that the greater the life change or adaptive requirements, the greater is the vulnerability or lowering of resistance to disease, and the more serious is the disease that does develop. The concept of a variable threshold of resistance and the necessity of having a special pathogen present may help to account for the differences observed in the acute infectious diseases. The concept of life change appears to have relevance to the causation of disease, the time of illness onset, and the severity of disease.

Clinical Applications and Primary Intervention

One of the questions arising from this research is: What, if anything, can be done to modify the relation between life changes and health changes? Individual counseling is the traditional mode of intervention and prevention. Here the life change concepts and the SRE can be used as a point for discussion in the supportive management of some patients.

Holmes has presented the following general list of preventive measures:

1. Become familiar with the life events and the amount of change they require.
2. Think about the different ways you might best adjust to the events.
3. Think about the meaning of the event for you and try to identify some of the feelings experienced.
4. Take time in arriving at decisions.
5. If possible, anticipate life changes and plan for them well in advance.
6. Pace yourself. This can be done even if you are in a hurry.
7. Look at the accomplishment of a task as part of daily living and avoid looking at such an achievement as a "stopping point" or a "time for letting down."
8. Remember, the more change you have the more likely you are to get sick. Of these people with over 300 Life Change Units for the previous year, almost 80% get sick in the near future; with 150 to 299 Life Change Units, about 50% get sick in the near future; and with less than 150 Life Change Units, only about 30% get sick in the near future.

These suggestions were given at the close of a one-hour nationwide television broadcast concerned with the relationship between life change and illness susceptibility. During the broadcast, the audience was told of the Social Readjustment Rating Scale. From a sample of 3000 requesting copies of the Scale, 225 were followed for the next two years. Life change, health change, and health care seeking behavior of this sample were examined for evidence of the impact of the television education.[28]

Although there was no significant difference in mean life change magnitude or in the distribution of life changes experienced before and after the broadcast, there was an increase of 23 to 38% in the proportion of people reporting no health change, no doctor visits, and no self-treatments in the year following the broadcast. In the second year, only 30% of the sample reported no health change or health care seeking.

Reports of health care seeking did not vary over time when health change was held constant. Both before and after the television program, 78% of all health changes were reported to a doctor.

The results of this study in primary prevention indicate that an overall decrease in the number of reported health changes can be achieved in spite of a constant level of life change magnitude.

Summary

1. A survey of some of the relevant literature indicates an intimate association between life change magnitude and the occurrence of a variety of medical and psychiatric diseases.
2. A study of the relationship of seriousness of illness to the amount of life change present at the time of onset of that illness reveals a significant positive correlation; i.e., the higher the life change magnitude, the greater is the seriousness of the illness which is likely to occur.
3. The life change magnitude, while predicting onset of disease, does not predict health care seeking behavior.
4. If one uses life change magnitude as a point of departure, preventive intervention is remarkably effective in increasing freedom from disease.

References

1. Meyer, A. The life chart and the obligation of specifying positive data in psychopathological diagnosis. In *Contributions to Medical and Biological Research,* vol. 2, pp. 1128-1133. New York: Paul B. Hoeber, 1919.
2. Hawkins, N. G., Davies, R., and Holmes, T. H. Evidence of psychosocial factors in pulmonary tuberculosis. *Am. Rev. Tuberculosis Pulmonary Dis.* 75:768-780 (1957).
3. Rahe, R. H., Meyer, M., Smith, M., Kjaer, G., and Holmes, T. H. Social stress and illness onset. *J. Psychosom. Res.* 8:35-44 (1964).
4. Stevens, S. S. *Psychophysics. Introduction to Its Perceptual, Neural, and Social Prospects* (G. Stevens, ed.). New York: John Wiley & Sons, 1975.
5. Holmes, T. H. and Rahe, R. H. The Social Readjustment Rating Scale. *J. Psychosom. Res.* 11:213-218 (1967).
6. Rahe, R. H. Life crisis and health change. In *Psychotropic Drug Responses: Advances in Prediction* (P. R. A. May and J. R. Wittenborn, eds.), pp. 92-125. Springfield, Ill.: Charles C. Thomas, 1969.
7. Rahe, R. H. Subjects' recent life changes and their near-future illness reports: a review. *Ann. Clin. Research* 4:250-265 (1972).
8. Casey, R. L., Thoresen, A. R., and Smith, F. J. The use of the Schedule of Recent Experience questionnaire in an institutional health care setting. *J. Psychosom. Res.* 14:149-154 (1970).
9. Celdrán, H. Unpublished data.

10. Bramwell, S. T., Masuda, M., Wagner, N. D., and Holmes, T. H. Psychosocial factors in athletic injuries: development and application of the Social and Athletic Readjustment Rating Scale (SARRS). *J. Human Stress* 1(2):6–20 (1975).
11. Tollefson, D. J. The relationship between the occurrence of fractures and life crisis events. Master's thesis, University of Washington, Seattle, 1972.
12. Petrich, J. Unpublished data.
13. Selzer, M. L. and Vinokur, A. Life events, subjective stress, and traffic accidents. *Am. J. Psychiatry* 131:903–906 (1974).
14. Padilla, E. R., Rohsenow, D. J., and Bergman, A. B. Predicting accident frequency in children. *Pediatrics* 58:223–226 (1976).
15. Rahe, R. H. and Lind, E. Psychosocial factors and sudden cardiac death: a pilot study. *J. Psychosom. Res.* 15:19–24 (1971).
16. Theorell, T. and Rahe, R. H. Life change events, ballistocardiography and coronary death. *J. Human Stress* 1(3):18–24 (1975).
17. Theorell, T. and Rahe, R. H. Psychosocial factors and myocardial infarction. I. An inpatient study in Sweden. *J. Psychosom. Res.* 15:25–31 (1971).
18. Rahe, R. H., Bennett, L., Romo, M., Siltanen, P., and Arthur, R. J. Subjects' recent life changes and coronary heart disease in Finland. *Am. J. Psychiatry* 130:1222–1226 (1973).
19. Lundberg, U., Tores, T., and Lind, E. Life changes and myocardial infarction: individual differences in life change scaling. *J. Psychosom. Res.* 19:27–32 (1975).
20. Theorell, T., Lind, E., and Floderus, B. The relationship of disturbing life-changes and emotions to the early development of myocardial infarction and other serious illnesses. *International J. Epidemiology* 7:281–293 (1975).
21. Paykel, E. S., Myers, J. K., Dienelt, M. N., Klerman, G. L., Lindenthal, J. J., and Pepper, M. P. Life events and depression. A controlled study. *Arch. Gen. Psychiatry* 21:753–760 (1969).
22. Paykel, E. S., Prusoff, B. A., and Uhlenhuth, E. N. Scaling of life events. *Arch. Gen. Psychiatry* 25:340–347 (1971).
23. Paykel, E. S., Prusoff, B. A., and Myers, J. K. Suicide attempts and recent life events: a controlled comparison. *Arch. Gen. Psychiatry* 32:327–333 (1975).
24. Wyler, A. R., Masuda, M., and Holmes, T. H. Seriousness of Illness Rating Scale. *J. Psychosom. Res.* 11:363–374 (1968).
25. Celdrán, H. H. The cross-cultural consistency of two social consensus scales: the Seriousness of Illness Rating Scale and the Social Readjustment Rating Scale in Spain. Medical thesis, University of Washington, Seattle, 1970.
26. McMahon, B. J. Seriousness of Illness Rating Scale: a comparative study of Irish and Americans. M.D. thesis, University of Washington, Seattle, 1971.
27. Wyler, A. R., Masuda, M., and Holmes, T. H. Magnitude of life events and seriousness of illness. *Psychosom. Med.* 33:115–122 (1971).
28. Holmes, T. H. Unpublished data.

Psychosocial Stress and Illness: The Odd Couple

Adrienne Barnwell, Ph.D.
Norman Hoffman, Ph.D.
Michael Koch, M.D.
Department of Pediatrics and Department of Psychiatry
St. Paul Ramsey Medical Center
Saint Paul, Minnesota

For more than 40 years, stress has been viewed as a factor which contributes to the onset of illness (Selye, 1936).[6] As interest in the association between stress and illness has grown, models of psychosocial stress have been developed to describe the ways in which social-environment changes can influence the individual's physical, psychological, and mental functioning. However, research on the association between psychosocial stress and illness yields motley results. The relationship between stress and illness does not appear to be a simple causal correlation. To complicate matters further, theorists and researchers have used different operational definitions of stress and illness, have chosen to examine different outcome criteria, and have focused on different subject populations. In addition, important parameters and constructs may be inadequately addressed or entirely overlooked in the stress-illness research.

Despite the semantic and methodological problems in the literature, the concept of stress has influenced our ideas about illness and therefore has had merit. It is highly plausible that certain life events are related to some forms of illness, but to date the data are equivocal. Whether or not it is profitable to continue seeking a connection between stress and illness seems to depend upon clarification of the constructs of stress and illness, and upon a broader conceptualization of those environmental and personal factors which may serve to inhibit or enhance the relationship between stress and illness.

PSYCHOSOCIAL STRESS

What is stress? Researchers and theorists do not agree on a definition, perhaps for good reason—stress seems to be a highly subjective construct.

What you view as a stressful event might be taken in stride by your neighbor and go unnoticed in another culture.

Rahe (1979) defines stress as *any* life change that requires adjustment on the part of the individual.[4] By this definition, both positive events (getting a job promotion) and negative events (getting fired) generate stress. Other investigators restrict stress to noxious stimuli or negative events.[5] Getting fired would be stressful; getting a promotion would not be. Still other writers operationally define stress not in terms of events, but from subjective reports of loneliness and nervousness.[3]

The problem in defining psychosocial stress may not be as formidable as it appears. The moral of the blindmen's encounter with the elephant may apply. The various definitions of stress do not necessarily conflict. Rather, each writer is approaching stress from a different vantage point. As a result, each definition emphasizes a somewhat different dimension of stress. If the definitions are combined, what emerges is a multidimensional construct which defies simplistic description. A review of the literature yields the following factors as parameters of stress.

The valence of an event is one dimension of stress. Any given life change may have positive, negative, or ambivalent impact—depending upon the individual's perceptions and needs. A death in the family may signal a financial windfall, a significant interpersonal loss, or both. Though Rahe claims that extremely pleasant events require nearly as much life adjustment as do unpleasant events,[4] there is a growing body of literature which indicates that only undesirable events are related to physical and psychological problems.[1,5]

Another dimension of stress is the amount of control the individual has over a critical event. Fairbank and Hough propose that the kinds of events associated with illness are undesirable changes within the person's control.[1] Thus, we would not expect a person to become ill if he is beset by "bad luck" or natural disasters, but if life changes include divorce, being fired, or otherwise failing to perform well, the risk of illness is increased.

The timing and duration of stresses may also affect health. Most theorists and researchers agree that life change events have a finite period of impact on a person's adjustment and health, lasting perhaps only six to nine months, with peak effects in the three weeks immediately following the event. In addition, the duration of a stress may influence its impact. A life situation of chronic stress is more likely to be associated with illness than are sporadic episodes of acute stress.[2] However, the state of our knowledge does not allow for precise comparisons between the cumulative effects of minor or moderate stresses over time and the impact of an intense stress.

A related issue involves the amount of change occurring at a given time. Amount of change refers to the total number of stresses experienced by the individual, but could also reflect the intensity and/or duration of the changes. Very likely, estimations of both the intensity and the amount of stress are subjectively based. Most studies presume that large amounts of life change are associated with adverse reactions. However, it is conceivable that too little stress could create problems for the individual. Stress may be similar to other psychological constructs, such as anxiety, in which optimal functioning occurs under moderate levels, rather than under high or low levels.

A final dimension of stress which has received relatively little attention is the specific type of life change one experiences. Instruments designed to measure stress have traditionally lumped together life changes in such diverse areas as health, work, family, personal life, social and community relations, and finances to arrive at a global stress score. Our own work suggests that a global stress score may obscure important relationships between specific stresses and health. Different types of life change may have independent effects on illness and health care utilization. For instance, a financial setback could increase health risks by affecting one's diet and housing, but could decrease use of expensive medical services. Also, it seems reasonable to assume that stresses confined to just one sector, such as job-related problems, constitute less of a threat than do stresses which cut across a number of categories, such as family, job, and financial problems.

It can be concluded that psychosocial stress is not a monolithic variable. Instead, it is a complex phenomenon which varies on the dimensions of valence, locus of control, timing, duration, intensity, amount, and category. Stress occurs within the context of the individual's life space, and therefore is subject to the influence of a host of other intervening factors, most specifically subject variables and environmental variables.

SUBJECT VARIABLES

How a person reacts to stress is of importance in any model of the relationship between stress and illness. We have already emphasized the role of the individual's own perception of an event as positive or negative, ambivalent or neutral, in defining stress. Individual differences are obviously also present in stress tolerance and in the ability to deal with adverse conditions. Sarason et al.[5] propose that the effects of life change may be mediated by the individual's overall perception of having control over environmental events, his sensation-seeking status or needs for stimulation, and his psychosocial assets. In addition, such factors as the person's experiential background, knowledge, sex, age, and socioeconomic status may affect not only his perception of stress, but the impact of stress upon him and his response to it.

Whether or not the individual reacts to stress with physical or psychological symptoms, and whether or not he then seeks medical care, may also depend on his attitudes toward health and illness. His readiness to be concerned about health matters, his perceptions of his own vulnerability to illness, and the implications of his symptoms, together with his beliefs about the efficacy of health care and its physical, economic, and psychological costs, may all influence the person's complaints and medical utilization when he is stressed.

SOCIAL AND ENVIRONMENTAL VARIABLES

A host of social and environmental variables may further complicate the relationship between stress and illness. The individual's milieu may affect his response to stress, disposition to illness, and readiness to seek medical care. So far, there is but a small body of data on these variables. The potentially powerful influences of subcultural or ethnic customs, beliefs, and pressures constitute a set of factors which have been largely ignored in stress research. The concept of social support is the one social factor that has been investigated, but it suffers from many of the same definitional and methodological problems as the construct of stress. Social support has been defined as the system of attachments among people which enhances competence in dealing with crises.[2] The dimensions of support include the closeness of relationships, the breadth of the social network, and the frequency or accessibility of contacts. The literature suggests that support from family and friends may buffer the impact of stress, and may reduce the risk of illness or even death. In our own work, we are finding that social support may also affect the individual's pattern of medical utilization.

In research on stress and illness, environmental variables may come into play which could distort the results of studies that focus only on psychosocial stressors. Living conditions in themselves may present physical stresses which would increase the likelihood of disease by exposing the individual to crowding, hazardous materials, pollution, insects and rodents, etc. For the most part, stress-illness research has relied on medical records to ascertain the occurence of ailments in times of stress. However, the individual's environment may curtail medical utilization if he has no phone or transportation, or if the medical resource is otherwise inaccessible.

THE CONSTRUCT OF ILLNESS

Throughout this chapter we have been referring to illness as if it was a clearly defined, dependent variable. It is not. In the stress-illness literature, physical illness is often confounded with health care utilization as a reaction to stress. Mechanic points out that it is one thing to show that stress affects the occurrence of morbidity; it is quite another to demonstrate that stress results in different reactions to symptoms and different patterns of seeking care.[3] A crisis may reduce our resistance to disease, or it may dispose us to seek medical help either as a means of coping with stress or because we feel less able to control illness when we are stressed. Because of the lack of consistency in the literature in defining illness, it is not clear whether the primary effects of stress are upon vulnerability to disease, behavior during illness, or both. Possibly, the impact of stress is greatest in cases in which the symptom is not severe and the individual must decide whether or not to seek help. "Should I see a doctor, or just rest and see if I feel better?" In this vein, Haggerty (1980) reports that the effects of stress upon help seeking may be more apparent for illnesses of moderate duration (two to five days) than for illnesses of brief (one day) or longer (five or more days) duration.[2] Stress may also influence the type of medical service that the individual seeks. Our own findings confirm Haggerty's [2] impression that in times of crisis, a person may make more use of easy entry facilities such as a hospital emergency room.

CONCLUSION

Until recently, the stress-illness linkage has been approached in overly simplistic or extravagantly global terms which obscured the complexity of the relationship. In addition, there has been a failure to give sufficient attention to the interplay of individual differences and social-environment factors which may affect both stress and illness. As a result, it is not surprising that literature generally indicates low magnitude correlations between psychosocial stress and illness. What is surprising is that the research does yield some consistent relationships. For instance, behavior signifying illness should be more likely to occur if the person views himself as having little control over his world and as being responsible for negative events which occurred in the past month, and if his life situation is chronically chaotic and lacking in social support systems.

In light of this discussion, and of the strengths and weaknesses of the current research, some recommendations for future work emerge. The most obvious is that operational definitions of all constructs must be more explicit and specific if we are to achieve more definitive answers in this complex, frustrating, and yet exciting area. While more focused studies considering specific stresses and their possible effects are most strongly encouraged, one must not demand that all investigators follow the same course of study. Research in this area is really in its infancy. Consequently, varied approaches and a breadth of research avenues should be encouraged. There is insufficient evidence that any single instrument, technique, or research design is sufficient to be utilized as a standard for stress-illness research. In other words, the full spectrum of investigative ingenuity is encouraged, but it should be focused in any given study. Given such diversity, one would also hope that there would be an integration of future work with past and present efforts. Some titillating leads already reported may be more profitable sources of ideas than beginning from new directions. Finally, studies which present positive findings should be replicated and expanded to determine whether the results are robust, and to assess the generalizability of the findings in terms of variables and populations. We have yet to unravel the complexities of the association between psychosocial stress and illness.

References

1. Fairbank, D. T. and Hough, R. L. Life event classification and the event-illness relationship. *Journal of Human Stress* 5 (3): 41-47 (1979).
2. Haggerty R. J. Life stress, illness and social supports. *Developmental Medical Child Neurology* 22: 391-400 (1980).
3. Mechanic, D. Some implications of illness behavior for medical sampling. *The New England Journal of Medicine* 269: 244-247 (1963).
4. Rahe, R. H. Life change events and mental illness: an overview. *Journal of Human Stress* 5 (3): 2-10 (1979).
5. Sarason, J. G., Johnson, J. H., and Siegel, J. M. Assessing the impact of life changes: development of the life experiences survey. *Journal of Consulting and Clinical Psychology* 46 (5): 932-946 (1978).
6. Selye, H. *The Stress of Life*. McGraw-Hill, New York, 1936.

Psychological Stress from Physical Disease

Michael Blumenfield, M.D.
Associate Professor of Psychiatry, Medicine and Surgery
New York Medical College
Valhalla, New York

Associate Director
Liaison Psychiatry Division
Westchester County Medical Center
Valhalla, New York

Just as life stress can very often be a precipitant or an exacerbation of physical disease, so can physical disease itself be a cause of major life stress. The impact of physical disease on the individual can be understood in psychological terms. Using the psychodynamic model allows a conceptualization of the immediate and deep-seated meaning of the impact of physical disease. It provides a model in order to explain what often appears to be "irrational" behavior in response to disease. An in-depth understanding of the personality of each patient is usually not available, but this does not mean that the personal meaning of the stress of the disease should not be acknowledged and considered by the treating physician. This approach does not neglect the stress that disease places on the family members and the entire social setting of the patient. Rather, it views the stress as it is experienced psychologically by the patient.

Instead of using the word *stress*, let us change it to an equivalent word, *anxiety*. This is a subjective emotion of unpleasure which is known to everyone. Freud considered anxiety to have a biological, inherited basis in which the human organism was congenitally endowed with the capacity for reacting with the psychological and physical manifestations which we call anxiety. (These physical manifestations have been discussed elsewhere in this book.) He noted that in man as in lower animals this capacity has a definite survival value for the individual. For example, a human being without the protection of his parents, if he were not frightened by anything, would soon be destroyed.[2] During the course of growth, the young child learns to anticipate the early advent of any traumatic, overwhelming, or unpleasureable situation with anxiety. This type of anxiety,

Freud called "signal anxiety." It is produced by a situation of danger or by the anticipation of danger. In psychodynamic terms as originally defined by Freud, its production is a function of the ego, and it serves to mobilize the forces at the command of the ego to meet or to avoid the impending traumatic situation.[5]

We have come to understand that the individual's subsequent emotional reaction is going to be determined by previous emotions and experiences. Thus, if we understand the meaning of this anxiety or stress, we will then be able to consider some of the psychological mechanisms which the individual will use in response to this experience.

SEPARATION ANXIETY

While some people feel that birth trauma is the prototypic experience for the psychological stress that an individual experiences, there is serious question as to whether memory pathways of any kind are functioning to allow specific impact of this human experience. Much more is understood about the separation experience of the developing child.[6] The infant at approximately 8 months of age first experience separation in relationship to the mother. This has been called the beginning of *separation anxiety*. Similar types of anxiety will be experiences in subsequent stages of life—toddling away from the safety of a caretaker, going away to kindergarten, going away to college, moving out of the house, getting married, experiencing the death of important people, etc. Some of these events may be traumatic to the individual. The response of a person to a particular separation or the response to the anticipation of a particular separation will be determined by whatever the person's previous experiences have been. The impact of physical illness will mobilize the separation anxiety in all patients. Certainly illness which requires hospitalization will lead to separation from people with whom the patient has been very close. Different people will have varying tolerances to this experience.

There is still another reason why illness brings out separation anxiety and that is because most physical illness will bring to the surface feelings about death and dying. While the thought of death can have a wide spectrum of psychological meaning to people, it almost always engenders feelings of separation. Death means separation from loved ones and thus ideation about death will evoke separation anxiety.

All types of separation anxiety originate from one's earliest experiences as a child. As mentioned, the prototype would have been experienced with the mother, but it will be reexperienced subsequently with both parents as well as with other people in various situations in the environment. We would expect that those people who can best tolerate separation anxiety will be those who as children had relationships which were built on trust and who were not traumatized with neglect or forced separation at a young age.

Obviously dependency needs will go hand in hand with separation anxiety. A patient with a physical illness may show a strong need to be taken care of. There may be a clinging and even a demanding hostile quality to the manifestation of these dependency needs. While this may be the usual personality style of the individual, it can also be a response to the impact of the physical illness which has mobilized separation anxiety in a previously relatively independent person.

CASTRATION ANXIETY

One of the earliest fearful experience of childhood occurs when toddlers at age 2 or 3 realize the anatomical differences between the sexes. They recognize that boys have penises and girls do not. Children will express concern about an injury that caused or can potentially cause this anatomical difference. This is an especially traumatic fear to the child because the genital area at this age has become a source of pleasure as well as a source of conflict because of prohibitions around it. At subsequent stages of development, derivatives of this experience are going to be manifested especially in the male. This anxiety, known as *castration anxiety,* can be experienced with any threat to the individual's well-being even if the threat is not to the genitals. This type of anxiety is not limited to the male especially since the origin of such a fear can be in the little girl's first belief that she was injured in some way and that is why she is different from boys. The first bleeding at menarche may revive these anxieties and can be experienced in the young woman as a feeling of mutilation. Under most circumstances with normal development these fantasies will become repressed. However, at times of sickness, the fears of genital injury enhance the castration anxiety which can come to the surface and cause anxiety in both sexes.

ANXIETY FROM NARCISSISTIC INJURY

From the earliest age, the child has a sense of self, which consists of a sense of bodily integrity, boundaries, and strength. As the child grows older, this sense of self is part of his confidence and security in his ability to function as an independent person. When a person feels threatened by physical illness, he or she can have a conscious or unconscious concern about the loss of his or her bodily integrity and strength. This is especially relevant when there is a fear of mutilating surgery or debilitating disease, or when there is a threat of death. The person views illness and any loss of function as a blow to his or her sense of bodily integrity and to his or her sense of wholeness. Such concerns cause a great deal of anxiety. In fact, when a patient feels a loss of bodily integrity, we can say that the patient is suffering a *narcissistic injury*. This feeling can be quite incapacitating.

SPECIFIC PSYCHOLOGICAL MEANING OF ILLNESS

Even though on the deepest psychological level the impact of physical illness will create anxiety that can be understood in terms of the three categories above, there are nevertheless a whole range of psychological meanings of physical illness to a particular person. For example, a threatened loss of sight or hearing can bring about extreme anxiety not only because of the realistic importance of these sense organs but because of the special value and meaning to the individual. As we described earlier, any surgery can reawaken castration anxiety and anxiety around fears of mutilation, but there is additional meaning, for example, when a woman undergoes a mastectomy or hysterectomy. Her sense of femininity and identity is threatened. Any understanding of the impact of such surgery will have to take into account her own sense of security and sense of herself as a person and specifically as a woman. Obviously there could be analogous situations with a man or with numerous other areas of disease.

Persons who have incapacitating cardiac disease and can no longer function as they have done in the past will have a strong personal psychological response. Depending on their personality structure and previous experience, this will be felt as a threat to their masculinity or femininity, a threat to their ability to be a parent or provider, a threat to their sense of adequacy, etc.

The meaning of the physical illness will also depend on the patient's experience with illness in his or her family. There is often identification with one's parents which leads to the expectation of having the same or similar physical disease and prognosis. Needless to say, the psychological meaning of specific symptoms under these circumstances can be very dramatic.

DENIAL

We have described how physical illness will cause psychological stress in the form of anxiety. There is a strong tendency to avoid this anxiety in any way possible. One method is to avoid the perceptions of the physical illness.

This is commonly attempted through the psychological mechanism of denial. Denial is usually directed against the external world. All people use denial as everyone tends to avoid painful reality until it has to be coped with. Just as it is possible to block out stimuli that come to the sense organs from the outside, it is also possible to block out stimuli that come from bodily sensations. Denial can be likened to the pupillary action of the eye. The iris constricts to avoid overstimulation from the retina from too much light. In a similar manner, the defense of denial tends to protect from overstimulation by excessive stimuli which would cause anxiety. It must be emphasized that denial is an attempt to protect. Denial becomes a dangerous mechanism when it prevents individuals from making some realistic assessment or action which might help them. For example, when a person denies the signs and symptoms of cancer, this is harmful to that person. Similarly, if a person denies the seriousness of crushing chest pain and attributes it to indigestion, this could delay life saving cardiac care.

DISPLACEMENT

A common reaction to physical illness, especially when it is experienced as some degree of a narcissistic injury, is anger. This can be a severe anger and a rage which may appear to be quite prominent to the people around the patient but not recognized by the person who is ill. The patient is frequently angry at himself for getting sick. However, experiencing this anger can be very painful and intolerable to the individual, and thus it can be displaced to the doctor and to the patient's family. In such a situation, we have a patient expressing an irrational anger and provocativeness to the people that he or she needs the most.

INTELLECTUALIZATION

Another reaction to illness which is quite the opposite of denial occurs when a patient tries to learn all he can about his illness. The patient attempts to control the disease by knowing about it. Such a patient can accumulate a great deal of information about his or her particular illness. Anxiety and fear are usually much greater when something is unknown. The reduction of those unpleasant emotions through increased knowledge seems to be the reason behind this response. In addition, some people have a personality style which causes them to try to keep control of every situation with this intellectual approach. It can be helpful to such patients if they are allowed to participate actively in their treatment and if they are kept informed about the progress of their illness.

The entire range of human response to conflict can be used in response to physical illness. This can be understood in a wide range of defense mechanisms. However the three mechanisms just discussed are often the most prevalent, obvious, and dramatic.

DEPRESSION AND GUILT

Even though the previously described defense mechanisms are used to varying degrees in response to physical illness, the patient will still experience a certain amount of anxiety. He or she will also become depressed. Depression will accompany all the types of anxiety that have already been described. The patient who is hospitalized may react to being isolated and lonely by becoming depressed. The loss of any significant object is going to lead to depression. The loss of a person, the loss of function, or even the threatened loss of function will lead to depression. There is a natural grieving process that takes place for some patients when they become ill. The thing that they often miss the most is their independence. Forced dependency on bedpan and caretakers can intensify depression. The threat that an individual will not be able to function in his or her accustomed role of breadwinner or parent can cause depression. In such situations, people may be experiencing a loss of self-esteem and may feel unworthy. When this happens, the individual is going to have a varying intensity of depression.

Physical illness may also activate feelings of guilt that will intensify the depression. The illness can be perceived as punishment for previous sins. This will be further demonstrated when we consider the fantasies that patients develop about their physical illnesses.

SPECIAL MEDICAL SITUATIONS

There are certain medical situations which have been demonstrated to cause particular types of psychological reactions.

Intensive Care Unit

In the modern intensive care unit, patients are hooked up to a variety of electrical devices including electrocardiogram and other physiological monitors. While some patients may be reassured by the continuous monitoring, there can be other psychological problems that develop because of distress in the ICU. Patients may suffer sleep deprivation, sensory isolation, and sensory overload, which can lead to a psychological disorganization with confusion and loss of touch with reality. Such a patient can show cognitive deficits and disorientation that resemble an organic brain syndrome even though there may not be an organic basis. The psychotic manifestations can include visual and auditory hallucinations as well as paranoid behavior. In addition, even patients in full touch with reality may become extremely anxious when they detect the usual movement artifact on the electrocardiogram monitoring screens. All patients should be given some orientation as to what to expect and what is happening around them while they are in the ICU.

Hemodialysis

It is an unusual situation for a person to be hooked up to a machine for blood perfusion a couple of times a week in order to survive. This is the situation with chronic hemodialysis, and the psychological responses of patients to this process have been carefully studied.[7] The first stage is called the "honeymoon period." This usually begins one to three weeks after the first dialysis and can last from six weeks to six months. The patient seems to accept the intense dependency on the machine and the procedure during this stage. There is still great stress and anxiety, but the patient is basically content, confident, and hopeful. The second stage is called "disenchantment and discouragement." The confidence and the hope have passed and the patient begins to feel sad and helpless. This lasts between 3 and 12 months. Often this stage begins after the patients find that they are not able to perform their usual activities and become depressed. They also feel guilty over diet indiscretions and begin to react with shame about their illness. The third stage of the patients' reaction to hemodialysis is the stage of "long-term adaptation," in which patients are able to arrive at some degree of acceptance of their limitations. They still have marked fluctuations in their sense of emotional and physical well-being, but there are longer periods of contentment alternating with episodes of depression of varying duration. During this stage the most commonly used psychological mechanism is denial.

TRANSPLANTATION

Modern medical science now offers the possibility of organ transplantation, with renal transplantation being the most common type. In such a case the patient may have to ask a parent, a child, or a sibling to donate a kidney. Family conflicts can be heightened at this time, often causing feelings of guilt on the part of both donor and recipient. Dependency conflicts in the parent-child relationship can be heightened by the actual dependency that is imposed upon the patient by the illness.

When the kidney that is donated comes from a cadaver there are inevitable fantasies about the dead donor. In each situation there can also be a question of how an actual or fantasied cross-sexual transplant will affect the recipient's feelings about his or her sexual identity. It is also possible that these various psychological factors may even influence the actual physical rejection of the new kidney. The transplant patient also has the difficult task of integrating a new organ into his or her overall body image.

REGRESSION

There is an inherent tendency of people to revert to early patterns of behavior and thinking. This will happen particularly in the face of anxiety brought about by physical illness. This regression will intensify the dependency needs of the patient. At times this may be helpful in allowing the patient to be cared for, while at other times it creates problems because the patient can make intolerable demands on the caretakers. This tendency to regress psychologically during physical illness will also affect the doctor-patient relationship. The doctor becomes experienced as an ommipotent parent who is expected to cure the patient magically. The patient can feel an irrational attachment of love to the doctor which can easily turn to the oppostie feeling if the expectations are not met.

FANTASIES ABOUT ILLNESS

In response to distress and the impact of physical illness, every patient will develop a fantasy about his or her sickness.[1] Each patient will have an underlying fantasy as to why he or she got that particular physical illness. Since illness facilitates regression, the fantasy will tend to be one that reflects childhood conflicts. It will also demonstrate the central conflicts and personality structure of the individual.

One of the most common types of fantasy is a retribution fantasy. A case example was a 38-year-old male with a nine-month history of sixth nerve palsy, headache, and nausea. The patient stated that he believed he had some rare disease because he had had sexual intercourse in Southeast Asia. He felt very guilty about this and recently told his wife that, in his mind, this was a punishment. He knew logically that his symptoms was not those of venereal disease, but nevertheless the belief persisted. Viewing illness as a punishment is not unusual. Guilt feelings from a previous period of life can be revived at a time of physical illness. These can intensify the feelings of depression which often also occur during physical illness.

Sometimes the fantasy will be built around ideas of inheritance. For example a 28-year-old female with asthma had strong feelings about why she and her younger brother had it and not her other siblings. She and this brother look alike and resemble a maternal grandfather. She believed that she "probably inherited asthma from my mother." There was also a great deal of anger toward her mother. She had always been close to her mother and had recently been trying to get her husband transferred to another city where the mother lived so she could again live near her. The fantasy that she constructed about her asthma reflected the conflict that she was having with her mother and the mixed feelings that she had directed toward her mother. These emotions may have actually had something to do with any psychosomatic causative factors in the onset of her illness.

The treating physician is able to obtain the fantasy about the physical illness from the patient by a sensitive, empathetic inquiry as to why the patient feels they have the particular illness. The information obtained at times will demonstrate a medical misperception about the illness which can be corrected, but more frequently will reflect the underlying conflicts and stress that the physical illness may be triggering in the patient.

BASIC MANAGEMENT

The physician is accustomed to an action-oriented approach to the management of illness. Therefore the use of tranquilizers and/or antidepressive medication seems natural for treating anxiety and depression that arise from the stress of physical disease. These medications do have a limited role in the management of disease, but the physician can often be much more effective through a careful, empathetic attempt to understand the patient and his or her response to the illness. This does not require a detailed psychiatric study of the patient. It does require a sensitivity to the patient's past personal history. This information and knowledge may be obtained in small doses at the bedside. It may be obtained through numerous office visits even over the course of several years. As previously described, it does mean that the physician should have a sense of how the patient has handled important milestones in life including major separations, traumatic events, deaths, and previous illness. The physician has to look for clues as to the patient's self-image and the patient's fantasy about his or her illness. Not only will this knowledge be helpful in the everyday management of the patient, but also the interest shown by the physician in obtaining it will foster the patient's view of the doctor as a caring, empathetic person. In fact, as the physician appreciates the significance of the emotional impact to the patient, he will actually become more of a caring, empathetic person. The patient's sense of trust and confidence in the doctor can often do more to relieve anxiety than any drug.

Since the mechanism of denial can be recognized by the treating physician as an attempt by the patient to protect himself from something painful, there need not be an effort to eliminate this defense without first understanding the nature of these fears. This very understanding and support on the part of the physician can often allow the patient to give up this defense.

The physician can often diffuse hostile and provocative behavior when he recognizes that this is displaced anger that the patient feels primarily toward himself for being sick. In such a situation, a gentle statement of how the patient must be angry at himself for being sick will often make the patient realize the intrinsic nature of this feeling. With this insight the patient may be helped to discontinue displacement of anger toward family and medical staff. However, with this insight depression is often experienced.

When there is a persistent free-floating anxiety or anxiety pertaining to particular fears that do not show response to the concern and understanding of the physician, minor tranquilizers such as Librium (chlordiazepoxide), Valium (diazepam), etc., can be used. Care must be taken not to substitute the medication for the interest and concern of the doctor. In some situations where the anxiety is severe or where the sedative effect of the minor tranquilizer is a problem such as in geriatric patients, a small dosage of major tranquilizers may be utilized. The major tranquilizers such as Haldol (haloperidol), Thorazine (chlorpromazine), Mellaril (thioridazine), etc., also become indicated in larger dosages when there are breaks with reality with psychotic manifestations such as hallucinations and delusions.

There usually has to be some kind of grieving process for whatever loss of function or loss of health takes place. The physician's role in this management is to be available, give reassurance that competent care is being provided, give input about the positive aspects of the medical prognosis, and show empathetic understanding of the "bad news." This latter point, while it may seem quite obvious, can be a key point in the management of illness. If the physician emotionally withdraws his interest and caring, the patient will feel abandoned like a child who feels its parent doesn't care.

As indicated previously, grieving and depression around physical illness are universal, and medication is usually not the indicated treatment.

However, medication may be useful in such depression under certain conditions. For example, patients who have had a history of significant depression running in cyclic phases without necessarily having a precipitating incident will often respond to antidepressive drugs such as Elavil (amitriptyline), Tofranil (imipramine), etc. Another indication would be the presence of vegative signs of depression such as significant decrease in appetite, alteration in sleeping patterns, and diminished psychomotor activity.

As with all medication, one should be aware of side effects, contraindications, and drug interactions of any tranquilizer or antidepressive medication that is used. Blood levels of antidepressants may be helpful since inadequate dosages are not uncommon.

Patients who are discouraged and depressed may feel like giving up. They can express or experience suicidal thoughts. Sometimes this is a manifestation of the anger that they are feeling toward themselves. The physician should never be afraid to ask the patient if he has such thoughts. It is a common misconception that such an inquiry will give the patient a new idea.

Psychiatric consultation is indicated in the management of medical patients when there is a concern about suicidal ideation. Other times such consultation can be helpful in the diagnosis and management of psychotic manifestation or severe anxiety and depression. However patients with mainly medical problems usually should be managed by the nonpsychiatrist. It is in the context of this doctor-patient relationship that the treating physician can be the optimal provider of emotional support.

One final important point should be made about basic management. It has previously been mentioned how sleep deprivation, sensory deprivation, and sensory overload can at times cause a clinical picture of cognitive deficits and disorientation which will resemble organic brain syndrome. While this can be true under extreme conditions, the usual stress and psychological impact of physical disease does not cause a confusional state. Whenever a patient shows disorientation, confusion, or memory and cognitive deficit, organic brain syndrome must actively be ruled out. The cause may well be metabolic, vascular, infectious, or malignant. A reversible and treatable etiology must not be overlooked, which can be the case if such symptoms are incorrectly attributed to the stress of disease.

References

1. Blumenfield, M. The psychological reactions to physical illness. In *Understanding Human Behavior in Health and Illness* (R. C. Simons and H. Pardes eds.). Baltimore: Williams & Wilkins, 1977.

2. Brenner, C. *An Elementary Textbook of Psychoanalysis*. New York: International Universities Press, 1955.
3. Bribing, G. L. and Kahana, R. J. *Lectures in Medical Psychology*. New York: International Universities Press, 1968.
4. Freud, A. *The Ego and Mechanisms of Defense*. New York: International Universities Press, 1946.
5. Freud, S. *The Problem of Anxiety*. New York: W.W. Norton, 1936.
6. Mahler, M. S. *On Human Symbiosis and the Vicissitudes of Individuation*. New York: International Universities Press, 1968.
7. Reichsman, F. and Levy, N. B. Problems in adaptation to hemodialysis: a four year study of 25 patients. *Archives of Internal Medicine* 130: 859 (1972).
8. Strain, J. J. and Grossman, S. *Psychological Care of the Medically Ill. A Primer in Liaison Psychiatry*. New York: Appleton Century Crofts, 1975.

Communication of Emotional Meaning: A Biopsychosocial Dimension in Psychosomatics *

Fernando Lolas, M.D.
Michael Von Rad, M.D.
Universitat Heidelberg
Federal Republic of Germany

The notion that psychosomatic dysfunction is frequently associated with disturbed or arrested individuation in the realm of communicative transactions has become increasingly accepted in recent years. Bearers of so-called psychosomatic conditions, many of whom are highly skilled at verbalizing, are frequently described as being relatively unable to represent their feelings through the use of appropriate words. Their use of verbal symbols lacks emotional participation, and adequate integration with cognitive processing is impaired. Their style of speech tends to be flat and meager in the use of emotionally laden metaphors.

Besides bringing the interactional style of patients to the foreground as a diagnostic indicator, some writers have proposed that alteration or arrested

*During the preparation of this chapter, the senior author was supported by the Humboldt Foundation, Federal Republic of Germany.

development of the functions of communication may eventually disrupt bodily mechanisms and result in disease. Although this etiological proposal might or might not be true, the essential point is that psychophysiological (psychosomatic) disorders present commonalities, that these commonalities are related to communicative style, and that persons afflicted by them could be identified and treated accordingly. From a clinical standpoint, this has come to mean that simple notions equating psychoneuroses and psychosomatic conditions within a unified model have to be revised. Current research, challenging traditional views on conflict or personality pathogenic specificity, has addressed the question about the "core dimension" that should be used for studying physiological derangement from a biopsychosocial point of view.

A successful application of the biopsychosocial model implies the selection of appropriate probing strategies of relevant data and the delimitation of an observational field in which these data can be gathered and their importance estimated. The aim here is to expand scientific inquiry beyond biological and psychological determinants of health and illness to the social matrix in which the individual develops, lives, and becomes ill. The central position of communication and interaction in this frame of reference leads one to expect that no research strategy can be said to be comprehensive until these factors are taken into consideration. One of the ways of doing this closest to the clinical setting is through the study of speech.

The relevant position of language in biopsychosocial research stems from its being the locus of encounter among biological, psychological, and cultural processes. It not only fulfills many different functions but represents a highly developed form of interpersonal reality, a reality which can be shared by individuals but which cannot be created by them in isolation. Since Freud, all forms of "talking cures" make explicit use of the bond created between therapist and patient by means of verbal communication.

Language can be approached from many perspectives. Structuralist and hermeneutical literary analysis, for instance, represent a vantage point in which the essential datum is and remains language in its immanence, as an idealized whole or a concrete work of art. It may or may not undergo processes of change or evolution, but they interest the researcher only marginally.

Although this form of approaching language has had a place in psychoanalytic and psychiatric research, it cannot replace, in our view, studies which depart from pure interpretation and aim at empirical explanation and hypotheses testing. Both are, to be sure, complementary aspects of one and the same effort, namely, the study of interpersonal reality as it is represented in language structure and function. A different emphasis, however, characterizes a pragmatic approach such as the one we have pursued in psychosomatic research: it concentrates on speech as spoken by a certain speaker, transcends language, and searches for the user of the language. Language is endowed, so to speak, with a "symptomatic" character and becomes modified by the person who uses it. It becomes parole, speech. The relevant aim of research is not so much the study of invariances—of laws—but rather the personal variation as influenced by psychological, biological, and cultural factors—rules. Hypotheses to be tested refer to persons and situations, not to language itself. The main assumption here is precisely this: that speech reflects some characteristics of the speaker in much the same way that it reflects a relation between signs and things, and possesses an implicit structure of relationships between signs.

When we refer then to empirical clinical research using speech as a biopsychosocial probe, we mean to imply an analytic process whereby we make inferences about the origin, causes, and effects of signs within the behavior in which they occur.

One of the most important advances in this field has been the introduction of recording devices. They allow the researcher to preserve what otherwise would be an evanescent exchange of words and to recreate the original scene as many times as he wants. Others not directly involved in the recollection of the data can participate in its evaluation. If recorded material is transcribed, speech and conversation can be studied as a written production. They become texts. Texts are linguistic artifacts which retain some of the features of the real interaction. They represent no more than relational structures of signs. A text can also incorporate, for instance, nonverbal or paralinguistic elements which undoubtedly play a major role in communication processes. However, since these are frequently difficult to quantitate, with no unambiguous coding principles and implicit—as opposed to explicit—rules, a great proportion of current research is being conducted on the basis of speech, or verbal elements alone. This is a deliberate constraint which clearly reduces the scope of the investigation and limits its conclusions. Not infrequently, verbal and nonverbal channels show different degrees of dissociation. When the researcher concentrates on the verbal text, he implicitly makes the assumption that this text contains what interests him most.

While it is evident that texts derived from medical encounters can be studied in an almost endless variety of ways, research informed by the theoretical framework delineated above (deriving from clinical observations on bearers of psychosomatic conditions) needs explicit definition of a dominant dimension. Since verbal expression of affect and fantasy is the relevant variable in this approach, the "observational axis" should be constrained to what can be considered a relevant cue in this regard. For this core dimension of analysis, we suggest the term *communication of emotional meaning*. It is obviously not limited to the study of a definite group of people, but it alludes to a general dimension of meaningful relatedness between persons during patient-doctor interactions.

It is useful at this point to recall briefly that we are employing the word *meaning* in its commonsense denotation of *use* or *application*. *Information* in this context refers to a mathematical measure of the operations (mostly yes-no decisions) that relieve uncertainty and specify the contents of a message in terms of its degree of redundancy. Meaning presuposses a behaving and interpreting receiver who can put to work the contents of the message, that is, incorporate it to his own behavioral repertoire and use it. In a dyadic situation, emotional meaning can be said to be conveyed when interacting partners experience distinctive affective or feeling states brought about by the contents of communication. All psychotherapeutic interventions rely on this dimension of emotional meaning; they differ regarding the importance they ascribe to unconscious elements or in the ways in which they conceptualize the establishment of the actual relationship (e.g., transference and countertransference). A comprehensive theory of emotional meaning must surely take their contributions into account, particularly when it comes to define the observational domain for empirical testing.

Our research has been guided by the notion that texts based upon psychotherapeutic interactions might constitute suitable research instruments insofar as they permit operationalization and quantification of relevant constructs. This approach certainly does not exclude others. It should be viewed as a complementary strategy possessing the advantage that it relies upon an undisorted natural function, complex enough to permit a clinically meaningful level of inference. The goal is here to complement and expand data obtained under controlled laboratory conditions by means of information with a high degree of ecological validity.

In order to accomplish this goal, objective criteria for quantification have to be used. By these we mean to imply procedures of high consensual validity which can be applied to the raw data, allowing hypothesis testing, replication, and prediction. Although texts can also be analyzed from the standpoint of nonquantitative features, quantification, when possible and meaningful, should be attempted.

From a clinical standpoint, it is not critical to draw distinctions between formal and content analysis techniques. It should also be kept in mind that the analysis of a text is somewhat different from the analysis of verbal behavior as such. In the form defined above, a text is already a selected sample of signs taken from the total interaction according to implicit assumptions of relevance. Thus, although many features of the actual interactional processes have proved to be relevant in psychotherapeutic research (such as, for instance, the study of pauses), we shall not deal with them here. On the other hand, many techniques applicable to texts would equally fall under the heading of formal or content analytic techniques.

Content analysis is a system of data reduction. It relies upon coding the original material (natural speech) into agreed-upon units. This "many-to-few" mapping of information contained in a text serves the purpose of transforming intuitive judgments into explicit rules. In this sense, the techniques of content analysis do not add anything to what a sensible reader could discover by just reading the text. The process of coding (which many an author identifies with content analysis) allows an objective, systematic, and quantitative description of the contents by making use of predefined categories. These categories can be selected or developed *ad libitum,* depending upon the purpose of the investigation. So-called classical techniques employ coding units (or categories) which are close to observable facts or which can be defined independently from psychological structure and situation: such as grammatical categories, "type-token ratio," etc. These techniques are highly reliable, but their relevance to the questions most often formulated in psychotherapeutic research is at best indirect. Since in this type of investigation, the "kind of speaker" and the "situation" variables are interesting, other techniques—pragmatic ones—offer several advantages. In these, the units of codification (or categories for coding) represent a definite state or character of the speaker. While using rather complex constructs as coding categories might demand accurate validation procedures, the process of ascribing elements in the text to predefined units is the same in classical and pragmatic content analytic techniques.

Affect expression and communication of emotional meaning have been studied by means of different forms of content analysis. We have already pointed out that the basic assumption here is the symptomatic character of the text to be studied; that is to say, the text reflects—in a proportional and representative way—the type and intensity of the affects an individual may be experiencing. All forms of content analysis with a pragmatic orientation share this assumption. They may differ, however, regarding the minimal unit which should be coded. Some authors argue convincingly that the word might be an appropriate coding element. It can be ascribed to categories by means of automatic devices, and on occasion contextual information might be misleading. Other techniques disregard single words and operate on the basis of statements or sentences, which include contextual elements but which up to now have not been routinely scored by computer. Provided comparable frameworks of reference are used for defining coding categories and some independent validation procedure is available, it is advisable to use as many techniques as possible for the study of the same text.

Communication of emotional meaning studied through content analysis of psychotherapeutic texts has been a variable in a few studies we have conducted. As previously noted, some patients afflicted by somatic diseases have been described as exhibiting—among other characteristics—a peculiar form of verbal affect expression. This is a negative characteristic in that these persons are described as lacking a certain capability that is taken for granted in most social interactions. This could explain why the phenomenon was not described earlier and only imprecise formulations were offered. Even the introduction of the term *alexithymia* to designate the interactional style of these patients has not brought systematic exploration to the forefront. Imprecise concepts may be descriptive but lack any hypothesis-generating power. It might well be the case that this overall description should be replaced by descriptive dimensions of a lower level of inference and closer to consensual validation. Communication of emotional meaning assessed through the study of speech might constitute one such dimension.

Our research sought to explore an implication of the alexithymia concept, namely, the difference between subjects in whom the presence of the characteristic was more probable and subjects in whom it was not so probable. It is important to keep in mind that the concept as such was not investigated. Neither support nor rebuttal can be said to derive from our investigations. What we investigated was precisely the communication of emotional meaning through speech, in the hope that this might be related to the basic theorization and in an attempt also to bridge the gap between an imprecise descriptor, and objective and reproducible ones.

The study of psychotherapeutic texts was accomplished by means of a pragmatic, context-dependent form of content analysis developed by Gottschalk and Gleser and extensively validated. Magnitude of affect depends upon frequency, personal participation, and closeness to an ideal construct (centrality), and is represented by weighting factors. Sentences are coded into affective categories: six forms of anxiety and four forms of hostility. Because of the validation process and the derivation of the coding categories, this instrument represents an objective tool for depicting communication of emotional meaning in texts.

The results showed that between two clinically defined groups (psychoneurotics and psychosomatic patients), remarkable differences in affect expression could be evinced for the interview texts. So-called psychosomatic patients showed quantitatively less affect during the interview than neurotics, as measured by the Gottschalk-Gleser method. Other results and rationale can be seen in earlier publications. These results, as we have already said, cannot be brought to bear directly on the theoretical clarification of the constructs employed for describing the interaction of some patients. However, they present a way of approaching the problem at hand, exemplify a methodological strategy, and lead us to suggest communication of emotional meaning as a useful variable in this regard. Provided further theoretical refinements are introduced, it may serve as a descriptive dimension in psychosomatic research which makes use of speech as an integrative biopsychosocial probe.

References

Gottschalk, L. A. (ed.). *The Content Analysis of Verbal Behavior: Further Studies.* New York: Spectrum Publications, 1979.
Lolas, F. and Ferner, H. Zum Begriff des impliziten Verhaltens. *Zeitschrift f. klin. Psychol. Psychother.* **26**: 223-233 (1978).
von Rad, M., Drucke, M., Knauss, W., and Lolas, F. Alexithymia: anxiety and hostility in psychosomatic and psychoneurotic patients. *Psychother. Psychosom.* **31**: 223-234 (1979).
Ruesch, J. *Semiotic Approaches to Human Relations.* The Hague: Mouton, 1972.
Stone, P. J., Dunphy, D. C., Smith, M. S., and Ogilvie, D. M. *The General Inquirer: A Computer Approach to Content Analysis.* Cambridge, Mass: MIT Press, 1966.

Terrorism as a Form of Communication: Biopsychosocial Stress.

A Working Report by Stacey B. Day* M.D., Ph.D., D.Sc.,
Hon. Fereydoun Hoveyda,†
Colonel William J. Taylor, Jr.,‡ Ph.D. and Committee

Terrorism is a form of communication identifying biopsychosocial conflict. In the sense that *conflict* underlies such forms of social stress, it is useful to recognize that an ability to understand the situations involved is a first step in focusing intelligent awareness on actions that stem from terrorism, since such actions have both a *perceptual* content and an adversary or conflict role. In a simple way it might be said that one man's terrorist is another man's freedom fighter. This ambiguity makes it necessary to appreciate that such forms of conflict are not new to our age and time, but that intellectual roots of countervailing argument have been dominant in adversary conduct in all nations, and in all systems of government and society, over all centuries. What is perhaps unique to our times are the forms of violence used, and the nature and circumstances of the threats perceived. From the viewpoint of an ordered society, solving differences via terrorist philosophies is frankly to be deplored. Apart from emotional resolution, it is highly unlikely that force without dialogue can achieve lasting solutions or arbitrate opposing viewpoints. Terrorist conduct, if persisted in, carries the characteristics of disease, being readily transferable from person to person, from community to community, and indeed from nation to nation. If there is any positive feature deriving from this form of social conduct, it is the recognition that intelligent understanding of social stress may contribute to developing *policies* directed to resolution of conflict issues at the

---

* Clinical Professor of Medicine, Division of Behavioral Medicine, New York Medical College, Valhalla, New York.
† Former Ambassador and Permanent Representative of Iran to the United Nations; Former Chairman Ad Hoc Committee on World Disarmament Conference, United Nations, New York.
‡ United States Military Academy. Permanent Professor, National Security Policy Studies and Director of the Debate Council and Forum at the Military Academy, West Point, New York.
§ See Appendix to paper.

core of the antisocial conduct. This paper discusses and presents, in a simple way, a number of important observations derived by an interdisciplinary panel of educators, legislators, international officers of government, citizens, and military officers, who met at Tarrytown, New York, on November 12, 1980 to discuss, in terms of biopsychosocial health, terrorism as a form of communication.

GUIDING PERSPECTIVES

Studies in terrorism require a broad range of analytical and synthetic skill, and are enhanced by an interdisciplinary approach, which brings together not only knowledge found directly in or derived from traditional sociological disciplines such as economics, political science, mathematical statistics, and educational thresholds, but includes appreciation of many so-called newer disciplines. Depending upon whether the approach to the terrorist problem is limited or not, these studies will include military logic, a broad understanding of the fields of communications including networking, simulated policy making (mathematical analyzing approaches), intercultural communications, appreciation of the conflict role of technology in modern societies, numbers (population) problems, and in a long-range view, commitment to national and international policies and actions, including the urgent need to develop the *military intellectual* with consequent ability to translate via *operations research* classical techniques of military management to civilian stress situations. Beyond and including these prospects are matters of planning global and interplanetary harmony through appropriate legal settlements.

A danger therefore in summarizing panel discussions is that an impression might falsely be encouraged that the problem has been solved or satisfactorily reviewed. It should be pointed out that in the view of our panelists, the content of terrorism studies has barely been visualized. Societies are usually a heterogeneous mixture of people with varying energies, goals, aims, pursuits, idealisms, grievances, sympathies, and diverse loyalties. To manage such a society, and to be capable of being both analyst and leader, is a professional challenge to the identity and existence of a given nation. It is indeed a modern nightmare and, for Western philosophies, well summed up in Taylor's primary concern with the so-called *democratic dilemma*. Terrorism is *not* a marginal but a *fundamental* problem. Democracy by its nature permits terrorism to flourish, but the optimal steps to defeat or eliminate terrorists threaten democracy itself. It could be argued that since we live in technocracies governed by order, regulation, and control, this latter point is to be relegated   to finer print—but in the United States at least, the constitutional role of the First Amendment cannot be ignored, and Hoveyda perceptively outlined legal jurisdictions in society that can in fact protect terrorists or potential terrorists.

Nonetheless to understand the psychology and social dimensions in which terrorism is manifest, it is useful to propose boundary phases which may facilitate explicit attempts to control the problem. In the view of Hoveyda, there are four forms of terrorism:

1. International
2. National
3. Political
4. Nonpolitical

Quite obviously the emotional development and content within each and every one of the phases is experientially broad and requires not only perceptive skills but deep knowledge of culture and intercultural communicative modes. To integrate all four phases is clearly a formidable problem and, as likely as not, is one of the principal reasons why such bodies as the United Nations are not in a good position to deal fundamentally with issues of terrorism. The sovereignty of nations, vetoes on Security Council votes concerning control of acts of terrorists, and attempts by some governments to gain or keep power, fortify our view that private analytical evaluations of terrorism are preferable to international, highly publicized accounts that in fact cannot, or will not, proceed to policies and action. In our discussion, David Schulte argued for the view that there is not much difference between national and international terrorism. His case centered about the five R's of terrorism:

1. Rejection of child by parents at an early age by desertion, hostility, etc. (less than 5 years of age);
2. Resentment—the child feels inferior because of lack of family (older than 5 years of age);
3. Rebellion—getting even with someone (parents or siblings)—the desire to hurt someone;
4. Retaliation—the first R that occurs outside the family: striking out against other races, religions, etc. (this is the only R that can be controlled by threats of prison);
5. Rehabilitation—a myth—cannot be done with prisons and by psychiatrists.

LIFE PATHS AND QUALITY OF LIFE

It might reasonably be argued that the sociological analysis of terrorism has never really been undertaken. Our own studies in an effort to contribute to the theoretical and methodological understanding of this form of social conduct have been through the fields of health communications and biopsychosocial health, which themselves have been largely unrepresented in the educational curricula of most university programs. In the mid-1960s when social activism required perceptive insight and understanding of biopsychosocial dynamics, there was not a department in the United States capable of dealing with campus turmoil and national/international unrest. To this day, despite the great importance of health communications, this discipline remains one of the smallest subset fields in the major medical institutions of this country. Together with an unconscionable distaste for military sociology, medical schools have set back by over 20 years fair ability to handle deviations from the norm that occur in society, which have not only wreaked great destruction but have done so at extraordinary cost, pragmatically and spiritually, and still show no sign of abatement or amelioration. In this sense, a recent publication in support of the military model by Sir Harold Himsworth, former secretary and deputy chairman, British Medical Research Council, for consideration of the military model to integrate expert health knowledge into the machinery of government is important. This position has been our own argument, developed in the creation of the model of the military intellectual as policy advisor and in governance. It is only by such renewed thinking, we argue, that in modern fields of education (including health and social conduct) subject to high technology and specialization, current concepts can be adapted to solve the problems we face, including terrorism. (Day).

The sociological tradition in medicine has been so weak as to have been nonexistent. It is only within recent years that integrated medical efforts (such as the International Foundation for Biosocial Development and Human Health and the Japanese Foundation for Biopsychosocial Health) have been launched to educate and to strengthen society to recognize what in effect have become new forms of disease or social illness. It is a critical need that these be identified more urgently than cytopathologic or molecular disease, for the whole quality of life of nations, and nationhood itself, from its inception at birth, is at risk. The substantive nature of our concerns not only is responsive to individuals and groups, but also relates to the policy process, for good social health must fulfill a function for the state and for the well-being of nations. Social health outreach, therefore, against terrorism must begin with the family and with the community.

In our overall educational philosophy we have been committed to the view that quality of life, mediated by education, leads to the concept of the whole man. Whole is holy or holistic or good. In this sense, primary education is of the utmost importance. Sciarreta and Stahl emphasized in their approaches to teaching infants and children the investigation of those factors in the educational process that contribute to or deter the development of a terrorist. If citizens could discriminate between right and wrong there might be fewer incidents of "terrorism spreading as fun," an example cited by David Schulte. Stahl, in discussing her experiences with young children, argued that the development of a terrorist began early in life and might well be reinforced by media exposure of a violent nature such as Saturday morning television. Without exception, the extreme importance of media in encouraging terrorism was emphasized (Belack, Blake, Day, Rondon). In this sense it should be pointed out that terrorism needs an audience and, in one way or another, psychologically, an audience must be provided for successful completion of a terrorist's goal.

The nurturing of human beings is of course a complex mix of sensitivity, culture, education, and social and political evolution and organization of societies. Not uncommonly, most societies have a need for powerful idealism, which requires a healthy and useful outlet invariably provided by the culture of the society. In the absence of this outlet there may be a turning back or reversion of individual energy into a form of internal terrorism, conceivably leading to suicide or, when applied externally, manifest upon the outer body of society as destructive or vengeful acts. Terrorism might well be to the sick body politic what fever is to the body of man. The translation and transfer of these energies and moods may be almost imperceptible. In such cases, the nation and the individual will react under circumstances of stress.

Nicaraguan revolutionary experiences (Rondon) revealed youngsters of 8, 9, and 10 years of age handling M16 submachine guns, commanded by a boy 14 years old, fighting against the American "because he is our national enemy." Such young fighters were resolutely committed to Liberty, Country, and Death! In urban ghettos a similar psychophysiological orientation can be met among girls (Rondon). In such urban slums, "it is all right to have a baby by 15," the thesis being that only the toughest are the best and so worthy of receiving recognition, irrespective of societal values, of which they may or may not know, and to which in many cases they have no access.

If society is willing to leave decisions about the lives of its citizens in the hands of 14-year-old children, one might well ask those who educate society, *What power rests in education? What are the goals of education? What are values for life?*

Communication as well as education is necessarily involved, especially for those in economically deprived circumstances. Terrorism creates its audience. It may also create power sources (Black Panthers; Liberation movements; even the FBI has been involved in illegal campaigns to encourage false propositions), all of which lead, in a context of forces, to polarization and often to face-down conflict positions.

Educationalists are obliged to deal with these and similar situations. They must pose such questions as, *What does it mean to be a human being?* (Stahl). *How can we help people to be human beings? What are the responsibilities of the individual in society?* They must also provide reasonable leadership, example, and resolution to acts of violence and to fear (be it political, criminal, or social) and must provide access so that legitimate grievances can be aired before dichotomy of purpose leads to terrorism. The democratic dilemma must be as much to examine itself as to permit agents of force to operate against it. The educational process must ask, Who cares? Who will move to address the problem? Who will identify the problem? Otherwise, it will be of no help simply to regret the nature of those in society who will strike out as haves and have-nots.

Education ameliorates the tendency to impose solutions by preparing the parties concerned to liberate themselves by reasonable communications, by finding outlets for pent-up energy, and by seeking forums at which all voices can be heard.

PROFILE OF A TERRORIST

Recognizing the enormous prospects for conflict, we have described a wide variety of traits marking the terrorist:

1. Terrorism seems to be as old as history. What is new is the age, sex, and social class of terrorists. Formerly, we had rulers and revolutionaries from the ruling class resorting to terror for political purposes. They committed acts of violence in violent times. Now terrorists frequently seem to be young people of upper middle class background, neither rulers nor oppressively ruled, not religiously motivated, and—a sign of our times—women as well as men. Terrorism is not sexist anymore. It is, however, politically oriented and made more dangerous by the vulnerability of mass transportation and the visibility of individual targets, as a result of their permanent highlighting by the mass media. (Professor Otto Pollak)

2. Terrorists are generally male, 22 to 25 years of age (with females mostly in supportive roles); urban middle class (or higher); some university work or a degree; many from families of professionals;

most recruited at universities, especially during the 1960s and 1970s. Most study the humanities, except in the Middle East, where they usually have undertaken technical studies. National terrorism does not flourish where rule is by terror. (Colonel William Taylor)

3. A person or group commits or threatens violence to instill fear, to influence another group, and to achieve political, criminal, or other goals. The lines between goals may intermix. (Carl Belack)

4. Terrorists are usually wealthy, highly educated students, often less religious than blue collar workers in the population. The rejection of values by terrorists may be a form of self-loathing in consequence of which they have no respect for themselves or for others. (Marc Kusinitz)

5. Terrorism starts at home and goes to the schools. (Benilda Jones)

6. The terrorist is not necessarily pathological. He may use misfits to do his violence for him. (Professor Harold Dettelbach)

7. Terrorism often initiates legitimate means of violence, e.g., SWAT teams vs Symbionese Liberation Army. (Dr. Cecil Blake)

8. Terrorists are well organized and often smart. They understand us better than we understand them. (Colonel James Pepile)

9. Behind the terrorist is a powerful idealism without an outlet. (Bradford Riley)

10. The basis of terrorism is society espousing values in which it does not believe. (Hon. Fereydoun Hoveyda)

Overview

Violence is the language of people who cannot be heard. So suggested Martin Luther King. An essential, therefore, of terrorists and terrorism, whether incited for political or economic reasons, is to create an attentive audience. Terrorism is in fact a matter of social communication. Where destructive capacity exists, we have considered terrorism a sickness within the terms of biopsychosocial health.

In dealing with situations of this nature, a sense of wisdom is demanded. Constitutionally the judicial system in parliamentary democracies is such that part of the same constitution which defends the victim protects the criminal. Sensibly, therefore, violence must be arrested *before* it is delivered upon the public. Legitimate grievances must be heard under protection of law. Personal probity is of the greatest importance (thus if we encourage an immoral climate in which to live, we can hardly expect criminals to be persuaded by rhetoric claiming that it is more desirable for people not to be criminals). Further, it is unrealistic to suppose that government by giving money can solve basic human issues in society. Government should not be saddled with problems dealing with personal hates and envies, often the seeds of terrorism. Constraint in criminal activities is more a matter of teaching societal values and standards and observing citizen respect than a matter of fiscal handouts for doubtful programs on human rights. Serious educational development and good biopsychosocial health are potentially more powerful than temporary giveaway programs without any underlying serious ongoing fulfillment.

In the matter of dealing with terrorism, in the views of this panel, step-by-step progress was preferred. Essentially the matter must be dealt with by both (1) short-term and (2) long-term programs.

So-called quick solutions, outside of cataclysmic events such as an atom bomb, are seldom effective. Short-term control of terrorism should be by repression. Long-term control will result from remodeling societies under improved biopsychosocial educational and health strategies, and by improved communicative and explicit understanding of transcultural civic and social values.

SUMMARY OF MAJOR IDEAS

1. Terrorism is a form of communication.
2. Terrorism is difficult to define. Likewise, it is difficult to define what a terrorist is and who is a terrorist. Such identification often depends upon the perspective of the individual (i.e., Day's observation that "one man's terrorist is another man's freedom fighter").
3. Terrorists are currently most often young, male, educated, and upper class.
4. Schools and parents have a great influence on whether values are instilled in a child so that he can discriminate between acceptable and unacceptable means of protest.
5. The elimination of authority figures and moral institutions contributes to the development of a climate in which terrorism can thrive.
6. Rogue nations (those that practice or support terrorism) should be isolated by the international community.
7. Terrorism requires an audience in order to be effective. Judicious use of media is necessary so as not to encourage terrorism.
8. The short-term strategy to fight terrorism is the repression of terrorists. The long-term solution is the establishment of effective means for people with grievances to air their complaints and demands, as well as effective programs to eliminate social and political problems

that breed terrorism. These ends can be attained by prudent understanding and comprehensive planning within the fields of biopsychosocial health.

References

Day, Stacey B.: *The Military Intellectual.* In *Health Communications.* Foundation, New York, 1979.

Day, S. B.: Culture and concept: the military intellectual. *Foundation One* (The International Foundation for Biosocial Development and Human Health 2(1):3-5 (1980).

Himsworth, Sir Harold. On the Integration of expert knowledge into the machinery of government. *British Medical Journal* 281: 1197-1199 (1980).

Hoveyda, F. The problem of international terrorism at the United Nations. *Terrorism: An International Journal* 1(1): 71-83 (1977).

Appendix of Conference Fellows
Colonel James Pepile, representing Major General Vito J. Castellano Chief of Staff to the Governor, State of New York, Division of Military and Naval Affairs.

Captain John Rondon, Salvation Army; Corps Officer in Bronx Citadel, Salvation Army.

Harold Dettelbach, Ph.D., M.D., Director of Professional Affairs and Government Liaison, Hoechst-Roussel, Inc., Sommerville, N.J.

Professor Otto Pollak, Professor of Sociology, University of Pennsylvania, Philadelphia, Pa.

David A. Schulte., Former Commissioner of Corrections and National Correspondent on Prevention of Crime and Treatment of Offenders, New York, N.Y.

Roger Sciarretta, Chairman of the Green Meadow Waldorf High School, Spring Valley, N.Y.

Ann Stahl, Chairperson of Nursery Kindergarten, Green Meadow Waldorf School, Spring Valley, N.Y.

Bradford Riley, Humanist and Poet, New York.

Cecil Blake, Ph.D., Assistant Professor of Communications, Department of Arts and Sciences, Howard University, Washington, D.C.

Benilda Armstead Jones, President of Camelia Contraction Corporation, Westchester, N.Y.

Marc Kusinitz, Ph.D., Assistant Editor, *Science World*, Scholastic Magazine, Inc., New York, N.Y.

Carl Belack, Advanced Technology Systems, Fairlawn, N.J.

The Community and Stress

Barbara Greenblatt, M.S.W., C.S.W.
Supervisor of Special Services
Department of Social Services
Rockland County, New York

Major social conditions such as inflation, underemployment and unemployment, divorce, and aging are sources of stress generating a condition of tension within an individual. A situation may or may not be stressful, depending on characteristics of the individual, the meaning of the event, and one's ability to manage the increased pressure.

Lazarus suggests using stress as a generic term to include the stimuli producing stress reactions, the reactions themselves, and the various intervening processes. The field of stress refers to the physiological, sociological, and psychological phenomena, and their respective concepts. *Stress* then becomes a collective term for an area of study in which environmental demands, internal demands, or both tax or exceed the adaptive resources of an individual, social system, or tissue system.[1] It is at this point that many individuals and families come to community agencies, seeking counseling or therapy to alleviate the stress from psychosocial problems and the disequilibrium experienced.

Historically, the family has been the central institution of society. Once extended to include at least three generations usually working and living together, we now find the smaller family units increasingly vulnerable and poorly structured to survive the stresses of life. Family isolation and the lack of lateral supports have led to the need for increased support from social institutions. Evidence has been presented which indicates that families whose economic well-being is marginal are more vulnerable to crisis. Koos eloquently portrays the marginality of living in such families:

> They need all of their energies and every cent they can earn in order to meet the day-by-day demands, and they know that their environment will make endless demands upon them whichever way they turn.[2]

This monograph offers an overview of the diversity of events precipitating increased stress in the community, targeting those situations that come to the attention of the social agency with considerable frequency and the services available to help an individual cope with stress.

Data on the problems and the nature of services required by children and families who receive public child welfare services list the following "most important reasons" in order of highest frequency: neglect, abuse, financial need, emotional problems of children, parent-child conflict, abandonment, and parental unwillingness to care for the child. It should be pointed out that the children in the national study were by no means all from severely disadvantaged families. Only two of five came from families supported by public assistance payments.[3]

SINGLE PARENT FAMILIES

Perhaps the most dramatic statistic is the unprecedented increase in the number of female-headed households with children. Of all American families, 13% are headed by single, separated, divorced, or widowed women. Female-headed families now represent the single largest subgroup of the population that lives below the poverty level. More than half of these families depend on welfare payments as a source of income. These women are faced with the demands of raising children alone, which causes physical as well as emotional exhaustion and, for some, the stress of "single again" identities.[4]

More than two-thirds of the parents of the six million children who lived with one parent in 1974 were reported to be separated or divorced. Divorce is experienced as painful and disruptive by all participants as they are rendered vulnerable by the stress of the divorce process.

If all of the parental responsibilities rest on the single parent, the "sole executive" risks psychobiosocial overload, a term that refers to the stress resulting from trying to meet excessive psychological, physical, and social demands. Sole executives must usually earn a living for their families. Some are unable or unwilling to do so and receive public assistance. Generally, public assistance affords an inadequate standard of living, however, and this inevitably brings considerable stress to families. The employed sole executive must deal with the challenge of both job and family responsibility. Failure to meet conflicting responsibilities can generate a great deal of stress within the family. The impossibility of one parent successfully performing the roles of two inevitably leads to stress. The single parent faces problems involving diminished financial resources, unemployment, child care arrangements, and social isolation.[5]

Support systems in the community include postdivorce parenting programs to help stem hostilities between divorced or separated parents, daycare centers, guidance centers providing career counseling, mental health clinics, social work agencies, and self-help groups focusing on issues such as child rearing, dating, sex, remarriage, financial management, legal rights, career planning and job opportunities, and feelings of abandonment, loss, and anger.

DOMESTIC VIOLENCE

Domestic violence cuts across economic, ethnic, educational, and social divisions. The victim seen may be anywhere from 16 to 60 years old. The victims of domestic violence cannot be stereotyped or categorized. Emergency refuge, treatment, and care are needed by victims of domestic violence to cope with the immediate physical and emotional consequences of abuse. Because physical violence is often an expression of anger and frustration, social services and financial assistance must be integrated to most appropriately and comprehensively address the conditions which may precipitate violence. These conditions may be related to employment, housing, child care, lack of respite or recreation, individual or cultural acceptance of violent behavior as a normal family mode of interaction, or individual psychological disability.

Women who have been physically abused by their husbands generally need a wide variety of services ranging from police protection and legal assistance to emergency shelter, counseling, and financial aid. Encouraged by federal legislation, preventive and rehabilitative services provided by various public and private agencies include: advocacy for employment and housing, alcohol and drug abuse treatment, homemaker service, day care, special education training programs for parents and children, and organized social activities.

CHILD ABUSE

Parents who physically abuse their children come from all socioeconomic levels. Referrals for assistance with these stressful situations come from a broad community base including relatives, separated parents against their spouses, police, probation officers, neighbors, doctors, and other hospital staff.

Families in which a child has been abused or neglected require particular kinds of support and help if the goal of preservation of the family is to be attained. People from several disciplines become involved in the care of these families. Child protective service workers, functioning within departments of child welfare, are a primary source of help. Public health nurses, pediatricians, and psychiatrists play important roles.

The child protective caseworker, through a diagnostic evaluation of the family, can determine whether or not it is safe for the child to remain at home. If the treatment selected is intensive casework counseling, the worker can provide help and supervision to assure the child's safety. If removal is necessary, the worker is able to initiate court action to achieve this.

Homemaker service and parent aides teach parents to manage their household and child-rearing tasks. Parents Anonymous, a nationwide self-help organization, offers immediate relief to parents who feel they are abusing or neglecting their children. Their goal is to establish, strengthen, and maintain a healthy emotional and physical coexistence between themselves and their children.

TEENAGE PREGNANCY

The problem of teenage pregnancy is currently of growing interest and concern in the United States because of the enormous and potentially devastating problems encountered by many adolescent parents and their families. There are major health, educational, employment, and social implications attached to teenage pregnancy and parenthood. Young teenage mothers and their babies face significantly higher health risks than women who are physically mature. The teenage mother is less likely to complete her high school education and more likely to experience unstable marriage; child abuse and neglect are more prevalent for younger parents. The long-term effects on the child raised in this environment are bound to have repercussions on the community. Lack of education reduces the potential employment opportunities of the adolescent and, in turn, may create dependency on public assistance.

The pregnant teenager or young parent usually comes to the social agency seeking relief from financial stress and requesting housing and health care. Services provided include pre- and postnatal care, family planning services, and a variety of counseling services related to pregnancy, parenthood, education, and employment.

THE HANDICAPPED CHILD

The financial pressure caused by providing care at home to a mentally or physically handicapped child is a major stress for many families. Since eligibility for financial assistance for medical expenses is linked to income, a special burden is placed on middle income families. The everyday stresses imposed by the presence of a handicapped child in the home are evident in the difficulties in obtaining babysitters and household help, and in the inability to partake of vacations and other recreational activities.

Respite services for short-term care and increase in access to public education for even the most severely handicapped children alleviate some of the stresses. Alternatively, the admission of a handicapped child to a health facility or a group home is a time of crisis for parents who may feel confused and defeated as well as relieved.

DEINSTITUTIONALIZATION

For more than 100 years, the most severely and chronically disabled mental patients in the United States were incarcerated in large institutions for part or all of the remainder of their lives. An increase in psychiatric outpatient and general hospital facilities, the use of drugs to control psychotic symptoms, new legislation designed to protect the civil rights of mental patients by limiting involuntary confinement, and the concept that community care was not only better but also cheaper than hospital care—all have contributed to the move toward deinstitutionalization.[6]

The families of psychiatric patients feel the impact of mental illness when they assume the function of care giver to the returning family member. They experience physical and emotional stress caused by the pressures of meeting the needs of the chronic patient who has returned to the community. Family members feel pain, bitterness, shame, antagonism, and a sense of being trapped. The behavior of the chronically mentally ill is often destructive to the family unit. There are feelings of familial abandonment and guilt if the individual is placed in a group home. In many parts of the country, the results have been that many of the patients discharged live in single room occupancy hotels or inadequately supervised boarding homes. Programs to help the mentally disabled cope effectively with their environment have been instituted in many areas. Caseworkers who provide advocacy and service coordination, community support centers offering day treatment, mental health clinics, rehabilitation workshops, and psychosocial clubs have greatly aided readjustment. However, lack of job opportunities, inadequate financial aid, and inappropriate housing are barriers to the success of community-based care and could be a contributing factor to the rate of recidivism.

CULTURAL ASSIMILATION

One of the problems faced by people migrating to a different society, assuming new identities, and adjusting to new forms of social interactions is to assimilate into a new culture. The experience of migration tends to weaken the family bonds that created a supporting network on which the family could always rely. To a growing extent, the family finds itself alone.

The Puerto Rican culture, for example, relies most strongly on the support of the extended family. Those who migrate are torn from these associations, and it is this disrupted family which is faced with the overwhelming task of easing the acculturation difficulties. The key to the stability of the family system is the virtue that Puerto Ricans call *respeto*. The husband provides support and authority because he has *respeto*; the wife is faithful and properly submissive, and the child obedient and dutiful, because they have *respeto*. When this fails, family stress and possibly disorganization are on the way.[7] An inability to provide for one's family, and cultural conflicts relating to the roles assumed by modern women, contribute to this disorganization.

Puerto Ricans will often only make use of social agencies or mental health services as a last resort. An impersonal institution is demeaning and alien to their culture. If no other source is able to resolve the difficulty, the Puerto Rican will seek the social worker's help so that an authority can be used to effect change.

Similar problems exist with other emigrants. When there is increased stress, the natural support systems, like the family, tend to break down. Additionally, since there is no unity among the different minority groups and no link to the larger community, these groups feel more isolated, alienated, and powerless. When the individual does not feel part of a larger group, his or her need to be protected is not fulfilled. For groups such as Hispanics and Haitians, language is another major factor in maintaining a separateness and is a barrier to the use of services.

The result is that frequently these uprooted families have difficulty coping with the stress of cultural assimilation. Attempts are made, in many communities, to extend services to these diverse groups with the provision of care by practitioners who come from similar backgrounds and can sensitize other service providers to the needs of these groups.

AGING

The aged poor, society's most vulnerable and disadvantaged group, have less than the average income, have more severe health needs, and because they frequently live apart from their families, have grave difficulties in coping with isolation and physical handicaps. Financial insecurity leads to anxiety over housing needs and medical care. The severity of these issues is increased by the elderly's lessened ability to cope with and withstand stress.

Guilt and recrimination may afflict family members who are unable or unwilling to provide care for an aged or disabled parent or relative.

Losses in every aspect of late life compel the elderly to expend enormous amounts of physical and emotional energy in grieving and resolving grief, adapting to the change that results from loss, and recovering from the stresses inherent in these processes. The elderly are confronted by multiple losses which occur simultaneously: death of a marital partner, older friends, colleagues, relatives; decline of physical health and coming to personal terms with death; loss of status, prestige, and participation in society; and, for large numbers of the older population, additional burdens of marginal living standards.[8]

An intense crisis may develop around the problem of retirement and the loss of identity as a productive worker. Some lonely retired elders turn to community agencies, seeking someone who will care for them in a way that will reestablish their past and substitute for a lost object relationship or occupation.

Community-based services for the elderly include: home care which may be nursing care, homemaker services, rehabilitation services, senior nutrition programs providing a hot well-balanced noon meal, Foster Grandparent programs, recreational activities such as senior citizen clubs and senior centers, volunteer programs such as the Retired Senior Volunteer Program whose members work at many community facilities, and legal services.

While the vast majority of older Americans are either capable of adequate self-care or have relatives or friends who can care for them, a minority are in need of protective services. Protective Services for Adults is a system of care designed to maintain individuals in the community as long as possible and prevent institutionalization. Local departments of social services are mandated to provide protective services to all individuals over the age of 18 without regard to income.

Referrals for protective services come from all segments of the community including offices for the aging, housing authorities, health providers, and social agencies.

Preventive services include: information and referral, physical and mental health clinics, income maintenance, housing assistance, recreational counseling, homemaker services, visiting nurses, home-delivered meals, legal assistance, money management, friendly visiting, hospital care, day care and foster home care, and in some instances guardianship.

It is evident from the array of services that can be found in many communities that there is an intensive effort being made to provide the resources needed to alleviate the stresses that exist in the community.

However, there are many people with unmet needs who, without special help, are unable to make use of services because they are unaware of, or afraid to ask for, assistance. Often families use available services primarily to meet emergencies. This pattern of use of services works against permanent solutions.

Most communities have service directories and information and referral services to connect the individual in need with the appropriate service in the community that may satisfy that need.

References

1. Lazarus, R. S., *Psychological Stress and the Coping Process*. New York: McGraw-Hill, 1966.
2. Koos, E. L. *Families in Trouble*. New York: Kings Crown Press, 1946.
3. Shyne, A. W. and Schroeder, A. G. *National Study of Social Services to Children and their Families*. Washington, D.C.: U. S. Department of Health, Education and Welfare, Publication No. (OHDS) 78-30150, 1978.
4. Wattenberg, E. and Reinhardt, H. Female-headed families: trends and implications, *Social Work* **24**: 460-467 (1979).
5. Mendes,H. A. Single-parent families: a typology of life-styles. *Social Work* **24**: 193- 200 (1979).
6. Committee on Psychiatry and the Community. *The Chronic Mental Patient in the Community*. New York: Group for the Advancement of Psychiatry, Mental Health Materials Center, 1978.
7. Fitzpatrick, J. P. *Puerto Rican Americans,* Englewood Cliffs, N.J.: Prentice-Hall, 1971.
8. Butler, R. N. and Lewis, M. *Aging and Mental Health*. St. Louis: C. V. Mosby, 1977.

Survey of Long-stay Patients in a State Mental Hospital—Description of Patient Population*

A. O. Odejide, M.D.
Thomas A. Ban, M.D.
J. David Schaffer, M.D.
Department of Psychiatry
University College Hospital
Ibadan, Nigeria

Department of Psychiatry
Vanderbilt University and Tennessee Neuropsychiatric Institute
Clinical Research Service
Nashville, Tennessee

Introduction

In their analysis of annual changes in the resident population of New York State mental hospitals, Brill and Patton [4,6] revealed that it had reached an all-time high of 93,600 in 1955 as a result of continuation of a long-term trend that had doubled the number of mental hospital patients since 1929. This upward trend was abruptly reversed in 1955 and replaced by a drop in resident population which continued with an increasing tendency for at least three years. The decrease in resident population gained significance from the fact that it was coincidental with the introduction of neuroleptic drugs.[2]

Comparing the hospital population of March 31, 1955 with that of March 31, 1958 (i.e., after three years of pharmacological treatment), Brill and Patton found an overall reduction of 2123 patients.[5] Nevertheless, further analysis revealed that in spite of the introduction of neuroleptic drugs, the number of patients hospitalized for ten years or longer had actually grown and the number of patients hospitalized over a five- to nine-year period had remained unchanged. On the other hand, the one- to five-year group had diminished by 27%. The reduction in patients hospitalized for

*Support for this project was provided, in part, by a grant from the Tennessee Department of Mental Health and Mental Retardation.

less than one year, however, was less than 8%. Similar findings were reported by Kelly and Sargant.[11]

The finding that the greatest reduction in psychiatric hospital population occurred in patients hospitalized longer than one, but less than five, years indicates that the most significant action of neuroleptics lies not in the increased speed of therapy but in the prevention of chronicity.

Whether the decrease in hospital stay in the psychopharmacological era is the tail end of a historical trend or a drug-dependent phenomenon has not been answered to date. [1,8,10,14,15] The fact, however, remains that even with optimal therapy a certain percentage of patients will still remain refractory and/or must stay in hospitals because of various factors including inadequate rehabilitational facilities in the community.

The purpose of our study was to identify the characteristics of a subpopulation with a possible rehabilitational potential, among these long-stay psychiatric patients. Social factors were not taken into consideration; assessments were restricted to psychopathological symptoms, pharmacological treatment, and abnormal involuntary movements.

Method and Procedure

The site of our study was the Middle Tennessee Mental Health Institute (MTMHI), formerly Central State Hospital, an accredited psychiatric facility with 867 patients providing services for a population of approximately 1.2 million people in the middle Tennessee area (1979 estimate).

On the basis of the severity of psychopathological symptoms and impairment in social functioning, long-term patients in the hospital are subdivided into four groups (levels) and assigned to corresponding programs. Levels I and II consist of severely ill psychotic patients with virtually no or only minimal hope for discharge, while levels III and IV consist of patients with increasing rehabilitational potential. The population of our study consisted of patients from levels III and IV in the hospital.

All patients from levels III and IV were interviewed and subjected to a neurological examination. In addition, the case records of patients were studied for the purpose of extracting relevant information. On the basis of all these data, the Diagnoses and Prescription Practices Schedule (DPP), the Psychopathological Symptoms Profile (PSP), and the Abnormal Involuntary Movement Scale (AIMS) were completed.

Results

Ninety-seven patients (Table 1), ranging in age from 20 to 62 years, with a mean age of 39.6 and a median age of 38.5 years, were included in the

TABLE 1. Sex, Age, Number of Previous Admissions, Duration of Present Hospitalization (in Months), Initial Diagnosis and Present Diagnosis (DSM-II) of the 97 Patients Included in the Study.

		MALES						FEMALES			
				Diagnosis						Diagnosis	
No.	Age (years)	No. of Admissions	Duration (months)	Initial	Present	No.	Age (years)	No. of Admissions	Duration (months)	Initial	Present
1	50	1	17	293.2	293.2	51	61	9	19	291.5	291.5
2	22	1	13	295.0	295.0	52	28	0	48	293.2	293.2
3	38	2	108	310.0	295.0	53	31	2	12	293.2	293.2
4	44	2	156	295.1	295.1	54	40	5	9	295.9	295.1
5	26	5	5	295.0	295.3	55	36	3	5	295.3	295.3
6	30	15	25	295.3	295.3	56	52	4	24	295.3	295.3
7	61	8	18	295.3	295.3	57	45	3	132	295.3	295.3
8	46	2	9	295.3	295.3	58	21	2	25	295.3	295.3
9	46	1	48	295.3	295.3	59	34	1	8	295.3	295.3
10	54	3	36	295.3	295.3	60	58	8	13	295.3	295.3
11	45	2	14	295.3	295.3	61	50	1	40	295.3	295.3
12	22	4	7	295.3	295.3	62	52	3	24	295.9	295.3
13	26	1	2	295.3	295.3	63	49	4	48	296.34	295.3
14	21	3	8	295.3	295.3	64	28	2	5	295.4	295.4
15	40	8	3	295.3	295.3	65	54	2	36	295.74	295.74
16	37	8	37	295.3	295.3	66	56	3	72	295.3	295.9
17	34	2	96	295.9	295.3	67	22	1	30	295.3	295.9
18	25	3	20	295.9	295.3	68	40	2	180	295.3	295.9
19	30	1	27	300.4	295.3	69	31	7	17	295.9	295.9
20	27	0	18	295.2	295.9	70	37	3	30	295.9	295.9
21	33	4	84	295.3	295.9	71	34	2	48	295.9	295.9
22	24	2	1	295.4	295.9	72	38	5	18	295.9	295.9
23	26	1	42	295.74	295.9	73	48	1	312	295.9	295.9
24	55	12	18	295.9	295.9	74	24	2	9	295.9	295.9
25	59	2	18	295.9	295.9	75	53	0	372	295.9	295.9

26	28	1	12	295.9	295.9
27	38	5	60	295.9	295.9
28	58	1	17	295.9	295.9
29	58	3	30	295.9	295.9
30	25	2	39	295.9	295.9
31	30	3	4	295.9	295.9
32	36	7	63	295.9	295.9
33	40	1	14	295.9	295.9
34	57	5	5	295.9	295.9
35	36	0	42	295.9	295.9
36	56	1	288	295.9	295.9
37	53	4	144	295.9	295.9
38	35	0	27	295.9	295.9
39	34	13	38	309.2	295.9
40	58	2	72	295.9	296.1
41	21	2	33	295.99	300.0
42	38	4	12	301.82	301.82
43	42	1	17	295.74	309.3
44	58	0	420	295.9	309.3
45	56	1	24	312.0	309.9
46	26	1	30	310.9	310.9
47	55	1	300	311.9	310.9
48	20	1	26	311.9	311.9
49	44	6	120	311.9	311.9
50	25	1	16	295.3	312.6

76	46	7	168	295.9	295.9
77	52	14	4	295.9	295.9
78	48	4	156	295.9	295.9
79	33	2	60	295.9	295.9
80	59	2	90	295.9	295.9
81	42	6	15	295.9	295.9
82	39	4	24	295.9	295.9
83	49	4	132	295.9	295.9
84	62	9	16	296.1	295.9
85	20	1	53	298.0	295.9
86	35	6	72	301.82	295.9
87	21	2	28	309.4	295.9
88	28	3	12	295.9	296.1
89	47	4	12	296.1	296.1
90	38	5	11	296.33	296.33
91	46	8	25	296.33	296.33
92	57	2	60	298.0	298.0
93	31	2	108	310.4	310.4
94	30	6	6	298.0	310.9
95	24	0	36	312.9	312.1
96	41	2	204	312.9	312.9
97	23	0	31	315.0	315.0

DSM-II DIAGNOSES

291.5 Alcoholic deterioration
293.2 Psychosis with epilepsy
295.0 Schizophrenia, simple type
295.1 Schizophrenia, hebephrenic type

(continued)

TABLE 1. (Continued

295.2	Schizophrenia, catatonic type
295.3	Schizophrenia, paranoid type
295.4	Acute schizophrenic episode
295.74	Schizophrenia, schizo-affective type, depressed
295.9	Schizophrenia, chronic undifferentiated type
295.99	Schizophrenia, other (and unspecified) types
296.1	Manic-depressive illness, manic type
296.33	Manic-depressive illness, circular type, manic
296.34	Manic-depressive illness, circular type, depressed
298.0	Psychotic depressive reaction
300.0	Anxiety neurosis
300.4	Depressive neurosis
301.82	Inadequate personality
309.2	Nonpsychotic organic brain syndrome with brain trauma
309.3	Nonpsychotic organic brain syndrome with circulatory disturbance
309.4	Nonpsychotic organic brain syndrome with epilepsy
309.9	Nonpsychotic organic brain syndrome with other (and unspecified) physical condition
310.0	Borderline mental retardation following infection or intoxication
310.4	Borderline mental retardation associated with diseases and conditions due to (unknown) prenatal influence
310.9	Borderline mental retardation with other (and unspecified) condition
311.9	Mild mental retardation with other (and unspecified) condition
312.0	Moderate mental retardation following infection or intoxication
312.1	Moderate mental retardation following trauma or physical agent
312.6	Moderate mental retardation associated with prematurity
312.9	Moderate mental retardation with other (and unspecified) condition
315.0	Unspecified mental retardation following infection or intoxication

study. Fifty patients (i.e., 51.5% of the total population) were males, with a mean age of 38.9 and a median age of 37.3 years; 47 patients (48.4% of the total population) were females, with a mean age of 40.2 and a median age of 39.5 years.

The number of previous hospitalizations for the 97 patients ranged from 0 to 15, with a mean of 3.3 and a median of 2.7. In fact, 70.4% of the total population had more than one previous hospitalization and 35.7% had been hospitalized more than four times. It was noted that the number of previous admissions tended to increase with increasing age. This tendency was statistically significant ($\chi^2 p < .01$).

The duration of present hospitalization in the 97 patients ranged from one month to 35 years with a mean of 57.1 and a median of 26.9 months. More than half (54.6%) of the patients had been in the hospital for more than two years, and almost one-fifth (18.5%) of the population had been in the hospital for seven years or more.

The 97 patients were classified at the time of admission to the study into 25 different diagnostic categories. Nevertheless, 73 patients (i.e., 75%) were diagnosed as schizophrenic (43 patients chronic undifferentiated, 24 patients paranoid, and 6 patients of other subtypes). None of the other diagnostic categories included more than four patients. When current hospital diagnosis was compared with the 22 different diagnoses given at the time of the first hospitalization, it was noted that in 68 cases (i.e., 70.1% of the patients) the hospital diagnosis remained the same, while in 29 cases (29.9% of the patients), the hospital diagnosis had changed. As a result of this, at the time of admission to the study, there was a decrease in the number of patients in 13 diagnostic categories (295.2, 295.4, 295.74, 295.99, 296.34, 298.0, 300.4, 301.82, 309.2, 309.4, 310.0, 312.0, and 312.9) and an increase in the number of patients in ten diagnostic categories (295.1, 295.3, 295.9, 296.1, 300.0, 309.3, 309.9, 310.9, 312.1, and 312.6); eight diagnoses present upon initial hospitalization were no longer encountered (295.2, 295.99, 296.34, 300.4, 309.2, 309.4, 310.0, and 312.0), while five diagnoses encountered were not present at the time of initial hospitalization (300.0, 309.3, 309.9, 312.1, and 312.6).

Discussion

Our findings that 75% of a subpopulation of long-stay psychiatric patients consists of schizophrenic patients correspond with the reported results from other surveys in chronic hospitalized populations.[3,7,9,13] The somewhat lower mean (39.6 years) and median (38.5 years) ages of the population than those encountered in most of the other studies may be explained by the separation of adult and aged (over 65 years of age) populations in the hospital, and the exclusion thereby of psychogeriatric patients from the sample. Another possible reason for the relatively young age of our patients is the site of the survey. Levels III and IV consist of patients with rehabilitational potential. If the survey had been carried out with the more severely ill patients of levels I and II, the average age probably would have been higher.

The significant correlation between age and number of admissions in our sample is probably related to the chronic course of psychiatric disorders encountered in the study population and to the improved prognosis of readmitted patients, recognized by Odegard [12] in the 1960s. He followed three separate groups of patients (1936–1939, 1945–1948, and 1955–1958) over a four-year period, and found that while there was no marked increase in discharge rate for the first admissions from 1936–1939 to 1945–1948, the changes of being discharged for readmitted patients decreased from the first to the second period. On the other hand, from 1945–1948 to 1955–1958, the discharge rates continued to rise, but in the 1955–1958 group, readmissions had the same chances for discharges as had first admissions.

In spite of their relatively young age and frequent hospitalization (37.7% hospitalized more than four times), 54.6% of the patients had been in the hospital two years or longer and 18%, seven years or longer. These findings are in line with those of Brill and Patton that chronic patients tend to accumulate over time in hospitals despite the overall decrease in hospitalized psychiatric populations after the introduction of antipsychotic-neuroleptic drugs.[5] While undoubtedly schizophrenic patients respond most favorably to neuroleptics, the facts remain that neuroleptics do not cure schizophrenia and not all schizophrenics respond in a similar manner to neuroleptic drugs.

Summary

Demographic characteristics of 97 long-stay adult patients with rehabilitational potential at a state psychiatric hospital have been described. The population was found to be predominantly (75%) schizophrenic. The mean duration of hospitalization was 57 months (median: 27 months), and the average number of previous admissions was 3.3.

References

1. Achte, K. A. The course of schizophrenic and schizophreniform psychoses. *Acta Psychiat. Neurol. Scand. Supp.* **155** (1961).

2. Ban, T. A. *Schizophrenia: A Psychopharmacological Approach* Springfield: Charles C. Thomas, 1972.
3. Berry, C. and Orwin, A. "No fixed abode." A survey of mental hospital admissions. *Brit. J. Psychiat.* 112: 1019-1025 (1966).
4. Brill, H. and Patton, R. E. Analysis of 1955-56 population fall in New York State mental hospitals in first year of large-scale use of tranquilizing drugs. *Amer. J. Psychiatry* 114: 509-517 (1957).
5. Brill, H. and Patton, R. E. Analysis of population reduction in New York State mental hospitals during the first four years of large-scale therapy with psychotropic drugs. *Amer. J. Psychiatry* 116: 495-509 (1959).
6. Brill, H. and Patton, R. E. Clinical-statistical analysis of population changes in New York State mental hospitals since introduction of psychotropic drugs. *Amer. J. Psychiatry* 119: 20-35 (1962).
7. Cooper, A. B. and Early, D. F. Evolution in the mental hospital: review of the hospital population. *Brit. Med. J.* I: 1600-1603 (1961).
8. Freyhan, F. A. Course and outcome of schizophrenia. *Amer. J. Psychiatry* 112: 161-169 (1955).
9. Gore, C. P. and Jones, K. Survey of a long-stay mental hospital population. *Lancet* II: 544-546 (1961).
10. Hobbs, C. E., Wanklin, J., and Ladd, K. B. Changing patterns of mental hospital discharges and readmissions in the past two decades. *Canad. Med. Ass. J.* 93: 17-20 (1965).
11. Kelly, D. H. W. and Sargant, W. Present treatment of schizophrenics. A controlled follow-up study. *Brit. Med. J.* I: 147-150 (1965).
12. Odegard, O. The pattern of discharge and readmissions in Norwegian mental hospitals, 1936-1963. *Amer. J. Psychiatry* 125: 333-340 (1968).
13. Rollin, H. R. Social and legal repercussions of the Mental Health Act, 1959. *Brit. Med. J.* I: 786-788 (1963).
14. Shepherd, M. *A Study of the Major Psychoses in an English Country*. London: Maudsley Monograph, 1957.
15. Stern, E. S. A statistical study of departures from a mental hospital. *Brit. J. Psychiat.* 116: 57-64 (1970).

Survey of Use of Psychotropic Drugs in Developing Countries

F. E. Vartanian, M.D.*
A. O. Odejide, M.D.*
W. H. Wilson, M.D.
T. A. Ban, M.D.

*Central Institute for Advanced Medical Studies
Moscow, U.S.S.R.*

*Department of Psychiatry
University College Hospital
Ibadan, Nigeria*

*Department of Psychiatry
Vanderbilt University
Nashville, Tennessee*

Introduction

During the past 20 years, pharmacotherapy with psychoactive drugs has been increasingly recognized as the most effective treatment and has become the most widely used therapeutic technique in the management of the majority of psychiatric disorders. Psychoactive drugs have rendered psychiatric treatment accessible for large patient populations even in countries with great limitations of available professional personnel. In spite of this, there is little comparative information available on the patterns of psychotropic drug use in different geographic areas. The purpose of this pilot study is to fill in, at least in part, this gap and to identify similarities and differences in psychotropic drug use in developing countries.

Methodology

A questionnaire was designed to collect information on the use of psychotropic and anticonvulsant drugs in the treatment of the following

*At the time of preparation of this paper Dr. Vartanian was Senior Medical Officer in the Division of Mental Health, World Health Organization, Geneva, Switzerland, and Dr. Odejide was a World Health Organization Fellow at the Clinical Research Service of the Tennessee Neuropsychiatric Institute, Nashville, Tennessee.

syndromes: hallucinatory-delusional, depressive, manic, and convulsive. Respondents were asked to list the three most frequently used drugs for each of the four conditions in order of preference. Treatment of the acute and chronic conditions was dealt with separately. Respondents were also asked to list the most frequently encountered adverse effects of psychotropic drugs.

Results

Of the 29 questionnaires sent out, 25 were completed and returned. Of these, 11 came from Africa, 9 from Asia, and 5 from Latin America (Table 1).

Presented in Table 2 are the total number of drugs listed by all respondents, the number of drugs listed from each geographic area, and the number of drugs listed in all three geographic areas. In spite of the large number of drugs listed, there are only a few drugs which are listed in all three geographic areas (an average of about 4 out of 13). However, the drugs listed in common are primarily those selected as first and second choice with third choice comprising most of the nonoverlapping drugs.

According to Table 2, chlorpromazine is the most frequently listed drug for the treatment of both acute and chronic hallucinatory-delusional conditions. Nevertheless, while haloperidol is listed about as frequently as chlorpromazine for the treatment of acute hallucinatory-delusional conditions, it is only listed half as freqently as thioridazine (the third most frequently listed drug in chronic conditions) for the treatment of chronic hallucinatory-delusional psychopathologies. On the other hand, trifluoperazine is listed about equally often for the treatment of both acute and chronic conditions.

For the treatment of both acute and chronic depressive conditions, amitriptyline and imipramine are listed with approximately the same frequency (in acute conditions, amitriptyline is listed more frequently than im-

TABLE 1. Number of Questionnairees Returned from Various Countries.

Africa		Latin America		Asia	
Egypt	1	Brazil	2	Japan	1
Ghana	3	Costa Rica	1	India	3
Kenya	1	Panama	1	Indonesia	1
Nigeria	4	Venezuela	1	Iraq	1
Senegal	1	TOTAL	5	Malaysia	2
Zambia	1			Pakistan	1
TOTAL	11			TOTAL	9

TABLE 2. Total Number of Drugs Listed, Number Listed from Each Geographic Area, and Drugs Listed in All Three Geographic Areas.

HALLUCINATORY-DELUSIONAL	ACUTE	CHRONIC
Total listed	11	16
Africa	7	8
Latin America	5	9
Asia	8	10
In common	4	5
DEPRESSIVE		
Total listed	16	17
Africa	7	12
Latin America	5	8
Asia	8	9
In common	3	4
MANIC		
Total listed	11	9
Africa	7	7
Latin America	5	6
Asia	8	6
In common	3	4
CONVULSIVE		
Total listed	12	11
Africa	8	6
Latin America	5	6
Asia	7	7
In common	3	5

ipramine, while the reverse is true for chronic conditions); trimipramine is the third most frequently listed drug. Nortriptyline is listed in all three geographic areas but with a lower frequency than trimipramine.

For the treatment of acute and chronic manic conditions, chlorpromazine and haloperidol are listed with equal frequency. In the treatment of acute manic conditions, thioridazine is the third most frequently listed drug; however, in the treatment of chronic conditions, lithium is the third most frequently listed.

For the treatment of both acute and chronic convulsive disorders, phenobarbital, diphenylhydantoin, and primidone are the first, second, and third most frequently listed drugs, respectively.

In Table 3 the frequency of listing the first, second, and third choices of drugs for the treatment of different acute and chronic psychopathological syndromes is given while Table 4 shows the order of preference in the use of the same drugs. Average rank was calculated by summing the number of

TABLE 3. Three Most Frequently Listed Drugs under Each Psychopathological Condition Regardless of Order of Preference.

	ACUTE		CHRONIC	
	Medication	Listed	Medication	Listed
Hallucinatory-Delusional	1. Chlorpromazine	21	Chlorpromazine	18
	2. Haloperidol	20	Trifluoperazine	16
	3. Trifluoperazine	18	Thioridazine	11
Depressive	1. Amitriptyline	22	Imipramine	21
	2. Imipramine	21	Amitriptyline	18
	3. Trimipramine *	7	Trimipramine	6
Manic	1. Chlorpromzaine	21	Haloperidol	21
	2. Haloperidol	20	Chlorpromazine	20
	3. Thioridazine	9	Lithium	13
Convulsive	1. Phenobarbital	22	Phenobarbital	22
	2. Diphenylhydantoin	16	Diphenylhydantoin	20
	3. Primidone	10	Primidone	14

* Not listed in Asia for acute treatment.

first, second, and third choices for each drug and dividing by the total number of respondents. The rank order of preference, with three exceptions, corresponds with the frequency of listings. The three exceptions are acute halluncinatory-delusional conditions where haloperidol is ranked first, although listed as second; chronic depressive conditions where the frequency of listing and rank order of imipramine and amitriptyline are reversed; and chronic manic conditions where lithium ranks as first and haloperidol as third.

Finally, the most frequently occurring side effects are listed in Table 5. As shown in this table, the most frequently listed adverse effects are extrapyramidal reactions reported by 96% of the respondents, followed by postural hypotension and dizziness reported by 40%, other autonomic effects, and akathisia (a specific extrapyramidal sign) reported by 24%. All remaining side effects are reported by 12% or fewer respondents. The various side effects are listed with approximately the same frequency in the three geographical areas.

Discussion

Corresponding with our results are the findings if Itil, Reisberg, and Simeon[1] based on a survey including 1059 respondents from 53 countries, that chlorpromazine is the medication most frequently cited for the treat-

TABLE 4. Average Assigned Rank for Three Most Frequently Listed Drugs as Presented in Table 3.

	ACUTE		CHRONIC	
	Medication	Average Rank	Medication	Average Rank
Hallucinatory-Delusional	1. Haloperidol	1.79	Chlorpromazine	1.67
	2. Chlorpromazine	1.85	Trifluoperazine	1.83
	3. Trifluoperazine	1.87	Thioridazine	2.60
Depressive	1. Amitriptyline	1.42	Amitriptyline	1.38
	2. Imipramine	1.74	Imipramine	1.58
	3. Trimipramine *	3.00	Trimipramine	2.80
Manic	1. Chlorpromazine	1.44	Lithium	1.36
	2. Haloperidol	1.82	Chlorpromazine	1.56
	3. Thioridazine	2.22	Haloperidol	2.26
Convulsive	1. Phenobarbital	1.74	Phenobarbital	1.45
	2. Diphenylhydantoin	1.84	Diphenylhydantoin	1.83
	3. Primidone	2.50	Primidone	2.50

* Not listed in Asia for acute treatment.

174

TABLE 5. Listed Side Effects.

	Africa 1	Latin America 2	Asia 3	Total
1. Extrapyramidal/Parkinson	9	5	10	24
2. Postural hypotension	5	3	4	12
3. Dizziness	1	3	6	10
4. Akathisia	2	2	3	7
5. Dry mouth	3	1	3	7
6. Blurring of vision	3	1	1	5
7. Excess salivation	1	2	2	5
8. Difficulty in initiating micturition	1	1	3	5
9. Amenorrhea	2	0	1	3
10. Photosensitivity	0	1	2	3
11. Constipation	0	0	3	3
12. Excess weight gain	1	0	1	2
13. Skin rash	0	1	1	2
14. Liver toxicity	0	1	1	2
15. Gum hypertrophy	1	0	1	2
16. Protrusion of the tongue	1	0	0	1
17. Blood dyscrasia	1	0	0	1

1. No. of respondents that did not answer the question = 1 (No. 1 Africa).
2. No. of respondents that tabulated side effects into (a) neuroleptics, (b) antidepressants, (c) anticonvulsants = 6 (Africa, 2; Latin America, 1; Asia, 3).

ment of schizophrenia, and amitriptyline together with imipramine for depression. In the treatment of mania, chlorpromazine was chosen by almost one-third of the respondents, while lithium was chosen by only one-fifth. Since the report of Itil, Reisberg, and Simeon[1] is based primarily on data from developed countries, one may suggest that prescription practices are not essentially different in the development and the developed world.

Conclusion

In a survey of psychotropic drugs used in 16 countries, it was found that most frequently listed and assumedly used drugs in acute hallucinatory-delusional syndromes were chlorpromazine, haloperidol, and trifluoperazine; in chronic hallucinatory-delusional syndromes, chlorpromazine, trifluoperazine, and thioridazine; in acute depression, amitriptyline, imipramine, and trimipramine; in chronic depression, imipramine, amitriptyline, and trimipramine; in acute mania, chlorpromazine, haloperidol, and thioridazine; in chronic mania, haloperidol, chlorpromazine, and lithium; and in acute and chronic convulsive disorders, phenobarbital, diphenyl-

hydantoin, and primidone. No essential differences in drug preference between Africa, Asia, and Latin America were found.

The most frequently listed side effects were extrapyramidal reactions,
postural hypotension, dizziness, and other autonomic effects. Similarly to
drug preferences, no essential differences between the frequency of listings
of side effects were found across the three continents.

If one takes into consideration the results of a recent report based
primarily on data collected from Western countries, there seems to be sufficient evidence to indicate that psychotropic drug usage is similar in the
developing and the developed world.

References

1. Itil, T. M., Reisberg, B., and Simeon, S. Use of psychotropics in the world. *International
   Pharmacopsychiatry* **13**: 39-49 (1978).

Scientific Evaluation of Oriental Approaches to Psychosomatic Relationships from the Viewpoint of Cybernetics

Hitoshi Ishikawa, M.D.
Chairman, Department of Psychosomatic Medicine
Tokyo University Branch Hospital
Tokyo, Japan

In the early days of psychosomatic medicine, its main theories and treatment modalities were those of hypnosis, psychoanalysis, and classical conditioning. Over the years however, these highly directive treatment
modalities have been changing in the direction of more patient-oriented,
nondirective approaches. For example, hypnosis has in many cases been
replaced by autogenic training; psychoanalysis seems to be steadily losing
ground to transactional analysis; and operant conditioning seems to be now
favored over classical conditioning by many of the world's physicians.

These changes reflect a common tendency for a shift from responsibility and control of the patient by the therapist, to responsibility and control of the patient by the patient himself. So, historically, we can say that the treatment of psychosomatic medicine is shifting from outer control to self-control.

With this shifting of control from therapist to patient, the need has arisen for a theory to account for changes within each individual patient. That is, we needed to find the principle of self-control within each individual. We found the cybernetics theory of Wiener and the general system theory of Bertalanffy to fit this purpose.

The theory of cybernetics is based on the principle of information theory and control theory, and it is the common theory of all the feedback systems. The general system theory includes the cybernetics theory, and it is also the common theory of other systems such as sociology, chemistry, physics, and mathematics.

From these two theories, we extracted four principles to be used in psychosomatic theory. We call this new theory *cybernation therapy*. It is composed of (1) the black box principle, (2) the feedback principle, (3) the open and closed system principle, and (4) the information and energy principle. The first principle of cybernation therapy is *the black box principle*. As we cannot analyze the mind and body relationship of humans from the standpoint of anatomy, we must analyze it from the input and output relationship of the human mind-body system, which in this case is considered to be the black box. With the black box principle, we diagnose the patient by the polygraphic method. That is, the output of the patient is recorded as GSR, plethysmogram, EEG, EMG, heartbeat, respiration, and blood pressure, while various stresses are given to the patient as the input. From the relation between input and output, we can diagnose the cybernetical property of the patient.

The second principle of cybernation therapy is *the feedback principle*. Feedback denotes the feeding back of output signals of the system as input to that system. Then as error or discrepancy is detected, the output can be corrected. By this feedback mechanism, the function of the organism can be automatically stabilized. The organism has two feedback systems. One is the external feedback system, which includes the extremities and sensory organs, and is termed the servomechanism. The other—the internal feedback system—includes the digestive, circulatory, and respiratory systems, and is called homeostasis. The external system is controlled by the voluntary nervous system, and the internal system is controlled by the autonomic nervous system.

The third principle is *the open and closed system principle*. A living organism is usually an open system, which means that it is capable of receiving information and energy from, and returning it to, the outer world. In contrast, mechanical systems are closed systems, which means they cannot exchange information and energy with the outer world. Bertalanffy stated that the equilibrium state of the open system is dynamic and the equilibrium state of the closed system is static.

The fourth principle is *the information and energy principle.* In this case, information means mental activity, while energy means physical activity. So the information and energy relationship is taken to be the relationship between mental and physical activity. In the information and energy relationship, we can recognize two kinds of relationships. The information system can control the energy system, or the information system can discharge the energy system.

In the external feedback system, the information system is the voluntary nervous system, while the energy system is the muscular and skeletal system. In the internal feedback system, the information system consists of the autonomic nervous system and the endocrine system, while the energy system consists of the cardiovascular, digestive, and respiratory systems.

At present, we are attempting to apply these four principles in the daily practice of psychosomatic medicine. From the diagnosis standpoint, it is impossible to diagnose psychosomatic disease in the standard patho-anatomical way. It is suggested that diagnosis should proceed from an analysis of the input (stress) and the output (reaction of the patient) relationship, i.e., the black box principle.

In cybernation therapy, the most important point in diagnosis is to give the patient an awareness of his bodily, mental, and psychosomatic relationships, i.e., the feedback principle.

Also, social factors such as job, family, and school situations must be considered, i.e., the open and closed system principle.

As for the information and energy principle, the information corresponds to mental activity and energy corresponds to physical activity. Thus the diagnosis of psychosomatic disease must include the analysis of the relationship between mental activity and physical energy.

In individual cybernation therapy, we are utilizing techniques such as GSR monitoring of autogenic training, biofeedback training, gestalt therapy, and in some cases TA script analysis. In autogenic training, we observe the mental states of patients by monitoring their GSR which corresponds to the input and output relationship, i.e., the black box principle. During autogenic training, which in some cases is monitored by biofeedback equipment, a control of the relationship between bodily and mental states can be achieved, in which case the feedback principle is in operation.

In some cases during the course of autogenic training, a discharging of physical, mental, and psychosomatic symptoms might occur. In such cases, we utilize TA, gestalt, and other methods to help the patient and encourage him to be open to the therapist and his environment (i.e., the open and closed system principle). At other times, in some cases, we adopt the use of TA script analysis and elicit behavior modifications. In other words, we attempt to set up a new information (mental) and energy (physical/bodily) relation according to the information and energy principle.

In group cybernation therapy, techniques include meditation, TA, gestalt, sensitivity training, music therapy, and bioenergetics. The members of group cybernation therapy must be anonymous (i.e., the black box principle). In this way, we do not feel it necessary to analyze patient participants in regard to their family environment or past history; focus is on the here and now.

In group therapy, awareness of the relationship between bodily, mental, and psychosomatic disorders is important, as is the case in individual therapy. Only the techniques are different. In both cases however we are using the feedback principle. Also, in group cybernation therapy, all participants are allowed to share and exchange their feelings concerning aggression, anxiety, fear, sorrow, etc., which corresponds to the open and closed system principle.

Finally, by use of group therapy, we can also employ the analysis of a participant's script and use behavior modification (i.e., the information and energy principle).

The author believes that cybernation therapy can be the common principle of all psychotherapy and behavior modification, and it can also be the common principle of both oriental and occidental approaches in psychosomatic medicine. For example, in group cybernation therapy it is possible to combine sensitivity training, transactional analysis, and gestalt therapy (occidental approaches) with Yoga and other types of meditation (oriental approaches). In this way, the characteristics of both oriental and occidental cultures can be combined. There are some significant differences between oriental and occidental approaches. For example, oriental approaches are more black box or phenomenological, while occidental approaches are more white box or analytical in nature. With regard to the feedback principle, oriental approaches emphasize internal feedback, while the occidental approaches tend to emphasize external feedback. In regard to the open and closed system principle, oriental approaches are more closed and occidental approaches are more open. As far as the information and energy principle is concerned, oriental approaches are seen as being more controlling and occidental approaches are considered more discharge oriented.

Finally, the author concludes that cybernation therapy can be the common principle in psychosomatic medicine, as it is quite comprehensive in its inclusion of both the oriental and the occidental approaches.

Summary

We have adopted four principles from Wiener's cybernetics and Bertalanffy's general system theory which we feel are suitable for analyzing psychosomatic relationships, and have made them the major principles for cybernation therapy. They are: the black box principle, the feedback principle, the open and closed system principle, and the information and energy principle. The position that Yoga treatment, such as we have experimented with, occupies in the total system of psychosomatic treatment has been examined from the viewpoint of cybernetics.

III
LIFE STRESS AND
THE PERSON
(HUMANISM)

Technological Stress and the Humanist

Bradford Riley
Director of Speech Training
Three Fold Foundation
Spring Valley, New York

When a poet speaks of stress on certain syllables in poetic structures he is usually speaking of emphasis, meter or feet, in his line of poetry. The modern poet who clashes with this "new age" is under the stress of a new muse.

The poet works with syllables and sentences. The smallest element of poetic structure, like a brick or a cell, is a sound. The next, more complicated element is the syllable. After syllables, further complications emerge: words, sentences, and finally fully structured poems. The poet flows into verses, into stanzas, and when he masters these fundamental tools he may become a creative artist.

At this level he has mastered more than the bone structure or cellular static points of sound and word. He breathes in entire thoughts; connects himself to a flow of feelings; reflects the actions of warriors, thinkers, men, women, children, the old, the sea, the air, the water, and the earth. He can rise up to the starry heights and listen to the voices of the twinkling stars. He may look upon man in his totality, and he becomes for us the interpreter of the Universe.

It is at this high stage of development that the poet is able to merge himself with the heart and soul and lifeblood of a single human individuality. The poet may uncover for us the hidden secrets of a long-forgotten petty prince—Hamlet. He may be able to piece together the puzzle of the centuries, and shape into moods, words, and reality man's struggle with evil—he may create a Faust.

To allow a human individuality to walk out upon the stage of life—to allow us to share his most secret hidden moments, his depths, and his heights—is to achieve the highest aim of true poetic art. To allow man to live fully in an interval of time, in a composition of art, is the true measure of poetic artistic achievement. To fail at this task, to fall short of this goal, is to cramp man; to cut him short; to insult, deny, or corrupt him; to create stress in our society. We must locate the stress and strain of the problem of poetry in our modern culture and show how the Romantics, or Milton, or Shakespeare, indeed the poets of all ages, have never before been faced with such obstacles as those confronting the poet in the nineteenth and twentieth centuries.

The nature of our technocratic society has allowed us to enter into an antirhythmical, or *a*rhythmical, interaction with something entirely new. Mechanics, technics, industry—all are aspects and sources of this new problem. The automobile, the strobe light, the blinking yellow traffic light, the jackhammer, the train, all our sudden stops and starts; computers, mimeograph machines, typing machines, printing presses, the stray jet diverted into your airspace—all make up the combined undertone of the new rhythms that never before existed. These new rhythms make up our sonic-electronic culture.

These patterns and nonpatterned interruptions and general noise influence the poetics of our modern culture, influence the music and art of our present world, influence the very breathing and pulse of our lungs and heart. It is here that healthy and unhealthy creativity merge and surge as backwash into our culture, as nourishment to the soul, or as poison to its life. (Consideration of the soul is in keeping with our assumption that there is a space in the human being for such a consideration to be justified.) All art can be considered the incarnate reflection of the soul-life of the human being and, going further, the reflection of the human tensions and values of a given age.

The problem with the freedom of the artist is that no proper yardstick has been detected out of which a human "norm" has been determined. I propose to erect such a yardstick for poetics, using the pulse and breath ratio of the normal human being, and to trace this yardstick back to the Egyptian and Greek eras in which our Western culture had its birth and where, in the Greeks, artistic achievement in its fullness is reflected.

What is the average number of breaths taken by a human being in one minute? It is between 16 and 18 depending on the conditions of stress that may prevail. How many breaths do we take in a day? The answer to this question should be placed concretely before our eyes in an equation looking like this: $18 \times 60 \times 24 = 25,920$. What did this number mean to the ancient Greek? It meant that one day of a man's life on earth is equivalent to one year of the Sun's cycle through the Zodiac, following the procession of the vernal equinox. Man's breathing rhythm is concretely linked to the entire Zodiac. Man is more than a mere speck of dust placed by chance into the Universe—his breathing rhythm gives his secret away. Now we can understand why the Egyptian priests chanted this hymn to the Sun:

Homage to thee, O Ra, at thy tremendous rising!
Thou risest! Thou shinest! The heavens are rolled aside!
Thou art the King of Gods, thou art the All comprising,
From thee we come, in thee are deified.

What of the human pulse? What is its relationship to the breath of the human being? There is a cooperative working of heart and lung. Otherwise the human being would have long since vanished from the earth. What is the number of pulse beats the average human being carries within him in one minute? Depending on factors of stress, the normal human being has 72 pulse beats to the minute. This makes a ratio of 72:18 which, simplified, is a ratio of 4:1. What does this ideal relationship mean for poetics?

In the Greek art of poetry the hexameter was the standard, or yardstick, of the culture. The poet of that time, to earn any merit whatsoever, had to learn to turn phrases and meter into hexameter. Although it appears that hexameter does not have to do with our previously established ratio of 4:1, you will see how it is related when we understand its construction.

The hexameter is constructed to look like this: -uu-uu-uu/-uu-uu-uu/. The significant factor in the construction of the hexameter is the human breathing and pulse ratio. The full reality in the line of the hexameter is this: long short short, long short short, long short short; breath; long short short, long short short, long short short; breath. The two breaths taken in the line are given the same time value as two dactyls; that is, one breath is equal to one (long short short). This gave the Greeks the experience of breath and pulse working together in their most ideal relationship. The two breaths within the line make up the full ratio of 4:1.

The Greek educator knew that the relationship of 4:1 was the healthy yardstick for anchoring his pupils into the magnificent order of the Universe. He pointed to the Moon's rapidly changing face, and in beautiful artistic refrains drew his pupil's attention to the rapid pulse and to how the Moon makes the feelings ebb and flow like the tides of the sea. The Moon's changing nutation brought man fullness or emptiness, but in the steady change of her countenance he heard the steady pounding pulse like the waves beating against the shore. In Shelly's version of the Greek hymn to Selene, we hear just a fragment of the powerful beauty and richness with which the Greek teacher imbued his understanding, and his pupils' understanding, of the relationship the human being has to the Moon. It corresponds to the steady movement of the blood flowing like a tide, living in the liquid sea. Even the mystery of woman's periodic menstruation found an intimate and artistic expression, but most important was the actual "scientific" factor of the ratio of 4:1 as the reality of Moon and Sun and Man:

> When the Moon divine from heaven is gone
> Under the sea, her beams within abide,
> Till, bathing her bright limbs in Ocean's tide,
> Clothing her form in garments glittering far. . . .
> Hail Queen, great Moon, white-armed Divinity,
> Fair-haired and favorable! thus with thee
> My song beginning, by its sweet music. . . .

The hexameter in its fullness lived in such poets as Empedocles, who gives us this fragment of his lost work:

> Only from saintly lips permit the flow of the fountain,
> Thou most honored muse, thou white limbed maiden O' grant me
> That which befits the ears of men in their fleeting lifespan,
> Send from the regions of faith the supple chariot song.

Or again the hexameter expressed in its epic grandeur:

> Straightway the Father of Gods stretched forth the glittering balance
> Laid in the Golden bowls two death-lots of fatal darkness
> The one for Pelios scion, the other for mighty Hector
> And grasped the center and weighed, then downward Hector's destiny
> Heavily foundered to Hades, and Phoebus Apollo forsook him. . . .

Longfellow tried to carry into reality the power of the hexameter, but perhaps the time had passed for it to be the voice and basis for representing man's harmony with himself and with the cosmos:

> Still stands the forest primeval; but under the shade of its branches
> Dwells another race, with other customs and language.
> Only along the shore of the mournful and misty Atlantic
> Linger a few Acadian peasants . . .
> While from its rocky caverns the deep-voiced, neighboring ocean
> Speaks, and in accents disconsolate answers the wail of the forest.

The technological world of the twentieth century imposes itself, or superimposes itself, over our environment, distorting and altering our previous, perhaps primitive, relationship to the Universe. Yet the pulse and breathing relationship of the human being still remains a yardstick for health. If the person suffering from asthma relates that hallucinations are evoked when the rhythm of his lungs is altered, if another feels he is afraid to breathe deeply in this polluted environment and is always threatened by asphyxiation—we know that our sensitivity to breathe is still active and has not changed, even while mankind has moved on in the advancement of the intellect. A hypertension can cause a sudden seizure of the lungs and make a person hyperventilate, altering in its wake his whole orientation to space and making health a question of relativity to breathing. Indeed, this 4:1 relationship of pulse and breath is so crucial that even slight alterations determine the mental and physical stability of a person. Man is suffering from his own theory of relativity—his healthy relation to his environment and to the cosmos depends on the relative adjustment of his rhythms. This is the basis of poetry.

The intellectual twentieth-century man is lost to the sensitivity of his connection to the Universe. His intellect shoots spasms of hyperaction into his lungs and causes them to alter their proper and healthy action. We have become disconnected from our intimate knowledge of well-being and have become people who are unable to breathe deeply; we have become shallow. We have become a shallow society and intellectually sanguine lovers of technics, and technics is unable to provide for the needs of human beings because human beings have given birth to technics out of their intellects. These same intellects have loosened themselves, in the head only, from the proper balance of human measure and mean.

If the hexameter gave us a minute-to-minute relationship, which could establish and unconsciously remain the basis of our physical and psychic health, then what does modern culture offer in its stead? The provision for a healthy pause to breathe deeply is built into the structure of the hexameter line. This interval is so totally abused that we have no rest built into our radio and television culture. The 60-minute TV program gives us perhaps 18 minutes of commercial breaks.* Perhaps the secret principle of the Greeks lies hidden and transformed here. What happens during the 18 minutes of commercial breaks of a 60-minute program doesn't allow us rest, or inhaling, or breathing, or interval, or pause; no, we must follow the crude and unrelated designs of the sponsors of the program.

---

*The FCC has recently lifted the previously established limit of 18 commercial breaks per hour to allow *unlimited* halts and interruptions into a regularly established 60 minute program.

All space is used up and all time is filled. Empty, silent spaces are filled as quickly as possible with potential-economic-profit pressure. This constant barrage of profit pressuring forces us into stress. The 60-minute program, like our breathing, is forced into the constant pressure of usage, utility, or need.

What good is sleep if it is mere pausing and emptiness? Why not take a pill to avoid that natural organic rhythm of sleep? We are like people who expect to take one breath when they are born and race through life before they have a chance to exhale. One could even say that death is a pause from life, and our fear of death may be just as misguided as our fear of sleep. Why must radio, television, and all other areas of life become like huge, overstuffed supermarkets, where products, no matter what they are, are all intellectually lined up and stacked to infinity?

The poet must bring out certain words or phrases in brighter light, and others in less; you might say he uses his artistic sense to create rhyme and reason, to create some order in the world. Yet he must live and act and write in circumstances of the twentieth century that do not allow for the most natural highlights and contrasts of life to appear. Everything is equally lit and placed and shelved. There is no good or bad, or right or wrong, except when the store manager for some unknown reason puts one item on sale and another not. The problem is that we are all subject to the pressure of space, time, economy; and art is not in the least a major concern. In fact, most things that are important to providing healthy works of art for humanity are crushed under the heels of utility. No art, or bad art, no breathing, or bad breathing, causes *stress*.

Think of the crowded city with its streets placed mathematically exactly the same width apart, each block the same size, squared and endless and closed in. There is no space for the individual to sense a unique form of architecture that appeals to his own uniqueness. Everything is squared and blocked and must, like the men and women who people it, remain uniform and set, with no identity.

Sculpture, architecture, painting, and poetry all begin to shout back their sense of poverty, isolation, terror, hopelessness, and confusion, while slowly but surely the computer and technics have so insinuated themselves into the human zone of life and health that we begin to assume ourselves less perfect, less ordered, less wonderful, than the gadgets we have created. Yet the gadgets take no breath, eat no food, speak no words but those that apply to practical, efficient use of our space and time; they make sure that any consideration of man as a being greater than time and space—because he rests, sleeps, dies, eats, and brings to life in his breathing and speaking worlds beyond time and space—is quietly and quickly distorted or made into a commercial industry the minute the intellect detects the possibility for profit. We create our own pressure. We block out our own lives and create values in dollars and cents that are not possibly to be achieved by mere satisfaction with spatial, temporal things.

It is right that the poet of today seeks his own way; that he doesn't rely upon the efforts of an ancient world. That ancient world relied upon the Muse of the poet's higher being. Today, anything man claims as his own besides his physical body is looked upon as fantasy. The poet of today is forced to create science-fiction myths in order to integrate the technology of the present with his innate yearning for a world free from this boxed-in state. But whatever the changing view of man is, we can isolate two diametrically opposed pivotal points that determine the present state of poetics; and until this conflict is won we must all live under the *stress* of artless art.

The past saw man as integrated into a Universe of Gods, planets, and Deities, himself sharing and helping higher and lower powers. The poet was no poet who did not write out of this expanded consciousness. A consciousness inspired and opened at one end by something greater than himself. Homer rarely began any new topic without the invocation, "Sing O' Muse," which did not mean he gave himself grand airs for being the most popular poet. He called upon a being who lived in the interval of his breath and pulse, and who could enter and inspire his words with truth, beauty, and goodness. This higher being, this Muse, knew the virtues of earth and the virtues of heaven. He knew the laws of the planets and the music of the spheres. He saw the human being before his birth and after his death as an eternal spirit.

In the present we have a totally different Muse. It is a power indeed. It must have fuel of some sort to function, be it electricity, gas, oil, or smashed atoms. It must have its roots in the earth. The printing press needs fuel to function on. The tape recorder and television and radio—all advanced forms of printing—need earth's power. The computer offers the finest service to this new form of art. With it we can compose music, write poetry, synthesize records, and integrate sounds never heard before. It offers itself to our service, with a long extension cord, to become our Muse for the earth.

The ultimate question of *stress* rests on whether or not we as mankind can handle these earthly forces. This great Muse. With the old Muse man had to handle inspiration from above; with this new Muse he must now reckon with inspiration from below. Now, nothing could be said against this new Muse, if it always had our best interests at heart. But we have invented this new Muse and given it a kind of psyche of its own. It comes from tiny minds that have never seen the planets and the stars and the sun, which we men are a part of, as anything but empty, void, and dumb space, filled with various distorted rocks. It sees no soul and knows no spirit, and its human values are rather cruel since it is not yet human and since we have not yet instructed it in what is human. This new Muse of the earth is power hungry for the earth. The *stress* factors of our age are bound up with pressing needs of technology and our inability to define the infinite heights and breadths of that term *mankind*.

When we turn off a machine, it is clinically dead. It is at rest again until we turn it on. If a man is at rest, be it between birth and death, waking and sleeping, or inhaling and exhaling, he is only clinically dead when his heart beat and breath have stopped. There is a difference between a dead pause for rest and a living pause for rest, and that difference is a matter of life and death. The machine is always clinically dead, but in the tiniest pause of a human being, new thoughts, new feelings, new ideals, new goals, can awaken. In the silence of the mind is infinite time and space. Wordsworth put it simply:

> I wandered lonely as a cloud
> that floats on high o'er vales and hills
> when all at once I saw a crowd,
> A host, of golden daffodils;
> For oft, when on my couch I lie
> In vacant or in pensive mood,
> They flash upon that inward eye
> Which is the bliss of solitude;
> And then my heart with pleasure fills,
> And dances with the daffodils.

Machines might give us more time to have vacant or pensive moods, but it appears that a "consumer" society seeks not to elaborate its inner potentials by drawing closer to a higher Muse. That higher Muse lives in each individuality and, through the breath, in what we see and hear more deeply. He works into our breathing and pulse, and loves the harmony and rhythms of the healthy human being. We are a society that has become afraid of inner rest, and technology has made us frantic. We seek Eastern religions for harmony of soul, instead of investigating and examining in full understanding our present state of crisis. We cannot turn back. We must find man's balance and his relation to the Universe of today by protecting and creating space for that which longs to awaken in humanity.

With crisis in environment and technology and psychology hammering at our door, I would expect to find a doctor grappling with these huge questions of health. Professor Stacey Day rises above and beyond the call of duty, as a poet and humanist.* He makes the simple comparison of the present with the past in these few verses:

Wordsworth! who doth see your crowd,
your host of golden daffodils
beside the lake, beneath the trees,
fluttering and dancing in the breeze?

Here where would you would wander
lonely as a cloud
where far flung highways
crowd your vale and hill?

Now are golden daffodils
closed in glass conservatory cages
where choral music pipes adjuvant notes
for men who will never comprehend
a symphony of yellow trumpets
silent in the festive free of lake and tree.

And who will wander as your cloud
that floats on high o'er vale and hill
and who will seek to find your crowd,
your host, your golden daffodils?

The poet must reckon with syllables and stress and meter. He had a Muse once that showed him bright worlds and deep depths of a world that has known miracles. The poet of today is in earth's shadow land. We may disconnect ourselves so utterly from the divine Muse we once knew that we begin to worship and adore the neon gods that Simon and Garfunkle spoke of. We may let the power and ambition of our technology grind our humanity into dust, simply because we could not bear to hear the sacred sounds of silence. If this comes to pass, then Shakespeare's prophesy will be all too true:

To-morrow, and to-morrow, and to-morrow
Creeps in this petty pace from day to day,
To the last syllable of recorded time:
And all our yesterdays have lighted fools

*Poems and Etudes by Stacey B. Day (CEP Publications), Montréal, Canada, 1968.

The way to dusty death. Out, out brief candle!
Life's but a walking shadow, a poor player
That struts and frets his hour upon the stage
And then is heard no more: it is a tale
Told by an idiot, full of sound and fury,
Signifying nothing.

Let us live in the hope that with the terrorism and suicide that mount each year, we are not creating a society of Macbeths. He was a man under stress. May we seek inspiration of a different order than the councillors he chose for his destruction.

The Art of Eurythmy and Rhythm

Alice Stamm
School of Eurythmy
Spring Valley, New York

After having given a lecture on the Gospel of St. John, the Austrian thinker and educator Rudolf Steiner asked a young artist if she could dance to what he had brought, especially that which was inspired from the mighty beginning of that Gospel—"In the beginning was the Word." This was in 1910 and soon after, indeed, the mother of a young girl interested in the art of movement asked Steiner if new impulses could flow into this art out of his life's work of Anthroposophy. He indicated that in language one could find a new and vital source for the art of movement. Gradually he developed the various movements of Eurythmy and since then, this young art has spread throughout Europe and is beginning to become known on this continent as well.

Eurythmy as an art embodies all the gestures inherent in language or music. Steiner was able to perceive these gestures as they arose when one spoke or sang. The delicate movements which the larynx and organs of speech or singing create when we utter sounds flow into the breath and air. These movements reveal an objective, lawful world of forms which remain true to their individual character but allow an unlimited possibility of expression. In the training, the Eurythmist learns to recreate these movements with the whole body. We can experience how language can communicate the loftiest ideals, the most intimate feelings, the fieriest impulses. We also can experience what lives *between* the words, the phrases, the unspoken words. The Eurythmist strives to express through the bodily instrument, and especially the arms, that inherent life and formativeness in language and music.

Eurythmy is done either as solo or group work to recited poetry or to music. Just as the poet uses the elements of language to create imaginations, moods, calling our attention to some detail overlooked, the Eurythmist attempts to create pictures through the gestures of language. Speech becomes visible as well as audible.

To illustrate this, let us take a word and try to build up a feeling for the movement of the sounds which can then shed light on the content embodied by the word. The word *mood* is made up of one vowel and two plosive consonants. The vowel *oo* when spoken awakens in us a sense of mystery, foreboding, even longing. It might be described as light trying to penetrate through darkness. The *m* brings a different experience. As a consonant, it tastes, touches, melts into the world around it, understanding this world but leaving it quite free. It overcomes boundaries, and establishes an inner harmony or middle with something. It appears in such words as moist, mother, musing, mold, and movement. The sound *d* also carries resistance in the speech, but here something quite different is present. This sound, with its "thudiness," defines—comes to rest at something definite. In the German language, the *d* sound appears in words used to point out, to specify, or to place. In English, the *d* has softened to *th* in such words as this, that, those. The *d* as gesture brings something to rest, affirmation, placement. A stillness and a solidity accompany it as qualities. The word *mood* then, evokes a total movement of feeling-into-something-mysterious-and-bringing-this-to-quietness. The sounds and gestures remain basically the same, but the artist must be able to create a myriad of moods with these basic gestures.

The Eurythmic gestures carry not only the formative power of the language but also all that lives in the soul and spirit of man. Lyric, dramatic, and epic poetry is expressed. The movements are conscious, never arbitrary; it is just this lawfulness which calls forth the greatest artistic freedom of expression.

The artistic Eurythmy is the source of the pedagogical and curative Eurythmy as well. The movement can be as precise and rhythmical as gymnastics but must always carry the elements of truth and beauty, ensoulment, and goodness. The gestures have a moral effect on those who perform them, awakening qualities in the little child which build up his creative nature. He awakens to the space around him, the gestures and moods in nature, and begins to breathe with them. He relates to this world in an artistic way, planting into his being the deeper rhythms of life.

In curative work with doctors, Eurythmy can be a great help in the treatment of illnesses related to the rhythmic system of the human being. It is here that we approach the problem of stress.

Stress refers to many things: in the world of rhythm, it indicates those syllables which are emphasized over those which are not. One speaks of long or short syllables. Here though, one can learn to experience the delicate tension between the stressed and unstressed syllables, and one can learn that the degree of stress immediately affects the degree of unstress. For instance, one can feel that the rhythm short-long has a greater tension than short-short-long. The inner strength needed to carry one stressed syllable is much greater than that held in two short syllables flowing into the long:

"Wĕ cóme, wĕ cóme, ănd yĕ féel oŭr míght"—how different is the "and ye féel" than the energetic "wĕ cóme, wĕ cóme." Something is awakened in the artistic self which creates a dynamic balance between the stressed and unstressed syllable, or words.

In Greek culture, Homer's genius flowed through the whole epical imagination carried by the dactyl. The words of the poem often free themselves from the rhythm, but the mighty hexameter carries the drama on the breath. Here not only does the individual rhythm create a dramatic tension, but the composition itself reveals a rhythmical interplay. Three dactylics flow into space followed by a pause; then again three dactylics answer. The imagination flows out through the longs; the shorts awaken the inner self to the pictures thus carried:

"Auθpú μοι εννεπε, Moῦρα,-πολυτροπον, ὅs μαλα πολλα."

The rhythms reveal then a threefoldness: a long or stressed part carrying a more imaginative or cosmic quality; a shorter or unstressed part which awakens the inner life to that which is stressed; and then a third and perhaps most important element, the tension or breath or space between the other two parts. According to the nature or relation between the longs and shorts, the space or tension in between takes on a variety of forms, of qualities. This is the vital nature of rhythm, not the stressed or unstressed but that which lives and is constantly in motion, in the space in between.

If we take rhythm more specifically related to the human being, we can begin to consider the whole process of breathing as such. Perhaps one can call human breathing something of an archetypal rhythm—exhaling, inhaling, systole, diastole, in-breathing, out-breathing. We rightfully are not conscious of this quiet daily breathing or of the moment in which we have breathed out and begun to breathe in. To go from the physical level to that of the soul, one speaks about outgoing persons or inward, comtemplative persons. Or we notice that our fellow's gaze is radiant and sparkling, or inward and cut off. We live between these two mighty poles of rhythm: our birth was an in-breath, our death is an out-breath. The space in between becomes the biographical expression of varying forms of rhythm. If we observe our own life, we begin to sense when we have felt the need to draw into ourselves after having extended ourselves; or we long to have the vacation be over, to get back into the swing of things.

Stress in our civilization has been placed more and more on out-breathing and avoids in-breathing or finds it difficult to cope with the in-breath. The guidelines for out-breathing are more clearly defined than the more subtle ones for the cultivation of the inner life. One is accustomed to unfolding into the world of the senses, the body social, daily tasks which become routine but very necessary. Even more difficult is the swing of the pendulum toward an inner life of the soul. Here the relationships of feelings, thoughts, impulses are often rather confused, chaotic, unclear. The difficult thing is that one *must* breathe in. Perhaps one of the deepest longings of mankind today is to breathe in so that the out-breath carries renewing forces into life itself.

Like all art forms, Eurythmy concerns itself with rhythm. Language carries two qualities which express this: the vowels which belong more to the inner life, and the consonants which relate more to the world around man. One might also say, mood and form, principles of expressionism and impressionism. All which comes to man as impression—thoughts, sense impressions, events around him, gestures in nature, will impulses—carries an element of form. His innermost reaction to these, his own self-expression, reveals something quite unique in the world. This is the nature of man's being: that he takes the impressions into himself and can make them his own and bring them again into the world, transformed, as expressions of truth, beauty, and goodness. He must, however, be able to experience that moment between the impression and his own self-expression. He must be free even for a split second to relate the outer with the inner; otherwise, the stress becomes one or the other, and who man is as an ego-being becomes lost.

Eurythmy as an art of movement challenges the student to relate to the world of gestures in such a way that they become his own, that what he expresses is not routine or pattern but constantly enlivened by inner experience. The language itself carries the elements found in breathing. To learn to awaken to the delicate tensions between the in- and out-breaths requires a long study. Gradually the organ of perception for this space can unfold. It is not something which chance gives but, rather, which dedicated work begins to unfold. The quality of breathing, the artistic nature of rhythm, begins to form the basis of the art of Eurythmy. It is the artistic expression of the space between the stressed and the unstressed living in language or music, and it can carry into expression all that the soul of man in his relationship to the spirit and to the world around him strives to articulate in ever-greater degrees of understanding and insight. Eurythmy is one form through which man can relate again to rhythm. Not just his intellect or fantasy, but his whole organism, is called upon to be active in the art of movement.

Goethe was able to capture the quality of breathing in the following short poem. Our translation is very free. May it serve to awaken again the space which lives between the components of rhythm.

In atemholen sind zweierlei Gnaden:
Die Luft einziehen, sich ihre entladen.
Jenes bedrängt, dieses erfrischt—
So wunderbar ist das Leben gemischt.

Du, danke Gott wenn er dich presst,
Und Dank' ihn wenn er dich wieder entlässt!

In breathing lies a twofold blessing:
Draw in the air and release it again.
The first compresses, the second refreshes—
Thus marvelously is the mixture of Life.
Give thanks then to God when you He would press,
And thank Him again when relieved of the stress!

Stress and the State: Technocracy and the American Magna Carta

Stacey B. Day, M.D., Ph.D., D. Sc.
New York Medical College
Valhalla, New York

Whether one believes in technometaphysics or not, the post-industrial world has certainly inherited a cornucopia of paradoxical givens—machines, management, automated processes, nuclear potentials, numbers and monopoly, exponential abbreviations of time, ballistic missiles, man-artifact systems such as armies and factories, to say nothing of such socially extreme variables as inherent in people and use-generated values, concepts of freedoms, rights, responsibilities, accountabilities, and convivial tools.

If this listing be not enough, one might well add such further questions as, Who invented the modern *State*? For what purpose was it invented? Who might appropriately best lead it? From whence derive its powers? Are they real or imaginary, permanent or transitory, heritable, vulnerable, or simply unendurable?

Whether or not one feels compelled to answer these and other questions, the truth is that few live virtually untouched or experientially uninvolved with these situations. Such ends as give rise to actions in our times are marked by contemporary *transformations*—transitions which may involve the individual and the society, science and/or the misuse of science, the structure and the nature of the universe, in whole or in part, and forces internal or external to any and all societies. For most of us these factors in our lives cannot be gainsaid.

What is perhaps then of keener interest should be *how* societies in general, and ours in particular, conceive problem solving methodologies for handling the growing dependence of people on such systems. If one casts a backward look to our social past, there is truth in Harold Laski's assertion that there have been two epochs in modern history in which mankind had to meet overriding challenges that erupted before his eyes, so to speak. Each of those provoked fundamental breakdowns of social relationships and demanded redefinition of social constructs in life attitudes of Western societies.

Of considerable note was the *Reformation,* which destroyed for all time the concept of a single Christian commonwealth that existed until the Middle Ages. Of closer import, to which in fact we still are heirs, although separated by three centuries in time, are the transvaluations fostered by the economic turnabouts engendered by the French Revolution.

Now, in the rise of modern so-called *superpowers*, we see new but old forces challenging our ideas. Technocracies are here if you will, economic processes are in train of revision, principles of government are being reforged, political philosophies ebb and flow, and State and Individual have been in so much of a flux that less than a century has seen the human adventure absolve Whiggery, Socialist Trade Unionism, Conservatism, Communism, Fascism, Maoism, Technocratic Imperialism, Neofascism, and any brand of social ideal save perhaps that of religion!

The social burgeonings of this last transformation constitute, I suggest, conflicts not so much to be resolved by political philosophies as by strategies of a new order of *cultural imperatives*. If a new order is to come, if new wine gives appetite to old tastes, safeguard and prospect in our times might wisely be counseled by life attitudes of people themselves as much as by political expediency testing unknown notions. The thesis of this essay is not so much to take issue with political provisions or choices as to inquire whether, for technocracies at least, the social and psychological strengths inherent in the tradition of peoples may not serve still to accommodate and handle the apparent paradoxes of the new technocratic imperatives. For the English-speaking nations at least, this *spirit* resides in the provisions of the Magna Carta, and for America, uniquely, in the First Amendment to the Constitution.

The First Amendment, I submit, is a thing of spirit. Its strength, wisdom, and fortitude are capable, I believe, of guiding all of the cultural transitions provoked by our times.

SOCIAL RESPONSIBILITY

One might argue that the First Amendment to the Constitution is a thing of spirit. In this sense, no matter what the nature of the State it cannot invade the spirit of the people. Secular or religious, autocratic or democratic, or whether the State is conceived to be a technocracy, the essential human strength as well as the power of the State is recognized by and in the First Amendment to the Constitution. In our times, we might best view ourselves, in a not necessarily adverse situation, as living within technocracies, by which I mean that the human core of our societies is conditioned by regulation and order. This reality demands that the society, on a voluntary or other basis, surrender some portions of its powers for the benefit of the State as a whole. In achieving this, individuals conceivably will be relinquishing privileges that they might have viewed as *rights,* and equally importantly the distribution of this relinquishing may not be metrically equally based on a strategy of numbers alone.

The postindustrial society, the thrust of emerging technologies, and the concept of "spaceship earth" have made it more imperative to recognize that it is as much through some surrender of the power of the people as by constitutional changes that Man and Machine may more easily share a harmonious coexistence.

Few would dispute the ideal State in democracy, yet the fact surely is that few or any people have lived in a "true democracy" since the days of ancient Greece, and it is doubtful whether even then history presented a notion of democracy democratic enough to satisfy an ancient heathern, "that is one who dwelt outside the city walls, on the heather, a heather dweller," or present day political speculators seeking an alternative form of living in the idealism or world of Rasselas, Prince of Abyssinia! Such simply does not exist for our times, and Rasselas, were he with us, would find the world beyond his vale of contentment an enigma grappling with problems of sustainable growth, numbers and population policy, energy and fuel consumption woes, arguments Malthusian and otherwise on states of the art of food production, concepts of national and international security, environment and boundary limits, ecobiological psychophysiology, and for his *business news of the day* gold is up and out, and reverse *capitalism* is throttling the industrial nations who have the means of production, the factories, serviced by the arch-devils who have the essence *for* production (the raw materials)!

If such a world of scrambled growth and growth-related fields can be intelligibly analyzed, metrical (that is measurable) interpretations might more easily derive from *regulation and order* of any system that profits by harmonizing social systems, under variable degrees of tolerance, of Machines and Man.

How such concepts may integrate into philosophic traditions of freedom and justice for society is the heart of the question provoked by our times. Such tradition, certainly in so far as English-speaking Western societies are concerned, derives from the sealing on June 15, 1215 at Runnymede of the Magna Carta, which over the centuries has served as a basis for social growth within constitutional law. Originally providing recourse against arbitrary arrest and enforced taxation, abuse of prerogative and power, and failure to redress grievances against life, liberty, and property, or to afford protection against arbitrary spoliation, the concept of justice was achieved in the subscription that

No freeman's body shall be taken, nor imprisoned, nor disseised, nor outlawed, nor be banished, nor be damaged in any way, nor shall the King send him to prison by force, except by the judgement of his peers and by the law of the land.

Fullfillment of these concepts is a privilege of the First Amendment to the Constitution of the United States of America.

Congress shall make no law respecting an establishment of religion, or prohibiting the free exercise thereof; or abridging the freedom of speech, or of the press; or the right of the people peaceably to assemble, and to petition the Government for a redress of grievances.

We might well view this in a Republic as the "right of the people to petition the King" for justice. The most compelling feature of this amendment rests not so much on what is set forth in its wording as on its interpretation and intent. The command of this article is that the Republic will not invade the spirit of the people. Here lies the strength of the Constitution and the concept of justice, but here also lies the responsibility of the citizen. It should be a reciprocal truth of the Constitution that if the State will not invade the *spirit* of the Individual, the Individual shall in like spirit, if society and the state of the Republic so warrant, surrender in good faith such unwritten power prescribed on his behalf when the survival of the Constitution and of the society is imperiled, or at command. It is the *intent*, not the order, of this amendment that this reciprocal goodness be justly shared, and perhaps in this mutual sharing, the concept of justice is the guarantee of freedom within technocracies, which as Man-Machine states require identical order-regulation controls. However, the concept of justice freely consented to may permit separate identification of differing ideologic technocracies which commonly today may face us in any of several guises—democracy, totalitarian autocracy, technofascism, or quite simply as "states based on law and order."

To the degree to which we understand justice in terms of the surrender of power within the Constitution, social and civic harmony is likely to be achieved.

CULTURAL TRANSITIONS AND TECHNOLOGY

Julian Huxley, in his essay "Tennessee Revisited," says that we have often been told that overall planning is incompatible with democratic freedom and individual initiative, but he says that "it is precisely in the U.S.A. that planning has been most conspicuously and most successfully democratic.

The best examples are in the Tennessee Valley and in the North-west Region along the Columbia River." As Huxley rightly says, it was in these areas that decentralized planning permitted people to participate via popular action and opinion toward ideas of development for the public good.

Conscience changes too in a changing world, but cultural, social, and economic pressures invariably remain as constants, and technological societies really present only a different plain upon which may advance more time honored forces, which strictly speaking seek to resolve the same question, progressing to what may be a new direction. How does a society keep in step yet not lose change of step? How does a society disturb the process of governance while not disturbing the whole process? How does a society deal with political aspects using culture as a tool? These questions are answered in some measure by integrating for syntheses between change and non-change.

This philosophy is no stranger to American thinking. John Dewey, unquestionably a preeminent figure in the history of education in America, and certainly a foremost philosopher of the nation, was in his times as much perplexed by the sense of divisions and separations as are many today.

That were, I suppose borne in upon me as a consequence of a heritage of New England culture, divisions by way of isolation of self from the world, of soul from body, of Nature from God, brought a painful oppression—or rather, they were an inward laceration.

Initially Dewey turned to Hegel for *synthesis* of subject and object, matter and spirit, the divine and human:

Hegel's treatment of human culture, of institutions and the arts, involved the same dissolution of hard-and-fast dividing walls and had a special attraction for me.

Though ultimately moving on from Hegel, Dewey, like all major thinkers of the last century—Engels, Marx, Feuerbach—for "genuine materialism," and most Western scholars have found that they have been obliged to deal in a post-Hegelian world with Hegel's "concept of spirit"—true spirit, culture, and morality—and that these concepts are vital in contemporary present-day thinking. Increasingly, the world is unified although diverse in its unity. "We the people" of the American Constitution are not exactly the *familia* of the Roman state, in which *famulus* meant not so much "the family" in our sense but the total number of slaves belonging to one man,* a meaning not overlooked by Engels in his *The Origin of the Family, Private Property, and the State.*

The *spirit* comes out of the people, but as J. B. Priestly remarked, "The people are not the masses." To be sure, "political religion always preserves a spiritual factor," which conclusion of Santayana was certainly known to Marx, but the chief advantage for technocracies descended from democracies is that the *quality of spirit* is inherent in their attitudes toward life, the "courageous endurance and reasonable compromise" of that prince of physicians, Wilfred Trotter.

Spirit, in terms of communication, for Trotter implies:

> Free play of mind, liberty of opinion, honesty are not only morally good but also sources of every kind of strength.

If the nature of the State is based on the spiritual as well as the pragmatic nature of Man, then no matter the technological thrusts of our present cultural transitions, economics, systems, or efficiency, society, which is not all bad or all good, will prevail by reasonable compromise and justice in the interpretation of the First Amendment to the Constitution. One repeats, the First Amendment is a thing of spirit. The State may have been invented, but its spirit is implicit in the *being* of men.

* Gaius: Familia, id est partrimonium = family is the patrimony, the inheritance.

Stress and the Military

Major Mitchell M. Zais
Assistant Professor
Department of Behavioral Sciences and Leadership
United States Military Academy
West Point, New York

Colonel William J. Taylor, Jr.
Professor
Department of Social Sciences
United States Military Academy
West Point, New York

INTRODUCTION

The traditional Spartan ethic of the military implies demands which are "excessive" at the margin. The professional military ethic has long placed emphasis on mission accomplishment over individual welfare, austerity, physical and mental rigor, and the unlimited liability of the soldier, extending to the risk of life itself.

Because of the unique aspects of military life, the military was at the vanguard in research into stress-related issues. During World War II extensive investigations were conducted concerning the relationship between stressors of the battlefield and combat performance. This research centered around the issue of battle fatigue, its source, and methods to overcome this phenomenon which could have such debilitating effects on combat motivation and on the willingness and ability of the individual service member to fight. Interest in and research on this topic continues.

There are three general categories of stressors in the military: those that are job related, those which derive from the military life-style, and those which are combat specific.

COMBAT-SPECIFIC STRESSORS

The military has long recognized the importance of stress reactions to combat and their significant, deleterious impact on combat effectiveness. These

Draft manuscript not to be quoted or attributed without the express permission of the authors. The views and conclusions expressed in this paper are solely those of the authors and do not purport to represent the policy of any government agency of the United States.

stress reactions are varied, ranging from soldiers who are absent without leave (AWOL) to those who inflict wounds on themselves, or who experience psychiatric breakdown. The latter category has received special attention based on general recognition of its relationship to combat effectiveness. For example, in ten days of fighting in Okinawa the 6th U.S. Marine Division suffered 2662 wounded in action (WIA) and sustained an additional 1289 (48% of the WIA) psychiatric casualties (Markey, 1973). More recently, during the 1973 Arab-Israeli War, almost 900 (60%) of the first 1500 Israeli casualties suffered solely from psychic trauma (Forissier and Darmandieu, 1976). Variously termed "shell shock," "war neurosis," or "battle fatigue," the incapacitating effects of combat stress have long been known to military leaders and medical personnel. Although various strategies for treatment of stress-induced casualties have been utilized by the military (Ingram and Manning, 1980), prevention has been much more widely practiced.

Studies conducted during World War II revealed that the single most important mechanism for sustaining the individual soldier during the stresses of combat was the *primary group* (Marshall, 1947; Shils, 1950). In the presence of a small group of cohesive and supportive men, the individual combat soldier withstands danger and deprivation which, if experienced on his own, would prove overwhelming. Accordingly, the military has established and continues to develop organizational policies designed to enhance cohesiveness and the formation of primary groups. These policies include: (1) training, deployment, and replacement of intact combat units or teams, as opposed to training individuals who are subsequently assigned to extant units; (2) encouraging junior leaders to maintain an attitude of protectiveness toward their subordinates; and (3) insuring that members of combat units spend as much time together as possible in all phases of life, which includes billeting (housing) by unit, eating by unit and, in fact, performing every feasible aspect of daily life in the organization within the context of the individual's five- to ten-person unit (e.g., the tank crew or rifle squad). Additionally, parades and military drill have as a primary purpose the development of cohesiveness and a sense of shared responsiveness to commands from the immediate leader. Unit athletic and social activities, which play a prominent role in the military life-style, are designed, to a large degree, to foster the growth of cohesiveness within fighting groups.

Military training at the lowest combat level is highly repetitive. This is because military leaders have known for centuries what has recently been proven by extensive social-psychological research. That is, the performance of underlearned tasks or new skills is impaired by stress, while the performance of overlearned tasks and skills is enhanced by moderate stress (Zajonc, 1965). Thus, even while under enemy observation and fire, the tank crew is able to perform the complex tasks involved in driving the vehicle and loading, aiming, and firing the main weapon simply because they have done it so many times together in training and practice. Infantry squad members are able to aim and fire their weapons and maneuver toward enemy positions, even while being shot at and while seeing their comrades wounded and killed, largely because they have repeated these drills so many times in training.

The rate of psychiatric battle casualties has been shown to be a function of both the intensity and the duration of combat. The military practice of periodically pulling units out of the front lines for rest and relaxation (R & R), particularly following prolonged periods of heavy fighting, is an effective technique for reducing the number of stress-related casualties. This unit rotation policy, practiced in World Wars I and II, and in the Korean conflict, was replaced during the war in Vietnam with an individual R & R and rotation policy. While this strategy reduced the ability of the individual soldier to cope with stress by weakening the primary group and unit cohesiveness, a different policy was designed to compensate for this loss. This policy was the 12-month rotation system in effect for the duration of America's involvement in this war. As reported by the noted military sociologist Charles Moskos (1969), the American soldier was sustained in the knowledge that, regardless of the ultimate outcome of the war, if he was able to survive for 365 days, for him the war would be over. This specific date, known in advance by every soldier, enabled him to accept and manage stressors that might, otherwise, have been incapacitating.

Finally, several other techniques, devices, and strategies have been developed and utilized by the military to assist the soldier in coping with combat-related stressors. Military chaplains play a prominent role in sustaining individuals during these times when death or disfigurement seems likely. It has been frequently noted that "there are no atheists in foxholes." The military has long recognized the value of *mail* in sustaining soldiers, and when letters are long delayed morale suffers accordingly. As a result, every effort is made to maintain timely delivery, even to the front lines. Finally, the soldier is sustained in the knowledge that the might and the resources of his nation are marshaled in his support. Military leaders strive to reinforce this message for the soldier. Should additional firepower or reinforcements be needed, they will be at his disposal. Should he be killed, no effort will be spared in recovering his body for an appropriate funeral with honors. The realization of this support diminishes the effects of stress and increases the ability of the soldier to face danger and death with confidence.

JOB-RELATED STRESSORS

The job-related stressors experienced in the military are similar to those in industry and include task overload, role conflict, role ambiguity, and competition. The principal difference is that task overload is the norm, is not engendered by a profit motive, and receives no protection from such devices as labor unions.

The military response to these job-related stressors has been less than overwhelming. To a large extent, recognition and acknowledgment of these factors runs counter to the Spartan ethos of the military. A result of failure to deal with these job stressors has been decreased satisfaction with military service and an alarming exodus of experienced midlevel officers and noncommissioned officers.

LIFE-STYLE STRESSORS

Another type of military-specific stress is increasingly being recognized as having a significant impact on our country's military forces and their subsequent combat readiness, morale, and mental and physical health. This type of stress stems from the unique aspects of military life in a noncombat environment. This life-style involves: (1) frequent uprooting of families and their transfer from military base to military base; (2) frequent changes of jobs, bosses, subordinates, communities, friends, schools, churches, and other sources of social-emotional support; (3) the common occurrence of family separations when husbands are overseas, at sea, or on maneuvers; and (4) the experience of living in foreign countries with unfamiliar customs, strange languages, and the consequent sense of isolation to which this experience can lead.

These life-style stressors caused by frequent moves have become increasingly important. The modern Army, for example, is increasingly a married Army; in 1979 about 83% of male officers and 57% of enlisted men were married. Given a long-term erosion of pay and benefits over the 1970s, clearly perceived as such in the military, the number of spouses forced to work has increased dramatically. Stress derived from the conflict between the Army requirement to move often and the need for stability of the working spouse has become a serious problem. A related stressor is family separation. Separations are caused by the necessity to station soldiers overseas where family members (called "dependents" in the military) cannot accompany them, for example, the one-year unaccompanied tour of duty in Korea. Also, there are extended separations for periods of weeks when Army units are required to depart the home base for field training. The Navy's equivalents, of course, are extended periods of duty at sea.

A second stressor in this category is the inherent regimentation of the military system in which the work environment and most aspects of barracks life for single soldiers, as well as many aspects of family living in Army communities for married soldiers, are closely prescribed by military regulations. Reveille formation in the morning, rigorous room inspections in the barracks while the soldier is away at work, inspections and required corrections of conditions in family community areas—these are examples of stressors unique to military regimentation.

A third stressor in this category centers on the military personnel system for individual career qualifications and advancement in rank. The individual's job assignment, commander or supervisor, and subordinates change frequently and unpredictably, undercutting primary group cohesion and creating uncertainties.

A fourth military life-style stressor results from time demands. The military workday and workweeks are open ended and highly dependent on accomplishment of the unit mission. If 12- or 16-hour days, seven days per week, are required for mission accomplishment in the view of a local commander, it will be so. There is no additional monetary compensation involved. The only limits on time required "on the job" are dictated by the prudence, leadership, and management ability of the commander and by the military system of appeals through the Inspector General system. Traditionally, the time demands of a soldier for the family or for leisure have been considered secondary to the mission.

A final life-style stressor is called "disconnectedness." It involves the separation from established networks of friends and family, and has been shown to be significantly related to health and even to mortality. An exhaustive, ongoing study by L. F. Berkman (1977), beginning in 1965 and involving 7000 adults has shown that:

For every age group and both sexes, more people with minimal social contacts died than people with many social contacts. This effect was independent of health status . . . or of socioeconomic status. Furthermore, people who were socially isolated were more likely to engage in poor health behaviors (smoking, drinking, overeating, irregular eating, inadequate sleep, etc.). But the *extent of one's social contacts still predicts mortality over and above the effects of any or all of these poor health practices.* Thus, likelihood of death can be predicted better by knowing how isolated or connected a person is than by knowl-

edge of the person's smoking history, even though smoking clearly increases mortality. The data warrant the . . . conclusion that *social and
community ties may be powerful determinants of consequent health
status.*

Since disconnectedness has a devastating effect on social and community
ties for all members of the military family, it follows that frequent moves,
family separation, and the attendant stress increase poor health practices
such as smoking and excessive drinking and even significantly increase the
likelihood of death. It would be hard to imagine a more pronounced effect.

While the military has long recognized the problems caused by combat-
related stress, it is only recently that the unique features of the military life-
style and normal job-related stressors have been acknowledged as being
worthy of attention. This is particularly true in the direct combat branches
of the services such as the Army infantry and armor, or among Air Force
fighter pilots and Marines. In these branches the ideal of "masculinity" is
all pervasive. Anyone who cannot cope with stress is often viewed as un-
manly. An admission of suffering from stress-induced problems has been
tantamount to admitting incompetency or, even worse, lacking machismo.
In the combat support and service support elements (those units not directly involved in combat), the macho ideal or identification has not been
incorporated into the cultural value system to such an extreme degree. As a
result, efforts to confront and deal with traditional sources of stress have
been more readily accepted and incorporated into military organizations
serving in indirect combat roles.

The military has developed a broad range of strategies for assisting
members to cope with stress. The military practices one of the most traditional methods of dealing with organizational members who suffer
dysfunctional consequences of stress—separation. Historically, both com-
missioned officers and enlisted members of the service have been separated
for stress-induced deficiencies in performance. Discharges from the
military under the general categories of "unfitness" and "unsuitability"
have often been used to identify those whose behavior was incompatible
with the stressful demands of military service. Frequently these inappropriate behaviors were stress induced and manifested in excessive alcohol
or other drug use, excessive fighting, irritability and demonstrated lack of
ability to get along with others, sleeplessness, and simply the inability to
perform routine tasks under the critical eye of a demanding and unsym-
pathetic sergeant.

Another common strategy for minimizing the negative effects of stress
has been practiced by the military. This technique is simply a regular

regimen of physical exercise which is normally a standard feature of military life. This has been done, of course, in the belief that physical conditioning is important because combat itself is physically demanding and that, to be maximally effective, soldiers need to be well conditioned. Only recently has physical exercise been shown to be such an effective stress-reduction technique.

Yet another method adopted by the military for helping selected members deal with dysfunctional stress is formal counseling. On almost any military facility, agencies exist to counsel service members who have drug and alcohol problems, family problems such as child abuse and marital difficulty, financial problems and excessive indebtedness, or simply emotional or personality disorders. These formal counselors, found in a multitude of agencies, include military psychiatrists, psychologists, social workers, and chaplains. The military's increasing willingness to provide these extensive formal support systems stems from a realization that its human resources are expensive and difficult to replace. One cannot simply "hire" another sergeant to take the place of one who has left the military because of a drinking problem, for example. Sergeants are grown and trained, and it takes years to develop one. Unlike a commercial or even governmental enterprise which can replace an engineer, lawyer, or skilled machine operator by offering appropriate incentives to those outside the organization, the military cannot replace its skilled members through lateral entry of people with transferable skills from outside the organization. Even a sergeant who is a computer operator normally will have military leadership responsibilities for lower-ranking enlisted people. In essence, it is cost effective and organizationally sound practice for the military to work with and assist its members in adjusting to stress through the provision of professional counseling services.

The stressors associated with frequent change of duty station, a salient characteristic of military life, were addressed above. The military has adopted both formal and informal strategies to deal with the stress associated with relocation. These informal methods are perhaps the most effective in providing the social-emotional supports which such situations demand. Informal support systems are characteristic of the military culture and tradition, and are summarized in the common military adage, "The military takes care of its own." A military family transferred to a new state or to a foreign country normally will be assigned quarters or housing on a military base. There they will move into a neighborhood of other military families of comparable rank, many of whom, like themselves, are recent arrivals. Almost no one will have been there for more than three years. To cope with this transient life-style and the attendant stress, the military community has developed norms which ease the strain of adjustment to a new community. New arrivals in the neighborhood are sought out and welcomed by the more established members. Military units to which service members are assigned go to great lengths immediately upon arrival to make recently assigned personnel feel welcome, comfortable, wanted, and supported.

Formal organizational practices are designed to foster unit camaraderie and a sense of cohesiveness. These practices include monthly parties held specifically to welcome new organizational members and to honor departing members; formal calls to the home of the new commander or boss; change of command and welcoming ceremonies; and formal sponsor programs wherein an experienced organizational member is designated to assist the newcomer in all phases of adjustment such as securing family housing, enrolling children in school, and introduction to work procedures. Unit or organizational wives' clubs provide social and emotional support and a network of friendships for wives who do not have the opportunities provided their husbands through work activities for friendships and interpersonal interaction. It is not surprising then that older military leaders decry the recent decline of these military traditions which have historically assisted military families in coping with the stressors which are an attendant aspect of the military life-style brought on by frequent moves and family separation.

In addition to these informal and traditional methods of coping with the stressors of the military life-style, the military has established formal agencies designed to accomplish this purpose as well. Various community service organizations, relief agencies, and recreational facilities are found on all military posts. These range from the Red Cross, which provides relief and travel assistance to military members in the event of a death in the family, to agencies which temporarily provide the basics for establishing a household (sheets, towels, kitchenware, beds) for families awaiting the arrival or shipment of their household goods. Additionally, craft shops, auto-hobby shops, gymnasiums, and other sports facilities provide outlets for stressors that might find relief in less constructive ways.

CONCLUSION

The unique aspects of military life are the source of three different types of stress. These are combat-related stress, job-related stress, and the stress arising from the exigencies of the military life-style. The Spartan ethic and the masculine ideal have impeded the military's ability to deal with these stressors effectively. However, traditional military practices have evolved which serve the function of decreasing the injurious effects of these stressors. Further, increasing military awareness of, and concern for, the impact of stress on the quality of military life and on the effectiveness of the military fighting force has been recently demonstrated.

References

Berkman, L. F. Psychosocial resources, health behavior, and mortality: a nine-year follow-up study. Paper presented at the American Public Health Association Annual Meeting, Washington, D.C., October 1977. Cited by P. Zimbardo, in *Psychology and Life,* 10th ed. Glenview, Ill.: Scott Foresman, 1979.

Forissier, R. and Darmandieu, M. The Yom Kippur War and the Israeli Armed Forces Medical Corps. *Medicine et Armies* 4(7): 633-642 (1976). Cited in Ingraham, L. H. and Manning, F. J. Psychiatric battle casualties: the missing column in a war without replacements. *Military Review* (Fall, 1980).

Ingram, L. H. and Manning, F. J. Psychiatric battle casualties: the missing column in a war without replacements. *Military Review* (Fall, 1980).

Markey, O. B. Tenth U.S. Army. In *Neuro-psychiatry in World War II (W. S. Mullins and A. J. Glass, eds.)* Vol. II, p. 633. Overseas Theaters, Office of the Surgeon General, Department of the Army, Washington, D.C., 1973. Cited in Ingraham, L. H. and Manning, F. J. Psychiatric battle casualties: the missing column in a war without replacements. *Military Review* (Fall, 1980).

Marshall, S. L. A. *Men Against Fire: The Problem of Battle Command in Future War,* New York: William Morrow, 1947.

Moskos, C. C., Jr. Vietnam: why men fight. *Transactions* 7: 1 (1969).

Shils, E. A. Primary groups in the American army. In *Studies in the Scope and Method of "The American Soldier"* (R. K. Merton and P. F. Lazarsfeld, eds.). New York: Free Press, 1950.

Zajonc, R. B. Social facilitation. *Science* 149: 269-274 (1965).

Stress and Science: Scientific Communication, Culture, and the Media

K. S. Sitaram
Professor and Chairman
Department of Radio-Television
Southern Illinois University
Carbondale, Illinois

Scientific communication is the process by which a scientist transmits specialized information to the nonscientist. Intercultural communication, on the other hand, is the process by which members of different cultures share their experiences.[1] Depending upon the nature of feedback from the audience, techniques of intercultural communication change constantly. While intercultural communication is a two way process, scientific communication tends to be one way. It flows from the specialist to the nonspecialist and from the researcher to the user. Because there is little feedback, scientific communication tends to stay specialized.

Scientific communication, however, is intercultural since the scientist and the nonscientist belong to different "cultures." Their value systems are not the same. Generally speaking, the scientist may not believe in the values of his/her family's culture. Many scientists define *the truth* as that knowledge which is confirmed by experimentation rather than by intuition or meditation. Most nonscientists learn *the truth* from their churches, religious books, and other authorities rather than from scientific experiments.

Scientific information is now being transmitted to legislators, administrators, the general public, and others mostly via the mass media. Movie stars and media reporters are interpreting science to the general public. Persons who specialize in radio, television, print, and speech communication gather data from the scientist or his representative, and transmit them to the others. Thus the media reporters act as gatekeepers between the scientist and the nonscientist. Journalists simplify information so that their audience can understand what they are saying. In their efforts to simplify, they may misinterpret science. They also report sensational rather than essential information. On the other hand, great scientists are not always effective communicators. They fail to enlighten the public on important aspects of their research. In order to make their research "scholarly," some of them make their reports scientific gobbledygook. Consequently, both the scientist and the media reporter contribute to our inadequate understanding of scientific subjects that affect our lives each day. The complicated nature of the flow of scientific information is shown in Fig. 1. We can understand the confusion in scientific communication better by discussing a few cases.

Genetic research. The public misunderstanding of genetic research, sometimes known as DNA research and genetic engineering, is explained very well by Michael Rogers in his book *Biohazards.*[2] Rogers tries to show how the entire area of DNA research has been reported inaccurately. In a way, the mass media have already programmed the general public to perceive the scientist as a weird and dangerous person. Movies like *Dr. Jekyl and Mr. Hyde* and *Frankenstein* are stories of experiments by crazy scientists. People do believe science can create such monsters as Frankenstein. Why should they support research that might create a monster which will destroy them someday? Rogers calls this fear the Frankenstein Syndrome. Hearings on genetic research conducted a few years ago in the City Hall of Cambridge, Massachusetts, reflect this syndrome very well. Legislators and the general public have been led to further misunderstanding of genetic research by scientists, since they have not been able to explain their own work in the common person's language.

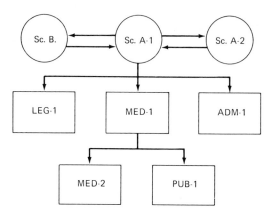

FIG. 1. The flow of scientific information from the scientist (Sc.A-1) to other scientists of his own specialty (Sc. A-2), scientists of other specialities (SC. B.), legislators in his own country (Leg-1), the media in his own country (Med-1), the administrators in his own country (Adm-1), the general public in his own country (Pub-1), and the media in other countries (Med-2).

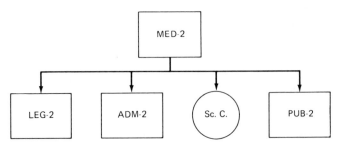

FIG. 2. The flow of scientific information from the media (Med-2) to legislators (Leg-2), administrators (Adm-2), scientists (Sc.C.), and the general public (Pub-2) in other countries.

Energy problem. This is one of the most confusing issues today. In spite of all the speeches by the President and appeals by television stars, people do not believe energy supply is a problem. Survey after survey has confirmed the popular disbelief in the problem. Most persons still believe the earth has unlimited deposits of petroleum, coal, etc. Although the reports are conflicting, each time a person speaks for or against the gasoline industry, that person appears to be highly credible. When audiences are caught between two equally credible sources, perhaps they sway their views so much that they cannot make up their minds.

SIDS research. Sudden infant death syndrome (SIDS) is a less known problem, but it affects many parents.[3] SIDS research is still in its early stages, yet some important information already is available. If parents of potential SIDS babies would use the available knowledge, some of the babies could be saved. However, the information is not available in a language that less literate and low income parents can understand.

Family planning. Information on family planning is available today in abundance. It is possible to have children by choice rather than by chance. In less developed countries, even the highly educated couple does not have access to information on contraceptives, "the pill," for example. Physicians and other family planning experts are not trained in communicating effectively with couples.

Agricultural technology. In the less developed countries, most farmers still do not take advantage of the abundant knowledge available on agricultural technology. For example, most of them do not realize that they can enrich the soil on their farms once they find out which mineral it is deficient in. By using simple equipment, they can test the soil themselves. Even this information is not easily made available. Agricultural experts give profound speeches as parts of Farm and Home radio programs, but farmers say that they cannot understand what the expert is saying.[4]

This brings us to the main point of discussion here. Scientific information today is transmitted by mass media. The President appears on television and gives his well-prepared speech on energy. The syndicated columnist writes a fine article on DNA research. The SIDS researcher publishes his findings in a neat pamphlet. Governments of overpopulated countries distribute millions of pamphlets on family planning.

Radio and television can be influential only if the messages are produced and transmitted effectively. Studies still show that face-to-face interaction is the most influential method of human communication. This is very much true in the less developed countries since most of their people are illiterate and poor, and cannot afford radio or television sets.[4] Only opinion leaders can inform and influence the people in their communities. Studies have also shown that the media barely inform their audience. Perhaps by continued efforts the media can even influence them, but this takes a very long time. The problem in these countries is that there are few opinion leaders in each community and they cannot inform the masses. The mass media are impersonal and cannot influence their audience instantaneously on matters such as family planning, genetic counseling, and agricultural technology.

In the developed countries, mass information comes instantaneously and in abundance. Only three communications satellites can transmit the same information around the world in less than one minute. Laser beams passed through a tiny hair-like fiber made of glass can carry television signals. A cable of less than one-half inch diameter containing these fibers can carry several hundred channels from remote stations. Data banks can spit out plenty of information in a few seconds. Each person is exposed to so much information that he is a victim of *information overload*. As Robert Merton points out, the overload may cause narcotization.[5] Consequently, the receiver of information does not take any action, he simply stays passive. The point is, mass media information given in such abundance may not influence the audience even in industrialized societies. In these societies, interpersonal communication is becoming so rare that even parents and children seldom talk with each other. In large universities, instructional television has partly taken over the function of teachers. While we know very well that face-to-face interaction can influence and motivate the public, we are still using mass media for scientific communication. Then, how can we transmit scientific information effectively?

Train the scientists. Scientists should be trained in effective public speaking. Why should all scientists learn to speak in public? Well, if they want the support of the administrator, the legislator, and the general public, they had better learn to communicate with them. In the United States, more than 50 colleges and universities offer courses in scientific communication, but most of these are journalistic writing courses. Those journalism students might not have taken even one course beyond Physics 101. None of the colleges and universities teaches scientific communication in face-to-face situations or via radio and television.

Develop courses. These should be courses specially designed to train scientists in techniques of communicating with the public interpersonally and through the media. Because the taxpayer pays for most research done at universities and other institutions, he/she has the right to know about that research. There should be special courses for science writers in the basics of the scientific area in which they write, speak, and broadcast.

This does not mean that the general public should know everything about the scientific research it supports. It is not even possible for the layperson to understand everything. The scientist should present the important points of his/her research that the public should know. These should cover all those aspects of the research that affect the public immediately and in the future. The scientist should be able to inform the various levels of the public using the technique appropriate to each level. Some of the areas that we all should know about are nutrition, contraceptives, biofeedback, energy, genetic counseling, laser technology, and common health problems. The fundamentals of intercultural communication should be a part of science courses since scientific communication tends to be intercultural. The scientist should also be familiar with the usage of the media, particularly television, since the way he/she presents information on the screen will have a lasting impact on the general public. Mass media, including television, are impersonal. They do not have the kinesthetic effect that interpersonal communication methods have. The media messages, particularly those on television, should be developed to make them personal. Television techniques could be used to make this medium more personal. Research in this area is much needed at this time.

Use universal terminology. Each discipline has its own terminology. Sometimes the terminology used in the same discipline may not be the same in two different countries. John Glenn is an "astronaut" in America, while he is a "cosmonaut" in Russia. Understanding a scientific discipline should not be limited to its specialists only. It should be available to anyone who would like to know. The scientist should be able to inform those that want to learn. The first requirement for this would be to develop a universal scientific terminology, something like the international nonverbal language that businessmen are now trying to develop. The terminology should be acceptable to all people no matter in which culture and under which political system they live.

Imbibe the scientific attitude. There are various ways to understand nature and so-called reality. From ancient times, philosophers have developed theories of acquiring valid knowledge. Greeks said that experimentation was the only way to know reality. Hindus said that meditation was the way. Buddhists emphasised intuition, and Moslems believed in reasoning. Cultures that originated from, or were influenced by, Greek thought developed a positive attitude toward any knowledge that stems from scientific thinking and experimenting. However, those cultures that were derived from Hindu thought accorded respect to knowledge that was based on meditation, and they looked down at science. They even went to the extent of saying that science is destructive. Buddhists took a moderate view and said that while experimental knowledge is important, the individual's intuitive abilities should guide him/her in finding valid knowledge. That is probably the reason why the East Asians, who are Buddhists, have a more positive attitude toward science than do the South Asians.

The point is that there are several ways to acquire knowledge. Young people should be trained to accept the idea that there are various ways to understand the world around us and that each culture has developed its own way of doing so. In order to understand science, a person would need the scientific attitude, or logical thinking, and respect for faultless experimentations. This scientific attitude should be imbibed at a very early age, and educational methods should be developed for this purpose.

Avoid ethnocentrism. Many scientists do not seem to be aware of what is being done in their area of specialization in other parts of the world. Some of them do not even want to know. If something is "not invented here," then they do not want to know about it. Others do not recognize scientists of other colors and cultures. They judge the scientific work of others using their own work as the standard. Such ethnocentric attitudes are partly responsible for the waste of time, money, and human resources in scientific research and education. If a particular research project is already being done by a capable scientist in another part of the world or by a person of a different color, effort should be made to support that research so its results can help everybody.

In the 1930s Mahatma Gandhi encouraged using methane gas for energy production. He knew cow dung was available in abundance in India and thought the farmers could use it. About 25 years ago, in a rural community called Nandi in India, a Gandhian was using bio-gas for burning light bulbs in his home. The gas was generated from a septic tank constructed in his back yard. Today, millions of dollars are being spent in the United States and other advanced countries on bio-gas research. Credit is not being given to those pioneers who originated the idea three decades ago. We should not hesitate to borrow ideas from others and recognize them, no matter to what country or race they belong.

Translate texts. Methods of translating books from other languages are in great need. Occasionally, one or two books from important European languages are translated into English, but what about translations from Japanese, Chinese, and Hindi? Perhaps an international task force under the aegis of organizations such as UNESCO, AAAS, and FASEB could come up with ideas for translation. A related problem is governmental control of the flow of scientific knowledge to and from other countries. Each government has some control on the export of such knowledge. Such controls should be loosened. The same task force can study this problem too and recommend ways of loosening these controls.

References

1. Sitaram, K. S. Intercultural communication: an overview. *Biosciences Communications* 4(6): 332-347 (1978).
2. Rogers, M. *Biohazards,* New York: Alfred Knopf, 1977.
3. Yamashita, T. S. and Goldberg, J. *An Application of Multivariate Analysis in Sudden Infant Death Syndrome in Chicago Area.* San Diego: American Statistical Association, 1978.
4. Sitaram, K. S. Some effects of radio upon the audiences of rural India. Doctoral dissertation, University of Oregon, 1979.

IV
LIFE STRESS, THE CHILD, THE WOMAN, AND THE FAMILY

Child Abuse and Stress: A Sociosituational Interpretation

Edward J. Hyman, Ph.D.
University of San Francisco
San Francisco, California

Overview

In this paper, the Child Abuse Neglect Syndrome (CANS) is described. Traditional models of the etiology of child abuse are outlined and discussed critically, as is the relationship of CANS to the General Adaptation Syndrome (GAS). Preliminary observations on an interactive multivariate model of child abuse conclude the paper. In that model, the interaction of social stress agents, of conditioning by situational and environmental factors, and of psychopathological and personality variables is suggested.

Child Abuse and Neglect: Definition and Description

Selye (1980) observes that one of the most difficult considerations in the systematic study of stress is providing an adequate definition of the concept. Research on the etiology and treatment of the Child Abuse Neglect Syndrome (CANS) suffers from similar complexities of definition. A broad and inclusive approach is suggested by Gil (Volpe et al., 1980), who defines abuse as either actions or inactions of individuals, institutions, or society, and the resultant conditions that inhibit the development of a child's innate capacities. Kempe and Kempe (1978) offer four specific agencies for the inhibition of these capacities: (1) physical violence against a child, (2) emotional abuse of a child, (3) physical and emotional neglect of a child, and (4) sexual victimization of a child. Employing these two approaches, one can consider the causal role of social stress agents as well as delineate deficiencies in the coping patterns of abusive parents. This paradigm also contains a potentially reflexive quality in allowing for an examination of the impact of the victim's reaction on further actions of the abuser.

The Abusing Parent

Abusive and neglecting parents can be understood to be the 20 to 30% of American parents who have difficulty caring for their children adequately (Kempe and Kempe, 1978). This includes highly pathological parents, abusive-neglectful parents, and poor parents who have potential difficulties. These parents are characteristically angry, indifferent, or seductive, with a pattern of abuse that corresponds to the particular personality predisposition. Parenting deficiencies arise in providing for the child's physical care, love, nurturance, mental development, and bodily development, and in aiding the child to organize and master experiences in his or her environment. Underlying these elements, Kempe and Kempe (1978) suggest, is a basic element of empathy. They argue that parents must learn to recognize the importance of the child's welfare and to credit themselves for having provided for the child's needs. Since parental needs will inevitably conflict with those of the child, parental sacrifices are necessary. The ability to postpone immediate gratification and make these sacrifices is based on a cognitive reward system, linked closely to empathy. This reward system is absent in most abusive parents.

Of all types of abuse, emotional abuse is the most elusive since it leaves no visible scars or marks. The most sensational indicators of child abuse are contained in gory pictures of maimed children. Equally debilitating in many circumstances are the emotional wounds children endure. "Scapegoating"—a phenomenon well known to family therapists—is among the more common forms of emotional abuse. Possibilities for emotional abuse, however, are almost infinite. Indeed, emotional abuse underlies to one extent or another all forms of child abuse.

The age of onset of abuse can be significant. Most children who are abused as infants are also abused during childhood. In such cases, subsequent experiences reinforce initial traumatic events. The abuser himself or herself, however, is most likely to have been an abused child. In times of crisis, when the external world or the child is producing stress excessive to the parent, the parent may revert to child-rearing techniques employed by his or her own parents. Though the parent may have consciously rejected these deficient parenting practices, the parent's reaction to extreme stress may be to revert to these patterns conditioned in early childhood.

The degree of stress associated with child rearing reflects in many cases the manner in which the child is perceived by the parent. The belief that a 6-month-old child is capable of controlling his or her behavior and defecates intentionally to harass the parent is obviously a misperception. This misperception reveals both an unrealistic assessment of the child's abilities and the parent's own insecurity in parenting. Most abusers view their children unrealistically, demanding too much or too little (or sometimes alternating between the two modes).

Abusive parents view physical punishment as both efficacious and appropriate. This orientation is frequently rooted in their unrealistic expectations of children to which we have just alluded. These parents often become discouraged when punishment fails to provide results, but they perceive no alternatives. They become depressed with the child's behavior and their own inability to modify it. A cycle arises characterized by punishment, deterioration of the child/parent relationship, frustration accompanied by depression, and further punishment.

Just as the abusing parent misperceives the child's abilities and intentions, and miscalculates the alternatives available for modifying a child's behavior, the abusive parent is also governed by a distorted self-image. These parents view themselves as worthless, bad and unlovable. This self-image is frequently associated with a misanthropic world view in which approval, affection, and pleasure are replaced by a distrust of an unforgiving, anhedonic, and cruel world in which anger and punishment reign supreme (Kempe and Kempe, 1978). The phenomenology of the childhood of abusive parents reveals some keys to this world view.

As children, abusers were frequently "problem" children who learned early that pleasure could be attained only at someone else's expense. They came to understand giving pleasure to someone else as denying it to themselves. This understanding carries over to their patterns of parenting and to their sexual relations, and is instrumental in the etiology of these two major facets of family dysfunction. As children, this perspective often made it difficult for them to develop lasting and meaningful friendships. Afraid of rejection and distrustful of their peers, these future abusers tended to withdraw from their peers or to engage them in bellicose interactions. Lonely as children, these future abusers were conditioned not to use human resources to which they had access. They often continue to ignore this access even after departing their hostile childhood environments. This constricted range of interaction may result in an impairment of mental and emotional functions, and can contribute to a predisposition to failure by the time the child enters school (Hyman and Wylie, 1980).

As adolescents, these abused children and future abusers experience a profound and ever-increasing need for love. This search for what Kempe and Kempe (1978) have refered to as "love at any price" often manifests itself in the discovery by the abused or deprived teenager of a similarly needy adolescent with a parallel familial background. Their generally premature, if not immature and ill-fated, marriage often compounds their frustration. They find that their distrust and immature misperceptions of human relations do not lend to a giving and fulfilling marital interaction. Their relationships often beckon analogy to Pieter Brueghel's *The Blind Leading the Blind*. Their increased frustration is often transformed into a set of unreasonable expectations for a newborn child. As their own parents had solicited a sense of their own success and self-approval from their children's acquiescence and compliant love, the next generation makes the same demands of its children. Love and approval are not forthcoming from the equally immature spouse, who is often most nonsupportive. In such cases, practitioners must emphasize the need of the at-risk or abusive parent to nurture himself or herself.

The Abused Child

The parents' childhood experiences, while crucial, are only contributory to the etiology of abuse. The particular history of the abused child, whether an unwanted child or perhaps the result of a difficult childbirth, is also of great importance. Infantile frailty is often a danger sign for abuse. The costs, emotional and financial, of caring for a frail infant often tax the limited coping skills of the parent(s). Mothers of infants who are treated for failure to thrive are often recognized as potential abusers. Other factors, such as the birth of a female child to parents who could not even think of having anything but a boy, also are significant. Parents who have led lives burdened by a perception of constant frustration and continued failure will view such a birth similarly. This additional frustration will contribute generously to the depletion of already limited parenting resources.

The child's developmental requirements of increased attention, social interaction, autonomy, and exploration increasingly begin to curtail the parent's freedom, particularly that of the mother. The abusive parent's expectations that the child will be pleasure bearing and will make only limited demands run up against the realities of children's developmental patterns. If the child refuses to allow the parent to curtail or restrict these developmental requirements, the child will be considered disobedient and bad by the parent. The child will be punished to assure that he/she does not wind up spoiled! Other difficulties in the child/parent interaction arise when the parent is too pathological to recognize the child's needs when they arise. Too depressed or psychotic to respond to the child's immediate needs, the parent may respond according to a schedule that conforms more to her needs than to those of the child. The necessary responsiveness of the parent to the child's expression of need is quashed. This frustrates the child's satisfaction and reduces the child's perceived efficacy in the world.

This also, however, precludes the parent from experiencing the potential satisfaction in the symbiosis of child rearing.

It is not surprising, if one considers the childhood conditioning of abusers, to recognize in many of them preadult reasoning. The mother who views her defecating 6-month-old child as willfully bad is not perceiving reality as mediated by adult reasoning. The impoverishment of social interactions in the early lives of these abusers often has deprived them of sufficient maturation to confront the burdens of adulthood, much less spousal or parental responsibility. These abusive parents are, by and large, immature and limited in their ability to cope with the demands of adulthood. They have difficulty in locating and maintaining employment, have few friends and a constricted or absent social support system, and are fraught with unrealistic expectations of themselves and their children.

Loss of a job, difficulty with the apartment manager, sexual intercourse interrupted by a child's late night cries, feeding problems with a child, or a child's ill-timed defecation may all increase stress to a level beyond the toleration of the abusive parent. Unreasonable self-expectations lead the parent to believe that he/she should be able to control and eliminate any of the child's problems. When the child cries at night and the parent cannot stop the crying, the parent perceives this as a deficiency in his or her parenting abilities. This self-perception itself contributes to increasing levels of stress.

Other factors may increase the stress that precipitates abuse. Impaired intelligence, emotional and mental disorders, excessive impulsiveness, isolation from the community (due either to interpersonal problems or to racial and cultural differences), chronic poverty, and social, ethnic, or racial discrimination can all interact to contribute to abusive behavior. The brutal or emotionally deficient childhood of the abusive parent often has induced a disordered life pattern of social and economic disadvantage (Kempe and Kempe, 1978).

The role of the nonsupportive spouse in the abusive syndrome should be amplified. The result of immature development and unreasonable expectations, the marriage of abusive parents is commonly unviable. Self-absorbed and needy, these parents have little energy or support to provide each other. The exhaustion and frustration of one parent is most often matched in intensity and kind by the immaturity and inability to cope of the other. Such people may actually parent better unfettered by a nonsupportive spouse.

In summary, the abusive parent/child relationship can be understood to have five major foci: (1) the abusive parent's childhood is characterized by emotional and/or physical deprivation or abuse often leading to physical, emotional, or intellectual problems; (2) abusers perceive themselves as unlovable, worthless, and bad; (3) children are perceived as unlovable, disappointing, frustrating, disobedient, and bad; (4) abusive parents display inadequate mechanisms to cope with stress or crisis situations; and (5) the lives of abusive parents are governed by social withdrawal, absence of adequate communication, deficient social support networks, and failure to tap sources of help (Strauss, 1979). In the next section, prevailing theoretical perspectives for analyzing these data will be discussed and an interactive multivariate perspective will be suggested.

Traditional Theoretical Models of Child Abuse

Traditional theoretical approaches to child abuse can be aggregated into three general categories:

Psychogenic perspective attributes a particular personality disorder or otherwise disordered behavior to a parent who is responsible for the abuse. Research findings, however, have not indicated great variance explained by distinct pathological patterns common to abusers. Analysis is of individual psychopathology.

Family-dynamics perspective is a systems and group dynamics model in which situational factors induce the family to sustain a pattern of physical discipline and violence to elicit compliance and obedience. In these families, physical violence may induce compliance to parental wishes that is otherwise unobtainable due to arbitrary, inconsistent, and capricious child-rearing techniques. Analysis is of family, interpersonal, and group dynamics.

Sociogenic perspective ascribes a broader etiology of abusive behavior than the family-dynamics model. Proponents of this view locate causality within the social system that sustains generalized patterns of societal violence and engenders belief systems which inculcate the values of social violence into an abusive family mileu. In this model, elements of social structure such as poverty, isolation, unemployment, and a generally impoverished quality of life are emphasized, as are significant epidemiological variables such as poor health status at birth. These are identified as inducing a level of stress that taxes the coping abilities of the parent(s). Analysis is of broadly conceived social variables that are neither interpersonal nor individually psychopathological.

Though elements of all these perspectives offer attractive features, a more comprehensive model appears to be appropriate at this stage of research. In the next sections, this author will present evidence and arguments for a multivariate interactive model that is called *social-*

situational. The theoretical orgins of this model can be located in the association of the behavioral patterns of abuse to the General Adaptation Syndrome (GAS).

Stress and Child Abuse: A Discussion

A formidable barrier to the conceptual formulation of a single stereotyped response to stress was overcome when research findings indicated a unique relationship between diverse agents of stress and nonspecific stressor effects (Selye, 1980). The findings suggested that qualitatively distinct stress agents differed only in their specific action, but shared a common stereotyped nonspecific stressor effect. In the process of establishing this conceptual formulation, researchers made two observations that are cardinal to our understanding of the relationship between the General Adaptation Syndrome and the Child Abuse Neglect Syndrome. Selye (1980) summarizes these observations as:

1. Stress agents differing qualitatively but of equal stressor potency do *not* necessarily elicit identical syndromes in different individuals.
2. Identical stress agents of identical stressor potential may elicit different responses, physiological and behavioral, in different individuals.

The selective enhancement or inhibition of various stress effects can apparently be explained by discriminative stimulus control reactions. Both exogenous and endogenous factors condition reactions among specific individuals. The stress effect of a specific agent is comprised of a nonspecific stressor effect and an effect specific to the given agent. The interaction of the specific and nonspecific effects in a given individual is further modified by the endogenous and exogenous conditioning to which that individual has been exposed.

These observations were instrumental in clarifying abusive and neglectful behaviors toward children as they are associated with the concept of stress. One troublesome aspect of early observations about abuse and stress was a clear tendency in the data that indicated the prevalence of negative stress agents in eliciting abusive and neglectful responses. In examining these data more carefully, additional intervening variables came to light.

Data on abusers appeared seriously flawed by the disaproportionate inclusion of lower socioeconomic (SES) samples. Though child abuse and neglect can be identified at all SES levels, incidents of abuse have traditionally been brought to the attention of authorities with undue frequency among lower SES groups. The reasons for this are manifold and include: the ability of higher SES groups to seek out private clinicians who have not been disposed to report the incidents; the relative prevalence of mental rather than physical abuse among higher SES groups; the ability of schools and other community resources in higher SES areas to respond earlier and more effectively to developing problems because of the relative absence of other social problems that are abundant in poorer communities; and the reluctance of law enforcement and social service agencies to take action against higher SES group members, whom they assume to be more responsible and capable of remedying problems than the poor. Accordingly, most of the data available reflect a disproportionately large sampling of lower SES groups.

This sampling problem is particularly important in understanding the CANS/GAS data. The lower SES group members who are most frequently identified as abusers have fewer positive stress agents in their lives than do higher SES groups. For example, they have less mobility in their jobs, purchase homes less frequently, receive fewer offers of employment, travel less frequently, and are less likely to receive significant promotions in their jobs or to inherit large sums of money. The paucity of positive stress agents in their lives provides little data to evaluate the relationship between positive stress agents and abusive behavior.

Two factors militate against undue generalization about the sole influence of negative stress agents in eliciting abuse. First, in the higher SES cases observed in clinical treatment, stress associated with positive stress agents (such as getting a new and much more responsible job) may elicit abusive behavior. Second, in lower SES cases in which positive stress agents have been active, they have been observed to elicit abuse and neglect. Though stressor effects depend on intensity, whether the agent is pleasurable or not, selective conditioning of negative agents must be understood to be common in the absence of abundant positive agents. This is the case for most lower SES groups and is most characteristic of identified abusers. In consideration of these data, however, one must consider the role of conditioning in eliciting particular abusive and neglectful behaviors among given individuals.

Though the level of the potential stressor may be as high for a positive stressor agent as for a negative one, conditioning in the case of identified abusers is virtually always for responding abusively to negative ones. The development of this pattern is readily understandable. Most abusers were themselves abused and learned these response patterns to negative stressor agents in their early developmental years. The situations with which their low SES parents had to cope were largely negative. The abusive responses of their parents were elicited primarily by negative stressor agents. This conditioning, as well as the paucity of positive stressor agents in the environment of the abuser, tends to limit the abusive response solely to negative stressor agents. In the case of an abuser exposed to both negative and positive stressor agents, early childhood conditioning may explain a selective response elicited only by negative stress agents.

Discussion of Theoretical Implications

Presenting the etiology of abusive and neglectful behaviors in this context demands a more complex theoretical model than any of the three traditional ones. Most obvious components are elements of both the sociogenic and the family-dynamics perspectives. The influence of stressful situations within the social structure is apparent to the seasoned researcher or clinician. Yet, the specific conditioning of abusive behaviors by situational and environmental factors in their childhood is operative in replicating these same abusive familial patterns in the families of current abusers.

Accordingly, a more complex and sophisticated model is advocated in which the interaction of particular socio-situational stressor agents and learned responses conditioned in childhood is integrated into a single *socio-situational model*. This multivariate model reflects the additional complexity of the interaction of nonspecific stressor effects as well as effects specific to the given agent(s) of stress in a particular social and historical situation. The response of an individual to such a situation depends on the strength of the specific and nonspecific actions of the stressor agents, and the reactivity of the individual as determined by conditioning factors. Such a complex multivariate model might also indicate the interaction of some particular psychopathological or personality patterns among abusers. In turn, these variables might reflect conditioning in the family system in childhood as well as idiographic personological variables.

Though this interactive multivariate model is not nearly as neat or simple as earlier theoretical models, its complexity probably reflects more accurately the intricacies of the etiology of child abuse and its relationship to stress. Multivariate research along these lines would presumably fill the void created by univariate research designs with more limited underlying theoretical paradigms, and will hopefully produce a more systematic approach to the collection of clinically useful data. Such a complex multivariate model can also accommodate historical change when incorporating longitudinal consideration of appropriate variables as they interact over time.

References

Hyman, E. and Wylie, E. Intergenerational and intrafamilial determinants of child abuse. Unpublished manuscript, American Child Abuse Prevention Society.

Kempe, S. and Kempe, C. Child Abuse. In *The Developing Child* (J. Bruner, M. Cole, and B. Loyd, eds.) 1978.

Selye, H. Evolution of the stree concept. *American Chiropractor* 37-91 (March-April) (1980).

Strauss, M. Family patterns and child abuse in a nationally representative American sample. *Child Abuse and Neglect* 3: 213-225 (1979).

Volpe, R., Breton, M., and Mitton, J. (eds.). *Maltreatment of the School-Aged Child,* 1980.

Child Advocacy: An Outreach Approach to Rural Children

Bonnie C. Bedics
Glen E. Goltermann
Department of Social Work
University of West Florida
Pensacola, Florida

Problems of rural families were largely neglected by human service professionals and government agencies until 1970. Pure experimental design research reports on human service delivery in rural areas are scarce. Therefore, the issues explored in this paper are based not on hard data or experimental studies, but on the soft data base that currently exists on interviews with several multidisciplinary professionals who work in the rural community, and on personal experience.

THE RURAL COMMUNITY

People in rural communities tend to be poorer and have poorer educational systems, poorer housing, less access to social service, higher infant mortality rates, and more chronic and orthopedic health problems than urban dwellers. They spend more on health care, but have less access to medical and mental health delivery systems than their urban counterparts do (*NASW News,* Frebruary, 1978). These problems result from declining populations or declining revenue for local government bodies. Despite declining enrollment and inadequate services due to limited funding, rural schools, churches, and social organizations resist consolidation. Consolidation is seen as comparatively expensive and elusive of local community organization control. Unfortunately, consolidation or regional planning is viewed as the death knoll of the neighborhood community. This attitude has caused a dearth of primary service delivery. As rural populations decline, services are terminated because of lack of clientele and revenue. Regionally planned services that would meet the needs of a large geographic area by combining client groups and resources have not met with success in many rural areas because of the identity needs of declining rural communities. Jealousy, possessiveness, fear of loss of control, and unfounded fears of rising costs (the myth of the bigger, the more expensive) have damaged efforts for regional planning for service delivery, thereby leading to the dearth of services in rural areas.

Some rural communities lack even the basic support services for their families. In systems theory, community is depicted as having independent but interrelated components. Such components include the individual family, economic services, social services, recreational services, educational services, health services, extended families, and friends. Because of the interrelatedness, a malfunction in or an absence of one of these components is bound to effect the functioning of the other components. In relating this to the rural community, we can assume that the unavailability of or inaccessibility to one or several of these basic service components puts more responsibility and stress on those service components that do exist and especially on the families.

Because of the interrelatedness and interdependence of these systems, human services workers, especially in rural areas, must begin to develop a philosophy of "community as client," for we cannot fully help a family that is malfunctioning until we help the family's community or support system to function.

Dealing with the community as client necessitates eliciting intercommunity cooperation and planning for the sharing of services, resources, and clientele. Funding is a major stumbling block not only because of the limited tax base of the communities but also because rural communities are virtually ignored when federal human service legislation is passed. Either funding needed for social and health services has not been made available, or the community does not have access to the funding, primarily because of the monolithic or fractional community power structure. In order to qualify for many available federal funds, a coalitional structure is essential.

THE NATURE OF THE RURAL COMMUNITY IN RELATIONSHIP TO HUMAN SERVICE DELIVERY

Rural community residents many times feel a sense of desperation for a better life while at the same time feeling comfortable with community and family familiarity. People are extremely proud and independent in overt behavior, yet yearning for someone to give them life alternatives to ease the pain of having limited resources. Residents hesitate to talk to outsiders, yet fear discussing personal problems with those they are familiar with because "the word would get out." A good possibility does exist that the word would, in fact, get out. Rural communities are characterized by a small, intimate style of living. Everyone in the community knows everyone else, and many are related. The members of the community are highly visible. A communication system exists in which the word spreads quickly and is usually exaggerated. Yet a wide range of behavior, even deviant behavior such as child abuse, is tolerated (Kirkland and Ivey, 1977).

Human service workers who live in rural counties have special problems. They are a part of the community system and virtually cannot go shopping without seeing a client. The community is likely to have an eye on the professionals, and standards of conduct will be higher for them than for the rest of the community. The professional service worker is likely to working, on a peer basis, with relatives of a client. Therefore, confidentiality in rural communities is a difficult issue. Rural communities may have few professional human service workers. Other workers are either paraprofessionals, untrained persons, or political appointees. The worker has to be professionally generic, yet have access to specialized services. The worker may many times fulfill the role of health worker, social worker, and community organizer.

THE RURAL FAMILY

The traditional concept of the rural family is that it is slightly larger than the urban family and is more likely to have close ties with an extended family, both for social interaction and for help—desired and undesired— than the urban family. The rural family is more likely than the urban family to be paternalistic and to have a traditional pattern of roles for the man, woman, and children of the family. Finally, the rural family tends to be politically conservative and socially tradition bound. Changes are slow in coming and not readily accepted.

Characteristics that describe the rural family are gradually becoming less distinct from those that would describe an urban family. As urban dwellers move into rural areas to live while commuting to the city to work, and as farmers and other rural dwellers are becoming more interdependent with the towns near them, the values and life-styles of rural and urban families are becoming more alike than different. Improved roads, transportation, and communication systems are great contributions to this gradual blending that has led to the term "rurban."

One can still readily distinguish three characteristics of rural family life. Distance among neighbors is great; resources for the family are limited—families are forced to be independent in function or to rely on extended family and neighbors; community boundaries are greatly expanded and vary with the family activity, but neighborhood communities are powerful in their ability to sanction individual family life-styles.

The characteristic of distance among neighbors needs little explanation but does lead to some conjecture on the effect of distance on rural people. Positive effects would include privacy, an opportunity to appreciate the aesthetics of nature, and space to produce food products for family consumption. This leads to a feeling of independence and self-sufficiency and to the belief that the poor rural American has a much better life-style than his urban economic counterpart.

One problem generated by distance for the poor rural families is that trips to school, recreation, medical, and shopping facilities must be carefully planned and budgeted for. An emergency trip might drastically affect the food budget for the month. Distance also leads to fewer social contacts with neighbors so that a child is generally taught social values and life expectations almost exclusively by the family and extended family who are his most frequent outside social contacts. This limited access to the values and life-styles of others tends to perpetuate a value for maintaining the status quo and limited life expectations for and by the children; that is, their life goals tend to be no greater than those of their parents so that little value is placed on an education beyond that which leads to the social and economic level of the parents. Distance can also be deadly, because of poor access to emergency medical facilities. As one man said, "If you take sick during the night or during a bad storm, you're just out of luck. I've known folks to die while waitin' to get through to the main road."

Limited resources, a second characteristic of rural life, means that the family unit assumes more responsibility for itself than it would in urban areas where the community would provide for religious education, recreating, counseling, and so on. Perhaps because the family does assume responsibility for its own or because there is little or nothing available for treatment anyway, there is a broader definition of "normal" among rural people. What a rural family might describe as "a little hard of hearing" might be designated a severe hearing loss by an urban family. A rural child might be "slow to learn," but an urban child would be "learning disabled." This is not merely semantic distinction but a distinction in degree of acceptance. The child may be deaf, but everyone knows it and compensates for it so that it is not problematic in their daily lives. Acceptance of problems becomes the pattern.

The third characteristic—expanded community boundaries—indicates that in rural areas characterized by scattered small communities, the rural family may use one community for shopping, another for the children's education, another for religious services, and still another for medical services. Somehow the rural family must adapt to being a participant in, but not a member of, several communities. The rural family is typically a member of a small neighborhood which may afford informal help in times of emergency and give the family an identity and a sense of belonging. However, for children from families who are poor—in the social, more than in the economic, sense—this small neighborhood can be damning: for in such small groups, family members bear the burden of the family reputation. Once that reputation is bad, all things bad are attributed to that family and its individual members. Examples of this are those welfare folks "who don't do nothing' but lay around and have kids so they can get more money." Therefore, the children are thought to be innately of low moral fiber. Another example, common in the Florida Panhandle area, is the exclusion from church groups and local club memberships of children from families who drink, because alcohol is satanic and evil, and therefore the devil is in the family.

In summary, distance, limited resources, varying community boundaries, and myths distinguish rural families from their urban counterparts.

CHILDREN'S RIGHTS AND ADVOCACY

Until very recently, children were viewed as property. Laws protecting children stemmed from the humane society's argument that children need the same protection levels of dogs, cats, and other animals. Unfortunately children's rights often are equated with the rights of pets—food, water, shelter, and so on. Children, especially in rural areas, are at times viewed as extensions of their parents and not as individuals in their own right. What the parents see as right for themselves is therefore right for their children. Children are often viewed, as in the Victorian era, as miniature adults and not as developing humans with different needs and different abilities from those of adults. The paternalistic structure of the rural family coupled with this view of childhood leads to a very strong sense of parental responsibility. Therefore, many rural families feel that they should have total control of the child's socialization process, and generally this view is supported and reinforced by the community.

Children in rural and urban areas are politically impotent and rely upon the human service professionals to advocate for them. Advocacy for children in rural areas presents problems peculiar to the nature of the rural community and to the rural family.

The rural child is more impotent than his urban counterpart for several reasons. Because of the distance between neighbors, the rural child may be invisible. He may conceivably be unknown to people outside of the extended family and unknown to formal organizations. Even though a birth may be recorded, there may be no community follow-up on the child because of unavailability of a service delivery system or limited personnel within a service delivery network. The parental and community expectations of obedience to, and compliance with, parental authority make children's rights, except for gross maltreatment, a nonissue. For the child advocate these conditions present delivery problems in that outreach efforts to locate families with children may be exhausting, and even when clients are identified, the advocate must use persuasion to change the attitude and life-style of the family and the community of the family.

The limited resources of a rural community pose problems for the child advocate. Once needs are identified, services to meet those needs may be nonexistent or barely accessible because of distance to the nearest community with that service. At times, meeting a need may actually deprive the child of the security of his home and the daily nurturing of his family. For example, children with severe learning handicaps may only have access to educational resources in a residential treatment center in a distant city. In situations in which services are not available in the community area, the child advocate may have to "take on" the community as a client and attempt to convince the community of its responsibility to provide services to its citizens.

Advocacy in rural areas is further complicated by the expanded community trend in rural living, contrasted with the rural community philosophy of ownership and noncooperative planning. To provide an effective, comprehensive service delivery network to rural children and their families, regional planning and funding are essential, since no one community has the financial or manpower resources to meet the needs of its children. For an advocate for children in rural areas, planned change involving cooperative efforts of citizens' groups, governing bodies, and social agencies from the region is essential. This takes time (an estimated two to five years for a major change), patience, and some expertise, It is noteworthy that the citizens of rural communities practice living in an expanded community, but community leaders and politicians have difficulty in recognizing this formally. The outreach advocacy intervention model is offered as an aid for planning and executing a change in a service delivery system for children and their families.

THE OUTREACH ADVOCACY MODEL
FOR INTERVENTION

This model indicates a nine-step diagnostic procedure beginning with a clear definition of the service gap and the population it affects (I). The next step may require some research or legal interpretation. If a federal, state, or local law mandates the provision of a service (II), the burden of the advocate is lightened because the sanction of the law validates his cause. This step may be complicated by wording in the law, such as "when a sufficient need is demonstrated." Further complications may be that the law only applies to governmental bodies receiving certain federal funds, or that the burden of proof may be on the plaintiff to show that existing services do not meet the specific needs of the client.

In identifying the etiology in the service gap (III), most frequently the gap originates on the state or community levels. At times, the state does not qualify for available federal funding for service delivery because of failure to comply with the mandates for funding. If the state is receiving funding for a service, where is the blockage? Must the local community provide matching funds? Must the community make some changes in its political structure to be eligible? Are community leaders not interested in or not aware of available funding for the service? At times the origin of the service gap is with the family. Because of religious beliefs or social values, the family will not allow the child to take advantage of an existing service. At times, misunderstandings or lack of knowledge blocks access for the child.

Intervention in a service delivery gap may occur simultaneously on several levels. The advocate must decide where he will be most effective and which effort will yield the desired results (IV). Based on the level(s) of intervention, he must recognize those agencies, people, or interest groups who may help or hinder his effort (V). The advocate should then assess the level of interest, positive or negative, for each person, group, or agency (VI). This assessment can be based on previous postures on similar problems and on the stated "reason for being" of the agencies or groups. Based on an assessment of the vested interest (VII) of the person, group, or agency, an intervention strategy should be formulated (VIII). An evaluation of resources—the advocate's in particular—should be made. He must ask himself what is needed and what he has available to accomplish it. Does he have the time, expertise, social or political power, community acceptance, contacts, and agency backing? Based on the degree of resistance or cooperation expected and on the strength of the necessary resources, a prognosis for success should be made (IX). If the prognosis is negative, the advocate should bolster his resources or choose an intervention level and strategy that may meet with success. Creating conflict, hostility, or a feeling of futility among community members will render the advocate impotent for other advocacy attempts in his rural community. Unlike his urban counterpart who can successfully use adversarial techniques for creating change on behalf of his client, the rural advocate will be more successful and acceptable to the community by using a collaborative approach.

References

Adams, Berg, Berger, Duane, Neill, and Ollendorff. *Children's Rights.* New York: Praeger, 1971.
Kirkland, J. and Ivey, K. Confidentiality: issues and dilemma in rural practice. Presented to Second National Institute on Social Work in Rural Areas, 1977.
NASW News (February, 1978).
Zeglinski, I. One earth, a changing world: global perspectives on social work education for rural practice. Presented to Second National Institute on Social Work in Rural Areas, 1977.

The Effect of Maternal Pyridoxine Deficiency on the Development of Atherosclerosis in the Child

C. I. Levene*, M.D., D.Sc., F.R.C.Path.
Department of Pathology
University of Cambridge
Cambridge, England

WHY IS ATHEROSCLEROSIS IMPORTANT AS A DISEASE?

The usual pathological description of atherosclerosis is confined to the changes in the aorta and in the coronary arteries. In the aorta, the lesions described range from fatty streaking (which many do not believe to be atherosclerotic in origin) to fibrous plaques localizing around vessel junctions and in the lower aorta, which appear to age by the filling of their centers with necrotic, fatty material and which may ulcerate, liberating their contents into the bloodstream. These ulcerated plaques may then become calcified and/or covered with thrombus. The overall difference between the young unaffected aorta and the old atherosclerotic aorta is that the latter is no longer distensible, having lost its elasticity. The lumen of the aorta is too wide for even the largest plaques to be able to narrow it and thus seriously impede the blood flow; however, the diseased vessel does lack the elastic recoil that the young aorta possesses. The consequences of this loss of elasticity are not often discussed, possibly because they are not clearly understood. However, a theoretical consideration of the role of aortic elasticity suggests that since diastolic recoil is responsible for the filling of the coronary arteries as well as the peripheral arteries, the loss of recoil must adversely affect these functions, unless, for example, a compensatory rise in blood pressure occurs. Is it possible that a feedback mechanism exists to guarantee adequate coronary filling and that such a mechanism would be brought into play by the loss of aortic diastolic recoil? Is it possible, for example, that this hypothetical feedback mechanism could be a cause of essential hypertension?

The effect of atherosclerosis of the coronary arteries themselves is more

*Member of the External Scientific Staff of the Medical Research Council, Department of Pathology, University of Cambridge, Tennis Court Road, Cambridge, CB2 1QP. England.

obvious; narrowing of the lumen of an end artery is plainly a harmful event, and one is therefore concerned about such narrowing in the coronary, cerebral, and retinal arteries—three vital end arteries—particuarly if thrombosis supervenes on top of a plaque to occlude the lumen. Death of myocardium or of the patient may occur as a direct cause of atherosclerosis of the coronary arteries, if excess demand is suddenly made on a narrowed vessel which is incapable of transmitting sufficient blood and which, being an end artery, has no alternative pathway. In the brain, narrowing of cerebral arteries may produce cerbral degeneration or death of brain tissue if the vessel is occluded by a thrombus; in the retinal artery, thrombosis will produce blindness. Elsewhere, as in the lower limbs, atherosclerotic narrowing of an artery may produce no symptoms if the collateral circulation is adequate—indeed, studies have shown that many people over the age of 40 have a symptomless occlusion of one of their major lower limb arteries. If blood demand exceeds the supply, pain on effort—intermittent claudication—may result, or gangrene, if the situation deteriorates, as it may in atherosclerosis complicated by untreated diabetes.

WHAT IS THE CAUSE OF ATHEROMA?

A simple answer to this question is difficult to give, first, because of the long period it takes for the disease to manifest itself clinically, and second, because of its undoubted multifactorial etiology. In this paper, I shall enlarge on one particular factor, arising before birth, which is perhaps the "priming factor," setting the scene for the ensuing complications, and which, if true, may be prevented by a slight modification of the maternal diet during pregnancy. First, though, I shall briefly review the various theories that have been postulated regarding the causes of atherosclerosis.

Virchow's Classical Theory

In 1856, Virchow, doyan of pathology and father of the Cellular Theory of Disease, propounded the view that the primary cause of atheroma (this term is used synonymously with atherosclerosis) was a degeneration of the arterial intima, followed, as a response, by fibrous intimal overgrowth.

In essence, it is difficult to see how this differs from the view that atherosclerosis is an aging process—that "man is as old as his arteries."

The Lipid Theory of Anitschkow

Atheroma, a word derived from the Greek and meaning gruel-like, applies to the appearance of the fatty material that fills the center of an advanced atherosclerotic plaque; in 1913, Anitschkow followed what must then have appeared to be a logical step, and fed rabbits a lipid diet—cholesterol—in an attempt to reproduce atherosclerosis experimentally. He did succeed in producing lesions which, it was claimed, resembled atherosclerosis, and this model has subsequently been widely used as the basis for an enormous amount of work, culminating in the "lipid theory" of atheroma. I believe that this line of work has taught us more about the metabolism of lipids than it has about the etiology of atheroma; moreover, with the exception of a small group of congenital hypercholesterolemic patients who do appear to be at greater risk of coronary artery disease, there is little hard evidence to support the lipid theory. However, this theory has managed to rally the strongest support during the past 50 years, although one suspects that this may no longer be the case.

The Mechanical Theory

Like the heart, the arterial system withstands great mechanical stress over a lifetime, and so it is not surprising that one view of atherosclerosis represents it as a response to mechanical stress; this includes several factors—anatomical factors such as the tethering of branches at their junctions with other arteries; rheological factors such as turbulence; gravitational factors stemming from man's upright stance; and finally, of course, an increase in blood pressure, considered by clinicians to be a major prognostic sign. One need only consider the association of pulmonary hypertension with atherosclerosis of the pulmonary tree, or observe the atherosclerotic changes commonly encountered proximal to the congenital localized narrowing found in coarctation of the aorta, to be convinced that hypertension must play a significant role in atherosclerosis, if only as an aggravating factor.

Intimal Hemorrhage—Winternitz

In 1938, Winternitz and his colleagues published their classical monograph which showed that capillaries, absent in the normal aortic intima, abounded about the edges of atherosclerotic plaques and were liable to rupture, producing intra-plaque hemorrhage. It is likely, in my view, that these fragile capillaries are a complicating factor in atherosclerosis but that they do not act as a primary factor.

The Thrombogenic Hypothesis—Rokitansky, Duguid

This theory was first advanced by Rokitansky, a contemporary of Virchow, who ascribed plaque formation to the localized imbibition of blood constitutents by the arterial intima—a "furring-up of the pipes." It was modified in 1946 by Duguid, who has, in his recent monograph (1976), enunciated as a principle of pathology the fact that thrombi which often form on the intima of arteries and become incorporated into the arterial wall, produce localized plaques that eventually cease to resemble thrombi histologically and take on the appearance of plaques. Duguid has argued from this that the incorporation of mural thrombi plays a significant part in the etiology of plaque formation, and his observations have been confirmed by many workers.

In 1951, Geiringer showed that the thickness of a plaque played a critical role in its subsequent history. Normally, in the aorta, only the outer part of the wall is supplied by very small blood vessels, the vasa vasorum, the inner portion of the aorta depending on the diffusion of oxygen and other nutrients from the blood itself. The adhesion of a sufficiently large mural thrombus and its subsequent incorporation into the arterial intima impaired the nutrition of the wall at that point; once the plaque reached a particular thickness, secondary changes took place at the most hypoxic region in the center of the plaque, resulting in fatty change, calcification, and a liability to hemorrhage from the capillaries, described by Winternitz, which had originally helped to organize the mural thrombus. A second point that Duguid has stressed is the difference between the texture of a rigid, intimal atherosclerotic plaque and the pliable pulsating vessel to which it is adherent; this point bridges the mechanical, thrombotic, and capillary hemorrhage hypotheses.

One question often asked of adherents of the thrombotic hypothesis is an explanation for the localization of the plaques at particular sites; one such explanation which various authorities have put forward has been that sites of medial weakness exist in the aorta and in the large arteries, but these sites are not evident except beneath the most advanced plaques where the media is found histologically to be greatly thinned. One means by which such perferential sites of medial weakness might be demonstrated is by distending a vessel that contains an atherosclerotic plaque sitting upon a normal-looking media, with formalin, at diastolic pressure. It became evident from such work that the usual appearance of the eccentric atherosclerotic plaque bulging into the lumen is in fact a postmortem artifact due to contraction of the media—and that the plaque normally bulges into the media where it is locally weakened and hence appears thinned, the lumen of the vessel being circular. This work tends to confirm the view that atherosclerotic plaques arise as repairs of shallow, focal aneurysms which have resulted from localized medial weakness; the cause of these weaknesses has remained obscure, but a possible explanation is now forthcoming.

Pyridoxine Deficiency

In 1949, Rinehart and Greenberg claimed to be able to reproduce atherosclerosis in monkeys by maintaining them for 2½ years on a chronically vitamin B_6-deficient diet. This experimental study was never taken up by other workers, as there appeared to be little rationale behind it; however, it is now possible to offer a feasible explanation for this observation, which will be dealt with shortly.

Water Softness

The observation that people living in areas supplied by soft water suffered from a greater degree of atherosclerosis than did those living in hard-water areas was first made by Schroeder in 1958 and taken up by the Crawfords later. Recent studies in the United States suggest that this factor may be a truly significant one.

Monoclonal Hypothesis—Benditt

On the basis of the presence in atherosclerotic plaques of a particular type of lactate dehydrogenase isoenzyme, Benditt has put forward the view that plaques are monoclonal in origin and are, in fact, smooth muscle cell tumors.

Sucrose Theory—Yudkin

A nutritional basis for atherosclerosis has been postulated by Yudkin, who has claimed that the relevant factor is excessive sucrose intake.

The foregoing views represent the bulk of the theories that have been postulated regarding the causes of atherosclerosis in humans; the two major ones are the lipid and the thrombotic theories. It is of interest to note that clinicians who need to treat patients suffering from coronary atherosclerosis consider that the three major risk factors are hypertension, smoking, and whether the patient suffers from congenital hypercholesterolemia.

THE ROLE OF PYRIDOXINE DEFICIENCY IN THE PATHOGENESIS OF ATHEROSCLEROSIS

The junction of the left anterior descending and the circumflex coronary arteries is one site in the human coronary circulation that is particularly prone to atherosclerosis and its sequelae. When a histological study of this site was performed in human hearts of all age groups, it was found that focal lesions of the internal elastic lamina—a localized splitting—commonly occurred in newborn babies and in stillborn infants before term (Levene, 1956). The significance of this finding was not apparent at the time; all that could then be said was that these elastic lesions conceivably represented visible areas of invisible underlying medial weakness—the medial weakness could not be demonstrated histologically because of the amorphous nature of collagen. The localized medial weakness did in fact exist had already been demonstrated by fixing the aorta and large musculoelastic arteries with formalin at diastolic pressure.

During the past 10 to 15 years, the work of a number of groups throughout the world has established the biosynthetic pathway for collagen; this protein, which forms the bulk of the media of the large arteries, plays a key tensile role in the maintenance of arterial integrity; the other protein that plays a tensile role is elastin. Emerging from three widely differing lines of research, a vital theme has become clear—that collagen and elastin, as major biopolymers, need to be cross-linked in order to fulfill their major functions in the arterial system. The three lines of work—osteolathyrism, the chemistry of elastin cross-links, and the effect of copper deficiency on the swine aorta—led to the finding that cross-linking of collagen and elastin is catalyzed by the same enzyme, lysyl oxidase; this enzyme acts by the oxidative deamination of particular lysine and hydroxylysine residues.

When it was discovered that lysyl oxidase required copper as an essential cofactor, and that aneurysm of the aorta with subsequent rupture occurred in copper-deficient swine, the importance of intact cross-linking became more apparent.

THE ROLE OF VITAMIN B₆

Lysyl oxidase, the cross-linking enzyme, is an amine oxidase, one of a group of enzymes whose inhibition by particular drugs has greatly advanced the therapy of mental depression. Close study of the cross-linking enzyme suggested that there were differences between these classical amine oxidases and lysyl oxidase, and eventually we were convinced and produced evidence that lysyl oxidase required a second essential cofactor, pyridoxal phosphate, for which vitamin B₆, pyridoxine, is a precursor (Murray and Levene, 1977). We have been able to show that vitamin B₆ deficiency in the chick produces a fall in lysyl oxidase in the aorta with a return to normal values by treatment with the vitamin.

It has recently become clear that pregnancy in women, which greatly increases the maternal need for vitamin B_6, induces both a maternal and a fetal vitamin B_6 deficiency despite the fact that the mother's daily intake of 2 mg of vitamin B_6 accords with the recommendations of the FAO. Recent studies by Lumeng and his colleagues, a large multidisciplinary American group, have shown that pregnancy induces a functional vitamin B_6 deficiency; this study is based on direct pyridoxal measurements in the maternal and fetal cord plasma rather than on SGOT levels, and the authors conclude that a doubling of the minimal daily requirements to 4 mg of vitamin B_6 would be necessary to prevent deficiency.

What is being suggested here is that these early focal lesions of the internal elastic lamina found in the coronary arteries at birth, at the site of predilection for the development of atherosclerosis in later life, represent the visible effects of the inadequate cross-linking of elastin and of the underlying medial collagen which leads in later life to classical atherosclerotic plaques. It is suggested that these early lesions result from malfunction of the cross-linking enzyme, lysyl oxidase, which in turn is due to a deficiency of the second essential cofactor, pyridoxal.

The reason for the localization of these sites of medial weakness is presumably anatomic and innate to the arterial system as well as to other sites of constant stress—for example, the pyridoxine-deficient chick shows severe lesions in the epiphyseal cartilages of the long bones. The mechanism by which the plaques develop on these sites of predilection includes, I believe, the deposition of mural thrombi among, no doubt, other factors, including possibly lipid.

The most significant point to be made is that it should be possible to prevent the formation of these lesions by doubling the present minimal daily requirement of vitamin B_6 during pregnancy from 2 to 4 mg. The findings of Rinehart and Greenberg, that chronically B_6-deficient monkeys develop atherosclerosis, are now easier to understand.

IS IT POSSIBLE TO PREVENT THE ORGANIZATION OF A THROMBUS AND THUS PREVENT OCCLUSION OR LUMENAL NARROWING?

Following our work on lathyrism, in which we had shown that the defect which produced skeletal deformity, avulsion of tendons, slipping of epiphyses, and aortic rupture, was an inhibition of the formation of collagen cross-links, we became interested in seeing whether the deleterious effects of fibrosis might be avoided by treatment with the *Lathyrus* factor, β-aminopropionitrile. Consequently, using experimental pulmonary silicosis in the rat as a model for a severe, progressive form of fibrosis, we were able to show that the therapeutic control of fibrosis was a feasible goal, although drugs less toxic than β-aminopropionitrile would be required (Levene et al., 1968).

If one accepts that the organization of mural arterial thrombi is a significant cause of lumenal narrowing, then it should be possible to prevent the organization of the thrombus into a rigid collagenous plaque by the judicious use of a suitable drug, with the result presumably that the pressure of the blood would rebore the lumen (Levene, 1963). It is to be hoped that a study of the enzymes and cofactors involved in the posttranslational phases of collagen biosynthesis will reveal suitable points for therapeutic attack, thus offering the clinician further options for at least 5 to 6 days following a nonfatal thrombosis of the coronary arteries.

References

Duguid, J. B. *The Dynamics of Atherosclerosis.* Aberdeen University Press, 1976.
Levene, C. I. The early lesions of atheroma in the coronary arteries. *J. Pathol. Bacteriol.* **72**: 79–82 (1956).
Levene, C. I. In *Evolution of the Atherosclerotic Plaque* (R. J. Jones, ed.), pp. 235–242. Chicago and London: University of Chicago Press, 1963.
Levene, C. I., Bye, I., and Saffiotti, U. The effect of β-aminopropionitrile on silicotic pulmonary fibrosis in the rat. *Br. J. Exp. Pathol.* **49**: 152–159 (1968).
Murray, J. C. and Levene, C. I. Evidence for the role of vitamine B₆ as a cofactor of lysyl oxidase. *Biochem. J.* **167**: 463–467 (1977).

Psychopharmacology in Children

Michael Koch, M.D.
Director of Child and Adolescent Psychiatry
Saint Paul-Ramsey Hospital and Medical Center
Saint Paul, Minnesota

The use of psychoactive drugs in children has developed more slowly than in adult psychiatry. Only after the useful properties of the stimulant, antipsychotic, and antidepressant drugs had been established in adult patients were these medications tried in child psychiatry. There continues to be controversy regarding their usage. Critics assert that the drugs used are ineffective or even harmful, that creative or troublesome children are unnecessarily being put into chemical constraints, and that reliance on psychopharmacology reduces the incentive to use other treatment methods (Rie, 1976). Drug treatment may or may not do any of these things, but it is necessary that the usefulness and dangers of drugs intended for use with children be carefully evaluated.

Drugs are seldom a definitive treatment in themselves; rather, when successfully used they make patients more available for other help. Usually it is best to obtain an untreated baseline before starting treatment because children frequently not only respond to reassurances and to placebo (Eisenberg, 1972), but also have a strong tendency for spontaneous cure (Levitt, 1971). The lowest possible dose should be started and then increased with close monitoring for clinical and side effects. Ordinarily this requires observations of both teachers and parents as well as interviews with the child. Parents should not be left in charge of dosage regulation, but it should be a matter of consensus between the family and the physician. If it is clinically indicated to exceed the package insert, guardian and, with adolescents, patient consent should be obtained.

There are several kinds of drugs useful in child psychiatry. It is advisable to know one or two drugs of a particular class well and, after starting one, to give it a fair trial.

STIMULANT DRUGS

Stimulant drugs should be considered for use with children who present with a nonpsychotic behavior disturbance dominated by short attention span, impulsivity, physical overactivity, and disruptiveness in school. These hyperkinetic symptoms are usually well established before entry to school.

The preferred stimulants for hyperactive children include methylphenidate (Ritalin), dextroamphetamine (Dexedrine), and magnesium pemoline (Cylert). Amphetamines were first used in the treatment of hyperactive children and are still popular. They and methylphenidate are both short acting (two to six hours), and some children require a second dose around midday. Systematic studies of dosage (Sprague and Sleator, 1975) suggest that many children will respond to a dose of methylphenidate as low as 0.3 mg/kg/day, or a total daily dose not exceeding 20 mg/day. It is likely that the reduction of motor activity is due to increased attentiveness and not a paradoxical response (Werry and Aman, 1975). Side effects, which occur in about 30% of patients receiving moderately high doses of either drug, typically include anorexia, delayed onset of sleep, and weight loss. Some data suggest that stimulants, especially Dexedrine, may inhibit growth. A recent investigation did not show any growth reduction in adolescents treated with stimulants as children (Gross, 1976), but it is important that height and weight changes be monitored on a growth chart. If weight loss persists despite attempts to lower the dose and temporary "drug holidays," it may be necessary to use other drugs (phenothiazines or tricyclic antidepressants) less likely to retard growth in patients who require drug treatment. Other side effects in some patients are irritability or mood changes and tearfulness.

Pemoline differs from the other stimulants in that its activity is delayed one to two weeks, it is long acting, and it can be given in a single dose. Because of the delayed response, many clinicians find it more difficult to regulate dosage. Also SGOT values may become elevated with pemoline, and it is necessary regularly to evaluate liver function. The significance of SGOT elevations with pemoline is uncertain; if they are persistent, the drug should be discontinued.

The duration of treatment with stimulants has not been clearly established. The symptom of hyperactivity does decrease markedly with age, but social and attentional handicaps frequently persist into adolescence. No data have yet revealed an increased prevalence of amphetamine abuse in children who have been treated with stimulants. Pemoline has no euphoriant effects at therapeutic levels and can be considered for adolescents who still require stimulant treatment.

Although the use of medication to manage behavioral disorders in children is still controversial, Klein et al. compared the results of behavior-modification techniques with methylphenidate treatment and found medication to be significantly better (Gittelman-Klein et al., 1976). Ordinarily both would be used, with drug treatment regarded as synergistic and not in competition with other treatment.

MAJOR TRANQUILIZERS

These drugs include the phenothiazines and butyrophenones. Although frequently used in adults with psychotic conditions, they are also used in child psychiatry for the management of hyperactive, aggressive behaviors, in childhood psychosis, and in Gilles de la Tourette syndrome. Children with conduct disorder who respond to these drugs show less aggressive behavior, are more manageable, and have fewer fights with other children. The usefulness of the drugs is generally limited by the high incidence of side effects at therapeutic dose levels.

In psychotic children, age of onset usually distinguishes childhood autism from schizophrenia. Stimulants usually worsen the condition of psychotic children and should be avoided. The major tranquilizers do not have a specific effect in autism but may be helpful in controlling sleep disturbance, overactivity, and mood lability, and in aiding behavioral control. With medication, school attendance becomes more possible with some psychotic children and institutionalization may be avoided.

Both young and psychotic children tend to be less sensitive to pheothiazines and haloperidol. Dosages range up to 500 mg daily for chlorpromazine (Throazine) and thioridazine (Mellaril); 10 to 15 mg for haloperidol (Haldol), fluphenazine hydrochloride (Prolixin), and trifluoperazine (Stelazine); and 40 mg for thiothixene (Navane). They can usually be given in a single evening dose and with fewer side effects. The most common unwanted side effects are sedation, dystonic conditions, and weight gain. Dystonic symptoms can be safely treated with diphenhydramine (Benadryl), and, if that fails, anticholinergic medication can be used on a p.r.n. basis. A transitory extrapyramidal rebound syndrome has been reported in psychotic children after withdrawal of antipsychotic drugs (Polizos et al., 1973). Neurologic symptoms are more likely with high-potency drugs such as fluphenazine or haloperidol than with drugs such as chlorpromazine or thioridazine. The former drugs should be avoided except when the dosage can be kept below that which causes extrapyramidal symptoms, because of the discouraging syndrome of tardive dyskinesia (an oral-buccal-lingual choreoathetosis), which is thought to be due to postsynaptic sensitization to dopamine as a result of the dopamine blocking activity of the drugs.

Haloperidol is well established in the treatment of Tourette's syndrome, where it reduces the frequency and severity of tics and vocalizations

(Shapiro et al., 1973). Low doses should be started, 0.5 to 2 mg/day, and then increased to higher levels until either attainment of the desired clinical improvement or side effects that cannot be controlled without reducing the dosage. Haldol should not be used to treat the common, usually transient tics of childhood. It and Navane have FDA approval for patients over 12 years of age only.

In addition, low doses of phenothiazines are used in many clinical settings for treating anxious children, usually without notable side effects. Their efficacy for this purpose is not documented, and there is much variability in clinical response.

ANTIDEPRESSANTS

Controlled trials of monamine oxidase inhibitors are rare in children, and tricyclic drugs are mainly in use. Again, the clinical indications for the use of these drugs in child psychiatry is not limited to depressive conditions.

The oldest and most frequent use of the tricyclics in children is in enuresis. Most enuretics will wet less often when receiving the drug, but many relapse once the drug has been discontinued. It is unlikely that they suppress enuresis through an antidepressant effect because the response usually occurs shortly after starting treatment.

The tricyclics have also been studied in systematic trials with hyperactive children (Rapoport et al., 1974). Most of these studies have shown them to be of some value, but they ordinarily produce significantly less improvement than methylphenidate and are not as well tolerated. Their effect on cognitive function suggests that they work by some action analogous to that of stimulants rather than by a sedative or antidepressant effect. Dosage is controversial because over 200 mg/day has been used in hyperactivity, whereas in the treatment of enuresis daily dosage usually does not exceed 50 to 75 mg. The usual side effects are dry mouth and constipation. Less frequently, children can become more irritable and tearful, and have weight loss. High doses can produce more serious side effects, namely seizures and cardiotoxic effects consisting of T-wave changes and lengthening of the P-R interval. Therefore, the Food and Drug Administration has ruled that 5 mg/kg is the maximum allowable clinical dose in children. Ordinarily it is best to not exceed 100 mg daily.

More recently, antidepressants have been used to treat emotional disturbance in childhood. Gittelman-Klein and Klein (1971) have demonstrated the efficacy of tricyclic antidepressants in treating pathological separation anxiety as seen in some school phobias. There was a lessening of observed depression, phobic behaviors, and somatic symptoms in the imipramine group, and it was thought that the drug acted by reducing symptoms of severe separation anxiety. Although the treatment is still experimental, there does seem to be sufficient evidence to warrant antidepressant drug trials in children who present with a phobic disorder, persistent mood change, and somatic symptoms. The drug effect may not be seen for several weeks, and medication should not be discontinued too soon. In addition, there must be a concurrent effort to increase the child's independence.

Lithium carbonate is widely used to treat and prevent relapses in adults with manic-depressive psychosis. There are uncontrolled anecdotal reports of its usefulness in children, and it has been used in adolescents with episodic, violent temper outbursts (Annell, 1969). It does not have FDA approval for children under 12 years.

MINOR TRANQUILIZERS AND SEDATIVES

Both of these types of drugs are widely used in children by family physicians. The benzodiazepines and antihistamines have a useful role in minor disturbances marked by disturbed sleep and anxiety. There are few published studies, and some investigators (Lucas and Pasley, 1969) found an increase both in anxiety and in disturbed conduct in prepubertal children treated with diazepam. Although safe, these drugs should not be prescribed for more than a few weeks. Antihistamines are sometimes used to treat anxiety and sleep disturbance, and commonly induce sleepiness at dose levels of 2 to 4 mg/kg body weight.

OTHER DRUGS

Anticonvulsants have at times been advocated for the treatment of behavior problems in both epileptic and nonepileptic children. To date, they have no demonstrated value except as an indirect result of better seizure control (Stores, 1975). Caffeine has had recent popularity in the treatment of hyperactivity, but controlled studies indicate that it is not a reasonable alternative to stimulant medication (Firestone et al., 1978).

Restriction of certain foods and additives from the diet has recently been popularized as a treatment for hyperactivity. Controlled studies to date suggest that this remedy is difficult to carry out and ineffective in most children studied (Werry, 1976).

References

Annell, A. L. Lithium in the treatment of child and adolescent. *Acta Psychiat. Scand. Suppl.* **207**: 19-30 (1969).

Eisenberg, L. Symposium: behavior modification by drugs. III. *Pediatrics* **49**: 709-715 (1972).

Firestone, P. et al. The effects of caffeine and methylphenidate on hyperactive children. *J. Am. Acad. Child Psychiat.* **17**: 445-456 (1978).

Gittelman-Klein, R. and Klein, D. F. Controlled imipramine treatment of school phobia. *Arch. Gen. Psychiat.* **25**: 204-207 (1971).

Gittelman-Klein, R. et al. Relative efficacy of methylphenidate and behavior modification in hyperkinetic children: an interim report. *J. Abnorm. Child Psychol.* **4**: 361-379 (1976).

Gross, M. D. Growth of hyperkinetic children taking methylphenidate, dextroamphetamine or imipramine/desipramine. *Pediatrics* **58**: 423-431 (1976).

Levitt, E. Research on psychotherapy with children. In *Handbook of Psychotherapy and Behavior Change* (A. Bergin and A. Garfield, eds.), pp. 474-494. New York: Wiley, 1971.

Lucas, A. R. and Pasley, F. C. Psychoactive drugs in the treatment of emotionally disturbed children: haloperidol and diazepam. *Compr. Psychiat.* **10**: 276-386 (1969).

Polizos, P. et al. Neurological consequences of psychotropic drug withdrawal in schizophrenic children. *J. Autism Child. Schizophr.* **3**: 247-253 (1973).

Rapoport, J. et al. Imipramine and methylphenidate treatment of hyperactive boys. *Arch. Gen. Psychiat.* **30**: 789-793 (1974).

Rie, H. Hyperactivity in children. *Am. J. Dis. Child.* **130**: 783-789 (1975).

Shapiro, A. K. et al. Tourette's syndrome: a summary of data on 34 patients. *Psychosom. Med.* **34**: 419-435 (1973).

Sprague, R. and Sleator, E. What is the proper dose of stimulant drugs in children? *Int. J. Ment. Health* **4**: 75-104 (1975).

Stores, G. Behavioral effects of anti-epileptic drugs. *Dev. Med. Child Neurol.* **17**: 647-658 (1975).

Werry, J. S. Diet and hyperactivity. *Med. J. Aust.* **2**: 281-282 (1976).

Werry, J. S. and Aman, M. Methylphenidate and haloperidol in children. *Arch. Gen. Psychiat.* **32**: 790-795 (1975).

Contemporary Working Women on the Treadmill

Mitzi L. Duxbury, R.N., Ph.D., F.A.A.N.
Professor and Assistant Dean for Graduate Studies

Susan J. Shelendich, R.N., B.S.
Research Assistant
University of Minnesota School of Nursing
Minneapolis, Minnesota

Labor Force Participation

Labor force participation by women has increased dramatically. The 1969 *Handbook on Working Women* noted that while the United States experienced equally large population increases for men and women from 1947 to 1968, the number of men in the work force increased only 16%. The number of women in the work force increased 75%.

During the 1970s the number of women in the work force continued to increase in vast proportions. Today, over 70% of all divorced women work, 60% of women separated from their husbands work, and 50% of married women living with their husbands work. The sharpest increase is seen in the case of women with children under 6 years of age. In 1950, only 12% of all women with young children worked outside the home. Now, 40% of all mothers with children under 6 are employed.

Women are showing up in jobs once held by men. In the decade from 1960 to 1970, the percentage of woman bank and financial managers increased from 12.4 to 31.6%, the percentage of lawyers and judges from 3.3 to 12.4%, and the percentage of physicians from 6.8 to 10.7%. The number of women awarded graduate degrees in business administration has grown fivefold in a decade (*U. S. News and World Report,* 1980).

Incomes

The lot of women has not improved, however, in spite of the broadened scope of women's enlistment in the work force. In the present as in the past, the pay and prestige afforded a work group decline, as participation by women increases (Bird, 1968). Compensation for work performed by women, compared to that of men, has decreased as women's participation in the labor force has increased. In 1955, the average wage for a woman was 64¢ for every dollar earned by a man in a similar job. In 1980, women earn 59¢ for every dollar earned by a man in a similar job.

Health Care

The cost effective contribution of nurse-midwives to high quality health care is often acknowledged. However, nurse-midwives could be lowering the cost of health care at their own financial expense. Second-class salaries and second-class working conditions are assigned to nurse-midwives, largely because they are women.

Rose's (1980) summary of the history of payment for obstetrical services illustrates the degree to which the sex of the caregiver determines the worth of services rendered.

Midwives of previous centuries provided free services, ostensibly because of the empathy they felt for those "whose hour had come." Over time, token goods or small amounts of money were provided to midwives for their services. When medical men entered the field, those men charged substantially higher prices for essentially the same services.

The cost of having a baby has soared in the last 30 years under the direction of predominately male obstetricians. Now, when health care costs have reached a crisis point, nurse-midwives (women) have rallied as advocates for client needs. Women and babies are healthier, and personal service is provided to the consumer at affordable costs. Nurse-midwives, however, receive little compensation for the responsibilities they shoulder: they often work 60 hours or more a week, have offices in "the basement of the Rear Annex," as Rose depicts it, and earn lower salaries than others with similar educational preparation.

Pediatric nurse practitioners, credited with providing high-quality cost effective care for children, were lauded for their efforts ten years ago at the height of the shortage of primary care physicians in the United States. Now, as the nation faces an oversupply of physicians, the American Academy of Family Practice calls for restraints on the practice of pediatric nurse practitioners. A 1980 position paper states that the practice of these independent nursing professionals should ideally be controlled by physicians! The worth of nursing (women's) services is thus belittled as it threatens to compete for more of the physician's dollar.

Contemporary Women's Values

Women in the United States in the 1980s continue to marry and bear children. They are also employed in the labor force in ever-increasing numbers. How do women view these dual commitments?

In 1970, sociologists Karen Mason and Larry Bumpass surveyed American women to explore contemporary women's sex role ideology by examining intercorrelations among attitudes and social and demographic variables (Mason and Bumpass, 1975). Statement areas of the questionnaires included desirability of traditional sex-based division of responsibilities, rights of women workers, consequences of maternal employment for the well-being of children, and various stereotypes about women and the conditions under which they are happiest.

They found that the gender role attitudes of never-married women under 45 were not organized into a unidimensional ideology. Rather, these women embraced different fundamental attitudes toward their roles at home and at work. Most of them favored a traditional division of labor at home. Toward work, they embraced an egalitarian ideal.

Choosing a traditional approach toward home responsibilities and an egalitarian approach to the work world places women in an impossible situation. Whereas most men support their work world accomplishments "propped up" by their wives, women tackle home and work simultaneously, and alone. The decision is not freely made, however, as societal and family pressures push women into the worst of both worlds.

Thus, an educated married woman's resolution of this career-family dilemma cannot be adequately evaluated without knowledge of her husband's resolution of the way he fits his work and his family into his life (Bailyn, 1972). In a study of 200 British university graduate women and their husbands, Bailyn found that the happiest women with careers and families were those whose husbands were family men rather than career oriented.

In the United States today, 70% of the men still believe that "unless it's an economic necessity, a family is better off if the woman of the house does not work" (*U. S. News and World Report,* 1980.) Apparently, women's preferences for traditional gender role ideology in the home is being influenced in large part by men!

Life on a Treadmill

Life on a treadmill is the logical consequence of women embracing a traditional role in the home and an egalitarian role in the workplace. Dual commitments compete for the limited time and energy resources of individual women, ensuring decreased productivity and precluding achievement and a sense of worth and accomplishment in either arena.

What is Life Like for Today's Working Woman?

The mythical ideal, as suggested by columnist Ellen Goodman, is that today's working woman rises each morning with enthusiasm. Breakfast is shared together by the family, and Mom, Dad, and the kids arrive at work and school on time and eager to begin the day. The typical working woman, dressed for success, engages in important work, executing command decisions. At the end of the workday the family reunites. A gourmet dinner is followed by a spirited political discussion involving the entire family. The working woman and her husband-lover retire early, whereupon she enjoys multiple orgasms until midnight.

The truth is that today's working woman, a nurse, for example, may rise at 5:30 A.M. after working an extra shift until midnight the previous evening. A load of laundry is tossed into the washer, dishes from two days ago are washed, the children are awakened and dressed. No one eats breakfast. The children are dropped off at the day-care center by 6:30 A.M. The wife-cum-nurse arrives at the hospital by 7 A.M., changes to scrub clothes, and spends her day in a busy, short-staffed ICU. She cares for patients and, quite frequently, saves lives. She orders medicines and supplies, cleans the unit, humors physicians, teaches interns, calms relatives, fixes equipment, and finds staff for the next shift. She doesn't take a lunch break; she works overtime to complete paperwork. This college-educated working woman is earning less money than many men working in the same building, who are high school dropouts.

By 5 P.M. she is back at the day-care center. She and her family enjoy yet one more macaroni and cheese dinner. She plays Candy Land with the kids; the loser cries. Her husband is watching "Monday Night Football" on television. The children are sent off to bed. The clothes aren't folded. The working woman falls asleep on the couch.

Much of life stress may result from exposure to the constant, unremitting negative effects of frustrated attempts to manage the common, everyday problems of life. Chronic daily stress, such as that experienced by many working women today, is often followed by burnout. This overwork syndrome of physical, emotional, and cognitive exhaustion hinders even the motivation required to achieve success and satisfaction at home and at work. Given the constraints imposed by today's societal norms, women's feelings about their roles at home and work, and men's current low level of involvement in the home, is there any reason to think that working women can anticipate any escape from their treadmill existence?

Prescription for Change

Lack of flexibility in the work world, the isolation of small modern families, and the "masculine is superior" attitude work together to support the inferior status of women. The attitudes perpetuate the vicious cycle of overwork, stress, and exhaustion in working women.

It is impossible to change the status of women without also changing the status of men. This hybrid model of change rejects the institutional structures present in both the workplace and the home.

The work world, and male attitudes, must adapt their demands toward women's needs if the full contribution of women at work is to be realized. Women are unlikely to abdicate their role in the home; consequently, daily coordination of work, home, and family will continue to be a high priority.

Employment policies can be changed to encourage options such as flexible work schedules and parenthood for both men and women. Child care facilities should be more readily available. Equal pay for comparable work should be a reality, not a dream.

Current gender role stereotypes limit the personal growth of men and women. To ask women to become more like men merely invites women to take the oppressor's role. Shared allocation of the tasks and responsibilities of child rearing and homemaking will enhance the lives of both men and women, and allow solution of the family-career dilemma for today's working women.

Summary

Social and economic forces of the past two decades have served to exploit women's talents in the marketplace. The net effect of 20 years of change has been a decline in the position of women in our society.

Current economic conditions in the United States demand labor force participation by many women. Such mandatory labor force participation in combination with traditional responsibilities in the home precludes high levels of achievement in either sphere and ensures that women are exhausted and stressed. The mythology supporting the inferior status of women has been reinforced, not erased, by the treadmill existence of contemporary working women.

Fundamental changes will have to occur in the relationships between men and women if the vicious cycle perpetuating exhaustion and stress in women's lives is to be interrupted. Gender role stereotyping obstructs maximum achievement at home and at work for men and women alike. Assumptions underlying current patterns of behavior between men and women need updating. Societal norms respecting the contributions of men and women at home and at work will ease the currently disproportionate burden carried by women.

References

Bailyn, L. Career and family orientations of husbands and wives in relation to marital happiness. In *Readings on the Psychology of Women* (J. M. Bardwick, ed.). New York: Harper & Row, 1972.

Battle of the sexes: men fight back. *U. S. News and World Report* 50-52 (December 8, 1980).

Bird, C. with Briller, S. *Born Female,* pp. 33-35. New York: Pocket Books, 1968.

Burke, R. J. and Weir, T. Relationship of wives' employment status to husband, wife, and pair satisfaction and performance. *Journal of Marriage and the Family* 279-287 (May, 1976).

Holstrom, L. Toward our liberation. In *The Two-Career Family,* pp. 153-181. Schenkman Publications, 1972.

Macke, A. S. et al. Housewives' self-esteem and their husbands' success: the myth of vicarious involvement. *Journal of Marriage and the Family* 41: 51-57 (1979).

Mason, K. and Bumpass, L. U. S. women's sex role ideology, 1970. *American Journal of Sociology* 80: 1212-1219.

Rapoport, R. and Rapoport, R. Dual career families: progress and prospects. *Marriage and Family Review* 1-12 (September-October, 1978).

Rose, P. A. How much is a nurse-midwife worth? *Journal of Nurse-Midwifery* 25 (6): 1-2 (1980).

A Population under Duress: Violence against Women

Mitzi L. Duxbury, R.N., Ph.D., F.A.A.N.
Professor and Assistant Dean of Graduate Studies

Diane K. Kjervik, R.N., M.S.
Assistant Professor
University of Minnesota School of Nursing
Minneapolis, Minnesota

Violence against women has become a way of life throughout the world. In our culture this violence is manifested in many ways, some specific to us, others general to humankind. This brief paper deals with certain etiological factors underlying the problem, describes forms aggression may take, and proposes some solutions.

VIOLENCE: RAPE AND THE SOFT KILL

Aggression takes myriad forms, both overt and subtle. Domestic violence, rape, and genital mutilation are overt manifestations; more subtle and pervasive psychological and sociological forms may be equally damaging. Steinmetz and Straus have maintained that "any social pattern as widespread and enduring as violence must have fundamental and enduring causes."

Throughout history, male envy and fear of women have ranked high among the fundamental causes of violence against women. Men may envy women for their greater resistance to disease, increased longevity, greater quantitative sexual abilities than males, and women's reproductive ability. Morgan identifies men's early fear of women in primitive times as being related to the mystery of reproduction.

The social forces that condone and/or nurture violence against women are manifested in the prevalent myths related to rape, socialization of the young, backlash to the women's movement (by the "moral majority," religious trends, police, and judicial systems) and, increasingly, the media.

One myth about sexual assault is that women who are raped have brought it upon themselves by dressing seductively, visiting places where they know the risk of rape is great, and then giving only half-hearted resistance to the aggressive approaches of strangers. This myth shifts the blame to the victim.

The fact is that rape is seldom provoked by the victim. Only 4% of reported sexual assaults, according the Federal Commission on Crimes of Violence, involve any precipitative behavior on the part of the victim, and indeed this precipitative behavior involved walking or dressing in a manner defined, simply, as "attractive."

Victims are of all social classes, ages, and races, with the reported age ranges between 6 months and 93 years. Up to one-half of all sexual assaults are committed in the victims' private residences.

It has been well documented that the primary goal of the rapist is not sexual gratification. Rather, rape is predominately an aggressive attack against a member of the population of women, a violence enacted upon the gender "female."

Another myth is that many reportings of rape arise from a woman's desire to have a man arrested in a moment of anger following a fight, through motives of vindictiveness or a desire for revenge. The facts show that only 2% of all rape calls are false reports, roughly the same percentage as in the reporting of any felony.

Although reports of rape are on the increase, many feel that most rapes (perhaps many as 98%) are never reported. The reason for this isn't hard to figure out. For one thing, police and courtroom procedures leave much to be desired in terms of comforting the victim and prosecuting the aggressor. The victim must relive her ordeal several times in the presence of police officers, detectives, counselors, prosecutors, and trial lawyers. She may be required to submit to polygraph tests and to intimate physical, and psychiatric examination. Her private life may be made public. Friends and spouse may doubt the veracity of her report. The burden of proof lies with her, the victim, and finally, more often than not, after her double ordeal, the rapist is set free.

THE KILL VICARIOUS

An alarming trend in the last few years has been in the increased portrayal and acceptance of violence against women through motion pictures and television. Many feel that this is related to the women's movement toward equality, that it represents a well-organized backlash against women.

Often the victims in films are independent, assertive, and successful women. The message here clearly is, "This is what you will get if you step out of line." One uniquely disturbing aspect of this pattern involves a recent trend in camera utilization. In some of the older, "violent" films, such as those of Alfred Hitchcock which portray women as victims, the camera lens presented to the viewing audience the victim's view of her pain and anguish. In a sense, the eye of the camera was the victim's eye. Today the tendency is to let the audience see and participate vicariously in assaults through the eyes and mind of the assailant. This can develop an empathy toward the aggressor. In a movie theater today, one may be startled, but is seldom surprised, to hear the audience shout, cheer, and applaud the aggressor. Contrast this behavior with that of earlier audiences whose gasps of empathy were for the victim.

A more subtle, less physically violent treatment of women is seen in many other films today. The highly acclaimed movie *Ordinary People,* about a woman who has lost her young son, depicts her as cold, unfeeling, and superficial. The surviving son and the husband, mutually supportive, together secure professional help to resolve the trauma induced by the child's death. They are able to cope and to grow. No support is available to the woman, and her grief and pain are not made apparent in the film. She is portrayed as an obstructor in the process of grief resolution in the husband and son. The media message is clear: "good" women are supportive of their families; they have no real needs of their own.

The production of sexist and violent X-rated films increases yearly. The National Coalition on Television Violence states that more X-rated movies than G-rated films (those designed for general audiences) were produced in 1980. About one-third of the films produced in 1968 were rated G, compared to only 4% in 1980.

In describing causal factors underlying violence against women, Brownmiller maintains that women are punished for *not* maintaining their traditional passive role. The media enlists in a vigorous effort to press this message home.

WOMEN'S SELF-CONCEPT: SOCIETY'S MIRROR

Mixed societal expectations of what a female should be create an unsureness within her as to what she should do to behave acceptably. Strength and self-assertiveness are seen as desirable characteristics of adults, but are not perceived as clearly feminine traits. Passivity and deference may be seen as proper feminine behaviors, but these are not aspects of healthy adult behavior.

The woman in a violent situation is faced with this dilemma and becomes immobilized from the stress of determining whether to submit to the abuse or to fight or flee from it. This immobility explains why at times a woman who is much larger and much stronger than her assailant submits to an attack without fighting back or getting away.

Stress-induced immobility leads to self-deprecation. The woman blames herself for her immobility and for the attack itself. The rape victim, the myth described above early implanted in her mind, may believe that if she had worn different clothes or walked a different route home she could have avoided the attack. Self-blame reinforces the immobility, or as Walker labels it, the learned helplessness.

The victim frequently expresses more concern for her attacker than for her own health. In support groups for rape victims, one of the initial concerns expressed by the women is that the men who raped them must feel awful about what they did. They must feel guilty and their lives must be in shambles. The focus on persons external to the self is easier than facing—and dealing with—one's own feeling of immobility and powerlessness.

The high frequency of rape and battering in this society and the unpredictability of when it will occur reinforce the woman's learned helplessness. Straus estimates that 50 to 60% of all married couples experience violence within their relationship. LeDray estimates that one out of every 50 to 100 adults experiences rape. Insofar as this figure may be derived from reported rapes, which are a fraction of the total number, the incidence of rape is probably much greater.

In Seligman's experiment in which dogs were given intermittent, unpredictable painful shocks, the dogs learned that no matter what they did they might experience pain. The result was immobility. Even when a way out of the situation was offered, the dogs made no effort to use it. As women receive frequent emotional abuse in terms of society's negative evaluations of them, together with episodic physical abuse through rape, incest, and battering, they learn to feel helpless against this violence; they do not try to stand up to it or get away from it unless strongly encouraged or directed to do so.

Learned helplessness diminishes one's self-esteem. A battered woman may feel increasingly culpable and unworthy as she continues to stay with her abuser. Efforts of helpers to point out what she is doing to herself by staying with the batterer augment her sense of self-betrayal. Similarly, a rape victim often blames herself for having been attacked. Victims of violence are under stress and react to this by displaying widely diversified psychological reactions. The pattern of the rape victim's reaction to the attack differs from the battered woman's pattern. A battered woman who is beaten at sporadic intervals over a period of time suffers from chronic stress as a reponse to what Walker calls the cycle of violence. The raped woman, during and subsequent to the attack, suffers from acute stress and anxiety.

Characteristically, the rape victim goes through three phases: (1) the acute reaction typified by shock, extreme anxiety, disorganization, and physical problems; (2) the outward adjustment in which extreme feelings are suppressed or denied and the woman returns to her normal daily routine; and (3) integration and resolution accompanied by depression, a need to talk about the rape, anger, and eventually a reality-based view of the incident (LeDray). Psychological reactions to rape often continue for years. Some women are not able to tell anyone about their suffering because of their personal shame, embarrassment, and self-contempt.

Walker identifies three phases in the cycle of violence: (1) a tension-building phase where minor physical battering incidents and psychological abuse occur; (2) an acute battering phase where the batterer loses control and the major physical attack occurs; and (3) a kindness and contrition (loving) phase where a calm exists between the man and the woman. The couple live in a state of extreme mutual dependence. The man believes he cannot exist without the victim as much as she believes she cannot live without him. Ten percent of the battering men in Walker's study killed themselves after the woman ended the relationship.

Following the battering cycle, the woman's victim role is solidified in the final phase, where the man behaves lovingly toward her. Having learned that the violent episode precedes episodes of loving behavior, she may provoke an attack in order to bring about this aftermath. In this way the woman may find a kind of stability, however precarious: unable to control whether or not she will receive physical abuse, she can determine when and where the abuse will come.

In summary, the psychological portion of violence against women begins long before any actual attack. Women learn to dislike themselves and to be victims at an early age. Correspondingly, men learn to be victimizers of women. The actual physical violence is the logical end point in the education of females as victims.

FREEING THE VICTIMS: A VIEW TOWARD CHANGE

Societal acceptance of violence against women must be challenged. Media portrayals of woman as victim and man as victimizer teach women and men how to behave. The exploitation of women's bodies in pornography and prostitution should not be passively accepted or ignored. Its destructiveness to the self-concepts of both man and woman must be acknowledged.

Victims of violence can be helped by having access to safe houses to which they and their children can retreat. Individual supportive therapy is helpful for some victims whose guilt, anger, and depression have immobilized them. Group treatment can also be effective. Walker suggests that battered women, who tend to isolate themselves from others, benefit from group interaction with other battered women in which they learn that their problems are not unique. However, Valenti says that in composing a group, a therapist should mix battered women with women who have general relationship problems, thus avoiding their being stigmatized by the label "battered woman."

Traditional couples therapy is not considered effective in dealing with battering relationships. As Walker says, teaching couples how to fight more fairly is not helpful. What they need to learn is to obviate loss of self-control. Walker has developed an effective behavior-oriented form of couples therapy, based on her cycle theory of violence, that aims to short-circuit communication patterns which precede the stage of violent outburst.

Victims need to think rationally about what has happened to them. Instead of blaming themselves, rape and battering victims must learn what societal views of women have done to create the atmosphere and expectation of violence. The victim also needs to learn that no behavior of hers (unless she strikes the man first in a life-threatening manner) justifies his violence. Even if she walked naked down a busy metropolitan street at 3 A.M., she would not deserve to be raped.

Battering victims should learn that there are alternatives available to them and to explore these alternatives. The process is gradual. Seligman's dogs had to be dragged out of their painful situation many times before they unlearned their helplessness. Similarly, a battered woman may go back to the batterer several times before she actually sees and believes that she has options.

Counselors should not be overzealous in pressuring women to leave the battering situation. Such pressure can paradoxically diminish the woman's self-esteem. The counselor should assist the woman in identifying the needs that may be fulfilled by the batterer and in finding healthful alternatives. The woman should be encouraged to identify her unmet needs and to think about how these could be met in the context of her overall well-being.

Clearly, it will be necessary to eradicate sexism, both rank and subtle, as well as the counterparts introjected within the personalities of both the victim and the victimizer, before violence against women ceases. Health care professionals are in key positions to help effect these crucial changes.

References

Kjervik, D. K. and Martinson, I. M. (eds.). *Women in Stress: A Nursing Perspective.* New
    York: Appleton-Century-Crofts, 1979. (Specifically, chapters as follows: LeDray, L. et al.
    Impact of rape on victims and families; Valenti, C. Working with the physically abused
    woman.)
Morgan, R. *Going Too Far.* New York: Vantage Books, 1979.
Steinmetz, S. and Strauss, M. (eds.) *Violence in the Family.* New York: Harper and Row, 1974.
Straus, M. A. and Hotaling, G. T. (eds.). *The Social Causes of Husband-Wife Violence.* Min-
    neapolis: University of Minnesota Press, 1980.
Walker, L. E. *The Battered Woman.* New York: Harper and Row, 1979.

Family Stress, Family Strength

Sara Taubin, Ph.D.
Associate Professor
Department of Human Behavior and Development
Drexel University
Philadelphia, Pennsylvania

Emily H. Mudd, Ph.D.
Emeritus Professor of Family Study in Psychiatry
Consultant in Behavioral Sciences
Division of Human Reproduction
Department of Obstetrics and Gynecology
University of Pennsylvania
Philadelphia, Pennsylvania

Families are social, cultural, and economic systems subject to overlapping,
interminable intrapsychic, interpersonal, and exogenous stresses. We have
selected for consideration three areas of diverse yet related stress: the
overloads of simplistic, contradictory, and provocative misinformation
about families, women, and fertility through the media; the mounting impact upon families of women's paid work outside the household; the
related problem of infertility management facilitated through couple
counseling. Additional major family stress is reported. Flexible behavior
and adaptive mechanisms in healthy families are summarized. Questions
are raised about the feasibility of national policies to anticipate impacts
and buffer families against excessive stresses.

Facts about Families: Definitions and Trends

Concepts of family are volatile mixtures of fact, myth, and sentiment. When a legal or demographic precision is required, family is defined as two or more people, related by blood, marriage, or adoption, living under one roof. Most people at some points in their lives fit into this traditional definition. Normal life transitions bring about other family arrangements for all of us. Yet definitions and statistics are often twisted out of context deliberately or through ignorance to confuse and arouse people (Glick and Morton, 1977).

For example, there is the repeated assertion that only about 13% of families are now traditional, nuclear families. Disbelief and shock greet this statement. What insidious changes must have happened if this shrinking minority alone supports our traditional heritage. Worse, 87% of us must live in deviant groupings which undermine values and disrupt society. In fact, the figure is lifted from a tabulation in which it applies to a particular segment of families composed of an employed father, an unemployed mother, and children under 15 years of age. A change in employment pattern or children turning 18 is a normal event, not a deliberate defiance of tradition. Traditional families are always a small percentage of households. Divorce statistics are also sensationalized and arouse anxiety.

A major concession to a broader view of family was made at the 1980 White House Conferences on Families. Recognition as families was offered to people living in enduring committed relationships. Representatives from every part of the country accepted this more inclusive label. To be named a family member seems to provide an identity, validate and stabilize relationships, and relieve the stress of alienation.

Goaded and misled by information drilled in by the media, "many conclude that something has gone seriously awry," according to Masnick and Bane (1980). Aware that rational responses to changing patterns are also possible, they analyze demographic data, chart long-term trends, and use the method of cohort analysis to correct misconceptions and predict probable changes through 1990. They suggest that the traditionalist families formed after the World War II were a temporary response to abnormal social events. Young families being formed now, they say, are returning to the following long-term projections that began more than half a century ago.

Later marriage (in the mid-twenties), a leveling off or small rise in divorce rates, and lower fertility are established patterns. Within a longer life, with more options at more numerous developmental nodes, people will have more complex and unconventional life histories. Before and after marriage, and for some between marriages, single life is on the rise, with or without children. By 1990 about two-thirds of households will be entirely adult, many of these solitary widows. Married couples will head up about half of the households.

Certainly changes, even when expressed in numbers, may be unsettling. On the other hand, as people move from one family type to another or set up new households, they develop greater flexibility, adaptation, and tolerance for stress. The realization that the ups and downs of personal life follow a cohort wave may in fact provide a sense of shared identity, connectedness, and strength. Women's attachment to careers, delayed childbearing, and an increased incidence of infertility are cohort experiences from which the demographic sciences develop neutral data and informed predictions. Responsible reporting could open the path to rational personal and public decisions.

The Continuing Impact of Women's Work

Making a living is in all accounts the number one stress in families. Managing money is a major problem. Changing work roles are a significant source of stress between women and men. Work and woman is the focus of this brief summary. Directly related to trends in delayed marriage, fewer or no children, and independent living arrangements is the significant increase in the number of women seeking full employment outside the family. Few statistics will be cited here since the pattern is complex and percentages are derived from overlapping or contradictory data bases. Age, marital status, education, the presence and age of children, and socioeconomic level are variables that affect individual decisions and group pressures in the labor market.

"A revolution in the impact of woman's work is on the horizon," report Masnick and Bane (1980). Better-educated women in large numbers will demand an equal share of the benefits of employment. Women now typically work part time, part year, and sporadically in low paid jobs. Working wives now contribute only about a quarter of family income. Fully employed women, on the average, earn less than men in equivalent jobs. The revolution yet to come is in women's attachment to careers, working full time, and accumulating lifetime fringe benefits packages.

The employment of mothers outside the family has traditionally been considered harmful to the family. Some blame the presence of women in the workplace as a major contributor to what they see as the general destruction of the family. A more reasonable examination reveals that much of the turmoil in families with working mothers results not from employment but from the dearth of support services for the women and their families. As one example, there are fewer than 2 million licensed day-care facilities for the more than 6 million children of working parents. Quality care is shockingly expensive. After-school care for older children is considered a family problem exclusively. An unmentioned problem is the mischief worked upon and by young people of high school age with time on their hands and few constructive opportunities. Questions about child care perplex the two-career family: is it desirable even if it can be found?

Stress is also generated within the couple (Skinner, 1980). Most husbands approve of their wives' working and enjoy the economic benefits. Their verbal support does not, for most couples, translate into the assumption of an equal share of housework and family responsibility. Men help out, even cheerfully, when asked. Truly equal contributions of time and effort elude most working couples. Family time in addition to work time drains women's personal lives. Unfortunately, in some families it comes to a choice between the marriage and the job.

Employers have been reluctant to acknowledge the stress people experience from their balancing act between job and family. Most jobs are not given the flexibility that would allow men as well as women to devote adequate attention to their family needs. From observing women's family and work requirements, men have become interested in the advantages of flex-time, job sharing, shorter hours, and paternity leaves. There is beginning evidence that when tried, cooperation between workplace and family benefits both.

The impact of women's employment on families has been continuously evaluated for two decades. Although the findings differ somewhat by population studied, there is substantial evidence that when wife and husband are pleased and support each other, the foundation is laid for a constructive marriage (Mitchell, Taubin, and Mudd, 1965) and for an equally positive result in the children. Certainly there is more money. In some cases, the mother's work is the only or major income. Children of working parents develop a work identity, and learn responsibility and independence. Most important, they expand their perception of female/male roles and partner relationship in marriage. The benefits for the couple include dual retirement incomes while both are alive. Men related to home and children, and women capable of financial management, have added insurance against the inevitable end of the marriage by death. The negative view of the wife's employment entrenched in the popular wisdom is that it may pose a threat to the husband's self-esteem, particularly if she gains prestige and status from her job or if her earnings exceed his. Changes in the power structure may bring increased conflict as employed wives tend to exercise more influence in decision making than do full-time homemakers. The pressures of work and family responsibilities may reduce the amount of time parents have to spend with children and with each other. A wife with an independent income may be more inclined to see divorce as an alternative to an unhappy marriage than a wife who is financially dependent on her husband.

These negative effects may be transitional problems of adjustment rather than permanent, long-term consequences. Conflict, for example, may be healthy in the long run, as it encourages husbands and wives to develop more effective communication patterns. Time pressures may force parents to find more constructive ways of relating to their children and to each other.

The overall impact on families of women's work outside the home is subject to many different interpretations. There is little doubt, however, that women will continue to seek paid employment for ideological as well as economic reasons. Projections are for an increase of 12 million women workers during the next decade. This means that by 1990, 70% of all women will be in the work force, accounting for one-half of all workers. It is intellectually untenable to expect that we will ever return to the traditional family with a wife who spends full time in the home and a husband who earns the living. Although the traditional pattern continues to be an option for some families, it is not and in all probability will never again be the norm.

John Kenneth Galbraith, for one, has documented the concealment of the housewife's substantial contribution to the economy. Her "shadow" work is unpaid and unpraised. Moreover, during the intervals of time when a woman may need, want, or be forced to leave paid employment, Galbraith asserts, she is manipulated into excesses of credit-financed consumption; stress compounds with the interest. He concludes that for housewives "to see how they are now used is to see that they need not be used. To see that they serve purposes not their own is to see that they can serve purposes that are their own."

Infertility Counseling to Reduce Stress

Unanticipated side effects and latent consequences reside within the most thoughtful decisions, helpful technologies, and benign behaviors. Certainly the education of women with subsequent career attachment cannot be faulted. Equally beneficial are the greater varieties and effectiveness of contraceptives, for they give men and women reproductive choices. Later marriage and childbearing have been documented as components in more stable marriages and better parenting. Singly and in combination, these contemporary realities have contributed to an increasing incidence of infertility. It is estimated that between 15 and 20% of couples will not have children, (Masnick and Bane, 1980); some are child-free by choice, others are bereaved and sincerely anxious for help.

Infertility is a complex couple problem, mixing physiologic and psychogenic, male, and female factors. Environmental causes of sterility have been documented, while new dangers are being identified and reported. Psychologic procedures and treatments are applied when no organic causes of infertility can be identified. Counseling may be useful when reproductive barriers are primarily sexual, social, or behavioral (Mudd, 1980). The role of stress in reproductive inability is readily perceived by the counselor, although the impact of emotional stress on reproductive physiology has not as yet been clarified.

While infertile couples differ widely, they are alike in many ways when they come for counseling. Their frustration in their lack of control over reproductive decisions is great. Many couples had been able to schedule the important events of their life up to the present. They are shaken by their powerlessness. They feel frightened and diminished by the medical and surgical procedures. They may feel drained, barren, and old if they have delayed childbearing. There is a tendency to place blame on past contraceptive practices, on each other, and/or on their physician. One or the other may be avoiding sex on schedule, or the male may become unable to ejaculate. Performing now is associated with failure. When pregnancy is delayed or does not occur within a year or so, both husbands and wives may become frustrated, short tempered, and full of anger.

Communication with the counselor enables anger to be released. This in turn eases tension. Social and sexual values are examined, and the dignity and self-esteem of both women and men, as well as their belief in each other, are restored. Options for bringing about the advent of a child through desired pregnancy, artificial insemination, or adoption are examined. Through these means some couples achieve their desired parenthood.

Women and men are both distressed by infertility, but understandably, the wife seems to suffer more. In a basic sense, pregnancy, birth, and the responsibility for new life belong in large part to the female. Women have enjoyed reproductive freedom as a right, and both they and their spouses seem to expect conception when desired. Counseling can help these couples tolerate frustration and find substitute satisfactions if necessary. Undesired infertility is a stress of major proportions to a couple. In the national perspective it does not rank high.

Major Stresses on Families Summarized

In 1980 the White House conference to examine family difficulties, strengths, and public policy issued its final report. Calculated attempts to disrupt and honest disagreements marked the four years of community, state, and national meetings. Nevertheless, the majority of the participants did find themselves in agreement on a range of issues. Five recommendations received major support. They reflect the gravest perceived national family problems. Priority is given to:

- Adoption by employers of such family-oriented policies as flexible working hours, negotiable leave time, shared and part-time jobs, and sensitivity to the effects of job location transfers.
- Efforts to stem alcohol and drug abuse through education and the media.
- Recognition of the financial contribution of homemakers, changes in tax codes to eliminate the marriage penalty, and revision of inheritance taxes.
- Tax policies to encourage care at home of the aged and the handicapped.
- Increased financial assistance to families with a handicapped member.

The proposed Equal Rights Amendment, abortion, and sex education issues also received recommendations as secondary listings. Just how far reaching and meaningful the proposals will be remains to be seen. Professional advocates for families and family members demonstrated remarkable tenacity and strategic acumen in diverting organized forces bent on subverting the purpose of the meetings. Implementation of the recommendations by public laws and private policies may be a long-range process. Family strengths were demonstrated by the participants and documented in the countless words of testimony. They were not examined as the conference had promised.

Family Adaptation to Stress

There is cumulative evidence of the presence of durable families, resistant to pervasive assaults of environmental stress. Their competence, flexibility, and adaptive skills are being studied (Mudd, Mitchell, and Taubin, 1965; Lewis, 1976; Mudd and Taubin, 1980). The finding that levels of discord, tension, and physical illness coexist with effective functioning should come as no surprise. Some individuals and families succumb to stress. Others are stimulated by problems, remain in control, and reorganize at even higher levels of family cohesion. A number of clear patterns for handling stress are cited in studies of varied types of durable families:

- They have a strong core of shared beliefs and values which stabilize the family. Yet they are not rigid and exclusive. Opinions or beliefs may be questioned and revised. Difference is respected.
- Activity, initiative, involvement, and commitment are repeated themes. Mental and physical health are constantly being refreshed and restored through education, cultural interests, body maintenance.
- The families have a clear stucture that distinguishes the generations. The couple is united, affectionate, and egalitarian. The children participate in decisions, but do not run the family.
- Problems are acknowledged and dealt with, but there seems to be a high threshold to stress. Such families generally perceive and report few stresses.
- Numerous affiliations are maintained with kinfolk, friends, and communities. A generosity of spirit is apparent.

Moderation and reality define stress-resistant families in their negotiations with external systems. When troubled, they use the options of seeking help from doctors, marriage counselors, and the clergy. A decade review of family stress and coping concludes:

As our focus shifts from trying to understand why families fail to how they manage or even thrive on life's hardships, we can envision the emergence of a wealth of research which will add in an appreciable way to our understanding of why families often do so well, with so little. (McCubbin, 1980)

Family Policy, Family Impact

For the next few years, at least, we might expect more than usual disarray in the interface between government and families. Those who appropriate for themselves the pro-family label are most vociferous in rejecting government programs and policies. Yet the major pro-family events in the country's history were the social security laws of the 1930s, the veterans' benefits of the 1940s, and the Older Americans Act of the 1960s, as examples. For most of us it is inconceivable to separate government from families; they are one and the same. The fact is that governmental pro-grams and policies have had and continue to have an impact on families (Mudd and Hill, 1956).

We conclude with some thoughts about stress, families, and public policy. First, responsible government must assume the backup support for basic family needs. For example, when unemployment insurance is ex-hausted, the provision of food, shelter, clothing, and health care may need to be coordinated by combined public and private sources. The issue is to insure that indispensable family-oriented programs are functioning effi-ciently and supportively.

Second, a new aspect is family impact analysis. This methodology is in-tended to determine the actual or probable positive/negative impacts of a given policy or program on families. Both the initial intent and its unan-ticipated or latent consequences are scrutinized.

The third trend is toward further research for family policy. Here the focus is to determine whether an emerging set of family patterns is likely to cause trouble. An assessment of consequences is made for the family unit, for individuals, and for society.

The family debate over the next few years will center on the questions: What is a family? What is the federal role? How can impact studies be con-ducted without creating new bureaucracies? What is to be done with research for family policy and impact statements when they are in hand? Will the popular media disseminate findings responsibly? In the present climate of hands-off families, will policy makers pay any attention to them? (Nye and McDonald, 1980).

References

Glick, P. C. and Morton, A. J. Marrying, divorcing, and living together in the U.S. today. *Population Bulletin* **32**(5): 2-39 (1977).

Lewis, J., Beavers, W. R., Gossett, J. T., and Phillips, V. A. *No Single Thread: Psychological Health in Family Systems.* New York: Bruner/Mazel, 1976.

Masnick, G. and Bane, M. J. *The Nation's Families 1960–1990.* Boston: Auburn House, 1980.

McCubbin, H. I. et al. *Family stress and coping: a decade review. Journal of Marriage and the Family* **42**(4): 855-867 (1980).

Mudd, E. H. The couple as a unit: *sexual, social and behavioral considerations to reproduc-tive barriers. Journal of Marital and Family Therapy* 23-28 (January, 1980).

Mudd, E.H. and Hill, R. *Memorandum on Strengthening Family Life in the United States* (Confidential). Washington, D.C.: Social Security Administration, Department of Health, Education and Welfare, 1956 (limited distribution).

Mudd, E. H. and Taubin, S. B. "Success in family living: a twenty year follow-up. *Journal of Marital and Family Therapy* (in press, 1981).

Mudd, E. H., Mitchell, S. P., and Taubin, S. B. *Success in Family Living.* New York: Association Press, 1965.

Nye, F. I. and McDonald, G. W. Family policy research: emergent models and some theoretical issues. *Journal of Marriage and the Family* **41**(3): 473-486 (1979).
Skinner, D. A. Dual career family stress and coping: a literature review. *Family Relations: Family Stress, Coping, and Adaptation* **29**(4): 473-482 (1980).

Stress: an Individual Nursing Perspective

Barbara L. Nichols, R.N., D.Sc.

President
American Nurses' Association
Madison, Wisconsin

To be a female and a nurse is to experience discrimination, prejudice, segregation, and power differences based on gender and occupation. In human terms it means feeling anxiety, frustration, and stress—a sense of being worn out, used up, spent, dissipated, drained, thwarted, and consumed.

Why is it important that nurses understand stress? First, nurses are partners in a health team that frequently encounters and treats the manifestations of stress. Second, the very nature of the work nurses perform may be stress producing on them. Third, the multiple roles nurses hold—wife, mother, and professional—spawn role conflict and ambiguity which may create individualized stress. Thus it is important that nurses have a clear conceptual understanding of stress and its relationship not only to nursing but to everyday life. Understanding stress becomes the basis for preventing and alleviating it both in nurses and in patients.

Most nurses talk about stress, many think they suffer from it, and all think they know what it is. But what is it? Stress in engineering terms is described as a body suffering strain as a result of being subjected to load or force. This definition is directly analogous to one of the ways stress is used in everyday language to refer to human beings.

Hans Selye, the leading authority on the physiology of stress developed the concept of stress as a physiological adaptation. He termed the external force which causes stress, the stressor. The most important features of his concept of stress are:

1. Stress is nonspecific—it can be evoked by many different stressors.
2. Stress represents a protective defense mechanism.
3. The defense mechanism itself may be maladaptive.

One criticism of Selye's concept of stress is that its concentration on the physiological basis of stress fails to account for individual differences which occur in real life. For this reason stress has also been studied by social scientists. Major concepts regarding stress from the social-psychological literature are:

- Stress emanates from demands made upon the individual partly by his environment, and partly by his internal physiological and psychological needs.
- Stress arises if there is an imbalance between the individual's view of the demand and his assessment of his own capacity to meet the demand.
- Stress brings into play coping mechanisms both physiological and behavioral which reduce the impact of the stressor.
- Stress arises in the organism whenever the demand for adaptation made on the organism departs from a moderate level.

The status of the nursing profession illustrates the first concept that stress arises from pressing requirements made upon the individual, partly by his environment, and partly by his internal physiological and psychological needs. Hospitals, the major employer of nurses, have been dominated by men who view nurses in sexist images of femininity. Physicians and administrators who control the health care working environment tend to view the nurse as having the attributes of housekeeper, wife, or mother doing whatever home and institution require. Any attempts by women to express nontraditional roles lead men to chastise women for stepping out of their roles of wife, mother, servant of man. Clearly, the fundamental image of nurses is deeply rooted in that of females. Consequently, the authority structure of the hospital replicates the authority structure of society: men are the decision makers, and women are the doers. At conflict in the hospital work environment is the nurses' decision-making authority. Within the hospital power stucture it is assumed that nurses have no independent authority to make decisions about when and how to apply medical technologies which are often their direct responsibility. Nurses have been cast in roles in which they frequently have to make decisions, some meaning the difference between life and death, but institutional rules recognize only physicians as having authority to make independent professional decisions about patients. Thus, as the doctor-nurse game illustrates, the authority structure in health care is designed to make nurses' actions and nurses' contributions to patient care reactive to physicians' judgments and orders and to employers' views of institutional needs and prerogatives. In practice, nurses must frequently make the decisions even though institutional rules deny them this authority.

The attitudes of nurses and of society toward the worth of their profession demonstrates the second concept that stress arises if there is an imbalance between the individuals' view of the demand and his assessment of his own capacity to meet the demand. From infancy, girls are trained to be passive and dependent. As they grow up, the culture continues to emphasize that women are more dependent and less competent than men. Likewise, the stereotypic image of the best nurse is somebody who is passive, attractive, willing to work hard for low pay, less competent than the male physician, and moderately trained. Nurses have not been viewed as having special intellectual expertise to contribute to patient care. It is perceived that what they do is more important than what they know. The need to keep nurses in their place by devaluing their knowledge and skill has been ongoing. Nurses are all too often viewed like women in general— as sex objects first then as productive workers.

Since World War II the functions and responsibilities of nurses have changed dramatically. While in the past nurses were primarily concerned with professional support and assisting the patient with activities of daily living, the nurse is now involved in the direct application of modern technologies. Nurses control and translate much of the available clinical knowledge to care for the seriously ill and are expected to make judgments about its appropriate use. Hospitalized patients are more acutely ill than ever before. Such patients are more dependent upon nurses in every respect. The nature of their illnesses requires the use of professional nursing clinical judgment, constant surveillance, and the coordination of services provided by others. Nurses must be able to distinguish the beginnings of life-threatening crises from routine discomforts and to take action based upon informed professional judgment. The current hospital structure provides little recognition of the significance of the nurse's role in clinical decision making. There has been minimal change in the nurse's sphere of authority in the care of patients. To cope with the stressors in nursing which flow from the low status of the work, and with the social, political, and philosophical stereotypes associated with the profession, nurses must understand that some of the frustration and dissatisfaction they experience comes from the environment in which they work.

A classic experiment by Hofling and others (1966) illustrates the third concept that stress brings into play coping mechanisms both physiological and behavioral which reduce the impact of the stressor, and documents Selye's view that the defense mechanism may be maladaptive. In the experiment, nurses were called upon to carry out a physician's order which was clearly inappropriate. Surprisingly, almost all of the nurses, until intercepted by the researcher, would have carried out the inappropriate order despite their recognition that it was probably not in the patient's best interest to do so. I believe this demonstrates dramatically the enormous stress experienced by nurses who agonize about whether their professional judgment is a legitimate basis for questioning a physician's order. This stress is one of the prime factors which contribute to the burnout syndrome discussed in the nursing literature (Storlie, 1979; Wandelt, 1980). I believe that it is an important factor prompting nurses to seek employment in other parts of the health field. The high nursing turnover rates reported by the nation's hospitals may in fact represent a coping mechanism. Quitting work or leaving a dissatisfying work environment divorces the nurse from stress evoked from the interplay of acutely ill patients and the absence of control to execute clinical decisions in the interest of patient care.

The fourth concept maintains that stress arises in the organism whenever the demand for adaptation made on the organism departs from a moderate level. In terms of carrying out the responsibilities of nursing, nurses must understand the effects of drugs on stress and the relationships among stress, mental and physical illness, and patient care. Stress is an important factor in variations in man's behavior, sick or well. Insufficient demand upon an individual can be as stressful as too much demand. There are a number of circumstances in which patients may be isolated and/or impoverished in sensory terms, for example, in private rooms or in intensive care units. This paper does not discuss in any detail stress caused by lack of stimulation or sensory deprivation; it is mentioned primarily to sensitize the reader to the fact that an impoverished environment may be as stressful as one which is excessively stimulating. Therefore, it is important for nurses to understand the relationship of stress to sickness and health. It may well be that the optimum state is not an absence of demand, but a moderate amount which is within the range of the individual's ability to cope. Selye says it best, "Stress should not and cannot be avoided. The art is to learn how to live a full life with a minimum of wear and tear. The secret is not to live life less intensely but more intelligently. Each individual must find his innate stress level and live accordingly." Each nurse must understand the effect of stress on her ability to effectively carry out her responsibilities.

In summary, much of the stress experienced by nurses emanates from the nature of the work itself and from the social, political, and philosophical stereotypes associated with the profession. Nursing will remain a troubled profession as long as decisions about the nurses' role and status are viewed in the light of restrictive social definitions of their proper place as employees and health care professionals. It appears that stressors in nursing could be brought into proper balance if nurses had more autonomy in the execution of their clinical judgments and expertise, as well as in the manner in which nursing work is organized and controlled in the hospital environment.

References

Hofling, Charles K., Brotzman, E., Dalrymple, S., Groves, N., and Chester, M. P. An experimental study in nurse-physician relationships. *Journal of Nervous and Mental Disease* **142**(2): 171-180 (1966).

Lazarus, R. S. *Psychological Stress and the Coping Process.* New York: McGraw Hill, 1966.

Selye, H. *The Stress of Life* 2nd ed. New York: McGraw Hill, 1976.

Storlie, F. J. Burnout: the elaboration of a concept. *American Journal of Nursing* **79**(12): 2108-2111 (1979).

Wandelt, M. A. *Conditions Associated with Registered Nurse Employment in Texas.* Austin: Center for Research, School of Nursing, University of Texas, 1980.

Geriatric Stresses

Otto Pollak, Ph.D.
Professor of Sociology
University of Pennsylvania
Philadelphia, Pennsylvania

Manifestations of aging surprise old people from year to year and sometimes in shorter intervals. Even if one conceives of the life cycle as presenting ever new challenges to one's power of adaptation, one is frequently under the delusion that one has met the last challenge, and can now experience a period of peace and rest. This, however, is not so; the restlessness of the human experience never stops.

Perhaps the most pervasive aging experience is slowing down. In middle years one is surprised that young people seem to walk faster than they used to; even if one is walking busily, younger people seem to bypass one without apparently being in a hurry. At first one reacts to this slowing down of one's walking speed with amusement, then with acceptance, and finally with irritation. It may have been fun to see a younger person who has bypassed you waiting for a Stop light to change, and to reach him or her before it does. It is a different experience when that person has made a green light and it changes before one can cross. It is a new surprise to find oneself considering taxis for distances which one used to walk as a matter of course, and it is another surprise to find oneself considering whether one wants to go out at all because walking has become physically difficult to the point of affecting one's self-image.

Slowing down also has a sexual aspect which may interfere with marital satisfaction. In the process of maturation men become slower in getting aroused, slower in getting an erection, and slower in reaching an ejaculation. Women, on the other hand, become more impatient to complete the act or at least to have their male partners complete it, because osteoporosis frequently makes the sexual act physically difficult for them and leaves them with backaches for hours or days to come. It is a paradox of human development that a frequent form of female dissatisfaction with intercourse, namely premature ejaculation of the male, turns into the opposite in old age. It can also happen that it is psychologically misunderstood. The slowness of the male may suggest to the female that she is not desirable anymore and may make her impatient; showing this impatience may then produce failure where she was anxious for fulfillment.

Other surprises in the aging process are equally stressful and seem equally difficult to handle, if not more so. Retirement, whether taken early or at the obligatory age limit, represents the challenge of a different use of time and of a different income, as well as a loss of legitimate encounters. The different use of time deprives the day of markers to which one has become accustomed. There is no morning train to make, no office to enter at a certain time, no specific time to go out for lunch, no specific time for going home. One's circle of associates becomes smaller, and if one appears in one's old working place to socialize with former colleagues, one finds oneself interfering with their schedule and, pretty soon, one has lost information about issues that currently concern them so that these encounters become sometimes unwelcome and sometimes forced. It is also difficult to be a guest where one was a person with a function and, conceivably, a person with power. One former executive expressed this to the writer by saying that upon retirement he became a "no person."

Retirement also affects marriages. People who have "dosaged" and conceivably tolerated their marriage only on the basis of a limited part of the day, find that they have to experiment with amounts of togetherness that they have known before only on holidays and vacations. Mutual irritation may result, and the retired person may have to seek office substitutes in public libraries, public parks, and taverns. Retirement is also usually connected with a decline in income that, under the impact of inflation, becomes ever more marked. While it was assumed in the past that we had made socioeconomic advances by providing retirees with 80% of their preretirement income, this is true only for the first year; afterwards, their income is constantly decreased in terms of purchasing power by the inroads of inflation. It is perhaps one of the most relentless surprises of the aging process that income becomes more insufficient from year to year. It has frequently been said that older people do not have the expense of bringing up children anymore and that this justifies their decline in income or at least makes it tolerable. What this frequently overlooks is the fact that the medical expenses of older people are constantly going up.

Older people acquire a new social role, the role of the chronic patient; this means regular visits to their doctor's office, regular health checkups, often special diets, and drugs which prevent water retention, control high blood pressure, supplement potassium deficits, etc. Perhaps one of the greatest stresses of advanced years is the regular health checkup which stimulates death anxieties on a routine basis, particularly in our civilization in which cancerophobia is kept alive by the mass media and by a stream of information about friends and relatives who have been attacked by this disease. The stimulation and restimulation of death anxieties in regular intervals by our modern health care system is in and by itself one of the greatest geriatric stresses that we know in our time.

Another aspect of old age stress is the loss of religiosity by many older people who in their prayers ask God to exempt them or their loved ones from terminal diseases and death, and find their prayers unanswered. It is, of course, a naive, if not infantile religiosity to ask God to arrange for exemptions from the working of his Creation. Still, it is frequently done with stressful ineffectiveness.

A common observation of the aging process relates to memory loss for recent events. One forgets where one has put things, one mislays checks before cashing them, one forgets names, one loses notebooks, and one must spend time finding what one has mislaid, looking up what one has forgotten, and reconstructing information that one has assembled. These memory losses produce irritation with self, and, in repetition, affect the self-image. They are probably one of the more bothersome aspects of the aging process, and coping with them takes large amounts of time from people who are aware that their time is running out.

Another aspect of aging is finding one's home too large or too unmanageable after the spouse has died, and the temptation is strong to move to more convenient quarters, preferably in a more pleasant climate. Relocation, however, deprives old people of easy contact with their friends and relatives, and throws them into new circumstances at a time when adaptability goes down. Actually, constancy is one of the greatest needs of people who suffer declining capacities, declining income, and declining social contacts. It is a losing battle best fought in one's home ground.

Unavoidable in the long run are losses in perception acuity, such as loss of hearing, deterioration of eyesight, and even diminution of the sense of smell and taste in advancing years. The writer has fought a long battle with hearing loss and made many adaptations to it. As a teacher, he had to change his methodology from classroom discussion to lecturing. He has shifted his luncheon engagements from going to restaurants to inviting people to his own home or office. He has been forced to come closer to people if he wants to understand them and, thus, to apologize for the invasion of their personal territory, and he has found that he can be a participant at parties only by raising topics of likely interest without being able to follow the resulting conversation. All these adaptations have seemed to be successful for a time, and all have become more burdensome as the years have gone by. As a simple vignette it might be mentioned that using a public telephone has become difficult for him, while he can still telephone successfully with his own personal equipment.

Climbing stairs in one's own household or in office buildings where the elevator is out of order becomes an undertaking which must be avoided as far as possible or accomplished with greater effort or more amount of time than other people have to apply.

In a marriage, these deficiencies frequently lead to a redistribution of roles: where one partner cannot function, the other must take over. In such situations, people who have been retired with unstructured time hanging heavily on their hands, find themselves suddenly pressed for time. Attention should be drawn also to the frequent experience that one lives in old age with anticipatory bereavement. Health checkups bring bad news; the obituaries in newspapers remind one of one's own mortality and the mortality of one's friends. Sometimes every week brings news of somebody having died whom you have known. Thoughts of dying replace thoughts of living.

For people with enduring marriages, the death of spouses becomes one of the greatest traumas of advancing years. Since women have a greater longevity than men, this stress frequently afflicts women rather than men. One could almost say that when we talk about old age, we talk mostly about old widows. Going to sleep in a bedroom which one has shared with a spouse for most of one's adult life evokes feelings of abandonment and loneliness for which the companionship of a marriage has provided little, if any, preparation. Since loneliness implies helplessness, widowhood, especially during the nighttime, is, during the period of transition, anxiety provoking to the point of despair. Strangely enough, the majority of women get over this traumatic experience quite well and lead fairly satisfactory lives after the shock of survivorship has worn off. Many such widows are inclined to reject the thought of a second marriage, even if opportunities should suggest themselves, not wanting to assume the responsibility of becoming a nurse-housekeeper to an aging man for a second time in their life. Widowers, however, seem to be less capable of adjustment to survivorship. It is frequently observed that they die relatively soon after the death of their wives. Apparently a long marriage develops a kind of nurture which leaves old men in a kind of emotional deprivation which they only rarely are able to overcome.

Increasing infirmity makes many old people dependent on their grownup and, in their turn, aging sons and daughters. They become dependent on them, not only for services such as shopping, cleaning, and health care, but also emotionally and financially. In the parent-child relationship, since many such relationships are conflicted, the reversal of power stimulates the expressions of old antagonisms, going back as far as child-rearing experiences. Old people, on the other hand, have in their infirmity a weapon of hostility with which to frighten sons and daughters who are, in turn, approaching old age. Giving a son or daughter to understand that in the visible future he or she will know by experience what it means to be old and infirm can stimulate death anxieties which, so far, have been repressed. Such negative interactions between sons and daughters in their 50s and 60s and parents in their 70s and 80s can produce guilt and anxiety on one side and increased loneliness on the other.

For those who ultimately need institutionalization because they are unable to care for themselves and do not have sons or daughters who can assume this care, institutionalization is the last resort. This, however, means care at the price of autonomy, submission to life in a total institution and, by the regulation of such institutions, a degree of dehumanization which people who have grown up in our individualistic society often find hard to take.

The task of presenting a survey of various manifestations of stress in the experience of older people does not imply that over a span of between 20 and 30 years, old people do not find many successful adaptations to their losses and do not experience feelings of mastery and heroism. However, even in successful coping with all experiences of loss, the energy spent on adaptations produces an undercurrent of fatigue which makes aging a period of intermittent exhaustion and recuperation. Finding time during the day to rest after an effort may make possible a new effort. However, in the long run, the fatigue of aging is cumulative, and people may become too tired to fight disease; they may maintain a diminishing life and may become, in the truest sense of the term, tired of living. At this point it may well happen that the wish to live turns into the will to die and that people give up cooperation with life-maintaining support systems such as nutrition and health care.

V
STRESS AND
SOCIOLOGICAL
PARAMETERS

Ecobiological Stress: Community Planning—A Cross-Cultural Model

Jiri Kolaja, Ph.D., Ph.Dr.

Department of Sociology and Anthropology
College of Arts and Sciences
University of West Virginia
Morgantown, West Virginia

This paper is an introductory analysis to community planning development, conceived in space and time dimensions. The concept of entropy has also been used in this chapter.

Having spent several months in Sarajevo, Yugoslavia two years ago, I was struck by the fact that this Bosnia-Herzegovina capital planned its population growth to 280 thousand but got 40 thousand people more.[1] Bosnia-Herzegovina is one of the six Yugoslav republics, and distinguishes itself because 40% of its population speaks the Serbo-Croatian language but, because of the Muslim religion, identify themselves as another ethnic group. Moreover the introduction in 1950 of workers' councils has normatively contributed to a distribution of decision making. Though the term *worker* is used, one can find these councils in all social organizations, e.g., hospitals, schools, or city government. The council functions as a small parliament, making decisions especially about employment and reward policy and the future development of the organization. One could therefore expect in Sarajevo considerable room for decision making.

The search of about 200 publications dealing with the problem of planning, several of them covering community planning, has disclosed that a common complaint has been the absence of a satisfactory theory. Let us refer to Le Corbusier though we could have pointed to Perloff, Kent, Bolan, or those who favor governmental planning like W. Leontieff or Woodcock.[2]

Le Corbusier is concerned with the plan for a whole city or region that is organized by universalistic and not particularistic criteria. There is a dominant, and let us not hesitate to say, visually dominant pattern such as a diagonal, a circle, or something else for the entire community. In Le Corbusier's way of thinking, there is not much room for an approach that would cater to individual preferences, as exemplified by Jane Jacobs.[3] Le Corbusier's plan is a visual-spatial orchestra and not an individual instrument stressed by Lindblom.[4] Note that we have touched here on one or possibly the basic issue of planning: How much should we plan, to what detail, and for how many items?

Inspired by a complaint that no generally accepted theory has yet been accepted, an attempt will be made to present some basic propositions that could later lead to a more acceptable theory, or at least to a theory that would be accepted by a larger number of planners. One more word of caution deserves to be advanced. The subject matter that is planned calls certainly for different theories or, stated more cautiously, a division of labor in our thinking and action could elicit more or less different theories of planning.

Let us consider two tendencies in our changing world—the organization of energy and entropy. The concept of entropy (i.e., that energy which is unavailable) is quite helpful. The second law of thermodynamics expresses it as follows: the orderly array of the constituent atoms decreases and thus an increase in entropy can be equated with an increase in disorder.[5]

Provided that the above is accepted, we meet the issue of unavailable and available energy. Planning is the business of developing different degrees of order that should be constituted by the available energy. Since the order in planning is conceived and developed by man, our first focus should be directed on the different degrees of order that planning can attain.

It appears that there can be two different structures of order. The first is a chain of events that recurs or partially changes, but does not cross or interfere with another temporal chain of events. By contrast, there can be a case where a chain crosscuts another chain of events. This has already been observed, for example, by Herbert Spencer, Ferdinand Tonnies, and others who have proposed that there has been an increase in the number of such intermixed relations. To differentiate between chains which intermix and those that do not, we shall designate the latter as *parallel* chains. It should be stressed that there has occurred an increasing number of parallel chains resulting in increased aspirations not to be overorganized or overcontrolled. It appears that we have been freed of some dysfunctional patterns of behavior represented by uncomfortable dress and unhygienic food consumption. There has been a growing desire to live a more natural and uncomplicated life. Parallelism appears thus as a countertrend to the drive to become more organized. If these two tendencies have been coexisting, a legitimate question arises: How have planners been dealing with such coexistence? There are two points to be advanced. First, there has been an increasing acceptance of the idea that one should plan for several possible problems which might arise in an entire area. Second, there has been a clamor for an extension of the time for which the plan should be developed. However, in contrast to social progress schemes of a century ago, there is more specific reasoning involved. One should particularize not only the problem, but also time. With our increasing knowledge of past events, our estimates of future events keep expanding.

Let us return to our prior argument and cross-classify the dimensions of space and time by further differentiating between now and here as well as later and away (at another location), as illustrated in Table 1.

To interpret the four possibilities given in Table 1, we note that cell 1 is now and here, while cell 4, its opposite, is later and away. These two cells display a convergence in time and space, but the same does not occur in cell 2 and cell 3 in which present time or later time is combined with away or present space. To visualize these instances, let us classify them against a person, a group, or an item of material or nonmaterial culture, as shown in Table 2.

To explain why a person or social organization has been classified as here-later or away-now, we propose, theoretically, that an acting person moves from the here position to, or projects to, a later time, however temporarily short it may be. Although if a group is referred to, the principal consideration is that persons are not in the same spot, they are away from each other, at least minimally, while sharing, for example, the same room or table. They, however, seek to communicate with each other at present-now.

When classifying here-later or away-now of Table 1 in regard to the material and nonmaterial categories of Table 2, it appears that the tangible culture is at present here but its uses are projected potentially to a later time. Nonmaterial culture—norms of justice, for example—is located away and best described by the term *transcendence,* but it is applied now.

In the above discussion we have conceptualized the action group and culture by combining local or distant space with present or distant time. One also can think of space or time as the difference between biological or

TABLE 1. Cross-classification of Space and Time.

| | | Time | |
		Now	Later
Space	Here	1	2
	Away (at another location)	3	4

TABLE 2. Cross-classification of Spatial and Temporal Variables with Social Phenomena.

Person	Social Organization	Material Culture	Culture, Nonmaterial
here-later	here-later		here-later
away-now		away-now	away-now

cultural analysis. A further theoretical advance should focus more on the tangible aspects of the spatial or temporal variables. Of course we do not mean that one should be engulfed in nothing but speculative procedure. However, we should seek to identify, at least in an approximate manner, values that underpin our projects and plans.

Therefore, let us consider project plans in terms of a spatial-temporal transcendence. From a spatial viewpoint, the plan can be realized in the same place as it was designed or figured out. It can, however, refer to a universal norm, e.g., an ethical norm. Note that in its temporal projection the norm is a universal, while in its spatial realization it becomes approximate, not perfectly realized. Yet if we conceive of time and space as nothing but existential dimensions, space can be thought of as gaining some temporal property, too. To realize a universal norm in space takes some time to achieve. Vice versa, acquired spatial properties—without some measurement, some differentiation that also is a spatial property, i.e., successiveness in time—would be inconceivable.

The above analysis suggests that the problem of development and planning ought to be analyzed in terms of space and time. Moreover, such an anlysis indicates that phenomena of personality, social group, and tangible and intangible culture keep developing according to different spatial and temporal schedules. In dealing with planning issues of these sociocultural phenomena, we first have to clarify, or we should seek to clarify, some basic concepts such as space and time as applied to person, social group, and tangible or intangible culture.

There is one more observation to be advanced in connection with our earlier reference to entropy. If the structuring of matter and the organization of inorganic and organic phenomena are decreases of entropy, then man's cultural effort embodied in planning is an ordering activity par excellence. It is worthwhile to think of planning as an activity that conceives of order as a potentiality and, on that count, as something that is a cultural order and yet not here in space and time. We should not hesitate to point out the transcendent nature of planning. It is a potential cultural order. In these two respects man transcends to another level of his life.

References

1. *Arch.* 1(2–3)(1963). *Sarajevo-Ekonomsko-urbani Razvoj* (J. Hadziomerovic, ed.). Sarajevo: Skupstina grada Sarajeva, Ekonomski fakultet i Arhitektonsko-urbanisticki fakultet, 1975.
2. Bolan, R. Mapping the Planning Theory Terrain. In Planning in America: Learning from *Turbulence* (D. Golschalk, ed.). Washington, D.C.: American Institute of Planners. Kent, T. J. Jr. *The Urban General Plan.* San Francisco: Chandler, 1964. Perloff, H. S. *Education for Planning: City, State and Regional.* In *Resources for the Future.* Baltimore: The John Hopkins University Press, 1957.
3. Jacobs, J. *The Death and Life of Great American Cities,* pp. 433-440. New York: Random House, 1961.
4. Lindblom, C. E. *The Intelligence of Democracy: Decision Making through Mutual Adjustment.* New York: The Free Press, 1965.
5. Entropy. *The New Encyclopaedia Britannica,* Micropaedia, vol. III, p. 911. Chicago: Encyclopaedia Britannica, 1977.

Acknowledgment. I wish to recognize the editorial help given by H. N. Kerr.

Helping Rape Victims in Rural Areas

Judith Ann Davenport
Joseph Davenport, III
Counseling Center
Mississippi State University
Jackson, Mississippi

Department of Social Work
Mississippi State University
Jackson, Mississippi

Social workers, human service personnel, and other concerned citizens have become increasingly concerned about rape, an act which is being reported with increasing frequency.[1] Little discussed for years, rape has emerged as a topic of serious, and sometime heated, discussion. A *Newsweek* article found that articles, television dramas, and books such as Susan Brownmiller's *Against Our Will,* have served to raise the public's consciousness of this problem. The article stated that:

> New perceptions of rape have inspired more than talk. Police have established specially trained sexual-assault squads. Hospitals have remodeled their methods of treating victims. State legislatures have revised their laws. Feminists, who have made rape a major concern, have organized "rape crisis centers" and "hot lines" that victims can call for help.[2]

Human service workers across the country have been involved in many of these activities. Over the past several years they have witnessed the presentation of papers at conferences, the publication of books and journal articles, and the articulation of ideas at numerous institutes and workshops. Many human service workers, especially social workers, have used their first-hand knowledge in meaningful efforts toward change. They have worked to humanize the process and procedures affecting the victim; they have called public attention to the problems and needs; they have helped to change laws penalizing the victim; they have helped to establish rape crisis programs and centers; and they have developed new approaches to helping the victim.

However, while these activities and efforts have been laudable, they have almost invariably reflected an urban orientation. For example, one urban approach is the establishment of a rape crisis center with full-time counselors. Unfortunately, such a model has little applicability to rural communities which generally do not have the need or finances for such a program.

This article describes a model for delivering rape crisis services to rural victims. It discusses (1) the use of an existing resource—the regional community mental health complex—to provide services, (2) the needs of rural rape victims, (3) the kinds of services required, (4) the selection and training of a rape crisis team, (5) the in-service training of the mental health staff, and (6) the all-important consultation and education activities necessary to gain community acceptance, understanding, and support.

Location on Program

Rape—a social and mental health problem requiring skilled intervention—was perceived as such by the clinical social worker directing outpatient services at the regional mental health complex serving rural east central Mississippi. The director, who possessed a master's degree in clinical social work, became interested in rape because of the increased attention to this topic generated by the women's movement and because of the problems presented by the agency's clientele. For example, three out of four women in one therapy group had emotional problems relating to rapes which had occurred many years previously. Not a single one of these women had mentioned rape as a problem when she first sought help. Their embarrassment, coupled with the lack of counseling services in their sparsely populated communities, prevented them from receiving help for years, although the available literature on rape strongly supports the need of prompt professional assistance.[3]

The mental health complex staff was faced with numerous questions. How many women were not receiving services for this traumatizing act? What kinds of programs and services were needed? What kinds of personnel were required to provide the services? What agency or organization should administer the programs and services? Who would find it? In short, what type of service delivery model was appropriate, feasible, and viable for this rural southern environment?

The mental health complex staff decided to develop the rape crisis service as part of the regional mental health program. Several factors contributed to this decision. (1) The need for such a service was originally identified by the social worker in charge of outpatient services at the complex. (2) No other organization indicated an interest in, or capacity for, developing such a program. (3) The complex was already widely recognized and accepted in a rural area where acceptance of new programs and services did not come easily.[4] (4) The complex's staff already included mental health professionals whose generic skills could be used to aid rape victims. (5) The other resources of the complex, such as the crisis line, mobile clinic, and outreach program, could be used rather than duplicated. The two previous reasons are extremely important in rural areas since they tend to be limited in funds and professional staff. (6) Finally, the reported and suspected incidence of rape, while significant, did not justify the creation of a new agency or organization even if resources were available.

This particular regional mental health program was headquartered in a small metropolitan area containing approximately 40,000 people. Its catchment area included seven counties, all of which would be considered rural, especially under the definition developed by Buxton, to wit:

> Rural is used as reflecting an area which lags behind in population per square mile, in education, in variety of experience and finally, in the power to control its own destiny, compared to larger urban areas.[5]

The catchment area would also fit within the definition of rural used by the National Institute of Mental Health: "Rural counties are by definition those located outside Standard Metropolitan Statistical Areas and having more than one-half of their population living in communities of 2,500 or less."[6] Mental health staff for this rural region included a consulting psychiatrist, clinical psychologists, clinical social workers, and a variety of paraprofessionals. Each county had one outreach worker with a B.A. degree or less.

Community Acceptance via Consultation and Education

It is perhaps a truism to say that any human service program must be accepted by its potential consumers before it can be fully and effectively utilized. Gaining such acceptance, especially on a sensitive issue like rape, can be most difficult in rural areas. Rural inhabitants tend to possess lower levels of formal education and may lack the sophistication of urbanites. They are exposed to fewer professionals and place more emphasis on the person rather than on his or her credentials. They frequently share a philosophy of rugged individualism, which emphasizes the resolution of problems without outside help. Such a philosophy may be less a result of cultural lag than a practical necessity for rural survival. Rural residents are also increasingly resistant to urban-oriented programs and services being imposed upon them. Like most Americans, they want to be involved in identifying their own problems; in planning, developing, and implementing their own solutions; and in controlling those organizations, programs, and services affecting their lives.

Rape, however, poses a special problem, even for the conscientious human service worker determined not to interfere with the community's wish to define its own problems and control its own destiny. The average rural area will have no groundswell of public opinion requesting rape crisis services. Any given area will probably not have a large number of rapes even though the incidence may be just as high as an urban area. Feminist groups, which tend to make rape an issue, are neither numerous nor strong in rural America.[7] Sensitive topics such as rape or homosexuality are generally not as freely discussed as they are in urban communities. In fact, a prominent member of the mental health complex's advisory board would not use the word *rape* in mixed company. Local physicians, ministers, and law enforcement officials would each see so few rape victims that they would not be inclined to push for a new service. Consequently, while rural rape is just as real as urban rape, and perhaps more damaging since there are fewer resources for the victim, it is seldom identified by the community as a problem requiring attention. Rather than letting an apparent need go unmet, it may be necessary to raise the consciousness of the community.

The director of outpatient services at the regional mental health complex decided to raise the community's consciousness through the consultation and education component of the program. This component, which is a required service of all community mental health centers, is perhaps the most important feature of this service model. In fact, Held, an expert on mental health in the rural community, stated that "the use of consultation and education services are prerequisities for, and directly related to, the ability of the mental health program to gain entry and become a vital part of the rural community."[8] Barriers such as narrow definitions of mental health, general rejection of modern health specialists, fears of becoming identified as mentally ill, and mistrust of outside professionals can hamper or even destroy a program if they are not identified and dealt with.[9] Implementing the rape crisis service in this case was expedited by using the existing and ongoing consultation and education program of the regional mental health complex. Building on such existing strengths was an important factor in beginning the program at the complex.

A crucial step was the involvement of county outreach workers. Many mental health programs require advanced degrees in the human services for their county outreach positions and consequently are frequently compelled to employ outsiders, who are not easily accepted by their community. This Mississippi program facilitated community acceptance by employing county residents. While only two of these people had even a bachelor's degree in a helping discipline, namely, psychology and social work, they were provided orientation, in-service training, close supervision, and consultation.

County outreach workers played an important part in discussing possible problems and needs with their county advisory boards. These workers were usually natives of the county in which they were employed, knew most advisory board members on a personal basis, and were well accepted and trusted by county residents. They served as an imporant link between the rural population and the regional mental health complex's professional staff, many of whom were from outside the region. Advisory board members were representative of their counties, and included businessmen, clergy, educators, physicians, and housewives. They in turn discussed the advisory activities with their families, friends, and acquaintances. Securing their input, understanding, and sanction was imperative if rape crisis services or any other proposed services were to be met with more than passive acceptance at best.

News articles were printed in regional and local newspapers, and information was conveyed through the regional television station and local radio stations when available. A rape crisis team, comprised of several professionals from the main center, spoke to many organizations such as civic groups, service clubs, women's organizations, and ministerial associations. Rural social work experts, such as Ginsbserg,[10] have emphasized the importance of service clubs in small towns and rural America. Horejsi notes that:

> These informed networks lack the sophistication and knowledge base of professionally organized programs but they do perform a valuable function and are usually "supported" by influential citizens and community leaders.[11]

Gaining the interest and backing of these groups is a great boon toward community acceptance. Furthermore, Horejsi warns that "if a new formal plan for the development of human services poses a threat to these informal service structures, it may encounter considerable resistance."[12]

> Team members also spoke with many key individuals such as hospital administrators, law enforcement officials, school counselors, and county health officers. Again, involvement of these people can spell success, whereas lack of involvement may spell failure.

> Educational efforts with individuals and groups should be localized or "ruralized" as much as possible. This does not mean that national statistics or examples should not be used. It does mean that in rural

Mississippi, the mention of a rape in Hot Coffee, Mississippi, carries more impact than the recitation of statistics showing a rape occurring every few minutes across the United States. Rural residents, who often associate rape with Chicago, New York, and Los Angeles, need to be reminded that rape also occurs in Hungry Horse, Montana; Sun Dance, Wyoming; and Long View, Mississippi; as well as on ranches, at crossroad stores, and along country lanes.

Educational efforts should also be personalized. The message should be that rape does not just happen to attractive young females who go places where they should not. It can happen to the minister's 6-year-old daughter walking home from school; it can happen to the teacher's grandmother at home; it can happen to the retarded sister of the department store owner.

Securing approval and sanction through this community-oriented approach was considered an integral and absolutely vital ingredient in the success of the program.

Problems and Needs of Victim

Neglected for years in favor of research on the offender, the rape victim is receiving an increasing amount of attention from social workers and social scientists. The pioneering efforts of Sutherland and Scherl, [13] followed by Burgess and Halmstrom, [14] and then McCombie, [15] have provided a valuable base on which to build. Fox and Scherl were able to identify predictable patterns of responses common to the rape victims in this study, including "(1) acute reaction, occurring immediately after the rape and usually lasting for several days, (2) outward adjustment, and (3) integration and resolution of the experience." [16] They developed a number of interventions aimed at helping victims work through each phase as smoothly and completely as possible.

Two California social workers built on this knowledge to develop comprehensive rape crisis services in their communities. Abarbanel[17] initiated a hospital-based program in Santa Monica, and Hardgrove[18] established an interagency approach in Pasadena.

Hardgrove found that the rape victim has a very specific set of needs. She characterizes these needs thusly:

After being raped, a victim needs to feel that she is safe and that she will not be brutalized further. She needs to receive medical treatment. She needs to be listened to and helped to talk about the experience and her feelings regarding it. She also needs to know certain practical information that will help her to decide what to do next. Should she report the rape to the police? What will happen if she does and if she doesn't? What kind of medical treatment does she need and why? What about pregnancy and venereal disease? If she is going to report the rape, what should and shouldn't she do so that the evidence will not be destroyed? What kinds of feelings can she expect to have about the rape and the rapist? What will she have to go through if she does choose to prosecute? Where can she get emotional support? Where can she go to get the help she needs and feel sure that she will not be treated in a suspicious, further brutalizing manner? In short, the victim needs safety, medical care, facts, and support.[19]

Arbarbanel found similar needs and stated that:

Rape victims clearly require a comprehensive range of services from persons in the field of medicine, law, and mental health. However, a woman who has been raped is in a state of extreme emotional crisis. She is not prepared to go to one place for medical care, another for counseling, and still another for information about her legal rights. Therefore, one agency must take responsibility for developing the program and for organizing and conducting additional support services.[20]

Rural victims, who have similar reactions and needs, also face problems more indigenous to rural locations.

Lack of anonymity and confidentiality can be more of a problem. Rape carries a certain degree of stigma everywhere, but the urban victim can usually work or travel without constantly encountering people who know her or about the rape. The opposite is true in small towns and sparsely populated regions. A person reporting or seeking help for a rural rape will generally know and be known by health and legal personnel. Everyone seems to know everyone else's business. Most of the people encountered in everyday life (e.g., grocer, mail carrier, next door neighbor) will know. This knowledge makes it more difficult to report the crime. If reported, the victim and her family may require extra help in dealing with their feelings and relationships.

Rural victims may face greater pressures from family or friends not to report the rape or press charges if the offender is another local because doing so could tear the social fabric of the community. People whose families in many cases have lived together, worked together, and worshipped together for generations are often reluctant to create a rift in the community. A controversial and heated trial could result in irreparable damage to social and business relationships. Such rifts can take generations to heal in small communities.

Objectivity in courtroom procedures is usually more difficult to obtain in rural areas. While feminists are succeeding in changing laws which permit questions about the victim's previous sexual activities, rural jurists frequently are already well informed about such background material. Such knowledge, especially when added to a relatively conservative philosophy of sex, often means that the woman with an unchaste reputation can expect little sympathy or support.

A victim from outside the local community frequently finds that it can be extremely difficult to prosecute and convict if the rapist is a local male. This is especially true if the accused is well liked and, in the South, a "good ole boy." In fact, the family and friends of one male accused of raping an out-of-state college student were reassured when a jurist, who happened to be a friend of the family, winked at them as she left the courtroom!

Additional problems emerge in the provision of services. As stated earlier, there is simply not the need or the resources for a full-time rape crisis center. Small rural hospitals frequently have no social work department at all, let alone one capable of providing a specialized rape crisis service as in Santa Monica. Unlike Pasadena which is served by an interagency network, the rural community will in all probability not have a YWCA, Family Service Agency, or Planned Parenthood Center. Local law officers will not be as well trained and their departments will not have special sexual assault squads or even female officers. Most rural communities, however, are served by regional community mental health programs and can utilize the personnel and services of this resource.

Personnel and Services

This rape crisis program in rural Mississippi utilized a rape crisis team formed from the complex's professional staff. The team, with one exception, was comprised of females since many rape victims have expressed reluctance to confide in a male after their experience.[21] A male counselor, however, is of value in helping a victim reestablish relationships with males and in helping spouses or male friends adjust.[22] Team members possessed helping skills and were well versed in crisis intervention techniques. They also attended special workshops on helping rape victims and visited other rape programs to enhance knowledge and skills.

Team members, available 24 hours a day, seven days a week, responded to referrals from physicians, hospitals, social agencies, victims, and outreach workers of the mental health complex. They answered crisis calls, saw "walk-ins," accompanied victims to hospitals, prepared them for courtroom procedures, and provided follow-up services. Crisis calls were accepted from, and services provided to, all counties in the catchment area.

County outreach workers were given in-service training on rape crisis counseling. Calls and referrals in the rural counties sometimes went directly to the main center and sometimes to the outreach worker. The worker dealt with the victim if possible or referred her to the team member on call if she thought the situation required a higher level of intervention.

It is most important that a victim have the option of contacting her county worker, the worker in the adjacent county, or a team member at the main center. While most outreach workers were females, some were not, and a local victim might prefer a female counselor from outside her county.

Also, clients may hesitate to seek help, including medical care, from local sources because of the lack of confidentiality. Horejsi noted when he worked for a satellite mental health clinic in a rural area:

> Some individuals or families preferred to drive fifty or sixty miles to a "strange town" in order to keep appointments with traveling mental health teams even though the team was in their own community on a regular basis.[23]

All victims received a psychosocial evaluation to determine their emotional and mental status. Those requiring the attention of the clinical psychologist or one of the clinical social workers were seen in their rural environment or at the main center if the client so desired. Outreach workers had easy access to professional consultation and supervision when needed. Supportive services were also provided to family members.

Unlike some urban programs,[24] volunteers were not used. Maintaining the necessary training efforts for volunteer staff in each county was not considered feasible. Training of volunteers operating the regional crisis line could be considered. These people, who already participate in ongoing training activities, handle incoming calls from the entire region and could be trained either to handle the calls or to refer them to the rape crisis team.

A word of caution might be in order here. While this model appears feasible and viable for many rural environments, the authors do not view it as a panacea or even the only alternative. Other arrangements, depending on local resources and needs, may also be successful and, if so, should be encouraged.

Mental health programs based on a medical model may provide adequate crisis intervention services but shy away from social conditions contributing to problems. Rape experts such as Holmes believe that a dualistic strategy of crisis intervention and advocacy is necessary.[25] She describes dualism as follows:

> First, an interventive strategy is needed to provide direct services to each victim, and second, there is need for a strategy directed toward

changing those conditions which contribute to the existence of rape as a social fact and which impinge upon the subsequent social functioning of rape victims as a group.[26]

She further states that:

Our feminist perspective suggests that rape be viewed as a crime of violence and/or power rather than sex, and as such, it is symptomatic of the unequal power relationships that exist between males and females in this society. Pragmatically then, the advocacy strategy is utilized in an attempt to protect the rights of rape victims to receive adequate, humane services, and to combat sexist attitudes and stereotypes which serve to maintain the status quo in relation to inequality between males and females.[27]

Such an approach will obviously not be endorsed by some mental health programs. Care should be exercised in initiating a rape crisis program at an agency unlikely to furnish more than crisis interventions services. However, if the regional mental health program is the only realistic possibility for a rape program, then crisis intervention without advocacy is probably better than no service at all.

Conclusion

The authors believe that rural rape victims have been neglected for too long and describe a model used to deliver services in rural Mississippi. This model circumvents the usual lack of funds and professional staff by building on resources already possessed by most rural communities—the regional community mental health program.

Skilled mental health professionals from the regional program form a team to provide community education, train center personnel such as the outreach workers, train community health and legal personnel, and provide specialized services to victims. Resources possessed by most regional mental health programs, such as crisis line and outreach programs, are used rather than duplicated in a separate program.

Overcoming suspicion of, and opposition to, a new service is accomplished through a community-oriented effort based on the existing consultation and education component of the regional mental health program. This approach to helping rural rape victims, while not a panacea, might well be emulated by social workers and human service workers in other parts of the country.

References

1. See, for example: Lipton, G. I. and Roth, E. I. Rape: a complex management problem in the pediatric emergency room. *The Journal of Pediatrics* 75 p: 859-866 (November 1969); Evard, J. Rape: the medical, social, and legal implications. *American Journal of Obstetrics and Gynecology* 3: 1977-199 (September 1971); *Suspected Rape,* Technical Bulletin No. 14. Chicago: American College of Obstetrics and Gynecologists, 1972; Fox, S. S. and Scherl, D. J. Crisis intervention with victims of rape. *Social Work* 17: 37-42 (January 1972); Schultz, L. G. The rape victim: implications for the social work curriculum. *Journal of Humanics* 1: 1-5 (Spring 1974); Davenport, J. A. Establishing a rape crisis program in a community mental health center in a small metropolitan area. Paper presented at the *Sixth Annual Conference, National Council of Community Mental Health Centers,* Washington, D.C. (February 25, 1975); and Davenport, J. A. and Davenport, J., III Role playing in a rape crisis program. Paper presented at the *Fifth Biennial Professional Symposium, National Association of Social Workers,* San Diego, California (November 20, 1977).

2. Rape alert. *Newsweek* 86: 70 (November 10, 1975).

3. Anonymous. Rape—a personal account. *Health and Social Work* 1: 90-91 (August 1976).

4. Good discussions on the importance of acceptance in rural areas may be found in: Buxton, E. Delivering social services in rural areas. *Public Welfare* 31: 15-20 (Winter 1973); and Ginsberg, L. H. Rural social work. *Encyclopedia of Social Work,* pp. 1128-1234. Washington, D.C.: National Association of Social Workers, 1977.

5. Buxton, op. cit., p. 15

6. *Characteristics of Federally Funded Rural Community Mental Health Centers.* National Institute of Mental Health, DHEW Publication No. (ADM) 74-6.

7. Although they are not as prevalent as in urban areas, rural feminist groups do exist. For a description of rural women's support groups, which have the potential to support rape crisis services, see: Young, B. D. Facilitating women's groups in rural Appalachia. In *Social Work in Rural Areas: Preparation and Practice* (R. K. Green and S. A. Webster, eds.), pp. 361-367. Knoxville: University of Tennessee School of Social Work, 1977.

8. Held, H. M. Mental health in the rural community. In *Human Services in the Rural Environment Reader,* (D. Bast, ed.), p. 47. Madison: University of Wisconsin-Extension Center for Social Service, 1977.

9. Ibid., pp. 46-58.

10. Ginsberg, L. H. Education for social work in rural settings. *Social Work Education Reporter* 17: 28-32 (September 1969).

11. Horejsi, C. R. Rural community-based services for persons who are mentally retarded. In *Social Work in Rural Areas: Preparation and Practice* (R. K. Green and S. Webster, eds.), p. 372. Knoxville: University of Tennessee School of Social Work, 1977.

12. Ibid.

13. Sutherland, S. and Scherl, D. J. Patterns of response among victims of rape. *American Journal of Orthopsychiatry* 40: 503-511 (April 1970).

14. Burgess, A. W. and Halmstrom L. L. *Rape: Victims of Crisis.* Bowie, Md.: Robert J. Bradley Co., 1974.

15. McCombie, S. Characteristics of rape victims seen in crisis intervention. *Smith College Studies in Social Work* 46: 137-158 (April, 1976).

16. Fox, S. S. and Scherl, D. J. Crisis intervention with victims of rape. *Social Work* 17: 37 (January 1972).

17. Abarbanel, G. Helping victims of rape. *Social Work* 21: 478-482 (November 1976).

18. Hardgrove, G. An interagency service network to meet needs of rape victims. *Social Casework* **57**: 245-253 (April 1976).
19. Ibid., p. 247.
20. Abarbanel, op. cit., p. 478,.
21. Kathy Akin, Marion Johnson, Cynthia Rutledge, and Karen Selestak conducted a "Rape Counseling Survey" at Mississippi State University to determine coed feelings about the use of counseling services following a rape. Of the 83 coeds surveyed, 58 (70%) indicated that they would seek counseling. Of these, 28 (48%) indicated that the sex of the counselor was not important, 20 (34%) indicated that they would prefer a female counselor, 8 (14%) indicated that they would only see a female counselor, and 2 (3%) indicated that they would prefer a male counselor. These findings tend to lend support to the belief that female counselors would be more easily accepted by a large number of female rape victims.
22. The role of the male counselor with a female rape victim is discussed in Silverman, D. First do no more harm: female rape victims and the male counselor. *American Journal of Orthopsychiatry* **47** 91-96 (January 1977).
23. Horejsi, op. cit., p. 378.
24. See, for example: Holmes, K. A. Dualistic strategies with victims of rape: advocacy and crisis intervention. Paper presented at the *Fifth Biennial Professional Symposium, National Association of Social Workers,* San Diego, California (November 20, 1977).
25. Ibid.
26. Ibid., p. 3.
27. Ibid., pp. 3-4.

Ethnic Stress: Some Sociological and Intracultural Aspects

Barbara J. Shade, Ph.D.
University of Wisconsin
Madison, Wisconsin

Barbara L. Nichols, R.N., D.Sc.
President, American Nurses' Association
Madison, Wisconsin

The shift in the social and economic participation of blacks during the 1960s and 1970s not only has had an impact on race relations in this country but also has added new dimensions of stress to black life. Prior to this time, black Americans spent a large portion of their time responding to or avoiding the customs deriving from the concept of "separate-but-equal" life-styles. Thus, the stress factors were related to such aspects as acquiring a house of their choice, finding travel accommodations, or acquiring admission to schools which afforded them the type of education they desired in spite of discriminatory practices. For most blacks, whether they lived in the North or the South, the primary focus of stress was battling the issue of segregation and discrimination.

Facing blacks of the 1980s, however, are the issues of:

1. A growing class division precipitated by upward social mobility of those with education and an accompanying diminution of opportunity and support for the black low-income population.
2. The growth of the black population into the major occupant of many of the nation's largest cities at a time when cities are faced with loss of political power, financial ruin, service and building decay, and growing crime rates. Saving the cities of America looms as a major problem that will have a significant effect on black individuals and families who occupy these cities which most other Americans have physically abandoned.
3. The constancy of low-level health depriving blacks of a sense of physical and mental well-being. Attempts to cope with chronic imperfect health tend tward habitual use of alcohol and drugs or excessive preoccupation with the supernatural on the part of black Americans. On almost every health index, statistics show that black Americans are disproportionately represented in terms of: life expectancy at birth, infant mortality, maternal mortality, nutritional deficiencies, chronic illnesses, physician and dental visits, and adjusted death rates for specific causes. Chronic poor health is as stress producing as the financial burden posed by sickness.
4. The integration of housing and neighborhoods, the job place, and the educational environment, which brings about the need for blacks to adopt new techniques for interpersonal relationships. Rather than having to confront the more obvious racial behaviors of past decades, blacks are now faced with the need to interact with people whose perspective of the world differs significantly from theirs and whose stereotypic attitudes and ideas about blacks are covertly manifested in their evaluation, relationships, words, and performance.
5. The persistence of racism despite the complex network of laws designed to alleviate inequities. To be black remains the basis for exclusion in many areas of American life. The legacy of the past sustains sanctions which deny access to power, limit the franchise, maintain

job discrimination, curtail the occupational ceiling, and provide inferior training or no training at all.

To discuss the concept of ethnic stress requires an examination of the various situations in which individuals of African heritage find themselves in the 1980s. Stress, while difficult to define, is most often perceived as any annoyance in environmental situations which requires some type of psychological or behavioral adjustment. For each black American the stress of daily life not only includes typical strains but also is compounded because of the racial group of which the individual is a member, the reaction to and perception of the problem, and the ability of the individual to tolerate frustration or stress. Thus, black Americans may have different stresses as well as different reactions to various situations which may or may not result from society's orientation toward their racial heritage. Within the framework of this paper, we will concentrate on situations involving education, social mobility, poverty, and sex roles.

Since the Supreme Court ruled in 1954 that separate schools for black children are *inherently* unequal, black teachers, students, and parents have been involved in a conflict which has produced an inordinate amount of stress. On one hand, all concerned felt that education was the road to equality and to the type of power which would eliminate the inferior stauts roles assigned to blacks. Yet on the other hand, the black community was asked to stipulate that all of the subsitute institutions which has served them so well, had produced numerous leaders, and had perpetuated and redefined black culture and history were, by the very nature of the fact that they were black run, inferior and unequal. So, although the change produced was necessary to remove the legal stigma attached to color which had promoted Jim Crowism, black Americans found it necessary to deny a part of themselves and to sanction the concept of group inferiority. In addition, it became necessary to overcome the great draining emotion of fear, particularly fear for the safety and welfare of their children who had to participate in the inauguration of the new concept of equal educational opportunity. It seems possible, based upon the personal accounts of those who participated, that the psychological ramifications of this stressful situation will have many far-reaching effects, particularly for the individuals who participated.

For those children who entered the desegregated colleges and public schools, another set of stress situations developed. Even today, young blacks feel not only the stress of competition but also the stress and frustration based upon the recognition that others view them as incompetent and unable to function according to standards. For many students, this becomes a self-fulfilling prophecy, or it establishes a stressful situation which, for blacks, might better be termed an anxiety reaction of "fear of failure." Closely akin to this situation are the covert hostility and racial insults of which black students become aware from fellow students or members of the faculty and teaching staff. For most, having been socialized not to respond overtly to these situations, this often results in an internalization of undirected hostility and a perpetuation of their own stereotypic attitudes toward whites which might prove somewhat detrimental to them in the future.

However, the most difficult situation, which seems to promote stress among Afro-American students in predominantly white situations, is perhaps the lack of a feeling of belonging. There are few clubs over which they can exhibit control, leadership roles are limited, and generally the student body has little understanding or knowledge of the culture and values which have meaning to a black American. The need to belong is a basic human need which every person, regardless of color, exhibits from the time of birth. As Sherif and Cantril summarize it,

> Every individual strives to place or to anchor himself as an acceptable member in his social milieu or in some social setting.[2]

Rare is the person who can maintain his/her morale or self-esteem in situations in which one faces continual disapproval from all others. This need to seek a sense of belonging in a desegregated school offers for many black Americans a tremendous souce of pressure and frustration with which they must cope. For those who are determined to change their economic and social status in the world, however, it merely provides practice and introduction to the type of stress and adjustments which they must make as they seek their goal of occupational achievement.

To be foreign born, Jewish, a black man or woman has previously been the basis for exclusion from engineering, science, law, architecture, banking careers, and the upper levels of the civil service. In addition, black Americans are characteristically subject to low representation in the health professions and are extremely underrepresented in the health profession's university schools. Despite these limitations, there has always been a core of professionals within the Afro-American community. Since the advent of civil rights legislation, the number of black professionals has increased.

Now Afro-American males and females are appearing in corporations, laboratories, institutions of higher education, governmental agencies, and in other white-collar positions in numbers as never before. With this increase in occupational mobility have come stress sources also not know previously. Although arriving in these positions with high expectations, great aspirations, and the desire to compete on an equal level, they soon experience stress from the emergence of new forms of "second classness." This second-class position either comes through the job assignment which essentially limits the work of these black Americans to those situations that have an effect upon minorities or other affected groups, or it comes through the lack of promotion to more powerful decision-making roles. Additional stress is generated when these individuals are confronted by the belief among their nonblack colleagues that black Americans are basically incompetent and inferior; therefore, they would not have obtained their positions without the affirmative action programs of the company or agency. Thus, although legal slavery has ended, the notion that dark skin indicates intellectual inferiority endures. Blacks find that the high visibility of color remains a crucial factor in limiting occupational mobility. Skin color becomes a pervasive stressor.

Cultural differences which emanate from diversity in perceptions, interpretations, and behaviors are another source of stress. Black Americans must continually switch language patterns, behaviors, and ideological viewpoints depending upon the particular role or environment in which they find themselves. This duality of life-style and interpersonal interactions produces a source of stress, no matter how adept individuals become.

The occupational roles to which many are striving provide the opportunity to have different life-styles, new housing, better educational opportunities for their children, and possibly new mobility foundations for succeeding generations. Yet these strivers often find themselves confronted by stress factors which emanate from the black community itself. Blacks left in the churning world of the ghetto and poverty often refer to this new socially mobile group as the "black bourgeoise," and with this term come all of the negative images and ideas perpetuated by E. Franklin Frazier. For those to whom this epithet is directed, it beomes a stressful guilt trip to be identified with those who have left the lower class, and it is even more stressful to realize that this advancement has not produced any more of a sense of belonging or acceptance. Those who meet the criteria of social success, therefore, become very much the marginal men and women who are alienated from the ghetto dweller and ostracized by the white middle class. Although many, as Macadoo has pointed out,[5] seem able to handle this situation the support of the kinship system which does not ignore them and still provides the social and emotional support necessary, it is, nevertheless, a stress point which each Afro-American who strives to enter the mainstream must face. This fact is immediately obvious when the student returns to the ghetto from college and finds that he or she is ridiculed or ignored by previous friends and acquaintances for being "uppity."

The reaction of black individuals in lower-class situations toward the black middle or striving class is not merely one aimed at imposing a sense of guilt. It is perhaps better interpreted as an indication of their own stress which derives from the concept of victimization. The concept of victimization implies that some people are used as means to other people's ends without their consent and that the social system is so structured that it can systematically by manipulated to the disadvantage of some group. The victim, his autonomy curtailed and his self-esteem weakened by the caste-class system, is confronted with identity problems.

Limited access to economic and political power makes it impossible for many blacks to acquire the money or education necessary for adapting and improving their life-style and life chances. In the "land of plenty," being poor is often equated with inferiority, laziness, primitiveness, lack of aspirations, and general failure. For those who are the object of these attitudes and portraits, it is a point of stress and conflict. For most of the individuals to whom these characteristics have been attributed, the ideas of hard work and of the acquisition of money, property, and social mobility have become as vital a part of their thinking as for those who are not enmeshed in the struggle for economic survival. Yet, the search for opportunity to actualize the dreams and ideas as others have done seems, for members of this group, to be met with constant obstruction. They are continually seeking work while having been forced out of a system which would provide the necessary skills. Their desire for status is evident, yet they are constantly reminded by welfare workers or law enforcement officials that they are a part of the lowest level of the stratification system; their strongest desire to better their condition is often thwarted by discriminatory practices. This type of confusing and conflicting situation creates severe psychological discomfort. The results are disillusionment, alienation, anxieties, and finally self-protecting adaptation mechanisms which may or may not be acceptable to those in the mainstream of society. It is, of course, into this classification that over half of the Afro-Americans and other minority groups in this country fall. When one considers the extreme dichotomies, pressures, and strains in which individuals who are both black and American find themselves, it is rather astounding to find that the suicide and mental illness rates are not higher for this group than they actually are.

Cultural values and background of blacks prohibit the giving way to stress in forms such as suicide and mental retreat. However, since stress is often seen as related to such physiological changes as increased blood pressure, increased heart rate, headaches, backaches, and other maladies, perhaps the alternative to these escape efforts is the internalization of stress which manifests itself in the high rate of hypertension among Afro-Americans. Certainly, recent studies seem to suggest this, as work done in several urban areas has reported that the incidence of hypertension is higher in blacks than in nonblacks in every age group.

Many researchers, of course, will attempt to suggest that blacks are genetically disposed to this disease. Others attempt to attribute its high incidence to diet and/or obesity. Dr. Charles S. Ireland of Howard University disagrees and attributes the preponderance of this disease to the strain of being black in a white-oriented society. In his studies and those of others, ecological stress resulting from skin-color discrimination, as well as the suppressed hostility among residents of an urban center, were found to contribute significantly to hypertension. Of course, lower socioeconomic status also seems to be a major contributor. As one physician in San Francisco pointed out in his studies of the relationship of stress to hypertension, blood pressure rates seemed to increase in direct proportion to the decrease in socioeconomic status. He thus discovered that if an individual was black and poor, the likelihood of having hypertension increased substantially.

Of the 60 million Americans with hypertension, according to a U.S. Health Department Survey in 1979, 50% of them were black Americans with the largest percentage being black women. One must thus wonder, under the circumstances, if the stresses and strains of being a black female in American society are so overpowering as to create a severe physical disability. Certainly the recent writings on this "double whammy" phenomenon, i.e., being black and female, seem to suggest that this is the case. Black women earn less than white women, who in turn make less than men—white or black. Although black women earn less, they are also much more apt to work than white women of the same age and education. However, in addition to this economic stress, black women must also adjust to social stresses which come from taking the primary responsibility for social institutions within the black community that effect political changes, and from raising children. The realities of these multiple roles and their burdens cause many personal difficulties.

This is, of course, not to say that the male member of the black community suffers any less as he attempts to meet the role expectations of being masculine in American society and also the requirements of adapting to street culture. Becoming an independent, assertive, achieving, and competitive member of the masculine sex—while being forced into the role of a conforming, warm, nonthreatening, cooperative character in order to achieve a place within a mainstream social system—can only be ego devastating and stress producing. Reconciling the role of male and that of black male as developed by mainstream society produces significant anxieties.

In summary, the major sources of stress for black Americans seem to come from multiple arenas. Of primary concern in this paper were the factors of dark skin color and diverse expectations from American society in general and the black community in particular. Together these factors create a severe strain on black individuals. As such, it would appear that a tremendous strength of character and some rather effective coping mechanisms have been extablished which permit not only survival, but also the continous development and progress of America's largest ethnic minority.

References

1. Blackwell, E. J. *The Black Community.* New York: Dodd Mead, 1975.
2. Coleman, J. C. *Personality Dynamics and Effective Behavior.* Chicago: Scott, Foresman, 1960.
3. Glasgow, D. *The Black Underclass.* San Francisco: Josey Bass, 1980.
4. Jones, R. E. (ed.). *Black Psychology.* New York: Harper and Row, 1980.
5. Macadoo, H. P. Black kinship. *Psychology Today* **12**:67–110 (1979).
6. Thompson, S. Hypertension: the silent killer of blacks. Unpublished manuscript, University of Wisonsin, 1980.
7. Williams, James (ed.). *The State of Black America 1979.* New York: National Urban League, 1979.
8. Wilson, W. J. *The Declining Significance of Race: Blacks and Changing American Institutions.* Chicago: University of Chicago Press, 1978.
9. U.S. Department of Labor, Office of the Secretary, Women's Bureau. *The Employment of Women: General Diagnosis of Developments and Issues,* 1980.

Television Violence—Pollution of the Mind *

George Dunea, F.R.C.P., F.R.C.P. (Ed.), F.A.C.P.
Professor of Medicine
University of Health-Science-Chicago Medical School
Chicago, Illinois

Director of the Department of Nephrology/Hypertension
Cook County Hospital
Chicago, Illinois

In recent years there has been much concern about the role of television in promoting antisocial or criminal behavior in children and adolescents— "Never before has so much violence been shown so graphically to so many."[1] This problem assumes enormous proportions in a world of changing values and life-styles where millions of people rely on television for information, education, and entertainment. For the nuclear family, the TV set has become the most reliable and least expensive of baby-sitters, but the wisdom of persistently exposing children to many hours a day of passive television viewing has been questioned, and the massive fare of mediocre commercial programs has been characterized as junk food for the mind— not necessarily harmful in itself but empty, superficial, and of little lasting value. Some have described television as an addictive drug that blunts children's sensibility and destroys their sense of morality, perpetuating dependencies and preventing normal development of skills, inner life, and fantasy. Some have wondered whether indeed our children are not becoming TV zombies, incapable of developing personal relationships, unable to read, to write, and to think.

The problem, in some respects, is not new. As early as 1910 parents were urged to supervise the attendance of their children at theaters and vaudeville shows. With television, however, the potential for serious consequences is enormously enhanced. As Professor Alberta Siegel recently pointed out, children formerly depended largely on storybooks and occasional theatrical shows for their instruction and education, and even the

---

*This contribution was held over from Volume II, *Companion To The Life Sciences*. It was received for publication 1979. (ED).

coming of the radio and the cinema had a relatively minor impact.[2] Television, however, has a much more widespread influence. With 96% of American homes having TV sets, children generally begin watching at the age of 3 to 4 years, the majority spending two, four, or even as many as eight hours sitting in front of the set.[1] At any one time of the day millions of children are watching television, and during one year a child may see as many as 20,000 commercials.[2] Television clearly has a profound effect on the child, by creating expectations of how people ought to feel and act, and by conferring status on certain individuals. It brings the child into the consumer world, provides models of behavior, illustrates patterns of social interaction, and teaches how conflict is resolved.[2] It has a great potential for influencing character development, and may be a potent cause of aggressive, antisocial, or criminal behavior.

The problem must be viewed against the background of a violent society, traditionally accustomed to frontier fighting and gangsterism and, more recently, to widespread urban crime and lawlessness.[3] In the United States, murder is one of the most common causes of death, the homicide rate being ten times that of Scandinavian countries.[1] More murders are committed yearly in Manhattan than in the entire United Kingdom.[1] There are an estimated 200 million guns in America, and every four minutes somebody is killed or wounded by gunfire.[3] Within the last two decades the homicide rate in some northern American cities has risen by over 300%, being responsible to a great extent for the decreased life expectancy of young, urban, nonwhite males.[4] The incidence of violent deaths in young people, especially in the 15- to 24-year-old age group, has increased alarmingly, and in many parts of the United States violence has become a way of life as well as a major health problem.[1]

A consideration of the impact of television requires an appreciation of the magnitude of the exposure to programs of violence. Rothenberg has pointed out that the average American child graduating from high school will have been exposed to some 15,000 hours of television as compared to 11,000 hours of classroom instruction.[3] He will have witnessed some 18,000 murders and many more incidents of robbery, arson, smuggling, beatings, and torture.[3] Children's programs contain six times more violence than adults',[2] and 25% of the industry's profit comes from the 7% of its programs directed at children.[3] Moreover, not only is television so much more accessible than the older forms of entertainment, but its overall character is different, so that whereas formerly violence was portrayed in the context of high tragedy, fantasy, or outright slapstick, modern television routinely represents violence and murder in the context of ordinary life, thus allowing a much greater identification with the murderer, the murdered, or both.[1] The potential for producing antisocial or outright criminal bahavior is consequently greatly enhanced, especially since the amount of violence shown by the networks has greatly increased in the past two decades. According to the National Parent-Teacher Association, some 70% of Americans currently believe that there is too much violence on television. Similarly, some 93% of doctors think there is too much murder and mayhem on television, and more than half suspect that they may be seeing in their offices the consequences of this excessive display of violence.

Some doctors have reported seeing increased aggression or anxiety in children, nightmares, injuries sustained while reenacting their favorite programs, or outright acts of violence. One child reportedly jumped from the roof while playing Batman; another was seen playing policeman with a loaded gun; and another set the house on fire after watching an incident of arson on television. In 1977 in San Francisco a little girl was raped by four boys shortly after the showing of a similar incident on television; in Chicago two teenagers burned a wooden cross on the front lawn of a black family half an hour after watching "The FBI versus the Ku Klux Klan"; and in Miami the lawyers of a 15-year-old youth convicted of first degree murder claimed their client was innocent because prolonged subliminal intoxication with television had produced a temporary state of insanity in which he felt that he was playing out a TV drama. Nor can the influence of television on true criminals be overestimated; in a recent interview in a Wisconsin prison, nine out of ten convicts admitted having learned new skills by watching television, with four out of ten actually attempting to commit the crimes they had seen there.

Beyond these anecdotal reports, numerous studies in the past 25 years have addressed themselves to the effect of television violence on aggressive behavior, and there have been at least eight congressional investigations since the early 1950s. Rothenberg in 1975 reviewed 146 articles representing 50 studies involving 10,000 children and adolescents, all showing that exposure to violence produced increased aggressive behavior.[3] Somers came to similar conclusions in her 1976 review, emphasizing in particular the findings of the two studies set up in 1968 and 1969 in response to public indignation over the rising incidence of crime, including the assassinations of the Kennedy brothers and Dr. Martin Luther King, Jr.[1] The first of these studies, by the Eisenhower commission, concluded that though television was not the principal cause of violence, it was a contributing factor and a matter of great concern.[1] The second study, by the Surgeon General's committee, was somewhat more equivocal, but most officials agreed that numerous studies had established a relation between television and antisocial behavior;[1] and Comstock expressed similar conclusions in a series of review papers issued by the Rand Corporation. The final word, however, probably belongs to Drs. Feingold and Johnson, who after receiving more than 1500 letters from concerned readers of the *New England Journal of Medicine* in response to Professor Somers' article, concluded that the "burden of proof that television violence does no harm lies with those who introduce such a potent force into the societal brew."[5]

The editor of the same journal, Dr. Franz Inglefinger, had already called television violence an unchecked environmental hazard and called for a boycott of products associated with the offending program.[6] Also joining in the antiviolence effort was the American Medical Association, with resolutions deploring excessive violence, supporting Dr. Rothenberg's pleas for "a cry of protest from the medical profession," and calling TV violence a mental health problem and an environmental issue. In 1977 Dr. Richard E. Palmer, president of the AMA, announced that he had asked the leaders of ten major corporations to review advertising policies that support programs containing excessive violence; and the AMA House of Delegates, representing some 200,000 doctors, also affirmed that television is "an environmental hazard threatening the health and welfare of young Americans and indeed our future society." In addition, the delegates committed the AMA to "remedial action in concert with industry, government, and other interested parties," and decided to "encourage all physicians, their families and their patients to actively oppose programs containing violence, as well as products and services sponsoring such programs."

Although the resolution carefully avoided the term *boycott,* a survey of 500 doctors showed that 52% thought that refusing to buy the sponsor's product was a very effective way of reducing TV violence, and a further 29% thought it was "somewhat effective." By contrast, only 30 to 40% of doctors believed that writing letters of complaint, boycotting certain programs or networks, or even government regulation would be very effective techniques. Yet these approaches may also have a place, and have been used or threatened by various organizations opposing TV violence. In 1977 the National PTA urged its 6.5 million members to keep a log of violent incidents on programs and send written complaints to the station and advertisers. It also warned the networks that unless the amount of violence was reduced, it would organize boycotts of programs and advertised products, file lawsuits, and ask for a denial of the license renewal of certain stations. In a similar move, the Southern Baptist Convention developed for its members a viewing log and a rating sheet with a preaddressed "immediate reaction" postcard, in order to "confront television's moral challenge" and "make heard the anguished cry of the American people." Later the national convention of the United Church of Christ also accused the industry of debasing American culture, degrading people, exploiting sex and violence, and falsifying human reality and values. And with other organizations such as the National Citizens Committee for Broadcasting joining in the campaign, there are now signs that the networks are beginning to respond to pressure and are eliminating some of the worst offending programs.

Yet, as might be expected, not everybody concurs with this approach, and some people have expressed concern about undue influence of pressure groups, interference with free speech, excessive government regulation, and impending censorship. One irate correspondent thought that the AMA would do better to direct its priorities to getting people to stop smoking and reduce the death rate from cancer of the lung. Network producers warned that "the industry was slowing down the violence to a degree that is dangerous," that a plastic television would breed a plastic society, and that pressure groups were "sanitizing violence" to a degree that would make it impossible to show the great works of literature and history without provoking an indignant outcry about excessive violence. Art imitates life, according to one producer, and another complained that television was being made a scapegoat for society's frustration over growing crime in the suburbs. However, others pointed out that the issue was not the violence in "Hamlet" or "Roots" but the gratuitous repetitive violence being produced in the assembly line of some of the television studios.

It now appears, however, that the pressure on the networks is beginning to be effective. In 1978 the National Citizens Committee for Broadcasting announced that 9 of the previous season's 12 advertisers of the most violent programs had greatly improved their overall standards by more selective buying. The study found a 9% decrease in the incidence of violence in prime-time TV programs and called this change "a rare public interest victory, with advertisers and networks responding to a broadly based but focused public concern." A study sponsored by the AMA also showed that after reaching an all-time high in 1976, television violence had dropped, almost reaching the record low of 1973. Yet excessive violence still appeared in more than two-thirds of all prime-time programs and in nine out of ten weekend morning programs; movies had become more violent; and there had been an increase of violent episodes between 7 and 9 P.M., in the so-called family viewing hour. The AMA study also indicated television's continuing cultivation of feelings of danger and mistrust, with heavy viewers being more likely to reveal pessimism and alienation, and to acquire locks, dogs, and guns for protection. Violence is still a pervasive factor in TV programs, according to a recent report of the National PTA, and the issue of how best to maintain adequate standards in a profit-oriented industry remains unresolved.

References

1. Somers, A. R. Violence, television and the health of American youth. *N. Engl. J. Med.* **294**: 811-817 (1976).
2. Siegel, A. Effects of television on children. Presented in Physicians training session on television and children, Chicago, October 29, 1977.
3. Rothenberg, M. B. Effect of television violence on children and youth. *J. A. M. A.* **234**: 1043-1046 (1975).
4. Rushforth, N. B. et al. Violent death in a metropolitan county. *N. Engl. J. Med.* **297**: 531-538 (1977).
5. Feingold, M. and Johnson, G. T. Television violence. Reactions from physicians, advertisers and the networks. *N. Engl. J. Med.* **296**: 424-427 (1977).
6. Inglefinger, E. J. Violence on TV: an unchecked environmental hazard. *N. Engl. J. Med.* **294**: 837-838 (1976).

VI
STRESS AND
CLINICAL DISEASE

Strain: Internal Physical Relations in Psychosomatic Diseases*

Wolfgang Zander, M.D.
Institut für Medizinische Psychologie und Psychotherapie
Technische Universität München
Federal Republic of Germany

Every psychosomatic illness represents a multifactorial process in which only one or perhaps two factors, albeit often relevant ones, are psychological in nature.

Generally speaking, we are concerned with four main groups of etiopathological factors:

1. Congenital somatic factors
2. Acquired somatic factors
3. Congenital psychological factors
4. Acquired psychological factors

These groups of factors are interrelated; in other words, the various factors exert a reciprocal effect on each other and can to a certain extent be substituted for each other. They form a cybernetic system. For instance, severe congenital organ damage, even without additional acquired pathogenic factors, prepares the way for a psychosomatic illness. In this case, the acquired somatic factor would be virtually or completely missing and the congenital factor, in contrast, all the more marked. Conversely, where there are strong environmental influences, the harmful congenital factor may be completely absent. Finally, all the somatic factors may play a very minor role, in which case the psychological elements assume correspondingly greater importance. The structural arrangement of the factors is shown in Fig. 1. In view of the foregoing, there can be no rational

*This article is a shortened version of the paper "Stress and Strain" in the series *Psyche and Soma,* Ciba-Geigy, Basle, 1978.

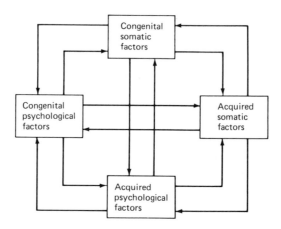

FIG. 1. Causal pattern of a psychosomatic disorder.

grounds for rejecting the idea that psychological causes related to neuroses may underlie morphological changes.

Moreover, two other psychophysical models have long been almost unanimously accepted in medical circles. They are Cannon's so-called emergency theory and Selye's stress model. Both workers have reported nonspecific physical manifestations of syndrome type. Whereas Cannon was interested in the changes brought about by acute influences, such as a fear of death, sudden anger, severe pain, or even acute hunger, Selye's research focused on the physical changes occasioned by sustained stress. Complicated as the function and course of the two syndromes may be, the secretion of adrenaline, the hormone of the adrenal medulla, the activity of the hypophysis, and the excitation of centers in the midbrain play a central role in both cases.

Although there are many scientific findings about the stress phenomenon and about Selye's General Adaptation Syndrome,[4] we know that even under "normal" conditions stress is a highly complex process. Although the humoral, neural, and morphological associations are complicated and some of them not yet fully investigated, they appear to be stylized processes controlled by the sympathetic nervous system. This is why some authors describe the physical responses as stereotyped and mainly nonspecific.

The basic course of stress can vary according to the circumstances. Individual aspects are of special importance in the case of stress due to mental and psychosocial causes, and Selye was already convinced that these stressors played the main role in man. Which psychosocial stimuli are converted into mental dis-stress depends on individual factors. Thus the normal psychological uneasiness experienced before dental treatment can, for example, result in particulary marked adaptation—the more nervous the subject is by nature and the worse his experience of earlier dental treatment. As Görres[4] so graphically put it, he will make a dis-stressor mountain out of a stressor molehill. In this connection, the term inner stressors has been used to distinguish these from pathogenic external psychological stimuli—the external stressors. These too can trigger off the General Adaptation Syndrome.

The discovery of the importance of psychosocial stressors and of internal stress for man led to the fact that these working hypotheses were often regarded as universal and sufficient also for the elucidation of psychosomatic diseases in a narrower sense. For the sake of factual clarity it is, I think, more sensible not to expand the concept of stress further, but to speak, in the case of psychosomatoses, of strain. For in practice, the constellations we most often find with our patients can only be described correctly with the help of knowledge about the psychology of neurosis, and in my opinion they transcend, therefore, all stress models.

Since Freud, we know that the primary causes of later changes in reactivity have their origins in earliest childhood.[5] These processes have been variously described and designated by different psychotherapeutic schools. However, the basic facts remain the same: the small child is frustrated in its needs by severity and/or overindulgence. Emotional development is impaired as a result, and the child acquires an early "imprint" which forms a basis for neurosis.

From histories of the origins of neuroses, the moment at which a small child experiences pathogenic frustration is known to play a decisive part. For instance, if a child is repressed at the oral phase (i.e., in the first year of life, or at the beginning of the second), a depressive structure is laid down in the form of a predisposing imprint; repressions at the anal or motor-aggressive phase similarly predispose to compulsive neurosis, while the hysterical structure arises through repressions at the phallic or oedipal phase. In later life, the depressive can resolve oral conflicts less well than other people and has difficulty in standing up for himself or grasping opportunities. The compulsive, neurotically structured individual, by contrast, has his later difficulties in aggressive encounters, and the hysterical generally in the sexual sphere. Our patients thus become ill in situations which are typical of their individual imprinting, their psychological structure. In this connection, it is by no means pure chance that determines which organ system is affected. Schultz-Hencke was the first researcher to put forward clearly differentiated views about the relationship between affect, impulses, needs, and the innervation of particular organs.[8] If we consider just two examples from the numerous possibilities, according to Schultz-Hencke's concept: an oral impulse involves the shared innervations of the mouth region and the upper gastrointestinal tract, while an aggressive impulse involves the innervation of the voluntary musculature. Thus, if a depressively structured individual later reacts to a subconscious oral problem by producing a psychosomatic syndrome, this will most frequently be manifested in the upper gastrointestinal tract, whereas the compulsive neurotic is predisposed to respond to repressed aggressive impulses with muscular symptoms.

Empirical studies further show that the later sickness-producing life situation is exceptionally often characterized by the triggering off of two diametrically opposed impulses or desires in our patients. They become victims of a so-called ambivalence conflict. This tends to be insoluble because one of the two drives is generally subconscious. An example may help to clarify the point:

A patient may fall ill if he seeks to struggle free from a partner yet, on the other hand, wants to be cared for by the partner. Because one side of the conflict, as already noted, is subconscious, our patient is not free to choose between independence and his desire to be cared for. A solution can often only be found with the aid of psychotherapy, since the latent side of the conflict is then revealed in the course of treatment. Without such insight, however, a state of mental tension continues to exist.

Yet how does the strain corresponding to such a state of mental tension—that is to say, the strain which represents the physical side of our patient's ambivalent reaction to a particular life situation—manifest itself? We have reason to believe that diametrically opposed psychological impulses correspond to antagonistic neurohumoral functional systems in the body. Just as the impulse to flight can be attributed to sympathetic stimulation, we know that the desire to be protected and cared for corresponds to parasympathetic stimulation. Alexander[1] was among the first to distinguish psychosomatic disorders associated with raised sympathetic or parasympathetic tone, and his teaching can be roughly portrayed diagrammatically, as shown in Fig. 2.

Empirical observations suggest that our patients most commonly become ill owing to certain life situations that lead to insoluble ambivalence conflicts which, because of their own particular earlier imprinting, the patients are unable to solve. Correspondingly, the respective organs are innervated by diametrically opposing and hence antagonistic systems. On the basis of these considerations, two different types of strain are conceivable in theory: the sympathetic or, alternatively, the parasympathetic tone, participating in the ambivalence conflict, can be suppressed. It is possible to

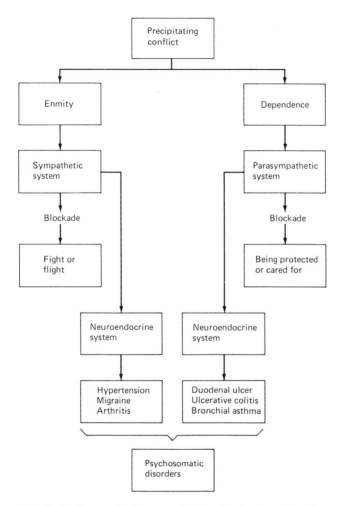

FIG. 2. Psychosomatic disease model (simplified), after Alexander.

portray the strain associated with suppression of aggressive (i.e., "fight")
impulses in simplified diagrammatic form, as shown in Fig. 3.

In contrast to this, suppression of the need to be cared for or to submit
could be diagrammatically illustrated on the lines shown in Fig. 4.
However, irrespective of the type of suppression, there is simultaneous involvement of the antagonistic innervations of the organ systems, and we
still know little about the circumstances in which the sympathetic and
parasympathetic nervous systems are equally active or in which one or the

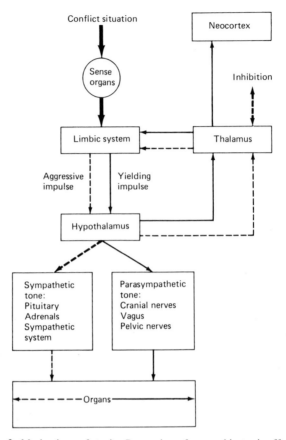

FIG. 3. Mechanisms of strain. Repression of sympathicotonic effect.

other predominates.* It is nevertheless easy to imagine that simultaneous excitation of agonists and antagonists can lead to dysfunction and eventually to morphological changes. This last point by no means argues against psychogenetic factors in the development of a disease. Despite all theoretical similarity between inner stress and strain, the important differences have presumably become more clear-cut.

The theoretical considerations thus far presented would, however, not suffice on their own if, in addition to the work on affect correlations and modern stress research, investigations into the subject of strain had not also already begun.

*This is only a rough draft of the concept. Since the recognition of alpha and beta receptors, we already know that antagonism exists in the adrenergic system.

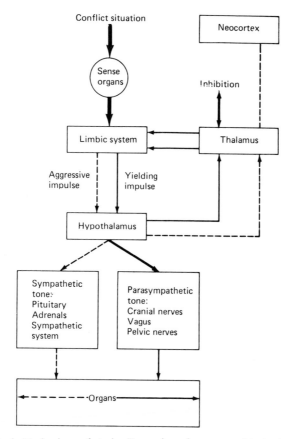

FIG. 4. Mechanisms of strain. Repression of parasympathicotonic effect.

In strain research—as may be understood from the foregoing—a patient is not exposed to any external stress factors, but is studied while undergoing a neurotic conflict. For example, Janus, to mention just one researcher, has measured the behavior of the blood pressure during psychotherapy in subjects with essential hypertension, and also the behavior of muscle action potentials in patients with cervical syndrome.

To show that strain research can also contribute to an understanding of the selection of the affected organ, I should like to describe the results of our own studies in duodenal ulcer patients. The presence of psychogenetic components is generally accepted by most specialists even in those patients whose ulcers are not caused purely by stress. By what mechanism emotional conflicts are able to produce a tissue defect at the stomach outlet or in the duodenum still remains an open question. In all, we have carried out deep psychological explorations in 77 patients, in all of whom the diagnosis had been confirmed not only clinically but also radiologically. In addition, 18 patients underwent gastroscopy. There were 55 men and 22 women, with an average age of 33 years. The average number of ulcers per patient amounted to nearly 3 (2.9), and the average duration of illness was about five years. All the patients could thus be justifiably described as ulcer sufferers.

By means of deep psychological exploration, it was possible to demonstrate a depressive-compulsive neurotic mixed structure as the relevant early imprinting in 86% of those studied. The development of this early childhood structure, however, showed some peculiarities compared with that of other patients of the same mixed structure. As small children, the patients had merely been prevented from actively asserting themselves, responding as individuals, or making demands. If the children were well behaved, they could wait patiently for their needs to be met without any activity on their part. They consequently developed what Schultz-Hencke called an oral behavior structure. Early childhood inhibition was further reinforced by the fact that it was a particularly strong taboo to covet anything that belonged to a brother or sister, or their corresponding substitutes. Sibling envy could not be entertained since it resulted in loss of love, or punishment. In the same way, aggressive encounters with brothers, sisters, or their substitutes were looked on as something to be punished, whereas struggle and achievement in other fields of life were thought of highly. From this there resulted an aggressive inhibited structure which only revealed itself in certain situations. In accordance with this very specific type of early imprinting, such individuals later tend to become ill in situations possessing the character of psychological "sham feeding."* These are situations in which subjects have to watch how others obtain (i.e., are fed with) just what they themselves want, but without actually being able to acquire it. No trace of the jealous indignation which others would experience in such a situation is displayed here, because of their early repression.

These relationships may be further clarified by describing the case of a 40-year-old woman patient who came to us with her second ulcer after frequently suffering from ill-defined stomach complaints since puberty. From her early history the following factors were of relevance. To outward appearances, the father was the dominating figure in the family but he soon

*Sham feeding was carried out on esophagotomized dogs by Silbermann of the Pavlov school. After two to three weeks he observed ulcer formation at the outlet of the stomach and/or in the duodenum.

went off to the war. He was kindly and caring toward the children and always brought them something when he came back from the front on leave. Apart from this, there could be no tidbits or other treats as the mother's meager budget would not run to them. The patient thus developed an oral complex which took the form of expectation from the open-handed man who gave if one only waited long enough. Otherwise the patient did not dare risk rebellion against the mother's strict authoritarianism. As the oldest child she had always to be sensible and to look after the three younger children. Other evidence for early repression of aggression was that she had been very afraid of the dark when she was 3 years old and also had a fear of thunderstorms that has persisted right up to the present. The following situation seemed to act as the trigger for her first stomach complaints when she was 14: her father died at this time, and her mother soon married an egocentric man who brought three of his own children into the family. The patient was now not only thwarted in her subconscious longing for paternal generosity, but things got still worse for her owing to the stepfather's low wages and the addition of three more mouths to feed. Moreover, the stepfather squandered on bouts of drinking the little money that the mother had saved for emergencies. However, in order not to upset her mother, the daughter remained silent.

At the time of her first florid ulcer, she also found herself in a—for her—typical life situation. She had been doing the bookkeeping single-handedly for a firm but was clearly being underpaid. After some years a male colleague was employed whom the patient had to train. This colleague was soon able to pull strings and obtain an increase in pay, but our patient denied being jealous of the man she had come to like. At the time of the second ulcer, she had changed her job, becoming sole bookkeeper in a largish fur business. As the owner made a caring paternal impression, she had not even inquired about her salary level—and again found herself in the position of being underpaid. Admittedly she was invited more often to her employer's home, which reinforced her subconscious longing for a giving father. In real life, she helped out her employer's wife in the house and saw for herself how spoiled the wife (previously also an employee in the fur business) was by her husband. However, as the employer's wife was a friendly, sympathetic woman, our patient—because of her early imprinting—did not feel envious in this case either.

It should not however be assumed here that the psychodynamic response to this fateful trigger situation consisted solely of jealous indignation. On the contrary, the psychodynamic response is of great complexity and, owing to other individual characteristics, also varies considerably from patient to patient. However, since this—almost always subconscious—emotional response has proved to be statistically significant as the central element in the whole pattern of causation, the history of our 40-year-old patient's illness has been presented here in simplified terms of jealous indignation.

As shown in Fig. 5, subconscious jealousy could be detected in 70 out of a total of 77 ulcer patients. In 33 cases these were mainly problems of possession; in 32 cases, of prestige; while interpersonal relationships played a part in only 5 cases. Among 77 control subjects suffering from other psychosomatic disorders, subconscious jealousy of this type could be demonstrated only in 6 individuals. (The demonstration of subconscious affects, desires, or needs is only possible by means of depth-psychology techniques).

Further observations now need to be made, however, to enable us to understand just why an ulcer should develop within this psychodynamic framework as a "strain effect" or "strain disease." Studies in man must by their nature be limited in extent, but it has been possible to combine a specific short interview with the necessary radiological investigation in 17 of the 77 patients, keeping the x-ray dose very low by the use of small-field radiography. When we carried out this combined x-ray/interview—which was divided into a standardized 11-point program—in our 40-year-old patient, the questioning three times produced a lightning response in the form of a violent, persistent spasm in the antral region of the stomach. This happened the first time when we spoke of subconscious jealousy of the employer's wife, a second time as discussion turned to how often the stepfather had indulged himself at the expense of the family and, finally, at the end of the interview when we again mentioned the situation in the fur merchant's house as a confirmatory check. No such changes could be observed in the stomach when any other points were touched upon. Similar findings of intensive antral spasm were demonstrated in 15 of the 17 patients. No

		TRIGGER SITUATION			
	Number	Jealousy		Others	None
Ulcer patients	77	70* Possession Prestige Relationships	33 32 5	4	3
Control subjects	77	6 Possession Prestige Relationships	2 4 Ø	67	4

*Statistically significant at the 1% level.

FIG. 5. Situations precipitating ulcer development in 77 patients.

single instance could be found in the control group. This finding was also statistically significant at the 1% level, as shown in Fig. 6.

That the antral spasm is not an incidental finding, i.e., not the result of something like general irritation in a disordered stomach, is confirmed by the following considerations. The spasm appeared exclusively in connection with matters relevant to the psychology of the patient's neurosis, i.e., only at the mention of the situation provoking jealous indignation. The reasons why this response could not be set off in two patients provide still further support for our hypothesis. In one patient, the combined x-ray/interview could, for extraneous reasons, only be carried out after considerable delay. The patient's life circumstances had meanwhile changed so much for the better that the precipitating jealousy no longer represented a problem for him. In the second case, the patient had deliberately remained silent about the relevant precipitating life situation during our preliminary exploration so that the particular problems underlying his jealousy could not be raised. During the combined x-ray/interview, the stomach did not respond with spasm even once, although a florid ulcer had been demonstrated gastroscopically. The relevant triggering situation could only be revealed later. It may thus be confidently assumed that one single strain element is concerned in this antral spasm—and not strain in general.

When the stomach responds in this fashion while the patient is experiencing the specific neurotic ambivalence situation, it is no longer difficult to imagine that the functional disturbance can eventually cause a tissue defect. Despite the relevant theories put forward by gastroenterologists we have consulted, further interdisciplinary research still seems to be required before the precise role of this spasm in the causal chain of ulcer formation can be determined. One thing has however already been shown by the studies so far carried out. Just as there are stress diseases brought on by psychological stress factors which then eventually follow their own organic laws, there are also strain diseases precipitated by neurotic processing of conflicts. Once started, they also have their own demonstrable changes and can develop somatic characteristics. That psychological factors can play a

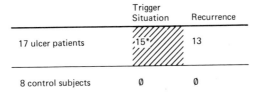

*Statistically significant at the 1% level.

FIG. 6. Spasm in the antrum.

relevant part in the etiopathogenesis of a range of conditions presenting as organic diseases may be regarded as confirmed by the work that has now been performed in this field.

References

1. Alexander, F. *Psychosomatic Medicine*. New York: Norton, 1965.
2. Ariens, E. F. Pharmakologie des adrenergen Systems. In *Das medizinische Prisma*, vol. 2. Ingleheim am Rhein: C. H. Boehringer-Söhne, 1970.
3. Cannon, W. B. *Bodily Changes in Pain, Hunger, Fear and Rage*. New York: 1929.
4. v.Eiff, A. W. *Seelische und körperliche Störungen durch Stress*. Stuttgart-New York: Gustav Fischer Verlag, 1976.
5. Freud, S. *Gesammelte Werke* (Collected Works). London: Imago Publ., 1940–1952.
6. Ganong, W. F. *Medizinische Physiologie*, Berlin-Heidelberg-New York: Springer Verlag, 1972.
7. Schmidt, R. F. Grundriß der Neurophysiolgie. *Heidelberger Taschenbücher*, Band 96. Berlin-Heidelberg-New York: Springer Verlag, 1976.
8. Schultz-Hencke, H. *Lehrbuch der analytischen Psychotherapie*. Stuttgart: Georg Thieme Verlag, 1951.
9. Schwidder, W. Psychosomatik und Psychoterapie bei Störungen und Erkrankungen des Verdauungstraktes. *Acta psychosomatica, Documenta Geigy* (1965).
10. Selye, W. The general adaptation syndrome and the diseases of adaptation. *J. Clin. Endocrin.* **6** (1946).
11. Zander, E.u.W. Die Neo-Psychoanalyse von H. Schultz-Hencke. In *Die Psychologie des XX. Jahrhunderts*, Band 3. Zürich: Kindler Verlag, 1977.
12. Zander, W. Psychosomatische Forschungsergebnisse beim Ulcus duodeni. Göttingen: Verlag für Medizinische Psychologie im Verlag Vandenhoek und Rupprecht, 1977.

Medical Applications of Biofeedback: With a Theoretical Background

Nelson Hendler, M.D., M.S.
Assistant Professor of Psychiatry
Psychiatric Consultant, Chronic Pain Treatment Center
Johns Hopkins Hospital
Baltimore, Maryland
Clinical Director
Mensana Clinic
Stevenson, Maryland

The use of biofeedback in clinical medicine and psychiatry is proliferating, and it has now been accepted as a reputable modality of treatment. However, as with all new techniques, there are many misconceptions regarding the mechanism of action and rationale for its application. Inherent in this concept is the need for proper patient selection and utilizing the appropriate modality of feedback for the disorder to be treated. Table 1 will serve only as a guideline for proper patient selection and treatment modality, but it is hoped that the theoretical information contained in this chapter will provide a conceptual framework which will allow the more innovative readers an opportunity to devise new and appropriate ways to employ biofeedback for the benefit of their patients.

By and large, the most replicable results are obtained with EMG and temperature biofeedback, while EEG and GSR are fraught with technical difficulties. After assuming that biofeedback *can* work, the questions then become why it works, how it works, and what the rationales are behind the application of this technique. This requires a review of neuroanatomy, because without this knowledge, one cannot understand the mechanism of biofeedback.

There are two coexisting nervous systems, and these are divided into a variety of functions. The major branches are the autonomic nervous system and the voluntary nervous system. It is useful to compare and contrast them. The autonomic nervous system is under hypothalamic and brain stem control; these are the centers within the brain that actually control what happens in the periphery. The voluntary nervous system is under cortical or, in some cases, cerebellar control (the cerebellar functionings are more automatic than the voluntary cortical control, but nonetheless there is

Table 1 *

Modality of Feedback	Part of the Nervous System Conditioned	Application	Rating
Galvanomic skin response (GSR)	Autonomic	Relaxation and stress reduction	N
		Lie detection	HS
EEG	Central nervous system	Relaxation	N
		Epilepsy treatment	HS
		Headache	N
Thermal	Autonomic	Migraine Headache	V
		Raynaud's disease	R
		Tinnitus	V
		Sympathetic dystrophy	HS
		Mixed musculo-skeletal-vascular headache	V
EKG (ECG)	Autonomic	Wolff-Parkinson-White syndrome	HS
		Premature ventricular contraction	HS
Heart rate (Pulse)	Autonomic	Anxiety and stress	V
		Hyperthyroidism	N
		Parasysmal atrial tachycardia	HS
Blood pressure	Autonomic	Hypertension	HS, V
		Migraine headache	N, V
Barometric (pressure inside or ouside a lumen)	Autonomic	Penile tumescence and erection	HS
		Ostomy patients for bowel control	HS
Electromyographic (EMG)	Voluntary	Stroke patients and muscle retraining	R
		Muscle tension headache	R
		Bruxism, TMJ	R
		Stress and anxiety reduction	V
		Sleep induction	V

RATING CODES:
R = Replicable results, reliable, and recommended.
V = Variable results, great differences in effect between clinicians.
N = Not recommended, too unreliable.
HS = Highly specialized—useful only at a research level with specialized equipment.

* The reader is referred to Vol. 3 and 4 of *Biofeedback and Self Regulation* (December 1978), which contains the task force reports of the Biofeedback Society of America.[18]

voluntary control). In most respects, autonomic nervous system functioning is automatic and unconscious: one does not have to think about breathing; one does not have to remember to tell the heart to beat. The voluntary nervous system obviously has conscious input: "I want to lift my arm," "I want to lift my leg," "I want to tense up the muscles," etc. The autonomic nervous system innervates smooth muscle—gut and blood vessels, for example—while the voluntary nervous system innervates striated muscle— the muscles of the arms, legs, back, etc. The autonomic nervous system usually has antagonism built in; that is, it has feedback within the system—parasympathetic actions conflict with sympathetic actions. On the other hand, the voluntary nervous system has sort of an unconsicious feedback mechanism—a cross-inhibition reflex—in which movement of one opposing muscle group produces the relaxation of the other opposing muscle group. Thus, one bends his arm and puts tension on the biceps, obviously one has to have a concomitant release of the tension in the triceps. However, this is done automatically. So, there are checks and balances in both of the systems and, in fact, one can consider this to some degree to be automatic and involunatry in the striated musculature, just as in the autonomic nervous system.

The autonomic nervous system uses acetylecholine for parasympathetic innervation, and epinephrine and norepinephrine for sympathetic nerve action. The preganglion synapse uses acetylcholine, and central control uses a variety of transmitters. The voluntary nervous system uses acetylcholine at a peripheral neurosynaptic junction between nerve and muscle, but its is very specific. Centrally, it uses GABA (gamma-aminobutyric acid), as well as glycine, to control the action of muscles.

The autonomic nervous system has many receptors on vessels and gut wall, and these respond to circulating hormones, as well as to specific neural input. This is a critical concept. The body does not need direct nerve innervation of the gut or blood vessels: these organs will respond to circulating hormones—hormones that come from the adrenal gland, the neurohypophysis, and the anterior pituitary gland. This is in contradistinction to the direct and specific connections found in the voluntary nervous system in which one nerve goes to one muscle, and if that nerve is cut, the muscle does not work.

The hormones that are circulating and affect the autonomic nervous system are all the catecholamines—dopamine, dopa, epinephrine, norepinephrine—and the indolamines (serotonin), as well as bradykinin, prostaglandins, and a variety of other vasoactive substances. The nerves and the muscles of the striated system and the voluntary system do not respond to circulating hormones. There is very little that gets into the synaptic cleft of the myoneural junction that makes it work, except the direct stimulation of the nerve.

The autonomic nervous sytem is under conscious control, and the patient is not aware of subtle changes. It can be altered by contiguity, which is a theory advanced by Guthrie that involves repeated pairings of a stimulus and a response, and by Pavlovian conditioning, which is merely the repetition of a pairing of a conditioned stimulus followed by an unconditioned stimulus.[1] An animal can actually learn, back one step from the unconditioned stimulus (fire, food, or whatever produces an unlearned response), and pair some previously neutral stimulus and make it have an effect.

The voluntary nervous system is under conscious control (with the exception of some cerebellar actions). Dr. Kamiya has advanced a notion of awareness, which indicates that once a person gains recognition of the fact that something is happening, he is on his way to being able to control it.[2] These responses can be reinforced; they can be operantly conditioned, and Skinnerian or (operant or instrumental) learning can occur.

The autonomic nervous system has proprioceptive sensors that are not readily in touch with the cortex. A person does not know what is going on in his carotid artery; he does not know what is going on in his vagus nerve. People do not have any real sense of these various physiological functions that are under automatic control until the abnormality is so severe that receptors, other than the normal proprioceptive mechanisms of the autonomic nervous system, come into play and tell them that something is amiss. This is in contradistinction to the voluntary nervous system which has a whole series of proprioceptive mechanisms built in: the gama motor loop, the cerebellar reflex arc—all of these tell an individual, via kinesthetic senses and proprioceptive senses, where his arm is in space. The voluntary nervous system tells a person that he can, in fact, get fine movement within his fingers and lets him regulate these things in a much more discreet fashion than he normally would with the autonomic nervous system. Hopefully, this differentiation between the two types of nervous systems gives one a clue about how one can train them. With this background, we can now consider what biofeedback is.

Very simplistically, it is merely an amplification of subtle changes in either the autonomic or the voluntary nervous system so that the subject can now become aware of certain physical changes going on within his body. It assumes he was not previously aware of these changes, and the measurement or the awareness affords the subject the opportunity to alter the responses he was experiencing and of which he was previously unaware. By displaying the physiological measurements using biofeedback instruments, researchers have amplified normal physiological responses and made them enter into one's consciousness; scientists have now given an organism the opportunity to exert some control over what is happening in its own body.

One other theory that should be taken into account is the difference between operant and classical conditioning, because without understanding this, a clinician cannot utilize biofeedback effectively. Operant conditioning—Skinnerian conditioning or instrumental learning—must have a reward, or it will not function.[3] Classical, or Pavlovian, conditioning does not need a reward.[4] Operant or Skinnerian conditioning is training a voluntary motion that is the response to a stimulus, but the response is voluntary. In classical conditioning, the response is a natural autonomic function; that is, it is unconscious. In operant conditioning, it is easy to extinguish or unlearn that response unless you get repetitive rewards. In classical conditioning, it is very difficult to extinguish or unlearn autonomically conditioned responses. In operant conditioning, the strength of the response and the rate of learning depend upon a type of schedule or (variable ratio and variable frequency) rates of acquisition, but in classical conditioning, many of the factors that influence learning are really directed toward the severity of the actual event that is the the unconditioned stimulus and the number of pairings. One can readily see a clear-cut distinction at that level.

Operant conditioning is used to condition the voluntary nervous system despite theoretical reports in the literature to the contrary. Certainly, one must employ classical conditioning to do any training of the autonomic nervous system.

Before proceeding further, one should consider some examples of classical conditioning. Dr. Horsley Gantt had trained some interesting dogs in his laboratory at Perry Point, Maryland and his farm in Virginia, and these have been well reported in the literature.[5] Gantt found that the more nervous or neurotic a dog is, the more the dog would respond to autonomic conditioning. For example, he would place a dog in a halter and find that the dog's heart rate was 80 or 100 beats/minute. As a person entered the room, the heart rate would jump to about 120 beats/minute. Why did the heart rate jump? These dogs had all been subjects in prior experiments, and one can only imagine the trepidation and anxiety the dog would feel being placed in the same experimental environment again ("What's he going to do to me now? Is he going to shock me? Is he going to stick me in the leg for blood?"). The presence of an experimenter was certainly not very soothing. Then the experimenter would approach the dog and, at this point in time, the dog would see that there was nothing in his hand, which was very reassuring, and the heart rate would drop back down to about 80 beats/minute, or maybe even 70 beats/minute. Then, as the experimenter began to pet the dog, the heart rate would drop down to 60 beats/minute —in some cases, 40 beats/minute. In some cases, with the more neurotic dogs, there would actually be cardiac standstill for as long as 4 or 5 seconds. This is a very interesting concept, because, in this experiment, the dog had not been reinforced, the dog had not been trained, but the dog had learned by association—simply by repeated contiguity (by repeated pairings) of an event with a physiological response. The dog learned that the presence or absence of an experimenter can influence his life, and he really responded very dramatically to this. Gantt called this phenomenon the "effect of person."[5]

Dr. James Lynch, at the University of Maryland, has carried this one step further and, in fact, has done research on people in intensive care units. Dr. Lynch found that the mere taking of a pulse in an intensive care unit would alter the pulse rate. Because these patients were continuously monitored, one could document this. These changes occurred even with unconscious patients, and indicated that the intervention of a person altered the pulse rate. This is another example of the effect of person.[6]

In another experiment, Hendler et al. demonstrated the effect of person with biofeedback patients.[7] They showed that the presence or absence of a clinician from the room can influence the response one is getting to the biofeedback instrumentation. With these constructs in mind, further practical considerations about biofeedback conditioning should be explored. Unconditioned stimuli are the first concern.

What are unconditioned stimuli? They are stimuli which are going to produce a response that normally or naturally occurs without prior training. One should consider something that produces an autonomic effect. As an example, food is an unconditioned stimulus, and salivation is an unconditioned response. Shock is an unconditioned stimulus—one does not have to learn about shock—all one has to do is be shocked once and the heart rate goes up. Do this repeatedly, and the event of someone preparing a subject for the shock already increases their heart rate. The real issue here is that the unconditioned stimulus is a naturally occurring event and the response is not within or under conscious control. Then, one can add a conditioned stimulus (a bell, a tone, whatever one wants) and present that prior to the unconditioned stimulus, so the sequence becomes bell then food, or bell then shock, and finally the resultant autonomic response— salivation, increased heart rate, etc. With this paradigm, some other considerations must be explored before the institution of biofeedback training. The next concept is stimulus generalization.

Stimulus generalization says that *any* bell will produce the same response in the subject, but the quantity and amount of the response are best when the tone of the bell is very similar or exactly equal to the tone of the bell that was used to condition the animal in the first place. So one can say that the animal responds to any bell (stimulus generalization), but the response is best to the very tone that was used to train him in the first place, which brings into play the concept of stimulus discrimination. Additionally, there are differing responses to different, but similar, stimuli. When an animal is conditioned to a bell instead of food, the type of salivation that is produced is different. When the animal salivates in response to food, he has both mucons and serons salivation—the thick, mucous type and the thin, watery type. When he is responding to just the bell (the secondary stimulus), it is only with the thin, watery kind. This fact now interjects a concept of primary and secondary rewards. Food or shock is a primary reward or a primary punishment—food being the reward and shock being the punishment. Then, the secondary reward can be conditioned and this can produce a response, but the response is not nearly as strong as the primary reward. These responses can be learned by the animal just by repeated pairing, and this is the concept of contiguity and repeated pairing which is essential to classical conditioning.

One other concept to consider is that of backwards conditioning. Backwards conditioning does not occur; one cannot offer the food, then the bell, and hope that the animal will start to salivate in response to the bell. However, the animal will learn that as it eats, it can expect to hear a bell ring. It does not learn that the bell is going to now bring on food, since this is not the sequence of events. There is no such thing as backwards conditioning. This concept must be borne in mind when one is training people on biofeedback. The final concept about classical conditioning seems simple, but it is critical: one needs a natural unconditioned stimulus to get a natural unconditioned response. Shock is one natural unconditioned stimulus; heat is another natural unconditioned stimulus; and cold is yet another. The unconditioned response is mediated by the autonomic nervous system; the more natural the unconditioned stimulus, the more natural is the unconditioned response. These are some very simplistic but basic concepts with which one must function when training people on biofeedback.

The second form of conditioning is operant, or Skinnerian, conditioning. This is used to teach a novel behavior to an animal when this behavior is not already in the animal's repertoire. As an example, imagine that one has a rat running in a cage, exhibiting random behavior. One begins to shape the behavior of the animal by rewarding the animal. As the random behavior becomes less random, the animal obtains more rewards and the behavior becomes even less random. What one has is a learned behavior: the animal can elect to use his behavior to get a reward. This concept is very important: he can *elect* to use his behavior; it is under his voluntary conscious control. The animal will learn that if he pushes the bar, he gets fed, and if he is full, no amount of reward is going to excite him because he has no motivation to pick up the reward. This behavior is well within the range of what Hull described as drive-reduction theory.[8] Hull's original work says that there are primary rewards—food, sex, sleep, avoidance of pain—which are in the realm of self-preservation; secondary rewards— money, control of the environment, etc.— which are things that one uses to acquire primary rewards; and tertiary rewards—praise, pleasing the experimenter, etc.

The further removed one is from a primary reward, the less rewarding is the impact of the substance or the experience. The use of food, sex, sleep, or avoidance of pain is very rewarding and reduces very basic needs on the part of the organism. This is within Hull's concept of drive reduction: the secondary and tertiary rewards are progressively less rewarding than the primary rewards. How can this be applied to biofeedback?

EMG biofeedback has probably been the most widespread application found in the literature. It seems to be the most replicable and has the broadest use in psychiatry, medicine, and dentistry. Why EMG biofeedback? Because EMG biofeedback makes the patient aware of what is happening in a particular muscle group, and the most frequent clinical complaints that respond to EMG biofeedback are muscle tension headache, bruxism, muscle spasm secondary to myofascial syndrome, and similar disorders. As a clinical example, in bruxism, muscle tension sensors are placed over the masseter muscle, and within two or three sessions the patients' headaches have stopped. Why have their headaches stopped? Because, for the first time, they have actually recognized that they grind their teeth.[9] Very often, when patients are atached to an EMG biofeedback machine and register muscle tension of 200 mV, they are told that normal resting muscle tension is 2 mV. The normal response is "My goodness! You mean my muscles are that tense here?" After three or four sessions, they can usually relax, and the headaches go away. However, the major part of this treatment is the recognition of a previously undetected tension within the muscles.

There is a complicated theoretical explanation for this improvement. The clinician has made patients aware of what they are doing with their muscles. They have been taught to reduce muscle tension which, in fact, may help them. They want to please the experimenter, so they reduce their muscle tension, and they find that the experimenter was not lying to them:

in fact, reducing their muscle tension did ease their pain, and that is rewarding. This produces both a tertiary reward (that is, pleasing the experimenter) and a primary reward (reducing pain), and now there are at least two reward systems in operation. This further facilitates retraining of a muscle group, by operant conditioning. By making the unconsicious become conscious, one now can control a specific muscle, and repetitive training and documentation by EMG biofeedback reinforce behavior by the operant conditioning method. Subsequently, one needs repetitive reinforcement sessions. If a patient does not continue to reinforce this type of behavior and unconsciously begins to tense the muscle again, the symptoms will recur. Two things can happen: (1) patients can have what is called spontaneous recovery, that is, after months of no reward, they can in fact remember what they learned while on the biofeedback machinery, or (2) they can extinguish the behavior (they won't remember or they don't remember how to reduce the muscle tension), and then they have to come back for reinforcement sessions. It depends on the person.

The above is a brief theoretical construct about why and how EMG biofeedback may work, which should be taken in the context of the voluntary nervous system and Skinnerian or operant conditioning.

The more difficult diseased are Raynaud's disease,[10] causalgia,[11] vascular headaches,[13] any damage to the vascular system or autonomic nervous system, irritable bowel syndrome,[14] and those involving any organs or parts of the body that are under autonomic control. Some authors feel that the autonomic nervous system is not amendable to operant conditioning per se. Black and others say that it is not appropriate to think of operant conditioning being utilized for autonomic training.[15] Before accepting this, consider for a moment the methods of vasoconstriction. Examine the pathology and the pathophysiology of Raynaud's disease, causalgia, and a variety of other disorders that have, in fact, damage to blood vessels or vasoconstriction as the manifesting problem.

The vessels can constrict in response to direct control of the autonomic nervous system; that is, stimulating a sympathetic nerve can cause vasoconstriction. They can respond to circulating hormones due to stress, other endocrinopathies, or even the common cold. They can respond to mechanical damage to the vessel—arteriosclerotic plaques, muscle spasm (which constricts the blood vessels because the blood vessels flow through the muscles), or anatomical occlusions. There are alpha 1 and alpha 2 receptors and beta 1 and beta 2 receptors that respond differently to epinephrine and norepinephrine. Sometimes these will dilate vessels and sometimes they will constrict vessels, and the action depends upon where the vessel is. Peripheral vessels do not respond in the same fashion as deep

STRESS AND CLINICAL DISEASE

muscle vessels, and neither respond the same as intestinal vessels or cerebral vessels. For simplicity, if one examines the response to epinephrine and norepinephrine in these vessels, using the teleological construct of flight and fight, then one can imagine that the body will not want blood in the gut, because an organism does not need to be actively digesting food at the same time that it is preparing to run. Therefore, vessels clamp down in the intestine, shunting the blood away from the gut. However, the body would want vessels in the striated muscle to be dilated, because it is anticipating the fact that it is about ready to run and it wants more blood flowing to these muscles. They dilate in response to this flight or fight response; the vessels in the skin really are not needed, so they constrict. One can now see how the body has mapped out this response to stress, and how vasoconstriction may be part of this response.

When one considers the mechanisms behind Raynaud's disease or sympathetic dystrophy, it seems that these disorders are amenable to biofeedback training. Very simply, because the manifestation of these disorders is reduced temperature in the hands, there is something to be measured and "trained." What are you conditioning when you make the temperature in the hand increase? Is it hormonal? Is it the release of circulating chemicals, such a norepinephrine, epinephrine, dopamine, dopa, serotonin, bradykinin, prostaglandins, etc.? This is not known, but it probably is not. Research conducted at Mensana Clinic, is conjunction with Dr. Ave Kowarski's pediatric endocrinology group at Johns Hopkins Hospital, addressed itself to just such an issue. Dr. Kowarski developed a technique for measuring norepinephrine in the plasma. By using an indwelling catheter with a constant withdrawal pump that removes blood at a regular rate, aliquots of blood for a set period of time were obtained. Norepinephrine levels were correlated with changes in finger temperature in a person trained to raise his temperature by biofeedback. In very preliminary work on only six subjects, there does *not* seem to be a direct correlation between changes in temperature in the fingers of the hand and changes in norepinephrine levels in the blood. However, other researchers found that epinephrine levels in the blood could be conditioned, and these may account for peripheral vascular changes.[16] Of course, further studies on the other vasoactive hormones are needed, as are a large number of subjects. In any event, it is more likely one is actually classically conditioning a descrete local function of blood vessel activity and this response does not seem to be generalized.

There is another set of disorders that manifest as reduced temperature in the hands or fingers, such as thoracic outlet syndrome, which is, in fact, a compression of vessels as they pass over the first rib. No amount of biofeedback training could help a patient with this disorder because the obstruction, or pathology, is mechanical; it is not to due to some inherent vasoconstriction in the peripheral vessels or a response to some circulating hormones. Based on the information currently available, it seems that disorders due to circulating hormones and mechanical damage to vessels do not respond to biofeedback. What does respond to biofeedback?

There are direct autonomic nervous system centers within the hypothalamus and within some areas of the brain stem. Research done in the 1960s by Hendler and Blake demonstrates that blood pressure increases can be produced by hypothalamic stimulation using either electical methods, angiotensin II, or other circulating hormones such as norepinephrine.[17] Since the hypothalamus sends projections to the cortex and the cortex sends projections back to the hypothalamus, a variety of central systems, among them the limbic system, which includes the temporal lobe and the lip of the cingulate gyrus, are involved in the central control of autonomic function. It is possible for the conscious cortex to exert control of hypothalamic or emotional centers, at least on an anatomical basis. According to this concept, it is conceivable that the cortical or subcortical control (actually the hypothalamic control) of autonomic function is probably the mechanism that accounts for the changes that are seen in thermal biofeedback when conditioning discrete vessel dilation. As an example, a case study of Raynaud's disease in a 45 year old man, is presented below.

A 4.5°C increase in temperature in the hands was effected after four 20-minute training sessions. After repeated training, the autonomic nervous system, or perhaps some cortical function controlling it, was conditioned, and this gentleman was able to return to work. He was able to function and the conditioning remained intact without his true conscious control. In other words, when the pain got worse, he did not have to sit down and say, "I now must concentrate and think of warming my hands." He, in fact, through some mechanism that he could not explain, was able to warm his hands. Now, what is that mechanism? Supposedly, the unknown event could be relaxation, or it could be reduced sympathetic tone from the central nervous system. Whether the cortex fed back to the hypothalamus to increase the temperature in his hand is unknown, but the concept is still there. To return to the paradigm of classical conditioning, this unknown event is an unconditioned stimulus—a natural event—and it produces a natural unconditioned response: a warm hand. Knowledge of the event (that is, relaxation, thinking of warm baths or of being in the desert) becomes a conditioned stimulus. This conditioned stimulus now gets paired with the unconditioned stimulus—again, an unknown event—and produces the conditioned response of a warm hand. Up to this point, the clinical response fits the classical conditioning paradigm, but it is not enough, because the conditioned response, the warm hand, is rewarding. It reduces pain. In the same way that muscle relaxation is rewarding for the person with tension headaches, so is this conditioned response of a warm hand. This feeds back to the cortical environment, saying "whatever you're doing—I don't know what you're doing—but whatever you're doing, please keep doing it, because it feels better," and then one gets the primary reward of pain reduction. This, in turn, reinforces more of the conditioned stimulus activity, that is, the conscious control of trying to warm the hands. Therefore, in order to understand thermal biofeedback in conjunction with learning paradigms, what one is really seeing initially is a classical conditioning paradigm and then, superimposed on that, operant conditioning due to the reward factor. This, hopefully, will serve as a theoretical framework for understanding what is happening when trying to condition the autonomic nervous system. Significantly, it differs from conditioning the voluntary nervous system. While the paradigm may not be accurate, it is one way conceptualizing the events that take place when biofeedback techniques are employed to treat physical disorders.

References

1. Hilgard, E. Guthrie's contiguous conditioning. *Theories of Learning,* 2nd ed., Ch. 3, pp. 48–81. New York: Appleton, Century-Crofts, 1956.
2. Kamiya, J. Operant control of the EEG alpha rhythm and some of its reported effects on consciousness. *Altered States of Consciousness* (C. Tart, ed.), p. 489. New York: John Wiley & Son, 1969.
3. Hilgard, E. Skinner's operant conditioning. *Theories of learning* 2nd ed., Ch. 4, pp. 82–120. New York: Appleton, Century-Crofts, 1956.
4. Gantt, W. H. Antonomic conditioning. *The Conditioining Therapies* (J. Wolpe, A. Salter, and L. J. Reyna, eds.) Ch. 8, pp. 115–126. New York: Holt, Rinehart and Winston, 1966.
5. Gantt, W. H., Newton, J. E. O., and Stephens, J. Effect on person on conditional reflexes. *Psychosomatic Medicine* 22:322–323, (1960).
6. Lynch, J. *The Broken Heart,* 1st ed. New York: Basic Books, Inc., 1977.
7. Hendler, N., Matthews, D., Avella, J., and Long, D. The effect of person on EMG biofeedback. *Abstracts of the Biofeedback Society of America—Annual Meeting,* Albuquerque (April 3–7, 1978).
8. Hilgard, E. Hull's systematic behavior theory. *Theories of Learning,* 2nd ed., Ch. 5, pp. 121–184. New York: Appleton, Century-Crofts, 1956.
9. Mangan, G. L., Murphy, G., and Farmer, R. G. The role of muscle tension in "repression." *Pavlovian Journal of Biological Science,* 15(4):172–176 (1980).
10. Sappington, J. T., Fiorito, E. M., and Brehony, K. A. Biofeedback as therapy in Raynaund's disease. *Biofeedback and Self Regulation* 4(2):155–169 (1979).
11. Blanchard, E. The use of temperature biofeedback in the treatment of chronic pain due to causalgia. *Biofeedback and Self Regulation* 4 (2):183–188 (1979).

13. Sargent, J. D., Green, E. E., and Walters, E. D. The use of autogenic feedback training in a pilot study of migraine and tension headaches. *Headache* 12 (4):120–128 (1972).
14. Whitehead, W. E. Biofeedback in the treatment of gastrointestinal disorders. *Biofeedback and Self Regulation* 3(4): 375–384 (1978).
15. Black, D., Kott, R., and Pavlovsky, M. Operant learning theory approaches to biofeedback training. *Biofeedback: Theory and Research.* (G. Schwartz and G. Beatty, eds.). New York: Academic press, 1978.
16. Natelson, B. H. and McCarty, R. Conditional catecholamine changes in rhesus monkeys. *Pavlovian Journal of Biological Science* 15(4):188–196 (1980).
17. Hendler, N. and Blake, W. D. Hypothalamic implants of angiotensin II, carbacol, and nor-epinephrine on water and NaCl solution intake in rats. *Communications in Behavioral Biology* A4 (1–3) (July-August-September, 1969).
18. Task Force Reports of the Biofeedback Society of America: (A) Psychophysiological disorders. (B) Vasoconstrictive disorders. (C) Gastrointestinal disorders. (D) Vascular headache. (E) Muscle tension headache. (F) Physical medicine. *Biofeedback and Self Regulation* 3 (4) (December, 1978).

Emotional Aspects of Heart Disease

Harold Geist, Ph.D.*
*San Francisco State
University, San Francisco, or Berkeley,
California*

Most professionals who work in the area of cardiac psychopathology at one time or another have heard of the work of Rosenman and Friedman in San Francisco. It occurred to me that perhaps there might be differences in personality characteristics of people with various kinds of heart disease, so without any preconceived notions, I set out to find out if indeed there were dynamic differences in patients with heart disease other than coronary artery disease. I chose four classes of patients: (1) those with arteriosclerotic heart disease, including patients with angina pectoris, acute myocardial infarction, and coronary artery disease; (2) those with hypertensive vascular disease, including essential hypertension, renal hypertension, and endocrine disturbance; (3) those with disturbance of conduction including sinoauricular and atrioventricular block; and (4) those with valvular disease including mitral stenosis, mitral insufficiency,

*Much of this work was taken from Harold Geist, *Emotional Aspects of Heart Disease* Roslyn Heights, N.Y.: Libra 1976.

aortic insufficiency, tricuspid stenosis, and tricuspid insufficiency. There were 124 arteriosclerotics, 75 males and 49 females with an average age of 58.7 years; 87 hypertensives, 36 males and 51 females with an average age of 54 years; 72 valvular patients, 41 males and 31 females with an average age of 41.5 years; 56 disturbance of conduction patients, 38 males and 18 females, average age 61 years. These were either patients in various hospitals in the San Francisco Bay area or patients with private physicians in this geographical area. There were a total of 339 patients, 190 male and 149 female with an average age of 53.8 years. These patients were gleaned from a variety of hospitals in the Bay area, mostly from the East Bay, and also from private physicians in the area. In the hospital, the diagnosis was made by the cardiologist, and for the private patients, the diagnosis was made by the physicians concerned.

The patients were given an extensive questionnaire assessing the following—date first noticed symptoms; anything unusual happening psychologically at the time; reaction of friends, relatives, and acquaintances to the heart condition; incidence of psychosomatic diseases in the family; self-concept in various areas; dreams and daydreams; personality of father, mother, and siblings; a complete work history; religious beliefs; indulgence in alcohol, smoking, drugs, exercise, and fatty foods previous to contracting the disease; and whether certain weather conditions, exercise, and emotional upset exacerbated these symptoms. All of the items were collated for each of the diagnostic groups.

In addition each patient was given four psychological tests—the Multiple Affect Check List, a Cardiac Adjustment Scale, the Tennessee Self-Concept Scale, and the Holtman Ink Blot Test. Each raw score for each scale of each test was used as a variable (only 15 of the Holtzman) scales were used), and a cluster analysis was done on all variables using the BC Try System of cluster analysis.

RESULTS OF QUESTIONNAIRE

Arteriosclerotics

The arteriosclerotics had a familial cardiac diathesis, mostly on the mother's side. Temper tantrums and tremors seemed to be two of the symptomatologies associated with hysterical psychosomatic psychopathology both as children and as adults. Although this group thought of themselves as either moderately or severely disabled because of their ailment, they had an unusually high regard for themselves and a stated good self-concept. In their growing and formative years, they got along well with all members of the family; the mother rather than the father was the disciplinarian. Their work history was good: they had worked for an average of ten years on the job and, according to their subjective reports, got along well with bosses and colleagues. They were either moderately or extremely religious, and the two elements which exacerbated their symptoms were exercise and adverse weather conditions.

Hypertensive Vascular Disease

In this group, heart disease was no factor. These patients perceived themselves as either moderately or severely disabled because of their condition. Headaches were predominant as a hysterical psychosomatic symptom both as children and as adults, with tremors present in childhood. A goodly majority of these patients got angry easily and also withdrew from difficult situations. In general they had a good self-concept and got along well with all members of the family when growing up. They had an excellent work record with an average of 14 years on the job, and according to their own assertions got along with bosses and colleagues. Emotional upset brought about an exacerbation of their symptoms.

Valvular Disease

In this group their heart disease was chronic (over two years). They thought their disease was either moderately or severely disabling. The majority of friends were moderately or greatly upset by their heart disease. A large number had lost their mother just previous to the appearance of symptoms. Headaches and temper tantrums were the hysterical psychosomatic symptoms which were present in these patients both as children and as adults. All of them had a good self-concept. All seemed to get along with their mother and father in their formative years, and in this group the father was the disciplinarian. Their work history was fairly good but not as good as the arteriosclerotics and hypertensives. All claimed to have gotten along well with colleagues and bosses on the job. A majority said their symptoms increased when they were emotionally upset.

Disturbance of Conduction

Most of this group was single as contrasted with the other three groups. There was a familial diathesis. The majority thought they were either seriously or moderately disabled. Relatives, friends, and acquaintances were quite upset by their heart aliment, so that it appears that this kind of cardiac disease does upset those surrounding the patient. Headaches, tremors, and temper tantrums exhibited by the other cardiac patients were not as unanimous in this group. The chief difference in the variables was in moodiness where half said they were moody and 37% said they were dependent. Their job tenure was relatively short. Of all the cardiac patients, this group got along less well with bosses and colleagues than the others. A significant number said their symptoms increased with emotional stress.

SPECIAL CONSIDERATIONS

Alcohol, Smoking, Drugs, Exercise, and Fatty Foods

In all the different kinds of heart disease, ingestion of fatty foods seemed to be a potent eating pattern just previous to their heart disease. Ingestion of either moderate or large amounts of alcohol prior to the heart attack seemed to be a factor in arteriosclerotic heart disease and valvular disease, but not in the others. In only those patients with valvular disease did smoking appear to be a factor. Since practically all of these patients exercised a good deal previous to their heart attack, it could not be ascertained whether lack of exercise might have an influence on the etiology of any specific kind of heart disease. Drugs taken previous to the affliction seemed to have no influence whatsoever.

RESULTS OF CLUSTER ANALYSIS

Three factors or clusters were obtained from the BC Try cluster analysis:

- Factor I—physical, moral, social, personal self-concept and self-worth; self-acceptance and self-satisfaction in general.
- Factor II—psychotic thought processes, pathological thinking, sexual dysfunction, and evidence of fear and sorrow.
- Factor III—fearful, discouraged, angry, with possible thought disorder (indicative of psychopathology but to a much lesser extent than factor II).

Factor I: The group which had the highest mean score on factor I was the valvular group, i.e., they had the most positive self-concept. Those who had the worst self-concept were hypertensives and disturbances of conduction with arteriosclerotics in between.

Factor II: The group which had the greatest psychopathology in the dimensions in which this factor was measured was the arteriosclerotic group, followed in order by the hypertensive, disturbance of conduction, and valvular groups.

Factor III: The valvular group of patients had the highest scores followed by the hypertensives, arteriosclerotics, and finally the disturbance of conduction group.

CONCLUSIONS

What can we gather from all this data? The group which has the *greatest psychopathology* was the arteriosclerotic group, with the accompanying syndrome of angina pectoris, acute myocardial infarction, and coronary artery disease. These are the people who have had what are commonly known as heart attacks. They should avoid what Rosenman and Friedman call "hurry sickness," excessive exercise, adverse weather conditions, and ingestion of alcohol. Physicians should take a complete family history in people suspected to have this disease, since there seems to be a familial cardiac diathesis. The patients who had the least psychopathology were the valvular disease patients who had the best self-concept. Because of recent surgery with artificial valve replacement, the outlook for these patients is relatively bright. However, on the questionnaire a majority said their symptoms increased when they were emotionally upset, so that even these patients must be careful to prevent such upsets. These patients did report ingestion of alcohol prior to their condition, so alcohol is to be avoided. Likewise, the valvular patients were the only heart disease patients to report a great deal of smoking previous to their heart attack. Hypertensives are those people who, strictly speaking, do not have heart disease but an illness highly related. Anger seemed to be a precipitating agent in this affliction, and emotional upset also brought about an exacerbation of their symptoms. This group also had a poor self-concept. Finally in the disturbance of conduction group, moodiness seemed to be prevalent, and members of this group had a spotty work record as contrasted with the other three groups. Physicians who suspect patients of having these disorders should take a thorough family and work history since these patients have a familial cardiac diathesis. It should be noted that all patient groups reported eating fatty foods and cholesterol-laden foods previous to their heart ailment, so that people who would avoid heart conditions should avoid such foods.

There are obviously many other so-called psychosomatic diseases such as bronchial asthma (closely related to the dermatoses), anorexia nervosa, obesity, ulcerative colitis associated with duodenal ulcer, various neurological dysfunctions, various endocrine and metabolic disorders, and now cancer. There are simply a host of therapies for all, specific for specific disorders (e.g., biofeedback and autogenic training plus medication for migraine). I think we have to fit the therapy to the patient, and there are really no hard and fast rules. One element in this whole field of psychosomatic medicine that has fascinated me is why in certain people the pathology goes to one organ and in another to another organ; why some people get headaches, some get dermatoses, and others heart ailments. I have the theory, since working with the rheumatoids and heart patients, that people have a congenital diathesis (i.e., people are born with some chemical or organic material, perhaps similar to an enzyme such as the rheumatoid factor of Engleman) and that with certain personality factors, the soil is fertile for the development of specific psychosomatic diseases. For example, Mirsky at the Carnegie-Mellon Institute at the University of Pittsburg has isolated an ulcerative factor which he found in ulcer patients. I think much more research must be done in all areas to get at the etiology and treatment of these diseases.

References

1. Friedman, M. and Rosenman, R. H. *Type A Behavior and Your Heart.* New York: Alfred A. Knopf, 1974.
2. Selzer, A. *The Heart, Its Function in Health and Disease.* Berkeley: University of California Press, 1966.
3. Rahe, R. H. and Paasiviki, J. Psychosocial factors and myocardial infarction. *Journal of Psychosomatic Research* **15**: 33 (1971).
4. Theorell, T., Linde, E., Fronberg, S., Karlsson, C., and Levi, L. A longitudinal study of 21 subjects with coronary heart disease. *Report No. 24, Laboratory for Clinical Stress Research, Stockholm* (November, 1971).
5. Geist, H. *Emotional Aspects of Heart Disease.* Roslyn Heights, N.Y.: Libra Publishers, 1976.

Psychosocial Stress and Coronary Artery Disease

Jonathan H. Stein, M.D.
John A. Ambrose, M.D.
Michael V. Herman, M.D.
New York Medical College
Valhalla, New York

That the relationship of psychosocial stress and coronary artery disease (CAD) must be seen within the context of industrialized, twentieth century society is both necessary and inevitable. Epidemiologically, CAD began to emerge as a significant public health problem in the United States and other Western societies in the early part of this century. Since the 1920s, there has been a precipitous increase in mortality rates from this disease. While there is recent evidence indicating a small, but perceptible decline in the mortality rate from this disease, it still remains the major cause of death in the United States. Accordingly, epidemiologic studies have attempted to identify those factors that contribute to the group and individual risk for CAD. Such factors as advancing age, male sex, elevated blood levels of cholesterol and related fats, hypertension, cigarette smoking, diabetes mellitus, family history of CAD, obesity, and physical inactivity have all been incriminated as contributory causes.

While these biologic risk factors clearly have great epidemiologic utility, the enthusiasm for them cannot obscure the fact that together they provide only a partial picture of the prevalence of CAD in the population and that, at best, they are an insensitive predictor of risk in the individual. Prospective large-scale investigation has shown that, with the passage of time, only a minority of the individuals who possess these risk factors are eventually afflicted with CAD. Equally disconcerting has been the fact that considerable coronary artery disease occurs in individuals who do not exhibit any of these risk factors. In fact, the present evidence indicates that the traditional risk factors account for only about half the cases of coronary artery disease seen on a worldwide basis.

The observation that the prevalence of coronary artery disease generally parallels the increasing complexity and ambiguity of social systems and hierarchies, both in animals and in man, implies the existence of other psychological and behavioral factors that may contribute to the pathogenesis of this disease. Indeed, it may well be that the psychosocial stress of modern society and individual behavioral adaptive capability to it are manifestations of the Darwinian evolutionary process of natural selection. Because adaptation is a process that may require thousands of years, it may well be that man has long to go in his evolutionary development before acquiring the capacity to cope adequately with the complexity and ambiguity of modern society. This hypothesis—that the psychological stress of modern society and the behavioral adaptation to it are related to the pathogenesis of CAD—is biologically and epidemiologically very tenable. It provides an explanation for the modern epidemic of the disease; it helps to account for the inadequacy of the biologic risk factors to predict the occurrence of CAD; and it is compatible with evidence that stressful psychosocial stimuli induce markedly different individual physiologic responses.

HISTORICAL BACKGROUND

The notion that psychosocial stress has profound effects on the cardiovascular system dates from antiquity. Celsus observed nearly 2000 years ago that emotional states could influence the heart. In 1628, William Harvey wrote in the Latin monograph *Exercitatio de Motu Cordis et Sanguinis in Animalibus:* "Every affection of the mind that is attended with either pain or pleasure, hope or fear, is the cause of an agitation whose influence extends to the heart." While eighteenth century English physicians such as Heberden, Parry, and Hunter were well aware of the deleterious effects that emotions could have on those with angina pectoris, it was not until Sir William Osler that a link was made between psychosocial behavioral patterns and coronary artery disease. In 1897, Osler wrote in the Lumelian lectures:

In the worry and strain of modern life, arterial degeneration is not only very common, but develops often at a very early age. For this I believe that the high pressure at which men live and the habit of working the machine to its maximum capacity are responsible.

The Mennigers were the first psychiatrists to recognize and publicize this relationship. They described the coronary patient as having strong aggresive tendencies that were usually successfully suppressed. Dunbar found coronary patients to be hard-driving, goal-directed individuals with a monodirective personality seeking refuge in work. Arlow emphasized the inner insecurity of coronary patients which, when combined with the inability of their accomplishments to overcome this feeling, drove them to strive incessantly for more success. Kemple further refined the psychosocial description of the coronary patient as aggressive, domineering, ambitious, and outwardly hostile despite the persistent effort to restrain this impulse.

In 1950 Stewart made a remarkably important contribution with his indictment of contemporary Western society, with its new and unfamiliar forms of socioeconomic stress, as critical to the mounting incidence of CAD. It was on the basis of this societal approach that Friedman and Rosenman proposed in 1955 their enormously important psychosocial model of the coronary patient. Their delineation of the coronary-prone Type A behavior pattern provided an integrated model that combined underlying personality traits of the coronary-prone individual with the behavior pattern that emerged from interaction with the social milieu of contemporary Western society. In addition to behavior pattern as a risk factor for CAD, considerable attention has recently been focused on the impact that various psychiatric and sociologic stresses have on the incidence of this disease. There is indeed a compelling body of literature that has emerged.

MECHANISM OF ACTION

If psychosocial and behavioral factors truly are risk factors for CAD, there must be a biologically plausible means by which to translate psychosocially perceived stimuli into physiologic responses that can induce cardiovascular pathology. The neuroendocrine system appears to provide such a means of access. Evidence from animal investigations shows that there are two fundamental neuroendocrine responses to psychosocial circumstances. Activation of the pituitary–adrenal cortical system with secretion of glucucorticoids generally results from social interactions that lead to downward displacement in the social hierarchy. Activation of the sympathetic–adrenal medullary system with secretion of catecholamines, the classic fight-or-flight reaction, generally occurs in response to social interactions that demand agonistic, aggressive behavior to meet a challenge or threat. That these two neuroendocrine responses occur in man and have important ramifications is clear. Both catecholamines and glucocorticoids have profound physiologic and metabolic effects that impact directly on the cardiovascular system. Indeed, the natural pathologic experiment of catecholamine excess in man, pheochromocytoma, includes among its clinical mainfestations hypertensive crises, arrhythmias, myocardial infarction, and myocarditis; the natural human pathologic experiment of glucocorticoid excess, Cushing's syndrome, includes atherosclerosis among its manifestations. Furthermore, there is reason to believe that the neuroendocrine system may participate in dynamic obstruction of the coronary arteries through coronary vasospasm.

Because of the complex nature of human psychosocial interactions, the role of psychosocial and behavioral factors in the pathogenesis of CAD in man is complex and elusive. Because it is a disease process that evolves slowly over an extended period of time, CAD poses major problems to epidemiologic and clinical investigation. Since our knowledge of the pathogenesis of atherosclerosis and the means by which the commonly accepted factors contribute to it is incomplete, guilt by association is about the best we can expect to establish at present. Furthermore, some of the psychosocial variables exert their risk potential on CAD not just directly, but indirectly as well, by influencing the biologic risk factors. Almost certainly, the risk factors, including the psychosocial factors, engage in a dynamic interaction that ultimately fosters atherogenesis. When the fundamental mechanisms of the atherosclerotic process and of the clinical expression of CAD are eventually described, it should be possible to establish a mechanistic rather than a circumstantial relationship between the psychosocial risk factors and CAD.

PSYCHOSOCIAL RISK FACTORS

There are a wide variety of psychosocial, sociological, and behavioral variables that demonstrate a possible relationship with risk for coronary artery disease. These variables can be categorized according to the following schema: socioeconomic indices; social mobility and status incongruity; anxiety, neuroticism, and reactive characteristics; life dissatisfaction and interpersonal problems; stress and life changes; and the coronary-prone Type A behavior pattern.

Socioeconomic Indices

There are clearly differences in the incidence and mortality from CAD in the populations of different countries. The United States and Finland have been shown to experience high rates of CAD, while Greece, Yugoslavia, and Japan have low rates. The obvious problem with such large-scale demographic studies is that they fail to distinguish the effects of such cross-cultural variables as genetics, society, and geography.

There have been numerous efforts to incriminate socioeconomic status and occupation as factors that predispose to CAD. Investigation has concentrated on such parameters as occupational position, level of education, marital status, religious affiliation, and religious participation. While findings have often been provocative, they have been too inconsistent to establish a definite pattern.

There are obviously substantial problems with the use of socioeconomic indices as predictors of risk for CAD. It appears that these gross social parameters are too distant from the crucial biologic processes involved in the initiation and development of CAD. It is considerably more likely that the individual's perception and response to his social environment elicits more significant physiologic responses with pathologic potential than does the individual's absolute position in the society. In general, demographic parameters tend to be inconsistent predictors of the risk of CAD.

Social Mobility and Status Incongruity

Social mobility indicates either intergenerational or intragenerational changes in a person's environment. Status incongruity refers to the condition of simultaneously having identifying characteristics of different social groups. These dynamic social variables are thought to generate internal conflict and disequilibrium.

While these parameters have shown some compelling associations, the data is still inconsistent. Social mobility has been implicated as a risk factor for CAD in a wide variety of settings and groups. It has been found in California, Pennsylvania, Illinois, and North Dakota; it has been seen in Japanese, Irish, and Yemenites who emigrated to the United States; and it has been identified in Finland and Israel. Similarly, status incongruity has been investigated as predictive of CAD. Positive correlations have been found in Illinois, Pennsylvania, Oklahoma, and Sweden. Unfortunatly, other investigators have found conflicting results. In Connecticut, no correlation between those variables and CAD was found, while in Hawaii an association could be demonstrated, but only when multivariate analysis with other variables was performed.

In summary, the available evidence suggests that these two variables—social mobility and status incongruity—may be valid predictors of CAD risk; however, the risk may be present only in certain places and times, only for certain presentations of the disease, or only when acting in combination with other variables.

Anxiety, Neuroticism, and Reactive Characteristics

In direct contrast to the socioeconomic indices, the psychiatric variables such as anxiety, neuroticism, and depression are directly reflective of the emotional conflict of day-to-day life. Consequently, these parameters more clearly implicate the central nervous system and are, thus, more biologically plausible.

For the most part, the evidence is compelling. Anxiety and depression have been found to be predictive of CAD risk in Connecticut, Massachusetts, Great Britian, France, Sweden, and Israel. Indeed, there is even evidence to show that in subjects about to undergo cardiac catheterization and coronary angiography, those with high scores for anxiety and depression are more likely to have severe angiographically demonstrable atherosclerosis. Other variables, such as hypochondriasis, sleep disturbances, emotional drain, and obsessive-compulsive disturbances have all been linked to CAD risk.

The major objection to the psychiatric variables is that they may ultimately be a manifestation of subclinical cardiovascular disease, and, thus, a prodrome rather than a risk factor for CAD. Whatever the physiologic substrate of these psychiatric conditions, there is an emerging body of compelling evidence to suggest that they may be legitimate predictors of CAD risk.

Life Problems and Dissatisfactions

Life problems and dissatisfactions encompass complaints about life circumstances and social environment. As such, this group of variables combines environmental stress and individual psychogenic response. In the United States, persons with CAD have retrospectively reported more work dissatisfaction, such as tedium, lack of recognition, poor relations with co-workers, poor working conditions, and low work self-esteem. Similarly, there is evidence to show that Americans in occupations with high average rates of dissatisfaction experience high rates of mortality from heart disease, but not from a variety of other causes. Prospective evidence has emerged from Israel showing that problems in the areas of finance, family, and work are predictive of increased risk of CAD; similar prospective findings have been found in Sweden.

This set of variables has the same intrinsic problem as the psychiatric variables—the difficulty of separating risk factor from clinical prodrome. Nevertheless, the association that emerges from prospective investigations is both epidemiologically very suggestive and biologically very plausible.

Stress and Life Change

There has evolved an extensive literature implicating painful or sustained environmental insults, such as death of a relative or work overload, as predictive of risk for CAD. The hypothesis underlying this association is that life changes induce stress which, in some way, depletes the individual's adaptive energy. It is more likely that environmental insults lead to the two fundamental neuroendocrine responses: activation of the sympathetic-adrenal medullary system because of threatening circumstances and activation of the pituitary-adrenal cortical system in response to uncontrollable circumstances producing helplessness.

Occupational stress and work overload have been incriminated as predictive of CAD risk. Numerous investigators have observed that a disproportionately large number of patients were working excessively long hours prior to experiencing myocardial infarction. Professionals in high stress categories of professional practice, as evaluated by their peers, appear to experience a higher incidence of CAD. Indeed, at the Kennedy Space Center in the mid-1960s, which must be the quintessence of occupational stress, there were findings of an inordinately high percentage of abnormal resting electrocardiograms and a moderately higher rate of sudden death.

Particularly striking is the observation that there is an increased mortality from CAD among widows, widowers, and others experiencing as recent death in the immediate family.

Perhaps, the most quantitative approach to stress and life change emerges from studies utilizing the Holmes and Rahe Schedule of Recent Experience. Subjects check the occurrence of events listed on the schedule that demand personal adjustment. The weighted values for the events are summed to produce a quantitative measure of life change. Retrospective studies have shown increased life change scores prior to myocardial infarction in Swedish, Finnish, and American subjects. While biologically very attractive, this set of variables awaits prospective confirmation.

Coronary-prone Type A Behavior Pattern

In 1969, Friedman defined the Type A behavior pattern in *Pathogenesis of Coronary Artery Disease* as:

A characteristic action-emotion complex which is exhibited by these individuals who are engaged in a relatively chronic struggle to obtain an unlimited number of poorly defined things from their environment in the shortest period of time and, if necessary, against the opposing efforts of other persons or things in this environment. This struggle has been encouraged by the contemporary Western environment because, unlike any previously known milieu, it appears to offer special rewards to those who can think, perform, communicate, move, live, and even play more rapidly and aggressively than their fellow men.

This definition of the Type A behavior pattern is important for both what it includes and what it excludes. Type A behavior is not tantamount to stress; it is neither a stressful situation nor a distressed response. Type A behavior is not to be confused with neurosis; it is not initiated, sustained, or distinguished by worry, fear, anxiety, or depression. Type A behavior is neither an abstract psychodynamic construct nor a reflex response to environmental stimuli. On the contrary, it is the consistent reaction of the psychologically predisposed individual to a challenging life situation. The Type A behavior pattern results from, and is sustained by, the interaction of the subject's intrinsic personality with a socioeconomic milieu that elicits a particular response to it.

Clinical recognition of Type A behavior pattern is traditionally accomplished by two means. The standardized structure interview of Friedman and Rosenman consists of a series of questions designed to elicit responses concerning facets of Type A behavior. While the content of response is important, the manner and tone of response is given somewhat more weight in the final assessment. The Jenkins Activity Survey is a self-administered questionnaire consisting of questions designed to elicit Type A characteristics. The former technique is generally considered to be more reliable, although it is more difficult to administer.

Type A behavior is recognized by its psychomotor components. Osler's description in the Lumleian lectures, of the patient with angina, serves equally well to describe the classic Type A subject:

It is not the delicate, neurotic person who is prone to angina but the robust, the vigorous in mind and body, the keen and ambitious man, the indicator of whose engine is always at full speed ahead.

The Type A individual demonstrates some or all of the following characteristics:

- Motor activities—the Type A person speaks directly to the point, in a staccato verbal flow, accenting words with a burst of volume. He tends to make frequent, forceful gestures.
- Drive and ambition—the Type A individual sets high standards for himself and others and is disturbed when they are not fullfilled. He is an effort-oriented person whose achievements give him little satisfaction.
- Feelings of competition, aggression, and hostility—the Type A in-

dividual is an inveterate competitor who competes as strenuously with himself as he does with others. Feelings of hostility and anger are easily provoked, despite efforts to restrain them.

- Time urgency—the Type A person is constantly engaged in an unending struggle to overcome the inexorably set constraints of time. He constantly strives to accomplish more and more within a framework that is constantly shrinking.
- Monodirective personality—the Type A individual is usually self-centered and egocentric. He is usually intensely dedicated to his job to the detriment of his family and other aspects of his life.

Probably no other psychosocial factor has received as much attention and as much confirmation as a predictor of CAD risk as has the coronary-prone Type A behavior pattern. The strength of the association between Type A behavior and the emergence of CAD is compelling. Prospective epidemiological evidence from the Western Collaborative Group Study, retrospective epidemiological evidence from Europe and North America, necropsy correlations, and angiographic associations offer replicable and consistently demonstrable evidence. It appears to be a risk factor with a high degree of specificity for CAD and not for other diseases. It also appears to be a behavior pattern that is discernible in young children, well before the appearance of CAD, thus suggesting that it is indeed a risk factor and not a prodrome of the disease. There is evidence to show that a biologic gradient exists; the more intense the presence of the Type A behavior pattern, the greater is the risk of emergence of CAD or the more severe its manifestations. Finally, it is a biologically plausible association. Not only does the neuroendocrine system provide the necessary link between behavior and the heart, but Type A subjects exhibit many of the biochemical derangements characteristic of patients with CAD. These include fluctuations in blood pressure, excessive catecholamine and ACTH production, increased lipid availability, and enhanced platelet aggregation. The evidence that the Type A behavior pattern is a risk factor for CAD is as valid as that for the other coronary risk factors. Indeed, a recent conference sponsored by the National Heart, Lung, and Blood Institute recognized this state of affairs when it appraised Type A behavior as a predictor of CAD of at least the same order of magnitude as hypertension, hypercholesterolemia, or cigarette smoking.

SUMMARY

The weight of evidence is now sufficient to justify the conclusion that psychological stress and behavioral factors are important risk factors for coronary artery disease. With the exception of the coronary-prone Type A behavior pattern, it is not entirely clear just which of the other variables will remain after careful, rigorous scrutiny. It should not be surprising that the best evidence is that of guilt by association; the same situation exists for the biological risk factors as well. Until we have a better understanding of the mechanism of atherogenesis and the manifestations of CAD, we cannot fully comprehend the means by which any of the risk factors contribute to CAD.

References

Friedman, M. *Pathogenesis of Coronary Artery Disease.* New York: McGraw Hill, 1969.

Jenkins, C. D. Behavioral risk factors in coronary artery disease. *Ann. Rev. Med.* **29**: 543 (1978).

Jenkins, C. D. Recent evidence supporting psychologic and social risk factors for coronary disease. *N. Eng. J. Med.* **294**: 987-994, 1033-1038 (1976).

Buell, J. C. and Eliot, R. S. Psychosocial and behavioral influences in the pathogenisis of acquired cardiovascular disease. *Am. Heart J.* **100**: 723-740 (1980).

Rosenman, R. H. and Friedman, M. Neurogenic factors in the pathogenesis of coronary heart disease. *Med. Clinics North Am.* **58**: 269-279 (1974).

Psychosocial Factors in the Onset and Course of Rheumatoid Arthritis

Malcolm P. Rogers, M.D.
Associate in Medicine (Psychiatry)
Division of Psychiatry
Department of Medicine
Brigham and Women's Hospital
Boston, Massachusetts

Assistant Professor of Psychiatry
Harvard Medical School
Boston, Massachusetts

Introduction

From the earliest time, clinicians have commented frequently on the associations between rheumatoid arthritis and psychological stress. For example, Sir William Osler remarked on the presence of "shock, worry, and grief" preceding exacerbations in joint symptoms. Rheumatoid arthritis and its variants represent a widespread problem. A national survey has indicated that approximately one-half of 1% of the population has definite rheumatoid arthritis. Over 100,000 children in the United States have juvenile rheumatoid arthritis. Approximately three times as many women as men are afflicted. In general, no consistent geographical, cultural, or climatic trends have been demonstrated in the incidence of the disease. The etiology of the disease is unknown, although intermediate immunologic mechanisms have been clearly demonstrated. Much of the research on the interaction between psychosocial factors and disease activity has been summarized in two recent reviews by Silverman[1] and Weiner.[2] In this chapter we will focus primarily on the potential role of psychological factors in both the onset and the course of the disease. The issue assumes greater importance in light of the interest in psychological perturbations in the function of the immune system.

Psychological Factors in the Onset of Rheumatoid Arthritis

Although there exists much anecdotal information concerning psychological factors, such as stress, in precipitating rheumatoid arthritis, attempts at more careful documentation have occurred only over the past 20 years or so. In investigating various categories of events that preceded or correlated with the onset of rheumatoid arthritis, Short and his colleagues[3] found that 50% in a series of 293 hospitalized patients with rheumatoid arthritis recorded one or more precipitating events which were distributed in the following manner: mental and/or physical strain, 27.3%; infection, 16.7%; exposure to cold or dampness, 10.6%; surgical operation, 5.5%; trauma, 5.1%; and pregnancy, 2.1% Of those reporting strain, 60% ascribed it to their occupations and 40% reported that a relative was ill or had died.

Some investigators, particularly of the psychoanalytic school, such as Alexander, have hypothesized that there are specific psychological conflicts which interact with some underlying biological predisposition to give rise to the disease. Alexander saw the origins of this conflict in restrictive and overprotective parents against whom the patient had rebelled and adopted a mode of covert hostility. He felt that a failure in this adaptive mode eventually resulted in the onset of the disease. By and large, however, most investigators have emphasized a more nonspecific emotional stress, especially since the work of Holmes and Rahe in 1967.[4] They demonstrated that changes in the psychological and social milieu are important as antecedents in a variety of illnesses, not only rheumatoid arthritis. The central hypothesis underlying this work is that life changes of major importance evoke psychological responses that are frequently associated with psychophysiologic reactions.

One of the more interesting and careful studies was done by Meyerowitz and his colleagues at the University of Rochester Medical School.[5] They investigated a series of eight sets of identical twins who were discordant for rheumatoid arthritis. Detailed psychosocial data obtained from five of the adult twin sets revealed that a period of psychological stress preceded disease onset in four affected twins. The stresses were characterized by a kind of "entrapment" in a restricting and demanding situation.

Rimón investigated 100 female patients with rheumatoid arthritis whose illness had begun less than seven years before the study.[6] Control cases consisted of 100 patients admitted to the same hospital during the same period and matched regarding age, sex, marital and social status, and duration of illness. He discovered that 37% of the rheumatoid arthritic patients had come from broken homes, a figure twice the national average at the time. In addition, he found that approximately a quarter of the patients had suffered from a previous psychiatric disturbance, about half of which were depressions. In terms of life stress factors, a significant major life conflict was found to exist in 55 of the 100 patients just prior to the first joint symptoms. In 12 other cases, life stress factors existed but were felt to be of minimal importance, and the remaining 33 patients had no clear life stress factors. The first group of 55 patients was called the major conflict group; the last group of 33 patients was called the nonconflict group. Rimón discovered some interesting differences between the major conflict group and the nonconflict group. The nonconflict group, for example, contained many more relatives with rheumatoid arthritis and, in general, showed a more gradual onset of the disease. In the major conflict group, exacerbations of the illness were closely related to life stress factors in 65% of the cases, whereas exacerbations in the nonconflict group were connected with important life stress factors in only 15% of the cases. Rimón hypothesized that there are two types of patients: one with previous psychiatric disorders and high life stress situations preceding the illness, and a second type with heavy genetic predisposition to disease in which life stress plays a relatively minor role.

In a closely related disease juvenile rheumatoid arthritis, there is also some evidence documenting an association between life stresses and the onset of arthritis. Heisel investigated 34 juvenile rheumatoid arthritics, comparing them to 68 control subjects.[7] The parents of each child filled out life change questionnaires pertaining to life changes during the year preceding the onset of disease. Heisel found the highly significant increase in life change indicative of stress in the juvenile rheumatoid arthritic patients. Two events stood out, one was hospitalization for illnesses not felt to be prodromal manifestations of arthritis such as tonsillectomy, and the other was the death of a family member.

None of these studies has yet been replicated, and all are hampered methodologically by retrospective investigations of the relationship between stress and onset of disease. However, not all studies have tended to confirm the relationship implied in these studies. For example, Hendrie and his associates performed a similar study of life change events in early adult rheumatoid arthritic patients.[8] Although life change scores were found to be higher among the rheumatoid arthritic patients than the controls, the difference was not found to be significant. Significantly increased stess was associated, however, with increased immunoglobulin levels.

It has been suggested that such life stresses might precipitate the onset of rheumatoid arthritis in susceptible individuals by some alteration in their immunologic system. It is interesting that virtually all of the initial precipitating events described by Short are associated with some diminution in immunologic competence.

Psychological Factors in the Course of Rheumatoid Arthritis

Apart from the issue of its initial onset, the question remains as to the role of psychological factors in influencing the course of the disease. There is both the possibility that psychological stress may alter disease activity by some internal psychophysiologic reaction and also the possibility that psychological stress may lead to altered behavior which might secondarily alter the biological activity of rheumatoid arthritis. Sleep deprivation, altered dietary habits, and altered levels of exercise, for example, might all result from psychological stress and potentially alter the degree of joint inflammation.

There is surprisingly little documentation of the interrelationship between psychological stress and disease activity. Many patients are convinced that there is such a relationship, in fact, frequently more convinced than their doctors. One recent study performed by Feigenbaum and his colleagues did look at the correlation between progression of disease and psychosocial factors associated with its onset.[9] They investigated 50 newly diagnosed young adults with rheumatoid arthritis. They compared disease progression over a five-year period between those patients with low stress levels at onset and those with high stress levels. They found a positive correlation between the high stress group and more rapid progression of disease as indicated by x-ray evidence of cartilage destruction.

Another study pertaining to this issue found that those patients whose disease progressed more slowly scored higher on psychological scales reflecting compliance, conscientiousness, perfectionism, denial or hostility, social responsibility, and strong moral principles. Those patients whose disease was progressing more rapidly seemed unable to use previous coping mechanisms, and were found to be more anxious and depressed and less compliant. They were also less able to control their anger and more socially isolated. These psychological findings, however, may be secondary to the course of the disease rather than a primary cause of it. It does not necessarily follow, however, that the greater the progression of disease, the more depressed and anxious is the patient.

Despite the uncertainties that remain, most clinicians and patients would agree with the view that, when emotionally upset, their tolerance for joint pain, discomfort, and the frustration which comes from lack of function is generally reduced. One patient described this when she said in response to a question about whether her own disease activity seemed influenced by psychological stress, "I think sometimes it could contribute . . . . I think if you get extremely upset, well naturally you start to feel bad and then if something aggravates you, it makes it worse . . . . I'm more conscious of my pain.'' From a practical standpoint, then, it is beneficial for most patients to reduce the level of distress in their lives in an effort to cope better with the demands of living with rheumatoid arthritis. Yet we cannot promise patients that by reducing levels of psychological stress they can produce remissions in their disease.

Summary

Frequent clinical observations by both physicians and patients over the years have noted the importance of psychosocial factors in the onset and the course of rheumatoid arthritis. Although there is no definitive proof that psychological stress precipitates the onset of rheumatoid arthritis, several studies provide strong suggestive evidence that, in some patients who are susceptible, psychological stress may play a contributory role in the onset of the disease. There is somewhat less evidence with regard to the effect of psychological factors on the course of rheumatoid arthritis, although some evidence suggests that greater psychological distress at onset may contribute to the more rapid progression of the disease. It is also a common observation that, when under increased emotional stress, patients have a somewhat lower tolerance for the pain and frustration of their disease.

References

1. Silverman, A. J. Rheumatoid arthritis. In *Comprehensive Textbook of Psychiatry II* A. M. Freedman, H. I. Kaplan, and B. J. Saddock, (eds.), 2nd ed. pp. 1694–1704. Baltimore: Williams & Wilkins, 1975.
2. Weiner, H. *Psychobiology and Human Disease,* pp. 415–494. New York: Elsevier North-Holland, 1977.
3. Short, C. A., Abrams, N. R. and Sartwell, P. E. Factors associated with the onset of rheumatoid arthritis: a statistical study of 293 patients and controls. *Ann. Rheum. Dis.* **8**:313 (1949).
4. Holmes, T. H. and Rahe, R. H. The social readjustment rating scale. *J. Psychosom. Res.* **11**:213 (1967).
5. Meyerowitz, S. Jacox, R. F. and Hess, D. W. Monozygotic twins discordant for rheumatoid arthritis: a genetic, clinical, and psychological study of 8 sets. *Arthritis Rheum.* **11**:1–21 (1972).
6. Rimón, R. A psychosomatic approach to rheumatoid arthritis: a clinical study of 100 female patients. *Acta Rheumatol. Scand. Suppl.* **13**:13–154 (1969).
7. Heisel, J. S. Life changes as etiologic factors in juvenile rheumatoid arthritis. *J. Psychosom. Res.* **16**:411–420 (1972).
8. Hendrie, H. C., Paraskevas, F., Baragar, J. D., and Adamson, F. D. Stress, immunoglobulin levels, and early polyarthritis. *J. Psychosom. Res.* **15**:337 (1971).
9. Feigenbaum, S. L., Masi, A. T., and Kaplaw, S. B. Prognosis in rheumatoid arthritis: a longitudinal study of newly diagnosed younger adult patients. *Am. J. Med.* **66**:377–384 (1979).

The Influence of Emotional Factors in the Development and Course of Cancer: A Critical Review

John R. Peteet, M.D.
Harvard Medical School
Boston, Massachuasetts

Galen taught that cancer preferentially affects melancholic women, and numerous authors have since contended that emotions such as grief, despair, and hopelessness contribute to the development of cancer.[1] In recent years, a variety of human and animal studies have attempted to shed light on the question.

Work with animals has provided perhaps the most direct evidence that environmental stress can influence neoplastic growth. Several investigators have described an increased incidence or size of induced solid tumors in mice and rats subjected to physical manipulation,[2] enforced activity,[3] crowding,[4] *or shock,*[5,6] while a few, working with different tumor systems, have reported opposite effects.[7,8] Ader and Friedman[9] found that the length of survival of mice subjected to manipulation depended on the timing of manipulation. Studies of survival in leukemic mice subjected to stress have yielded conflicting results.[10,11] Findings of animal studies have been difficult to compare because of the use of different strains of animals, types of tumors, and forms of stress used; the role of psychological stress per se has been difficult to assess since different forms of stress used produce varying proportions of physical and psychological effects.

Hormonal mechanisms have been invoked to explain many of the effects of stress on tumors in animals. Confinement produces adrenocortical hypertrophy and gonadal atrophy in mice,[12,13] and some stress-associated alterations in tumor growth have been reproduced by the administration of steroids or beta-adrenergic agonists.[14] However, these effects have not been entirely abolished by adrenalectomy, which suggests that there may be other mechanisms involved as well.[2,14]

Changes in immune function have also been demonstrated in response to stress. Mice subjected to confinement have shown splenic and thymic involution[12] and (in males) decreased reactivity to antigenic stimulation.[15] Protective effects on anaphylaxis have been observed after anterior hypothalamic lesions in guinea pigs and rats[16] and after confinement in mice.[12]

In humans, a recent study comparing 26 bereaved spouses with controls matched for age, sex, and race found decreased lymphocyte transformation to phytohemagglutinin and concanavalin A in the bereaved group at six weeks, but no changes in T- and B-cell number, serum protein electrophoresis, immunoglobulins, alpha-2 macroglobulin concentration, autoantibodies, delayed hypersensitivity (or mean serum concentrations of thyroxine, T-3, cortisol, prolactin, or growth hormone measured at a single point in time).[17] Another study,[18] attempting to correlate personality factors with immune function in 150 patients undergoing breast biopsies, found elevated levels of IgA in patients described as showing "extreme suppression of anger," as compared with normal controls and those who showed a pattern of "extreme expression." However, the same authors have also speculated that elevated levels of IgA in patients with metastatic breast cancer may be a secondary immune response.[19]

Dozens of studies have attempted to identify distinctive patterns in the history or personality of patients with cancer, using interviews and a wide variety of standardized psychological instruments. Hopelessness,[20] difficulty expressing anger,[21] masochistic character,[22] unresolved losses,[23] and disturbed relationships with parents[24] are among the many findings which have been reported to characterize patients with cancer. The majority of these studies are retrospective and have failed to take into account the influence of the illness itself on the findings. The few prospective studies to date, some of which claim to have predicted a diagnosis of cancer, have not controlled for intermediate variables known to be associated with increased risk of cancer, such as the extent of smoking or alcohol abuse (or, in the case of carcinoma of the cervix, age at first intercourse). In most studies, psychological assessments have been either subjective or based on a few test data.

Recently, better designed studies have attempted to correlate psychological measures with tumor progression, as measured by length of survival or time until development of recurrence. Derogatis et al.[25] reported, in a group of 35 women with metastatic breast cancer, increased anxiety and feelings of alienation in those who survived longer. They postulated that these patients "externalized" stress more effectively and called for further investigation of their findings using patients matched for both histologic type and stage of disease. Similarly, Greer et al.,[26] in a prospective study of 69 consecutive patients with $T_{0,1}$ $N_{0,1}$ M_0 breast cancer using a variety of psychological measures, found that 75% of those who responded to their diagnosis at three months with "denial" or a "fighting spirit" were alive without recurrence at five years, as compared with only 35% of those who responded with "stoic acceptance" or "helplessness-hopelessness." Unfortunately, the initial psychological assessments and the five-year medical evaluations of their patients were less than complete.

A few authors[27,28] have reported an increased number of separations or other losses prior to the diagnosis of cancer, but these reports have been uncontrolled and have not been confirmed.[26]

The lack of convincing evidence that psychological factors contribute directly to the development or course of cancer has not prevented workers from advocating psychological approaches to preventing or treating the disease. In the last century, Walter Walsh[1] advised those wishing to avoid cancer to choose the professions of the Army, Navy, and church over those of the bar, medicine, and dentistry, which he felt were more associated with emotional strain. Recently, psychological approaches to treatment developed by the Simontons have received widespread publicity. On the premise that patients who survive cancer longer are psychologically stronger and more flexible, the Simonton group has advocated psychotherapy, relaxation, imagery, and guided fantasy to improve the results of conventional treatment.[29] In a group of 225 patients with metastatic cancer of several sites treated in this way, they have reported an improved median survival time relative to average figures derived from the literature.[30] Unfortunately, their study failed to take into account several important variables: patient selection factors, differences in concurrent medical treatment and psychological state, and histologic type and stage of tumor.

While approaches such as the Simonton's promise hope and a sense of control over what remains for many patients a very threatening illness, they risk adding to the unrealistic burden of responsibility which many patients feel when they develop cancer. The intimate relationship between mind and body makes it reasonable to assume that emotions can influence the growth of tumors in more than one way, but further research is needed in order to establish the nature of the links in such a chain of influence. Future work needs to take into greater account at least three major sources of complexity:

First, neuroendocrine, immune, and emotional functioning is dynamic and varies over time. Corticosteroid production has long been known to follow a circadian rhythm; recently developed techniques for continuous monitoring and analysis of blood samples have brought the potential for greater understanding of the patterns of normal and abnormal secretion of a number of hormones. As Rogers et al.[31] pointed out, many immune parameters vary as a function of time. Finally, the timing of psychological assessment in relation to hospitalization, biopsy, or discussion of major treatment options is more important than has often been recognized.

Second, cancer is a heterogeneous group of diseases with a wide range of risk factors, hormonal sensitivities, and responsiveness to radiation or chemotherapy. For some forms of cancer, emotions may exert their greatest effect via shaping a life-style which entails exposure to known risk factors such as smoking or use of alcohol. By the same token, emotions may exert their major effect on survival through their influence on decisions about the aggressiveness of treatment or compliance with recommended treatment.

Third, the precise direction in which life events influence an individual's emotional state depends on both his personality and his past experience of similar events. Studies which depend on isolated measures of attitude, psychopathology, or life changes risk focusing on secondary phenomena and oversimplifying complex relationships among personality and environmental variables. Improved means of assessment are needed which will both adequately characterize the basic psychological state and makeup of the individual and allow objective comparison with the findings of others.

In summary, a long anecdotal tradition and a growing number of studies of the relationship between emotions and the pathogenesis of cancer have produced intriguing but inconclusive results. The complexity of the issues involved poses a number of challenges for further research.

References

1. Kowal, S. J. Emotions as a cause of cancer: eighteenth and nineteenth century contributions. *Psychoanal. Rev.* **42**: 217-227 (1955).
2. Van den Brenk, H. A. S., Stone, M. G., Kelly, H., et al. Lowering of innate resistance of the lump to the growth of blood-borne cancer cells in states of topical and systemic stress. *Br. J. Cancer* **33**: 60-78 (1976).
3. Stern, J. A., Winokur, G., Graham, D. T., et al. Effect of enforced activity stress on the development of experimental papillomas in mice. *J. Nat. Cancer Inst.* **23**: 1013-1018 (1959).
4. Riley, V. Mouse mammary tumors: alteration of incidence as apparent function of stress. *Science* **189**: 465-467 (1975).
5. Sing-Mao, L. Effect of neurosis on appearance and development of induced mammary gland tumors in rats. *Fed. Proc. Trans. Suppl.* **22**: 1241-1244 (1963).
6. Amkraut, A. A., and Solomon, G. F. Stress and murine sarcoma virus (Maloney)—induced tumors. *Cancer Res.* **32**: 1428-1433 (1972).
7. Reznikoff, M. and Martin, P. E. The influence of stress on mammary cancer in mice. *J. Psychosom. Res.* **2**: 56-60 (1957).

8. Ray, P. and Pradhan, S. N. Brief communication: growth of transplanted and induced tumors in rats under a schedule of punished behavior. *J. Nat. Cancer Inst.* **52**: 575-577 (1974).

9. Ader, R. and Friedman, S. B. Differential early experience and susceptibility to transplanted tumors in the rat. *J. Comp. Physiol.* **59**: 361 (1965).

10. Levine, S. and Cohen, C. Differential survival to leukemia as a function of infantile stimulation in DBA½ mice. *Proc. Soc. Exp. Biol. Med.* **102**: 53 (1959).

11. Kaliss, N. and Fuller, J. L. Incidence of lymphatic leukemia and methylcholanthene-induced cancer in laboratory mice subjected to stress. *J. Nat. Cancer Inst.* **41**: 967-983 (1968).

12. Marsh, J. T. and Rasmussen, A. F. Response of adrenals, thymus, spleen and leukocytes to shuttle box and confinement stress. *Proc. Soc. Exp. Biol. Med.* **104**: 180-183 (1960).

13. Christian, J. J. Effect of population size on the adrenal glands and reproductive organs of male mice in populations of fixed size. *Amer. J. Physiol.* **182**: 292-300 (1955).

14. Peters, L. J. and Kelly, H. The influence of stress and stress hormones on the transplantability of a non-immunogenic syngeneic murine tumor. *Cancer* **39**: 1482-1488 (1977).

15. Jaosoo, A. and McKenzie, J. M. Stress and the immune response in rats. *Int. Arch. Allerg.* **50**: 659-603 (1976).

16. Luparello, T. J., Stein, M., and Park, C. D. Effect of hypothalamic lesions on rat anaphylaxis. *Amer. J. Physiol.* **207**: 911-914 (1964).

17. Bartrop, R. W., Lazarus, L., Luckhurst, E., et al. Depressed lymphocyte function after bereavement. *Lancet* **1**: 834-836 (1977).

18. Pettingale, K. W., Greer, S., and Tee, D. E. H. Serum IgA and emotional expression in breast cancer patients. *J. Psychosom. Res.* **21**: 395-399 (1977).

19. Pettingale, K. W., Merrett, T. G., and Tee, D. E. H. Prognostic value of serum levels of immunoglobulins (IgG, IgA, IgM, and IgE) in breast cancer: a preliminary study. *Br. J. Cancer* **36**: 550-557 (1977).

20. Schmale, A. H. and Iker, H. Hopelessness as a predictor of cervical cancer. *Soc. Sci. Med.* **5**: 95-100 (1971).

21. Blumberg, E. M., West, P. M., and Ellis, F. W. A possible relationship between psychological factors and human cancer. *Psychosom. Med.* **16**: 276-286 (1954).

22. Bacon, C. L., Renneker, R. E., and Cutler, M. A psychosomatic survey of cancer of the breast. *Psychosom. Med.* **14**: 453-459 (1952).

23. Reznikoff, M. Psychological factors in breast cancer. *Psychosom. Med.* **17**: 96-105 (1955).

24. Thomas, C. B. and Duszynski, D. R. Closeness to parents and the family constellation in a prospective study of 5 disease states: suicide, mental illness, malignant tumor, and coronary artery disease. *Johns Hopkins Med. J.* **134**: 251-270 (1974).

25. Derogatis, L. R., Abelokk, M. D., and Melisarotos, N. Psychological coping mechanisms and survival in metastatic breast cancer. *JAMA* **242**: 1504-1508 (1979).

26. Greer, S., Morris, T., and Pettingale, K. W. Psychological response to breast cancer: effect on outcome. *Lancet* **2**: 785-787 (1979).

27. Greene, W. A., Young, L. E., and Swisher, S. M. Psychological factors and reticuloendothelial disease. II: Observations on women with lymphoma and leukemia. *Psychosom. Med.* **18**: 284-303 (1956).

28. Greene, W. A. and Miller, G. Psychological factors in reticuloendothelial disease. IV: Observations on a group of children and adolescents with leukemia. *Psychosom. Med.* **20**: 124-144 (1958).

29. Achterbert, J., Matthews, S., and Simonton, O. C. Psychology of the exceptional cancer

patient: a description of patients who outlive predicted life expectancies. *Psychotherapy: Theory, Research and Practice* **14**: 416 (1978).

30. Simonton, O. C., Matthews-Simonton, S., and Sparks, T. F. Psychological intervention in the treatment of cancer. *Psychosomatics* **21**: 226-233 (1980).

31. Rogers, M. P., Dubey, D., and Reich, P. The influence of the psyche and the brain on immunity and disease susceptibility: a critical review. *Psychosom. Med.* **41**: 147-164 (1979).

Migraine Headache

Harold Geist, Ph.D.
San Francisco,
State University
San Francisco, or Berkeley, California

Although migraine headache is one of the most common and distressing of human disorders, its nature and pathogenesis have escaped satisfactory searching analysis. Grimes [1] found that of 15,000 individuals examined in general practice, 1200 were so afflicted. Lennox [2] found an incidence of 5.4% of migraine among 20,000 medical students and nurses. In his series of migraine patients, 61% were able to recall that some relative also had attacks of "sick headaches." The most outstanding feature of the migraine syndrome is periodic headache usually unilateral in onset, but which later may become generalized. The headaches are associated with irritability and nausea, and very often photophobia, vomiting, constipation, and diarrhea. The attacks are *associated with irritability and* catalyzed by scotomata, hemianopia, unilateral paresthesia, and speech disorder. The evening before the attack is often characterized by a feeling of well-being, talkativeness, and high spirits. The duration of the attack may be a few hours to several days, and the headache can be of any degree of severity. In the interval between attacks, gastrointestinal symptoms—particularly constipation—may occur. Migraine may appear at any age, although commonly it appears during adolescence. No age, social, intellectual, or economic group is immune. On appearance, a migraine patient may look ill, his or her features implying dejection or suffering. He or she may be supporting his/her head, with a hand pressed against the painful region. The face is occasionally red, but regardless of superficial color, the temporal, frontal, or supraorbital vessels on the painful side are distended. The quality of the headache is initially a throbbing ache, which later on may become steady. The headache may be of short duration and low intensity, of long duration and low intensity, or any combination of the two. Photophobia always accompany high-intensity headaches. The sites are primarily temporal, supraorbital, frontal, retrobulbar, parietal, postauricular, and occipital. Anorexia is a very common accompaniment of migraine headaches. In some patients there are prodromata such as visual and other sensory disturbances, paresthesia, aphasia, and anomia.

The mood disorders that precede and accompany migraine are prostration, dejection, and depression. The patient is unsocial, irritable, and irascible. His judgment is poor, and he is impulsive and hostile, directing his hostility toward those dependent on him. During the headache, his memory, attention, and concentration are poor. One of the outstanding features of migraines is that they occur in periods of letdown. They occur during the first days of holidays, on Sundays, and on the occasion of a planned social engagement.

Wolff and others studied clincially, the personality dynamics of subjects with migraine, by asking them to describe their symptoms. They found that the personality features and reactions dominant in these individuals are feelings of insecurity and tension, inflexibility, conscientiousness, meticulousness, perfectionism, and resentment. This inflexibility and perfectionism which begin the pulsations of the artery is sufficiently decreased whether by ergotamine tartrate, epinephrine, pressure, or some of the newer methods such as biofeedback, hypnosis, autogenic training, etc.

Henzyk-Gat and Rees [3] examined the hypothesis that psychological factors may contribute to the etiology of migraine in that specific personality traits may serve as predisposing factors and stressful emotional experiences may serve as precipitating factors. Epidemiological methods were used to obtain the sample in order to avoid the bias which may result from a study of selected groups. Evidence was obtained from this study that patients presenting themselves for treatment at special migraine clinics are not fully representative of migraine sufferers in general. From a survey of 1895 members of the Civil Service in London, a sample comprising 50 women migraine subjects was taken. These were matched, in control situations, with similar groups who were not afflicted with migraine headaches. Further matched groups were also studied, namely, 89 women migraine clinic patients, to see whether or not their characteristics were similar to those of the originally selected migraine subjects. Nineteen male asthmatic Civil Service workers were studied to ascertain whether or not they, as sufferers from a different psychosomatic disorder, displayed personality characteristics similar to the migraine subjects. Two hundred thirty-seven individuals were interviewed to obtain a detailed personal history, medical history, and family history. Several psychosomatic tests were given: the Eysenck Personality Inventory, an abridged form of MMPI, and the Bass Burkee Hostility Guilt Inventory were completed by each subject.

Evidence was presented that emotional stress can act as a precipitating factor in migraine, since over one-half of the 120 attacks recorded during a two-month period of observation were related in time to an overt stressful event, and in one-half of the random sample, migraine began for the first time during a period of emotional stress.[3]

Sacks [4] believes that many migraine attacks are regressive, or a negative retreat, and are found in hypochondriacal personalities; these attacks are presented to the therapist in the context of either real or imaginary physical complaints, characteristic of hypochondriacs. He also believes that certain kinds of migraine, particularly those that tend to occur during the menstrual cycle, tend to bind or circumscribe painful or recurrent feelings. If the migraine did not occur, these feelings would recur the rest of the month. What Sacks calls "dissociative" migraine occurs in people who, on the one hand, give a brave, bland reaction of bravado totally out of context with the environment and, on the other, exhibit pseudomasochistic behavior of suffering. Here the migraine personality is isolated from the remainder by repression and denial. Sacks compares this with the hysterical personality; migraines, however, are encapsulated in physiological mechanisms, while hysterical symptoms are encapsulated in delusional material or the imagination.

The latter types of migraine are characteristic of people who have chronic repressed rage and hostility (characteristic of other psychosomatic diseases). Sacks also refers to "cumulative migraine" in which there is an ambivalent identification with a migrainous parent, partially refuting the genetic theory of migraine. These latter two types of migraine are particularly amenable to psychoanalytic treatment. When the hostility is turned inward (the former), we get a self-punitive kind of reaction, and it is these people who most need some kind of therapy.

Finally, psychologically speaking, migraine may be considered an expression of feeling which is denied direct expression in other ways.

MANAGEMENT AND THERAPY OF MIGRAINE

The treatment and management of migraine has been one of the great enigmas of modern medicine, psychiatry, and clinical psychology. This has centered around two procedures: those that tend to end and those that tend to prevent the headache.

It is generally conceded that vasodilation of the cranial arteries is the cause of the pain in migraine. Thus, purely medical measures have been employed such as pituitrin, ephedrine, benzedrine, epinephrine, caffeine, hypertonic salt solutions, and ice caps over the affected vessels, which will sometimes afford relief.

Likewise, pressing the finger over the affected vessel will sometimes give relief. Breathing 100% oxygen, since it has a vasoconstrictor effect on cerebral vessels, will also occasionally bring relief. Intramuscular administration of ergotamine tartrate early in the course of the migraine headache will also give fairly prompt relief, if followed by bed rest two hours after the administration. Side effects are sometimes experienced, such as nausea and vomiting, temporary numbness of the hands or feet, and tightness of the muscles around the neck and thighs.

For the alleviation of mild headache, medical therapy includes acetanilide, acetophenetidin, and aspirin; for the relief of moderately severe headaches, codeine phosphate is used; for the treatment of a very severe headache, codeine sulfate is used. Although ergotamine tartrate is probably the most effective medical (pharmacological) therapy, physicians are wary of using it because of its side effects. More recently, *para*chlorophenylalanine has had good results; experts in the field think this is so since it is a depletor of serotonin. Pathological serotonin metabolism is thought to cause migraine.

Nitroglycerin, erythrol tetranitrate, acetylcholine, and methacholine have been used to alleviate the pain of migraine, primarily by lowering the system's blood pressure and reducing the amplitude of pulsations of the cranial arteries.

Since, in some patients, dilatation of the temporal artery or periarterial infiltration has been shown to later cause at least an accompaniment of the migraine, ligation of the artery has been shown to bring relief. When the pain is cause by dilatation of the common carotid artery, ligation of the middle meningeal artery has been shown to cause relief.

Drugs that induce sleep or relaxation such as bromide salts (not used much anymore), barbiturates, acetanilide, antipyrine, and phenacetin have had some use, but certainly are more a temporary sedative than a cure.

Various kinds of diets, particularly the ketogenic diets of epilepsy, have lessened the frequency of migraines.

Some people think the migraine is the result of a pituitary disorder, but this has not been experimentally proved. Others believe that there are gastrointestinal disturbances or allergic abnormalities, and consequently treat patients in those areas, but again these theories have not been proved.

More important than the purely medical and pharmacological aspects of migraine are the psychological and psychiatric. The first, of course, is the avoidance of circumstances provocative of the migraine. Each patient is a rule unto himself, and while such things as a flashing light may induce a migraine in one patient, loss of sleep, a missed meal, or excessive, inhibited anger will induce headaches in others.

The therapeutic interview and just plain listening are of great importance in the therapeutic regimen. As in other functional psychopatholgy, very often this will radiate to other areas of the patients's life and help to drain the pent-up accumulation of stresses and tensions which precipitated the migraine in the first place. The therapist must be aware of the kind of patient who needs his migraine or is so attached to the migraine way of life that the headache, in effect, becomes his friend. (This is not indigenous to migraine alone but also to other areas of psychopathology, particularly hypochondriacal symptoms.) Here the therapists must be careful in disclosing the underlying reasons for this state of affairs, since the exposure of these may be more painful than the migraine itself.

PREVENTION

The prevention of migraine is principally psychological and psychiatric. The therapist should make the potential patient become aware of his tension, and recognize his fatigue and his feelings of dissatisfaction and frustration. His encouragement of relaxation and discouragement of obsession with work and responsibility are especially important in the prevention of migraine. Alvarez, who has written extensively about headaches, says that "it is better to be a healthy, happy rancher than a headache ridden professor." It is important for people who already have migraine that the therapist investigate those periods when the headaches are most frequent and those periods when they are less frequent in order to get at the life situations which may precipitate the migraine. Relief from anxiety and tension is the permanent preventative measure. Frequent pauses during work are essential in order to relieve the results of obstacles characteristic of migraine patients. Excessive preoccupation with work is pathognomonic with deep-rooted feelings of insecurity. It has been noted before that migraines often occur during letdown periods. It may be desirable to arrange the holiday or recreation period just after the work period and arrange the work so that there is a slowdown just before the holiday. Perhaps in planning the holiday this way, some energy can be invested during the holiday. Likewise, at the end of the holiday, there should be a gradual resumption of work. This has been shown to mitigate or eliminate migraine.

Both vigorous exercise and sexual intercourse (under the right conditions) have been advocated by some as preventative measures in migraine.

The most effective drug in the prevention of migraine is one recently introduced called methysergide (lysergic acid butanolamide). However, one must be careful of such side effects as disorders of neurological dysfunction, elevation of blood pressure, breathlessness, and pleuritic pain. Belladonna has been found to have a therapeutic prophylactic effect in some instances.

NEWER THERAPEUTIC PROCEDURES

Biofeedback, hypnosis, autogenic training, and various relaxation therapies have in many instances relieved migraine headaches. It has been found that a combination of biofeedback and autogenic training is usually the most efficacious, by this must await the results of rigid, controlled studies.

I investigated a number of patients with migraine headaches in the San Francisco, California Bay area, ranging from 18 to 60 years in age, all in the middle socioeconomic group, with a sex distribution of 10 males and 20 females. They were given an extensive questionnaire involving such things as various factors prior to symptomatology (e.g., stress, loss of close relative, difficulty with career or money). Various psychosomatic symptoms suffered either as a child or as an adult (tics, enuresis, etc.) were also assessed. Familial background was obtained, along with an extensive work history. Four psychological tests were also given: the Multiple Affect Check List, the Cornell Index, the Tennessee Self-Concept Test, and the Holtman Ink Blot Test. The results of the questionnaires wer collated, and the mean scores were computed for each of the scales for each of the tests.

In summary, there seems to be a familial diathesis with migraine patients, with a tendency for it to occur on the mother's side. It is quite a disturbing affliction to the patient and somewhat less upsetting to friends. About one-fourth of the patients had headaches as children, so most of the migraines developed in adulthood. As in many other psychosomatic ailments I have studied, particularly rheumatoid arthritis, people with migraine were unable to express rage and about half of them got angry very easily. They were a conforming group who were ambitious and persistent and said they were clean. In their formative years, the mother was the disciplinarian. Not surprisingly, when they got emotionally upset their migraine headaches became worse, but surprisingly, various external stimuli such as light and temperature changes triggered the headaches in a goodly number.

What these tests did show is that these patients were a moderately depressed group, who were confused, in conflict, and considered themselves maladjusted and neurotic. They also had an obsessive compulsive diathesis and were generally immature and according to the Holtzman could not tolerate stress.

References

1. Grimes, E. The migraine instability. *M. J. and Rec.* **137**: 417 (1931).
2. Lennox, W. G. *Science and Seizures.* New York: Harper Brothers, 1941.
3. Henzyk-Gat, R. and Rees, W. Psychological aspects of migraine. *Journal of Psychosomatic Research* **17**: 141–153 (1973).
4. Sacks, O. *Migraine, The Evolution of a Common Disorder.* Berkeley: University of California Press, 1970.
5. Geist, H. Personality dynamics of migraine patients. *Health Commun. Informatics,* **6**(6) (1980).

The Stress of Chronic Pain

Nelson Hendler, M.D., M.S.
Assistant Professor of Psychiatry
Psychiatric Consultant, Pain Treatment Center
Johns Hopkins Hospital
Baltimore, Maryland

Clinical Director
Mensana Clinic
Stevenson, Maryland

Selye is the acknowledged leader in the field of stress research. It was he, in 1936, who published the first paper in which the concept of a generalized stress reaction was introduced.[1] Selye has further refined his work and now defines many life events as stressors, which are experiences that produced a generalized stress reaction in an organism.[2] This generalized stress reaction is manifested by a variety of hormonal changes, associated with physiological manifestations. If the stress is prolonged, there are distinct anatomical changes that can occur, even to the point of creating disease and subsequent death. There are a great many examples of this sequence of events in psychosomatic medicine, and one only need think of the stressors of a businessman's life, which produce a variety of hormonal changes that can eventually manifest as ulcers or cardiovascular disease. Selye further expands upon his concept by delineating another type of stressor, that which produces eustress, the kind of response one has to good or positive events that occur in one's life.[2] Despite the fact that all concerned would consider the event as a beneficial occurrence, the body responds to this good stressor with a generalized stress reaction that is remarkably similar to the type of stress reaction seen with other types of stressful events. This eustress reaction can have many of the same physiological manifestations as negative life events. One only has to think of the cardiovascular response to "falling in love" to recognize that this concept, first advanced by Selye, is not at all farfetched. As Selye further indicates, the bad stressors in one's life produce the type of response that one most often associates with a stressful event, and this is called a distressful response to external events. The most important consideration one must bear in mind when considering Selye's work is the fact that both eustress and distress have remarkable similarities in terms of the physiological response that they evoke within an organism.

Holmes and Rahe have expanded upon Selye's concepts, and have devised a life events chart.[3] On this chart, they list a variety of normally occurring life events, such as the death of a spouse, divorce, acquiring a mortgage, buying a new home, getting a new job, having a car accident, etc., and make no attempt to distinguish between life events on a eustressful or a distressful basis. The common denominator on the life events chart is the fact that each event represents a significant change in a person's life, and it makes no difference whether it is a good or a bad change. This is a primary concept for understanding stress, since one must now take into account the fact that any change, which brings with it the phenomenon of producing an unknown quantity in someone's life, can be stressful for an organism. This only reinforces the early concepts of Selye, and underscores the similarity between good and bad events, simply because either type of event will produce a change in someone's life. One may now conceptualize stressful events as those that produce uncertainty and project an element of the unknown into someone's existence.

Joseph Brady, of John Hopkins University School of Medicine, has expanded on the above-mentioned concepts, and interjected the notion of volition and choice as another variable that produces stress in someone's life.[4] In a now classic experiment, Brady devised an apparatus that restrained two monkeys side by side. Both monkeys had an appliance which gave them a shock, and the shock was administered only after the presentation of a signal or light. The only difference in the situations of these two monkeys was the fact that one had a bar, which he would press within a certain set period of time after the presentation of the light, that could prevent the application of the shock to both of the monkeys. The "worker" monkey was forced to sit passively by, awaiting the outcome of the "executive" monkey's decision. It is significant to note that both monkeys received the same amount of shock, but one had control over the environment and was faced with making decisions, while the other was forced to abide by the decision of the first. Despite what one may intuitively think, it was the executive monkey that developed ulcers, while the worker monkey sat passively by and was forced to take whatever the consequences were of the executive monkey's decision. Now, an additional variable is introduced into the mélange of stress response. This variable is the ability to exert influence or make decisions about one's fate. Paradoxically, the ability to influence one's environment seems to be more stressful than accepting whatever one is assigned. This analogy can be applied to real life situations for humans only if one recognizes that the passive, dependent role of worker monkey is not stressful as long as one accepts the situation and makes no attempt to alter it.

Unfortunately, many experienced and knowledgeable writers in the field of psychosomatic medicine have neglected the impact of chronic pain on a person's life. They neglect to take into account the type of stress that pain can produce in and of itself and, as a consequence, of the alterations it can produce in a person's life. Very often, and quite mistakenly, patients are said to have "psychogenic pain" when a physician cannot find an etiological mechanism for the pain or when, in the physician's judgment, the pain "couldn't be that bad." Obviously, this judgmental attitude is equally as subjective as the experience of chronic pain, since all writers freely admit that pain is indeed a subjective experience. A great many myths have crept into the psychiatric literature, especially pertaining to pain, and many well-known authors have ascribed the sensation of pain to underlying psychiatric difficulties. What they neglect to consider is the premorbid (prepain) adjustment of the individual and the possibility that pain itself can produce stress and psychiatric disorder. Certainly Selye recognizes this and in the Foreword to *Coping with Chronic Pain,* he mentions the stress of pain that he must now endure in his own life, due to two artificial hips.[5] Norman Cousins, in his book *Anatomy of an Illness,* devotes an entire chapter to the impact of pain on one's own life, using the example of the extreme pain of lepers.[6] He most accurately describes the difficulty with which an individual accepts the recognition of a noxious sensation for which there seems to be no relief or, even worse, no explanation. Bonica, in the Foreword to the book *The Diagnosis and Nonsurgical Management of Chronic Pain,* tells the ravages of pain on society in general, and of the personal toll that pain can take in someone's life.[7] For people who know Bonica, they know that he is talking from personal as well as long-standing academic experience. Finally, one of the great leaders in the field of pain research, Dr. Ronald Melzack, has delineated the various hormonal components associated with pain.[8] As might be expected, these are remarkably similar to the hormonal correlates of a generalized stress reaction, and include the release of ACTH, as well as endorphins and enkephalins. There are many difficulties encountered when one attempts to measure pain, and obviously any attempt at a correlation between stress and pain would be futile. Both seem to be totally subjective responses, and even though there does seem to be some distinct physiological and hormonal changes associated with both, the quantification of these responses only tells the degree to which a certain organism responds to the stimulus of pain or stress, but does nothing to quantify the stimulus *per se.* This is a critical concept, since it freely admits that any attempt to measure pain is useless, and the only item that has any significance is the individual's *response* to the pain.[9] This same concept applies to stress in general, since the same stressor, applied to two different individuals, can produce two totally different and distinct physiological responses, both in quantity and in quality. To further expand upon this concept, one must bear in mind that threshold differences for pain vary dramatically between individuals, and may be based on purely biochemical factors (levels of β-endorphins or enkephalins), or may be dependent on sociological and cultural parameters. Additionally, personality characteristics, as well as psychological state at the time of pain, also determine the response that an individual will exhibit to the stimulus. It is now important to make a distinction that is critical for the understanding of pain as a stressor in someone's life. Acute pain does not produce the same type of effect as chronic pain does. The distinction between acute and chronic pain can be differentiated on an anatomical basis, as well as a psychological basis. Obviously, acute pain does not produce the same psychological stress as chronic pain. Acute pain is over in a matter of minutes, hours, or days. This does not allow the stimulus (stressor) to make a change in the person's life which is one of the criteria, discussed above, that is necessary to produce stress. Therefore, one would expect that acute pain would not change a life events score if one tabulated a person's problems on the Holmes-Rahe table. However, chronic pain truly does begin to change a person's life. The changes are not immediately apparent, and the entire process is a slow, evolutionary, and most insidious one.

There are four distinct phases to the chronic pain process which parallel, to a great degree, the type of response that a person sees in a dying patient, as so well described by Kubler-Ross.[7,10] If a normal individual, who is well adjusted prior to the acquisition of the pain, begins to experience chronic pain, he undergoes four very distinct and temporally definable stages in response to it. The first stage, which occurs between 0 and 2 months after the acquisition of the pain, would not produce any clear-cut psychological problems, because during this stage, the person expects that his pain will get better. Since the person's life has not changed in any great degree, nor is he expecting the pain to exist on a permanent level, the impact of acute pain as a stressor is apparent only on an immediate basis, but not on a protracted basis. However, if the pain is not corrected, and persists longer than 2 months, it enters the subacute phase, which usually lasts between 2 and 6 months but may last as long as a year. It is during this stage that persons with pain begin to fear that the pain they experience may last for their lifetime. This fear produces a great deal of stress, and they become overly concerned with bodily function and have manifestations of anxiety. It is during this stage of subacute pain that subtle psychological changes begin to manifest, and people become more irritable, have difficulty with sleep, and begin to experience sexual problems. During this subacute stage, patients exhibit the fear that is often associated with pain, and pain really becomes a stressor in their lives. The third stage of pain is the chronic stage. This stage usually begins after the pain has existed for a period of 6 months or longer. This stage may last anywhere between 5 and 8 years, and is recognized by the profound depression associated with the pain. By the time a person enters the chronic stage of pain, he has begun to realize that the pain will be permanent and that health professionals will be unsuccessful in their attempts to treat it. Even though he fervently hopes that the pain will subside, the patient recognizes that this is an unlikely possibility. By now, the stress of pain has produced depression, anxiety, sleeplessness, and heightened irritability, and has created problems for the patient on his job and at home. Thoughts of suicide during this stage of chronic pain are not uncommon. By now, the chronic pain has become a firmly entrenched stressor, creating life stress that is remarkably frustrating for an individual. During this stage, the individual exhibits all of the traits and characteristics of the executive monkey, and makes heroic efforts to find a diagnosis of the pain or an appropriate place for treatment. Patients become quite well read and well versed about their disorder if the diagnosis is known, or suggest readings to physicians in an attempt to assist them in making a diagnosis. They will try any new treatment modality offered to them, and one senses an element of desperation in their attempts to make one final effort to rid themselves of the pain. Also, they exhibit a great deal of hostility, anger, and resentment, since the denial stage has long since disappeared in the subacute phase of their process. By the time a person in chronic pain reaches the fourth or subchronic state, he has had his pain between 3 and 12 years. It is during this stage of their pain that patients begin to acquire the characteristics of the worker monkey. They begin to passively and almost philosophically accept the fact that the pain will be with them for the rest of their lives. By now, the hostility, anger, resentment, and depression have been resolved. They are left with a quiet sense of desperation, but not the overt manifestations of the psychological problems produced during the subacute and chronic stages. By this stage, pain has become less of a stressor, but is still a stressor nevertheless. However, usually by this stage, patients have acclimated their life-styles to adapt themselves to the ever-present pain. On balance, one can see that the entire experience of chronic pain is indeed a devastating life event.

When considering the response of the chronic pain patient to his plight, one must bear in mind that what has been described above is the response of a normal, well-adjusted person who had no psychiatric problems *prior* to the onset of chronic pain.[11] Again, it is most important to recognize the concept that chronic pain produces psychological and psychiatric problems in a normal, well-adjusted individual. The fact that the stress of chronic pain is able to create psychiatric problems in a normally well-adjusted person can only lend credence to the theory that pain itself is a powerful stressor. When this stressor is superimposed on the changes in life events that it also produces, the overwhelming effect of chronic pain becomes awesome. There are many changes in life situations produced by chronic pain. The following discussion delineates the most frequently found problems, and makes no pretext of being comprehensive, but only representative.

One of the least talked about changes in a person's life, but one of the most important to the average person, is the alteration of sexual activity produced by chronic pain. Very often, a chronic pain patient will report that the pain has eliminated any desire for sex, and this loss of libido is usually associated with either a fear of being injured during the sexual act or the actual impact that the pain has on the limbic system structures associated with sexual desire. Additionally, the partner usually expresses a fear of injuring the patient during the course of lovemaking, and even if the patient exhibits some degree of sexual interest, their partner is often very reticent about engaging in sexual activity, for fear of hurting the patient further.

Chronic pain also destroys self-esteem. The person in chronic pain finds himself unable to function in a normal job or in the performance of household chores. Additionally since sexual activity is curtailed, the net result is for the injured or pained partner to feel he has not lived up to his end of the marriage contract. Very often this self-admonition is expressed during the course of psychotherapy, and is usually associated with an inadvertent role reversal that occurs. If a man is injured and experiences chronic pain as a consequence of the injury, he usually finds that he cannot work or perform sexually as he used to. For persons engaged in manual labor, or where physical activity is a large part of their job, this usually results in the loss of the job, with the subsequent reduction of income. If the man finds that he cannot carry groceries into the house, but is forced to ask his wife to do so, he becomes the subject of derision in his neighborhood and, for himself, feels that he is "only half a man." A female suffering from chronic pain often expresses her inability to "function as a wife" as one of the major stressors in life.

If a chronic pain patient is unable to function, he obviously must depend upon other people for assistance. This evokes all of the dynamics associated with dependence. Typically, the person resents the other person on whom he is dependent. However, he is afraid to express his resentment for fear that the other person may go away. Additionally, chronic pain patients usually state that they feel a degree of jealousy toward those on whom they depend. All this creates a rather ambivalent psychological stress, because, while patients appreciate the fact that others are taking care of them, they concomitantly resent this. They become afraid to get angry at their helpmates, and when they finally do, the explosion is typically disproportionate to the event which has triggered the anger. Being placed in a dependent role only serves to further the stress created by chronic pain.

One of the often neglected considerations of chronic pain is the financial consequence that people suffer as a result of it. A great deal has been written about the "compensation neurosis," which is an attempt to derive financial gain as a result of an injury on the job or an accident for which another party is liable. However, very little has been written about the chronic pain patient who undergoes financial hardships as a result of inadequate compensation, disability insurance, or the absence of both, in association with an inability to work. More importantly, if a patient desires to return to work, has had a back injury or some other form of chronic pain, and is engaged in any form of manual labor, the mention of these disorders almost virtually guarantees him exclusion from employment. Very often, patients are told that hiring a person with a previous record of back surgery or chronic back pain will raise their health insurance rates, as well as their workmen's compensation insurance payments. Therefore, it is conceivable that a patient with chronic pain, who does seek gainful employment, will be denied this privilege. Finally, patients who were engaged in manual labor and had been earning reasonable salaries will sometimes be rehabilitated. Unfortunately, they are very often rehabilitated for a job that is physically less strenuous, with a concomitant reduction in payment as a result. Conceivably, a stonemason earning $20,000 a year, or a man "working high steel" and earning $25,000 a year, will be unable to perform these arduous tasks. After vocational rehabilitation, they may be assigned to a job paying approximately $8,000 to $10,000 a year, as a timekeeper or salesman. The financial loss as a result of this can be devastating, and obviously is a great stressor in a person with chronic pain.

Sleep disturbance as the result of chronic pain is an additional stressor in someone's life. For a variety of reasons, a pain that prevents someone from getting to sleep at night, or awakens them from sleep several times during the night, is bound to produce symptoms of fatigue, irritability, and occasionally depression. In fact, a great many of the neurochemical transmitters involved in sleep regulation are also intimately associated with pain perception and depression. A more thorough discussion of this matter is available in other references,[7] but suffice it to say that enhancement of serotonin, by the use of tricyclic antidepressants of the teriary amine class does provide some degree of symptomatic relief. In any event, disturbances in sleep may be as much a manifestation of the stress of chronic pain as they are the result of the chronic pain itself.

One of the most consistent findings of chronic pain patients is the presence of depression at the chronic stage (6 months to 8 years). In fact, depression is such a consistent finding that its absence in a patient experiencing chronic pain should immediately suggest an underlying psychiatric disorder, whereby the patient is utilizing the pain to his advantage, rather than suffering the stressful consequences of it. As one might imagine, the multiple stressors created by the presence of pain and the pain itself are enough to create depression in someone, especially when one recognizes that the stress or chronic pain will be permanent. According to many authors, the incidence of suicidal ideation and of suicide attempts is higher in chronic pain patients than in the general population. As mentioned above, one must be particularly careful to assess the premorbid adjustment of the patient, and if no psychopathology was evident prior to the acquisition of the pain, then one can be comfortable with the notion that chronic pain created the depression in that person. The notion of a "depressive equivalent" has validity only if there was a preexisting etiological mechanism that would predispose one to the depression, prior to the acquisition of pain. This particular psychological explanation for pain has been overutilized, even though the original definition of the existence of such a disorder was a brilliant piece of psychodynamic psychotherapy. As might be expected, there is a great deal of anger involved in the dynamics of the depression, usually directed at the person himself for having acquired the pain, or toward the person who created the pain for them (as a result of an accident), or finally, toward God, as the chronic pain patient tries to find an answer to the question, "Why me?"

Another consistent finding about chronic pain and the stress it produces in someone's life is the fear expressed by the patient. The fear usually centers around the pain itself. Will the pain get worse? Will the pain make me crippled? Is there something undetected that might be cancer? Is there something wrong with me that the doctors won't tell me about? These questions naturally evolve from the condition of chronic pain, and the stress that it produces. However, as one can see, the fear of the unknown, one of the critical elements of stress production, is abundantly evident in patients with chronic pain.

One of the most difficult questions associated with chronic pain is the litigation surrounding it. This is especially true within the United States, because of our overactive tort system. The inability of legislatures to recognize the necessity for no-fault insurance has created a most profitable industry for a variety of physicians and attorneys. Litigation may take the form of workmen's compensation hearings, where legitimate or illegitimate grievances may be brought before a commissioner in an attempt to seek reimbursement for an on-the-job injury. Additionally, automobile accidents or personal injury accidents, with the resultant liability suits, give rise to legal action. For every person who abuses the legal system, there usually is a victim as well. Very often, chronic pain patients suffer the brunt of the misuses of this system since pain is a subjective problem, and the absence of any quantifiable diagnostic tests makes any claim very suspect. As one might imagine, the unknown quantity of a legal settlement interjects an additional note of stress into the already complex picture of a chronic pain patient.

Because of the subjective nature of pain, a chronic pain patient is often subjected to accusations and doubts. Since pain is not a visible symptom, a pain patient typically is the recipient of a comment like "you look so good, how can you be in pain?" If litigation is involved, and if the patient is receiving some sort of financial support, even though it is far below what he normally might earn, there are always suspicions and accusations regarding his motivation for "remaining ill." The distrust voiced by family and friends only serves as one additional stressor in the already overwhelming stress life of the chronic pain patient.

While the chronic pain patient might be the recipient of doubts, he himself also has doubts. These are usually directed toward the medical profession, since its members obviously have not cured the chronic pain problem. Very often, the chronic pain patient is considered a "bad patient" who has not gotten well after surgery, and must face the accusation from the surgeon that "I can't find anything wrong with you. It must be all in your head, so go see a psychiatrist." This effectively helps remove the hope for any future treatment and further adds to the stress of chronic pain. Depending on the stage of chronic pain, the patient either will submit to the pronouncement that nothing more can be done or will continue to seek additional medical assistance. In either circumstance, pain still remains a markedly evident stressor

The final and perhaps most important consideration is the marital discord and family disharmony created by chronic pain. For all of the above-mentioned reasons, the chronic pain patient begins to find himself alienated from family and friends, and it is a rare spouse that does not begin to experience some resentment toward the patient with chronic pain, after being encumbered for a number of years by the problems associated with the complaint. Perhaps it is the very subjective nature of pain itself that creates so many conflicts. If the disorder of pain were visible, such as an amputated leg, then the basis of complaints and the resulting difficulties would be evident for all concerned. Unfortunately, this is not the lot of the chronic pain patient, and this serves to produce an additional stress on him as he attempts to prove to family and friends the existence of his pain. This is especially difficult in the absence of any family support, and the stressors injected by the problems of chronic pain serve to increase the divorce rate among patients with this disorder.

In conclusion, one can see that chronic pain is associated with a variety of stressors, all of which can manifest as distinct events in the life event change scale of Holmes and Rahe.[3] However, if one superimposes chronic pain onto a previously disturbed individual, the picture becomes even more complicated. Again, it must be emphasized that it is impossible to accurately measure pain *per se*, so some scales have been devised to measure the net effect of pain on a person's life. By utilizing indirect measuring instruments, one can get a modified Holmes and Rahe scale specifically designed for chronic pain. One such instrument is the Hendler Screening

Test for Chronic Back Pain Patients developed by Johns Hopkins Hospital Chronic Pain Treatment Center.[9] Utilizing this test, one can divide chronic pain patients into two broad categories: (1) those who are experiencing additional life stresses as a result of their chronic pain, and (2) those who are using their chronic pain (i.e., patients who had preexisting psychiatric difficulties which predisposed them to exaggerate the problems in their life, purportedly produced by chronic pain, but really ascribable to their own personality disorders). While other life events are easily definable as stressors, with the concomitant psychohormonal changes associated with them, chronic pain is indeed one of the most complex life event changes that an individual can experience, and it is equally difficult for a clinician to dissect the various components of this Gordian knot of pain.

References

1. Selye, H. A syndrome produced by diverse nocuous agents. *Nature* **138**: 32 (July 4, 1936).
2. Selye, H. *Stress without Distress,* pp. 26-27. New York: J. B. Lippincott, 1974.
3. Holmes, T. H. and Rahe, R. H. The social readjustment rating scale. *Journal of Psychosomatic Research* **11**: 213-218 (1967).
4. Brady, J. Ulcers in "executive" monkeys (reading from *Scientific American,* Oct. 1958). In *Frontiers of Psychological Research* (S. Coopersmith, ed.), pp. 250-253. San Francisco: W. A. Freeman, 1964.
5. Selye, H. Foreword. In *Coping with Chronic Pain* by N. Hendler and J. Fenton, pp. xi-xii. New York: Clarkson N. Potter, 1979.
6. Cousins, N. Pain is not the ultimate enemy. In *Anatomy of an Illness*, Ch. 4, pp. 89-107. New York: W. W. Norton, 1979.
7. Bonica, J. J. Forword. In *Diagnosis and Nonsurgical Management of Chronic Pain,* by Nelson Hendler, pp. vi-ix. New York: Raven Press, 1981.
8. Melzack, R. Quel est le role du stress dans le processus de la douleur. In *Stress—De Grands Specialistes Respondent* (S. Bensabet, ed.), pp. 72-74. Paris and Evreux (Eure): Hachette, 1980.
9. Hendler, N., Viernstein, M., Gucer, P., and Long, D. A Pre-operative screening test for chronic back pain patients. *Psychosomatics* **20** (12): 801-808 (1979).
10. Hendler, N., Derogatis, L., Avella, J., and Long, D. EMG biofeedback in patients with chronic pain. *Diseases of the Nervous System* **38** (7): 505-509 (1977).
11. Hendler, N. Psychiatric aspects of chronic pain. In *Textbook of Neurosurgery* (J. Youmans, ed.), Ch. 116. Philadelphia: Saunders & Co., 1981.

In Praise of the De-stressing Effects of Health Spas

Professor Zdenek Votava, M.D., Sc.D.
Sanatorium Helios, Strbske Pleso
Czechoslovakia, C.S.S.R.

Contemporary society, and individuals within societies, increasingly have been characterized as overworked, nervous, tired, and stressed. Modern life, in its quality, seldom brings those elements of calm known to earlier generations. We live, most of us, in complex societies in which communication is absolutely essential. We are obliged to develop intercultural communications, person to person, and we strive to develop competent "space for communication" (after S. B. Day) in which daily affairs can be conducted. Yet trivial surpasses that occur in one's occupation, in one's family, and even in such relatively innocuous events as a trip by car or by train, may provoke disturbing sequences which cause neurosis, stress, and various tensions.

Over the last two decades the pharmaceutical industry has developed increasing numbers of drugs directed toward allaying these neuroses—anxiolytics, ataractics, and minor tranquilizers have been used for these purposes. From the original tranquilizer, meprobamate, to diazepam and more recent compounds, increasing claims have been aired for *effectiveness without addiction*. All of these drugs cause sedation in patients, and inhibit life activity and pleasure. They may also encourage addiction and dependency.

Quite naturally, many patients need medical care and appropriate counsel. To give pharmacologic therapy may be an oversimplification of their need. Frequently such patients could profit more by advice on how to live more healthy, outgoing lives; how to regain an active mental outlook; and how to proceed about their affairs without the use of drugs. A stay in a specialized health spa can often be extremely beneficial to many of these patients.

THE CZECHOSLOVAK HEALTH SPAS

Czechoslovakia is a small country in the middle of Europe. As in many European nations, the tradition of balneotherapy has long been associated with this republic. Some of its spas were renowned several centuries ago, e.g., Karlovy Vary (Carlsbad), Marianske Lazne (Marienbad), and Piestany became world famous in the treatment of gastrointestinal, respiratory, and rheumatic diseases. Other spas have arisen, over the years, in some of the most beautiful localities of Czechoslovakia. Great forests, mountains, lakes, and fresh air return patients not only to sound somatic health but also to good psychic health.

Jesenik Spa (Grafenberg) in Moravia

There are several health spas in Czechoslovakia dedicated to the treatment of neuroses caused by stress. The most historically famous is Jesenik Spa, previously known as Grafenberg, which is located on the northern border of Moravia in the Jesenik Mountains (Altvater Mountains).

This spa has a most interesting history. One hundred and fifty years ago, a young boy by the name of Franz Priessnitz, lived with his father on a small farm bordered by large forests in which there were many crystal clear springs and rivulets of running water. Working as a woodcutter in the forest, Franz one day observed a doe with a wounded leg, submersing its limb into the cold water of a spring in order to encourage healing. Some time later, he himself was injured, and he resorted to the same treatment which had been used by the doe. His injury was healed and he affirmed that the healing effect was the result of the natural spring water. Soon, his method of treatment, using mountain spring water, became popular for the treatment of many diseases, including hysteria, neurosis, and mental disorders.

The medical success of the Priessnitz Treatment spread rapidly throughout Europe. Patients of all classes, including the aristocracy, sought help, and Priessnitz developed his cure into a therapeutic regimen that included long walks in the surrounding forests, physical work (i.e., woodcutting), and inculcation of "toughness" by washing in cold water just outside the forest! Such procedures—strange to aristocratic people who were accustomed to comfort and service—had suprisingly good effects, and frequently neuroses, hysteria, and other stressful situations were fully cured.

After the death of Franz Priessnitz in 1865, his family continued his tradition, augmenting the therapy with medical experts. As patient demand increased so did accommodations and facilities at the spa. After World War I, Sanatorium Priessnitz was constructed, and balneotherapeutic procedures were installed—hydrotherapy, inhalation, massages, etc. At the end of the World War II, the name of Grafenberg was changed to the

Czech name Lazne Jesenik, and all buildings were improved to develop the most modern medical facilities, which led to its reputation as an international spa. New laboratories were built for electrotherapy, electrosleep treatment, physical exercises, psychotherapeutic methods, etc. These procedures, along with prescribed diet and a favorable natural environment, created good preconditions for successful therapy.

Main indications for therapy at this spa include nervous and mental instability provoked as a result of psychic overloading and repeated stress situations. Other medical conditions, including diseases resulting from disorders of metabolism, endocrinopathies, and nonspecific diseases of the respiratory tract (chronic bronchitis, bronchial asthma), have also been treated with success.

Despite its worldwide reputation and long-standing tradition, Jesenik Spa remains a quiet location, behind a ridge of high mountains, affording shelter from stressful life and tumult, in an environment of clean springs, streams, wide forests, and air fresh with the smell of pines and alpine meadows. Located at a height of 650 meters above sea level, this spa has a very favorable climate and is particularly agreeable during the months of September and October.

Strbske Pleso Spa in the High Tatras of Slovakia

Another wonderful place with de-stressing facilities is Strbske Pleso Spa in the High Tatra Mountains of Slovakia. The High Tatra Mountains form part of the Carpathian Circle in the north of Slovakia and rise in terraces to a height of more than 2000 meters above sea level. The main ridge protects the southern slope of the Tatras from north winds. The terraces are turned to the south and catch the maximum of the sun's rays, so that a warm climate is created, and the ambience is suitable for a health establishment.

In this region, at an altitude of 1350 meters above sea level, the modern new Sanatorium Helios was opened to the public in 1976; it is located a short distance from the large mountain lake Strbske Pleso.

Patients are drawn to the mountains to admire the beauties of nature, to relax within the sound of the restful wind in the forest ranges, to inhale the pure air, and in this peaceful setting to gather new strength for the daily wear of life.

A feature of this spa is the rather small range of average day and yearly temperatures. During the winter months, particularly in January, frequent so-called temperature inversions occur, in which the temperature on the slopes is higher by 5 to 10°C than that in the lower regions of the same district. The sun shines for about 2000 hours annually, which is a relatively large amount of sunshine for a location at this altitude.

A further feature of importance is the amount of electricity in the atmosphere, which creates a desired "aerosol" composition. In yearly averages, ionization of air occurs at higher altitudes and is accompanied by large quantities of positive electricity—which have a revitalizing effect on the organism.

In Yoga terminology, this is the principle of energy called *prana,* which is energy that may be obtained by breathing pure mountain air with high positive electrical loading. On the basis of this psychophysiology, the *prana-yama* doctrine was elaborated many years ago in India. The essence of the doctrine is to teach the initiate how to restore good self-health, by correct breathing habits and the inspiration of pure air containing bountiful *prana* energy.

The physiologic effects of mountain climates should be included in the catalogue of stimulating thresholds to augment the vitality of the human person. Seasonal changes can be observed, and the ambient, unspecified impulses which act gently, and with time, are able to change the responses of the human body in, for example, the direction of improved resistance to psychic stress. Doubtless, other important biological factors are at work—freely abundant ultraviolet radiation, the radiations from the sun, etc., but all together serve as powerful de-stressing forces.

Sanatorium Helios at Strbske Pleso is particulary devoted to the treatment of nonspecific respiratory diseases such as chronic bronchitis, bronchial asthma, allergic diseases, and neuroses. The sanatorium is equipped with modern facilities for balneotherapy, including swimming pools for adults and children, electrotherapy, massages, and inhalation therapy. An important part of the therapy includes wandering in the surrounding forests and moutain region, in keeping with the instructions of a consulting physician.

SUMMARY OBSERVATIONS

On the basis of our experience, the opinion is expressed that a stay in specialized spas can ameliorate and improve neurotic and psychic states caused by the stress of life. The duration of treatment is most important, and should extend for a period of four to six weeks. Certainly a period of less than four weeks has less value. A week is necessary for acclimatization to high altitudes and for adjustment to differences in climate. After such a regulatory phase, patients feel well, and favorable therapeutic effects commence. If maximally developed by spa therapy, good conditioning remains for a long time after the patient returns home. A system of repeated annual therapy is recommended for optimal lifetime good creative health.

Index

aaas, 218
abusing parent, 222
accidental injury, 113
acclimatization, 387
accommodation
  in neural behaviors, 18
  property of, 19
acetylcholine, 31
acquired psychological factors, strain, 317
acquired somatic factors, strain, 317
acth, 8, 26, 67, 355
action potentials, 30
action, benzodiazepines, 51
actions that stem from terrorism, 145
activation, 83, 84
activation research, 87
acts, control of, terrorists, 147
acts of violence, 150
acupuncture, 27
acute depressive conditions, 171
acute hallucinatory-delusional conditions,
  171
adaptability, 9
adaptation, 4, 14
adaptive behavior, 87
adh, 25
adolescents, 223
adrenal cortex, 26
adrenalectomy, 66
adrenaline, 8, 35
adrenocortical enlargement, 4
adrenocorticotrophic hormone, 8, 27, 105
adulthood, 5
adversary conduct in nations, 145
adverse effects of psychotropic drugs, 171
advocacy, child, 230
aerosol composition, 387
afferent connections with thalamus, 21
Afro-American, 304
age, 66

Age of Information, ix
age of onset, abuse, child, 222
age related changes in physiology, 68
agencies, community, 154
agent, stressor, 4
agents, diverse nocuous, 3
aggressive behavior, 12
aging, 159, 277
aging process, 239
agonists, 322
agricultural technology, 214
akathisia, 173
alarm reaction, 4, 26
alarm signals, 7
alcohol, 11, 51, 344
aldosterone, 8
alexithymia, 143
allergic diseases, 387
allergy, 65
alpha receptor, 31
alpine meadows, 386
altering sleep, 38
altitude, spa location, 386
altruistic egoism, 12
altvater mountains, 385
ambivalence conflict, 320
amendment, first, 147
America, rural, 294
American cities, 310
American parents, 222
American soldier, 205
America's largest ethnic minority, 308
amines, biogenic, 49
amitryptaline, 171
analgesics, opiate, 29
analyzing psychosomatic relationships, 180
analysis, ix
  transactional, 176
analyst and leader, 146
analytic neurosciences, 13